D1006114

JUST ANOTHER SOUTHERN TOWN

JUST ANOTHER SOUTHERN TOWN

MARY CHURCH TERRELL AND THE STRUGGLE FOR RACIAL JUSTICE IN THE NATION'S CAPITAL

JOAN QUIGLEY

OXFORD
UNIVERSITY PRESS

OXFORD
UNIVERSITY PRESS

Oxford University Press is a department of the University of Oxford. It furthers
the University's objective of excellence in research, scholarship, and education
by publishing worldwide. Oxford is a registered trade mark of Oxford University
Press in the UK and certain other countries.

Published in the United States of America by Oxford University Press
198 Madison Avenue, New York, NY 10016, United States of America

Library of Congress Cataloging-in-Publication Data
Quigley, Joan.
Just another southern town : Mary Church Terrell and the struggle for racial justice in
the nation's capital / Joan Quigley.
pages cm
Includes bibliographical references and index.
ISBN 978-0-19-937151-8 — ISBN 978-0-19-937152-5 — ISBN 978-0-19-937153-2
1. Terrell, Mary Church, 1863–1954.   2. African American women civil rights workers—Biography.
3. Civil rights workers—United States—Biography.   4. African Americans—Biography.
5. African Americans—Civil rights—History.   6. African Americans—Segregation—
Washington (D.C.)—History—20th century.   7. Washington (D.C.)—Race relations.
8. Washington (D.C.)—Biography.   I. Title.   II. Title: Mary Church Terrell and
the struggle for racial justice in the nation's capital.
E185.97.T47Q54   2016
323.092—dc23   [B] 2015009744

1 3 5 7 9 8 6 4 2

Printed in the United States of America
on acid-free paper

Printed by Edwards Brothers, USA

For Martha

Besides, you ain't going North, not the real North. You going to Washington. It's just another southern town.

—Ralph Ellison, *Invisible Man*

Contents

JUST ANOTHER SOUTHERN TOWN

Prologue

January 27, 1950

For Mary Church Terrell, Thompson's Restaurant was the rendezvous point, the place to meet her colleagues. A party of four, they gathered on a late January day in 1950, after the noon rush. Inside, in a public cafeteria a few blocks from the White House, about two dozen patrons lingered. Outside, streetcar tracks crisscrossed Fourteenth Street, NW. In a city designed to emulate Paris, with monumental boulevards and public spaces, the corridor near Thompson's did not inspire postcards. A canyon of banks and storefronts, it pulsed with taxis, cars, and pedestrians: men in fedoras, jaywalking, rushing somewhere else.

Terrell, a former suffragist, had lived in Washington for sixty of her eighty-six years. As a charter member of the National Association for the Advancement of Colored People, she knew the city's topography and history, its checkerboard regime of exclusion and inclusion. She also knew how little had changed for the better—and how much had changed for the worse. Down a block from Thompson's, at F Street, stood Garfinckel's, a bastion of chic for First Ladies and the capital's gentry with gowns by Balenciaga, Balmain, and Dior. A block from Garfinckel's loomed the Treasury Department, where Terrell's late husband Robert H. Terrell—a graduate of Harvard College and Howard University Law School—had worked before President Theodore Roosevelt, also a Harvard alumnus, tapped him for a municipal judgeship in 1901. Just beyond Garfinckel's and across F Street rose the Beaux-Arts profile of the Willard Hotel, where in February 1861 Abraham Lincoln stayed before his first swearing-in ceremony, finalizing cabinet appointments and his inaugural address.

Farther south, across Constitution Avenue, opened the grassy expanse of the Mall, punctuated by the Washington Monument, and to its north, above the Ellipse, the White House. At the eastern edge of the Mall was the dome of the Capitol, whose restaurants barred African American customers. At the opposite end, overlooking the Potomac River, sat the Lincoln Memorial, at whose dedication ceremony in 1922, orchestrated by Chief Justice (and former president) William Howard Taft, American guests were confined to a segregated seating area.

Thompson's Restaurant harkened back to the prewar era, with floor-to-ceiling plate-glass windows and an art-deco canopy. Overhead, at 725 Fourteenth Street, NW, a sign fashioned the establishment's name with script lettering. Founded by John R. Thompson in 1891, the cafeteria was part of a chain catering to office workers, with fare such as frankfurters, corned beef, and rye bread from the company's bakery. At its peak thirty years earlier, just after World War I, the enterprise boasted more than one hundred restaurants in cities from Chicago, the company's base (the founder had grown up on an Illinois farm), to New York. But by midcentury, beset by competition, aging facilities, and a dwindling clientele, Thompson's had abandoned its signature five-cent cup of coffee and imposed a two-cent price increase, the first such hike in almost sixty years.

For Terrell, the appeal of Thompson's did not spring from its menu. Nor was she drawn by a sense of thrift, a value she espoused in theory if not always in practice. Rather, she was drawn by the chain's seating policy. From an office just down the block, two District lawyers, David Rein and Joseph Forer, had agreed to represent her, without charge, as she defied Thompson's practice of refusing service to blacks. They had also taken on as clients her three hand-picked companions: the Reverend William H. Jernagin, a Mississippi native who had spent almost four decades as pastor of Mount Carmel Baptist Church in Northwest Washington; Geneva Brown, the secretary-treasurer of the United Cafeteria and Restaurant Workers Union; and David H. Scull, a self-professed Quaker who served as president of the Washington Fellowship, an interfaith organization devoted to racial and religious understanding. The Washington Fellowship letterhead listed Mrs. William O. Douglas, the Supreme Court justice's wife, as a sponsor.

At roughly 2:45 p.m., Terrell, Brown, Jernagin, and Scull filed through Thompson's double glass doors. Inside, wedged into an L-shaped space with plain walls, tiered glass shelves rose above a railing. One at a time, customers nudged their trays along the rail, with selections showcased from waist-high to eye-level. Beyond the cafeteria line, in a window-filled area, diners sat at cloth-covered tables.

Jernagin, an octogenarian who stood about five feet tall, went first, taking a tray and cutlery. From one of the tiers, he selected a piece of cake. Brown, a thin African American woman, followed Jernagin, placing silverware and a napkin on her tray and choosing a salad. Terrell fell in place after Brown. With her high cheekbones and white hair, Terrell radiated propriety and elegance, carrying herself like a dance teacher.

At the end of the queue, Scull, the only white member of the group, spotted a waitress behind the counter beckoning to someone in the corner. As Scull watched, a man, clad in a white uniform, came forward and stood in front of Jernigan, ahead of him in line, and introduced himself as the manager. In a voice they could all hear, the manager told Jernagin that he and the other African Americans could not eat in the restaurant.

With his spectacles and a slight stoop, Jernagin projected frailty. But in practice, he was a fitness enthusiast, steeled by a regimen of homemade juices and workouts on an exercise cycle. During his first ministry in Oklahoma at the turn of the century he was known as "the fighting parson." In 1944, after a uniformed Virginia officer ejected him from a train for refusing to sit in a car designated for African American passengers, he filed a lawsuit seeking to invalidate segregated railway travel. Now, inside Thompson's, Jernagin proved the wisdom of the group's decision to send him first, like a paratrooper dropped behind enemy lines.

"Why not?" he asked the manager, whose name was Levin Ange.

"Because we don't serve colored people here," Ange replied, adding that to do so would violate the laws of the District of Columbia and public policy.

"The company is refusing to serve me merely because my face is black?" Jernigan asked.

That was the reason, Ange told him. He added that he had nothing against him personally, but that company policy wouldn't allow it.

Even as President Harry S. Truman was leading the world's strongest country in a global crusade for democracy, the manager of Thompson's Restaurant was invoking the decades-old logic of Jim Crow, with its architecture of racial inferiority.

What was happening at Thompson's came as no surprise to Terrell, who had navigated Jim Crow and the complexities of race for more than eighty years, since her childhood in post–Civil War Memphis, Tennessee. Washington, her adopted home, had long imitated the South. And that outlook, she knew, was a liability in foreign affairs, especially when restaurants refused to serve diplomats from countries such as Africa and India, treating dark-skinned envoys as if they were American blacks. Now, in the aftermath of World War II, in the midst of a cold war against Soviet totalitarianism, the specter of racial inequality in Washington had given her leverage. She had no intention of backing down.

"Do you mean to tell me that you are not going to serve me?"

The manager apologized, again saying that it was not his fault and that it was his company's policy not to serve Negroes. Terrell, an 1884 graduate of Oberlin College, had once considered training as an attorney. To her regret, with battles over segregated dining cars and state universities erupting in federal courts, she had not. Now, as if she couldn't help herself, she flipped into cross-examination. Was Washington in the United States? she asked the manager. Did the Constitution apply there?

"We don't vote here," replied Ange. His response was quite true. Residents of the District of Columbia, who lived amid elected officials and foreign dignitaries, who coexisted with the federal government and its employees, had no representation in Congress, no right to vote in presidential elections. Even in their own civic affairs, with no mayor or city council to elect, they had no voice—and had not had one since 1874, when Congress took away their voting rights.

For Terrell, having braved the cafeteria and met with opposition, there was nothing left to do, no recourse other than retreat. So along with Jernagin, Scull, and Brown she left, without further incident. She had achieved what she had needed to achieve.

★ ★ ★ ★ ★

The Washington of January 27, 1950, a century and a half after its inception in 1791, still bore the physical and psychic scars of slavery. The ten-mile-square federal territory had been commandeered from slivers of Maryland and Virginia, both slaveholding states. From the outset, their influence (and laws) held sway in Washington. Slaves helped build the White House and the US Capitol. Slave pens occupied the site across the street from what would become the Smithsonian Castle, whose red sandstone would be quarried by slaves. And as early as 1809, four years after Congress—which had jurisdiction over the capital under the Constitution—rejected a measure to free the capital's slaves, an aide to President James Madison warned him that foreign ministers would behold, on Washington's streets, the "revolting sight" of "gangs of Negroes, some in chains, on their way to a southern market."

Even free blacks were at risk when they ventured into the nation's capital. In 1826, a free African American man from New York, visiting Washington as a tourist, was arrested and jailed as a fugitive slave. Under a Maryland law dating to 1719, the capital's presidentially appointed marshal had authority to sell a runaway—or any other African American inmate, even a free man—into slavery if he could not finance his incarceration costs, meaning the expenses of his own confinement. After New York governor DeWitt Clinton interceded, sparing his constituent, Congress proposed shifting prison fees from inmates to the locality that ran the jail. When Georgetown residents objected, Congress shelved the plan. (Solomon Northup, another free black man visiting Washington from New York, would not prove so lucky; in 1841, he was kidnapped in the capital, transported to the South, and sold into slavery.)

Still, throughout the decades leading up to the Civil War, slavery and Washington coexisted, albeit uneasily, fueling cries for reform, recriminations, and compromise measures. In 1827, for example, the Washington Abolition Society denounced slavery's "deleterious influence" on the capital's welfare and prosperity. Congress barred African Americans from the Capitol grounds the following year, including not allowing them to attend performances by the Marine Band on the terrace. During his single term in the House two decades later, Abraham Lincoln authored an 1849 bill to ban slavery in the capital. The year after that, as part of an effort to forestall sectional conflict, the Compromise of 1850 abolished Washington's slave trade, though not slavery itself.

During the 1860s, however, with the nation fractured by secession and war and Lincoln in the White House, radical Republicans in Congress refashioned Washington into a model of freedom and racial parity. They started by eradicating slavery. On April 16, 1862, Lincoln, over opposition from local white residents and officials, signed into law the District of Columbia Emancipation Act, which liberated Washington's 3,100 slaves and ended, in antislavery parlance, "the national shame" of bondage in the capital. The following month, Congress required Washington to establish public schools for African American children, placing the facilities under the watch of the Interior Department secretary, who appointed a board of trustees. On January 1, 1863, Lincoln issued the Emancipation Proclamation, freeing slaves in the Confederate states.

With sympathetic legislators entrenched on the Hill, and the capital encircled by a network of forts, Washington's African Americans—long-term residents, refugees from the South, recent arrivals seeking work—mobilized for racial equality. Black soldiers, whose enlistment cemented their commitment to sacrifice their lives for their country, pressed for unrestricted access to the capital's newly established streetcars, which barred nonwhite passengers or confined them to a car for "Colored Persons." Congress complied in 1863 and again the following year, banning race-based exclusion of passengers from two separate streetcar lines in the capital and then on all common carriers in the District in 1865. Meanwhile, in April 1864, African American Washingtonians, a majority of whom had been free before the war, petitioned Congress for local suffrage—nine months before lawmakers on the Hill passed the Thirteenth Amendment, which outlawed slavery.

During the postwar reconstruction of the mid- and late 1860s, as Congress and the states weighed a trio of constitutional amendments extending citizenship rights to freed slaves, Washington continued to function as a vanguard and testing ground, heralding reforms before the rest of the nation. Between 1865 and early 1870, the states debated ratification of the Thirteenth Amendment; the Fourteenth Amendment, which guaranteed all citizens equal protection of the laws; and the Fifteenth Amendment, which outlawed race-based voting restrictions. But in January 1867, three years before the states ratified the Fifteenth Amendment—the last of the three postwar amendments to secure such approval—Congress provided for universal men's suffrage in the capital, extending the vote to black males, over the veto of Andrew Johnson, a Tennessee Democrat who had become president after Lincoln's assassination. (Washington's white male property owners had enjoyed local voting rights since the early 1800s, though the property requirement was later dropped.)

Washington's black men, meanwhile, used their votes to transform race relations. In biracial elections, they coalesced around reform-minded white Republicans who, in 1869, passed a local law barring discrimination in places of public entertainment—targeting the widespread local practice of segregated seating in white-run concert venues, even for performances by African Americans. After blacks gained representation on the city council, local legislators expanded the ordinance in 1870, adding restaurants, bars, and hotels, and imposing a $50 fine for violations. By 1872, the ban extended to bath houses, barber shops, and ice-cream parlors, the fine for violations had doubled, to $100—coupled with a one-year license forfeiture—and, by 1873, facilities had to be the same for all "well-behaved and respectable" customers. Collectively, the measures aimed to eliminate slavery's legacy of inequality in the nation's capital, removing obstacles to integration and racial equality in public places.

But with Ku Klux Klan violence surging in the South, Congress's embrace of voting rights for the capital's black men proved short-lived. In 1871, signaling its retreat from Reconstruction, Congress imposed a new regime on Washington, replacing its mayor and council with a presidentially appointed governor, a half-elected, half-appointed legislative assembly, and a five-member, presidentially appointed board of public works, overhauling the city from a self-governing entity into something like a federal possession, where residents could only vote for delegates to one house of their bicameral legislative assembly and a non-voting member of the US House. Then, only three years later, amid mounting concerns about corruption, municipal debt, and the perceived unfitness of African Americans for the responsibilities of full citizenship, lawmakers on the Hill dismantled Washington's legislative assembly, disfranchised all of its voters—black and white—and installed at the city's helm three presidentially appointed commissioners. (Those changes became permanent in 1878.) In a very short time, Washingtonians—black and white—had lost the right to choose their elected officials and govern their affairs. In the rest of the country, the Constitution apportioned US Senate and House members among the states, and, under the strictures of federalism, the states retained sovereignty over local affairs. However, in the federal capital—as the Thompson's manager had correctly told Terrell, and as Terrell already knew—Washington residents, who did not live in a state, had no say in their own governance, no representation in Congress, no locally elected officials.

The antidiscrimination laws, meanwhile, withstood retrenchment of their own. At first, in the early 1870s, local prosecutors enforced the ordinances, bringing cases in police court. (The prosecutions were later reversed or thrown out, but not for reasons related to the validity of the underlying statutes.) The laws languished on the books, not expressly repealed, but fell out of fashion and into disuse, especially after Woodrow Wilson's inauguration in 1913 touched off a wave of segregation, including government cafeterias and bathrooms. Local officials, who shared the racist proclivities of southern white congressmen, had little incentive to prosecute Washington restaurants for declining to welcome blacks.

By January 1950, race barriers had carved Washington into zones of prohibition and taboo, like a city in the Deep South. African American residents, who by now composed 30 percent of the District of Columbia's population, also accounted for roughly 70 percent of its slum populace, tuberculosis deaths, and felony arrests. Congressional investigations of Washington's alley dwellings—and the occasional reforms that resulted—dated back to the Civil War, as the *Washington Evening Star* noted in an editorial on June 4, 1949. "And photographs of them, with the Capitol in the background, have been published in every State and many foreign lands."

In the workforce, most of the capital's black wage earners toiled in unskilled occupations, as janitors, laborers, cooks, and servants. Washington's streetcar company—which, by act of Congress dating back at least to 1865, had to maintain integrated passenger cars—refused to hire African Americans to drive them. There were no black mechanics or linemen working at the telephone company. Department stores hired only white women as retail clerks, even if customers from both races patronized the enterprise.

Across Washington, blacks and whites studied in separate schools, went to separate movie theaters, and played on separate playgrounds. Downtown restaurants denied blacks service. Some relegated African American customers to a separate section, where they had to stand, while white patrons sat and ate their meals. Only at Union Station, or inside government office building cafeterias—quietly integrated during Franklin D. Roosevelt's administration—could blacks and whites sit side by side.

Yet with southern Democrats thwarting progress in Congress, almost two generations of Washingtonians had grown up knowing little else. In recent weeks, with a midterm election scheduled for November, Truman had revived his push for civil rights, courting support from northern blacks. In his annual State of the Union address, broadcast live over television and radio on January 4, 1950, a few weeks before the incident at Thompson's—and less than two miles away—he promised, as he first had in 1948, to support federal civil rights legislation. The contrast highlighted the degree to which Washington existed on the border and on the cusp: between North and South, between its past as a regional city and its emergence as the strategic and diplomatic epicenter of postwar global democracy, between its legacy of practicing Jim Crow and its future symbolizing the struggle for racial equality. International politics and race were intertwined. At the twentieth century's "midpoint," Truman said, the United States had emerged at "the center of world affairs," and yet Communists, in their quest for power, magnified "our imperfections," seizing on "setbacks" and "delays" in our effort to "secure a better life for our citizens." In a supper speech to congressional Democrats eight days later, he promised to fight for the party's 1948 platform, which included a civil rights plank. And on January 17, during a meeting with civil rights leaders, who were in town for a conference sponsored by the NAACP, he signaled his support. "We can't go on not doing the things that we are asking other people to do in the United Nations."

Still, in a city parsed by gender and race, inertia prevailed. The *Washington Post*, one of the capital's three white dailies, filled its front section with bulletins from the State Department, Congress, and abroad; amid the articles, advertisers hawked suits, tuxedos, and flights to Miami and California. Giant and Safeway, locally prominent grocery stores, advertised in the A-section, too, touting their steaks and bacon. The "Women's News," relegated to a separate section, brimmed with articles about teas, luncheons, parties, cooking, and interior decorating. In Georgetown salons, women withdrew upstairs after dessert and men huddled downstairs, like characters in an Edith Wharton novel.

In recent days, the impasse over civil rights had virtually receded from view, as reporters tackled a bigger story: Secretary of State Dean Acheson's refusal, at a press conference on January 25, to turn his back on Alger Hiss, a former State Department employee whom a federal judge had sentenced to five years in prison for perjury. The sentence, which came only days after a jury in New York had convicted Hiss, stemmed from allegations that he had lied when he denied funneling secret departmental documents to Whittaker Chambers, a former *Time* magazine editor and war-time courier to a Soviet spy ring. On Capitol Hill, meanwhile, two members of the Joint Chiefs of Staff testified that Washington would likely be a high-priority target during a nuclear attack. And Congressman Adam Clayton Powell Jr., a New York Democrat and one of two African Americans serving in the House of Representatives, denied having any ambition to run for governor. "As a Negro," he said, "I can go no higher."

Representative Richard M. Nixon of California took to the House floor the following day. Nixon was a member of the Committee on Un-American Activities, whose investigation had spawned Hiss's indictment. In an eighty-minute speech, he claimed to have evidence of a widespread subversive conspiracy operating inside the federal government, where American officials spied for the Soviets with the knowledge of high-level officials who refused to act. When he finished, colleagues on the floor and spectators in the gallery gave him a standing ovation.

★ ★ ★ ★ ★

Rain soaked the capital early on January 27, with forecasts calling for snow. Deep inside the *Post*, a chart mapped the hourly radio schedule, from Arthur

Godfrey, the ukulele-playing host of a daily program, to "The Lone Ranger" and "Ozzie and Harriet." At 10 p.m., WMAL planned to air a live boxing match from Madison Square Garden, pitting the middleweights Rocky Castellani and Ernie Durando. Harold C. Urey, a Nobel Prize–winning chemist, was slated to discuss the hydrogen bomb on WTOP at 11 p.m. And for late-night television viewers, "Great Fights" on WNBW promised footage of a 1921 heavyweight-title bout between Jack Dempsey and Georges Carpentier.

Three blocks north of the White House, delegates convened for the morning session of the Women's Patriotic Conference on National Defense. Representing a coalition of organizations, including the American Legion Auxiliary, they shared an aversion to Communism. And the night before, inside the Statler Hotel, they had listened to a speech from Truman, who appeared before the conferees at 10 p.m., capping what even he conceded had been a jam-packed day. In fact, since delivering his State of the Union address, Truman had juggled a crush of events and obligations: four press conferences, his annual budget message to Congress, special messages to Congress on tax policy and synthetic rubber. Earlier in the week, he and First Lady Bess Truman had toasted his newlywed vice president, Alben W. Barkley, at a fête attended by Washington heavyweights, including four senators, three Supreme Court justices, and J. Edgar Hoover, the director of the Federal Bureau of Investigation.

And just before 5 p.m. on January 26, the Trumans slipped into the Washington Cathedral to watch as Edith Cook Snyder, the twenty-four-year-old daughter of Treasury Secretary John W. Snyder, exchanged vows with a former White House aide, Major John E. Horton. First Daughter Margaret Truman, the maid of honor, hovered nearby, clad in a spruce green taffeta and marquisette gown, with a sweetheart neckline and three-quarter-length sleeves. Afterward, more than 1,000 invitees poured into the Chevy Chase Club, where they nibbled on smoked oysters and southern baked ham.

In his remarks to the delegates, Truman had refrained from responding directly to Nixon. Instead, he defended his foreign policy to contain Communism, saying his only ambition as president was to bring world peace. Totalitarian states believed in government for the few, he added, but American democracy fostered the welfare of everyone, not just those at the top.

That morning, the conferees heard from Nixon, who said the country could not afford another Hiss case. He also called on Truman to establish a nonpartisan commission charged with probing the loyalty of government officials. "I want this whole business raised above partisan politics and I want to see Communism cleaned up," Nixon said.

★ ★ ★ ★ ★

In the law office of Forer and Rein, located down the street from Thompson's, Terrell and her colleagues narrated the details of their experience. Line by line and paragraph by paragraph, their accounts of what happened at the restaurant would serve as the basis of a set of affidavits, each a one-page document to be signed and sworn before a notary public. Collectively, the statements would buttress a case against Thompson's for violating the Reconstruction-era prohibitions on refusing to serve African Americans. Still, even with the affidavits, Terrell and the lawyers could not sue Thompson's on their own. The statutes bestowed enforcement authority on Washington's local prosecutors, who worked in an entity known as the Corporation Counsel's Office. Those lawyers, whose ranks included long-time Washingtonians not known for progressivism on race, would have to act on Terrell's behalf.

As a legal theory, reviving the antidiscrimination ordinances had surfaced more than a year earlier, in a publication titled *Segregation in Washington: Blot on Our Nation*. The ninety-one-page report, released in late 1948, bore the imprimatur of the National Committee on Segregation in the Nation's Capital, whose ranks included former First Lady Eleanor Roosevelt, Minneapolis mayor Hubert H. Humphrey Jr., and Walter White, the executive secretary of the NAACP, the largest and most influential of the civil rights organizations. Citing speculation by unnamed attorneys, the committee observed that the statutes "may still be technically in full force and effect." Six months later, members of the Washington chapter of the National Lawyers Guild, an association of public-interest attorneys founded in 1937 to advance the causes of labor, civil rights, and human rights—and deemed a "Communist front" by the House Committee on Un-American Activities in 1944—wrote the capital's commissioners, urging them to enforce the Reconstruction-era laws.

Inside the NAACP's New York headquarters, though, Washington's segregated restaurants commanded little attention. Thurgood Marshall, a Baltimore native who served as the NAACP's special counsel, was in charge of implementing national legal policy, and the organization and its leadership faced more pressing matters, including litigation challenging segregated public graduate schools, whose fate lay before the Supreme Court. In late December 1949, while pushing its agenda in court and on the Hill, the

NAACP had repudiated so-called Communist front entities that were seeking to crash its civil rights conference in Washington. And the National
Lawyers Guild—which had supported enforcing the capital's antidiscrimination laws—had already earned such a label.

As proponents of contesting Jim Crow in Washington, where southern
lawmakers held sway, Terrell and her confederates stood virtually alone. At
this point in her life, though, more than halfway through her ninth decade,
she had amassed years on the periphery, vying for change from the margins.
Born in 1863, the year of the Emancipation Proclamation, she grew up in
Reconstruction-era Memphis, the daughter of former slaves, both of whom
apparently descended from their white masters. As one of three black
women in her class at Oberlin, the famous liberal arts institution—and the
nation's first college to admit both men and women—Terrell pursued a four-
year degree, which required her to master Greek. Her father, Robert Reed
Church, envisioned a life of abundance and ease for her, like the one his
wealth, based in prostitution and real estate speculation, had enabled her to
know as his daughter. Instead, a year after graduating from Oberlin, she left
Memphis and took a job teaching at Wilberforce University, a historically black institution located in Wilberforce, Ohio. A few years later, after
moving to Washington, she met her future husband, Robert, at a high school
where they both taught. Eventually, they became engaged, and, after a
Memphis wedding in 1891, settled into a home on Corcoran Street, NW,
near Logan Circle. But as a married woman, untethered to the vocation that
had defined her, Terrell battled despair, deflated by a string of miscarriages
and the monotony of housekeeping and errands. Within a few years, as
racial violence surged across the South, she launched a career as a reformer,
public speaker, and writer.

Over the decades establishments aside from Thompson's had declined to
serve Terrell, dating back as far as a drug-store soda fountain during the
Wilson administration. Still other venues, including the Mayflower Hotel,
had welcomed her without reproach, foiled perhaps by her gentility and
light-skinned complexion, causing even some southerners to mistake her
for white. In recent years, however, Terrell had seen the intransigence of
Washingtonians, including white women, deepen on integration.

In her public persona, Terrell feigned imperviousness to the slights.
"I have never allowed myself to become bitter," she wrote in her autobiography, *A Colored Woman in a White World*, written and published a decade
before the Thompson's incident. In private, though, she seethed.

That same afternoon, about an hour after Thompson's had refused to serve Terrell, Truman faced the press corps in his White House office. At 4:05 p.m., he opened with an update: he had accepted the resignation of his special counsel, Clark M. Clifford, who had worked in the White House since 1944. The announcement did nothing to distract the journalists. "Mr. President," the first reporter asked, "regardless of the outcome in the upper courts, will you or will you not turn your back on Alger Hiss?" "No comment," said Truman. After punting a query on a proposed 25 percent excise tariff on cameras—he told the questioner to read his recent tax message—he fielded another inquiry, again pertaining to the Hiss story. Truman bristled. "No, there is no point in asking any other Alger Hiss questions," he said. "They are not asked with good intent, and I don't intend to answer with good intent." Laughter erupted. Still, the press circled back. "Do you approve Secretary Acheson's statement?" asked another reporter. "No comment," replied the president.

Truman took several more questions, including one about a speech delivered the previous evening by Senator Harry F. Byrd, a Virginia Democrat who accused the president of guiding the country toward socialism. A reporter asked whether Truman would entertain a compromise on civil rights. Earlier in the week, Drew Pearson, whose syndicated column ran in the *Post*, had written that Senator Richard Russell, a Georgia Democrat, might be willing to reach a deal on some of the president's civil rights proposals. Truman dismissed the report, referring to his 1948 speech. "My compromise is in my civil rights message."

The next question stemmed from a United Press report stating that Truman was mulling whether the United States should construct a hydrogen bomb—and claiming that Russia might already be building one. The "awesome weapon," the article said, could prove many times more lethal than the atomic devices, based in uranium and plutonium, which the United States had unleashed on Hiroshima and Nagasaki to end the war in the Pacific. A reporter asked if the president could say something to the American public about a "super bomb." Truman rebuffed the inquiry, saying he didn't think anyone had authoritative information. "I make that decision and nobody else."

In Tucson, Arizona, Supreme Court Justice William O. Douglas dispatched a string of letters, dated January 27, 1950. As an assemblage, they evoked his background and interests. To an ever-increasing degree, more than a decade into his tenure on the Court, his attention lay elsewhere, especially in world travel and foreign affairs.

With a two-paragraph missive, Douglas declined a request to preside over a moot court at Yale Law School, where he once taught. Separately, he thanked a Cape Town, South Africa, resident for comments on a speech he made two years earlier and which *Reader's Digest* had reprinted. And, in a note to an assistant secretary of state, he shared a portion of a letter he had received from a Syrian resident, whom he had met in Soueida the previous summer, while traveling in Syria, Lebanon, Iraq, and Persia to cull material for a forthcoming nonfiction book about the Middle East. "He has summarized succinctly the ideas which I brought back from my trip," Douglas wrote.

From temporary desert quarters, in a four-bedroom stucco home with a swimming pool, Douglas was nearing his fifth month of convalescence. In early October 1949, just before returning to the capital, he had been riding a thoroughbred on a wild game trail in Washington's Cascade Mountains. The horse had reared and Douglas lost control and both horse and rider plummeted down the slope, leaving Douglas with a slew of fractured ribs and a punctured lung.

Douglas, a fifty-one-year-old native of Washington State, thrived on out-door adventure and risk, the legacy of a childhood fraught with financial insecurity and illness, including a severe malady—he claimed it was polio—before he turned two. The son of a Presbyterian minister, he was five when his father died, leaving his mother and elder sister and younger brother to support themselves in turn-of-the-century Yakima, an agricultural city in southern Washington. During their summer vacations, he and his siblings toiled in the Yakima Valley's orchards, where they earned their pay by the box, picking berries, cherries, apricots, peaches, and apples. In the off seasons, with no fruit to harvest, Douglas sold scrap metal to junk dealers and combed alleys and garbage cans for burlap bags, which he sold to local produce growers.

His high school's valedictorian, Douglas won a scholarship to Whitman College in Walla Walla, Washington, where he worked part-time as a waiter, janitor, and jewelry-store clerk and sent money home to his mother. After graduation, and two years as a high-school teacher, he gained admission to both Harvard and Columbia Law Schools and set out by freight train for New York. At Columbia, where President Nicholas Murray Butler de-nounced race hatred, Douglas's peers included Paul Robeson, a Phi Beta Kappa graduate of Rutgers College who lettered in four varsity sports as an undergraduate. Robeson, also the son of a Presbyterian minister, grew up in segregated Princeton, New Jersey, attending a blacks-only elementary school.

One of a handful of black law students at Columbia, he played professional football on weekends to supplement his income. After graduating in 1923, he worked briefly at a New York law firm—where a stenographer refused to take dictation from him because he was black—and gravitated toward the theater and activism.

Douglas, meanwhile, graduated at the top of his class in 1925 and, after brief stints in private practice on Wall Street and in Yakima, joined the law faculty at Columbia and then Yale. In 1934, he left New Haven for Washington, where he policed Wall Street from the newly created Securities and Exchange Commission, landed a spot at President Roosevelt's poker table, and squared off against Dean Acheson, then an attorney in private practice, during an SEC investigation of the New York Stock Exchange. After FDR nominated him, Douglas joined the Supreme Court in 1939, at the age of forty.

For an attorney of his stamina and ability—Douglas prided himself on his work ethic and efficiency, his capacity for concentration and physical exertion, his intellect and photographic memory—Roosevelt had bestowed the ultimate accolade, a career-capping appointment. Yet within months of landing on the Court, Douglas chafed at its isolation; it seemed to him to be a repository for old men. Among his new colleagues was Chief Justice Charles Evans Hughes, a former New York governor, presidential candidate against Wilson in 1916, and secretary of state during Warren G. Harding's administration. Like a long-distance suitor, Douglas peppered Roosevelt with letters, proposing a variety of schemes, including joint activities between the justices and the cabinet, ranging from baseball to salmon fishing. When one of the tribunal's periodic recesses ended, he proclaimed himself "shackled and sad."

Beset by restlessness, Douglas waded into Washington's nightlife, its swirl of stag functions, embassy receptions, and black-tie dinner parties. There, amid the 1940s East Coast Establishment of New Dealers, Ivy Leaguers, and diplomats, Douglas stuck out—a former fruit picker with an affinity for western hats. In a city awash in bourbon, Scotch, and cigarettes, he stood slump-shouldered, his hands jammed into the pockets of a rumpled suit jacket.

Even during his prolonged recuperation in Arizona, Douglas battled unease, as if he feared his infirmity and exile might calcify into permanence. Notwithstanding his injuries, he cajoled a friend to join him in a few months, during the Court's upcoming summer recess, on a five-hundred-mile horseback ride from the Russian border to the Persian Gulf. In letters to Chief

Justice Fred M. Vinson, a Truman poker buddy and former Treasury secretary, Douglas bemoaned his inactivity, saying he was afraid of growing "rusty." In a letter to Harold L. Ickes, the former Interior Department secretary, Douglas trawled for gossip. "Save a luncheon for me so we can get caught up on all the doings," he wrote. Privately, in correspondence with a former Yale colleague, he lamented the Court's apparent ability to function without him.

In less guarded moments, with a book slated for release in April—a memoir about the Pacific Northwest titled *Of Men and Mountains*, Douglas tended to his reputation as an outdoorsman, the basis of his burgeoning career as a writer. The Associated Press ran a wire photo of Douglas seated in his Yakima hospital room, clad in a western shirt, with papers in his lap and a pen in his hand. In Tucson, Douglas posed for another AP photographer, kneeling next to a hobbyhorse.

Back in Washington, while Vinson postponed oral argument in a railway segregation case until Douglas returned to the Court, and Robeson railed against racial discrimination in the capital, Douglas's colleagues took pot shots at their missing associate. He made an easy target. Justice Felix Frankfurter, another FDR appointee, clipped the Yakima-hospital photo and relayed it to Justice Robert H. Jackson, still another Roosevelt pick. In private, Frankfurter's intensity veered into derision, especially for rivals and brethren whom he believed fell short of his standards. In a handwritten note to Jackson on Supreme Court letterhead, Frankfurter wrote, "Cheer up, Bob!" in mock celebration of the prospect of Douglas's restoration to health. Frankfurter also sent Jackson the hobbyhorse image, shorn from the *New York Herald Tribune*. "From your correspondent at the front," he wrote.

Elsewhere inside the Court, Edith Allen, Douglas's secretary, tackled a stream of tasks during her boss's absence. Over Christmas weekend, she had dispatched a rifle, by express special delivery, to New York's Waldorf Hotel. From there, a member of the shah's delegation oversaw the firearm's return to an official, stationed at the US embassy in Tehran, who had traveled with Douglas the previous summer. She also balanced Douglas's checkbook, assembled materials for his income tax return, wrote a check for his $571 tax bill, and tabled four other bills until he received his paycheck. "It is a miracle that I was able to get a correct balance[,]" she wrote him on January 5, "and your check book looks like a doodler's nightmare."

The following day, in a letter dated January 6, Ickes urged Douglas to take care of himself: stay away from horses, listen to his doctors, and focus on getting better. As an ex–New Dealer and staunch ally of African Americans, a leading voice against discrimination in Washington, and an underwhelmed observer of Truman's Supreme Court appointments, Ickes wanted Douglas back on the bench, anchoring the Court's liberal wing, especially with civil rights cases surfacing on the docket. "This makes it all the more important that you should come back when you are able and take part in the brawl," Ickes wrote.

What Mary Church Terrell had started inside Thompson's Restaurant on January 27, 1950, would engage the nation's attention in the years ahead, when legal proceedings in the Supreme Court would alter the country profoundly. It was both a local affair—a particular cafeteria on a downtown Washington street refusing to serve an elderly black woman—and a national one, with repercussions outside the capital, across the South, and beyond. Washington was just another southern town in its treatment of African Americans, but after World War II, it had become the focus of the world.

Inside Thompson's, Terrell had sensed a reaction, a collective scrutiny, as if for those who stayed behind something had happened. Something had happened for her, too, and not just the indignity of being snubbed by the manager. She had gone to Thompson's for a reason: refusing, in a public and orchestrated way, to yield to Jim Crow—a system propagated by whites to make her and other blacks feel different, unwanted, and unequal. To that culture, embedded in Washington and across the South, she too was saying no. She was setting up a confrontation, triggering a legal challenge that would take her from Thompson's to the law office of Forer and Rein, from the local courts to the federal judiciary, and ultimately all the way to the Supreme Court.

Mary Church Terrell's life had roots in slavery, and her story spanned civil rights from the Emancipation Proclamation to *Brown v. Board of Education*. Her case against Thompson's helped usher in *Brown* and school integration, uniting a fractured Court behind Justice Douglas, one of its most polarizing members, to confront the specter of segregation at its doorstep. With her outing to a downtown restaurant, an almost ninety-year-old woman emerged at the forefront of irreversible change. She did so in the heart of Washington, a few blocks from the Truman White House and about two miles from the Capitol, just by trying to walk through a cafeteria line. After nearly a century of political calculus and capitulations, judicial lapses, indecision, and resignation, she sparked, finally, resistance.

I

On to the Battlefield

A few minutes past 10 a.m. on June 25, 1884, after the orchestra fell silent and the honorees and guests had been joined in prayer, Harvard University's president, Charles William Eliot, addressed the convocation. Inside Sanders Theatre, where students and spectators had gathered for commencement exercises, Eliot announced the name of the first speaker: Robert Heberton Terrell. The audience burst into applause. Terrell, clad in a black robe, strode to the dais. A wave of acclaim enveloped him, from his peers in the class of 1884 to curious onlookers and female invitees.

From the stage, Sanders, a 180-degree venue with a vaulted ceiling and room for about a thousand students, opened into a polygonal amphitheater, stretching upward from wooden seats amassed at the center, like pews facing an altar. Modeled after Christopher Wren's Sheldonian Theatre at Oxford University, the space boasted acoustics that could project the human voice with clarity and resonance. Overhead, an inscription from the Vulgate, a Latin rendition of the Bible, read: "They that be wise shall shine as the brightness of the firmament; and they that turn many to righteousness as the stars for ever and ever."

Terrell acknowledged the crowd with a bow. On the platform, the dignitaries included Massachusetts governor George Dexter Robinson, a Harvard alumnus. Robinson had arrived in Harvard Square earlier that morning in a coach-and-four, escorted by the Lancers, a volunteer cavalry militia mustered for the purpose of defending the Commonwealth and, once a year, shepherding its highest elected official to Harvard's commencement. For the occasion, the troops appeared as they had since before the Civil War, when they fought with the Army of the Potomac: mounted on horseback, clad in blue breeches and scarlet tunics, trimmed with gold buttons and epaulets.

Terrell, the son of former slaves, had written his speech out longhand. At the top of the first page, in his fluid cursive, ran the title: "The Negro Race in America Since Its Emancipation." He signed his name only on the back of the last page, rendering it as "R. H. Terrell."

Sanders Theatre anchored the eastern end of Memorial Hall, a monument to Harvard men who fought for the Union and died during the Civil War. Situated on a former playing field, a triangular-shaped wedge bordered by Cambridge, Kirkland, and Quincy Streets, the hall presided over the community like a medieval cathedral, with traceried windows, a 190-foot tower, and an exterior facade rendered in crimson brick and yellow sandstone. Alumni raised $370,000—one-twelfth the university's endowment—to finance its construction. Oliver Wendell Holmes Jr., an 1861 graduate who was wounded three times while serving with the Massachusetts Twentieth Volunteers, composed a hymn for the cornerstone-laying ceremony in 1870. "Give their proud story to memory's keeping/Shrined in the temple we hallow today."

In stone and glass, the edifice reflected the scope of the school's, and nation's, losses. Inside the Memorial Transept, with its sixty-foot Gothic vault, white marble tablets bore the names of fallen students and alumni. In the adjacent dining room, a stained-glass scene depicted a warrior, with a sword and red banner, exhorting his followers. Known as the Battle Window, the two-panel rendering was donated by the class of 1860, which had lost twelve members during the war—including Colonel Robert Gould Shaw, the commander of the 54th Massachusetts Infantry, the Union Army's fabled African American regiment. A decade earlier, as a teenage refugee from Washington, D.C., Terrell had waited on undergraduates in the then–newly opened refectory, which one of the architects, a Harvard alumnus, touted as the world's largest college dining hall, patterned after the great halls at Oxford and Cambridge. Inside the nave-like expanse, with ash paneling, hammerbeam trusses, and a cornflower blue ceiling, students sat at tables topped with white linen cloths. African American servers, clad in white jackets, ministered to their needs, ferrying courses and accompaniments, a cornucopia of soup and fish, butter and fresh milk, sliced roast beef and ice cream.

Terrell was born on November 25, 1857, in Orange County, Virginia, a rural area near Charlottesville, bracketed by rolling hills. Over the course of his life, he betrayed little inclination to return there, professing, well into adulthood, antipathy for rural settings and reticence about his childhood, including whether he had been born into slavery. Given the timing and circumstances of his birth, it seems likely he was, though he was careful in his public life as an adult not to say so directly. He did grow up, however, knowing cruelty and deprivation. By one account, he was given the job, as a four-year-old, of transferring turkeys from one section of an enclosure to another. When he inadvertently allowed a fence bar to fall and kill two of the birds, his grandmother whipped him until he passed out and kept beating him until he regained consciousness. By the same chronicle, he was ten before he mastered the alphabet.

Eventually, the family settled in Washington, D.C. As a boy, he attended the capital's segregated public schools, including an institution named for Charles Sumner, a Harvard-educated radical Republican senator from Massachusetts who championed integration of Washington's streetcars and schools, as well as a federal civil rights bill, which he introduced in 1870, that would have extended similar privileges to citizens nationwide, regardless of color. When Terrell turned sixteen, he fled to Boston and landed inside Harvard's dining hall, where students encouraged him to continue his studies. Five years later, in 1879, he enrolled at Lawrence Academy in Groton, Massachusetts. In an article for the *Student's Aid*, published on March 9, 1880, he reveled in antiquity, extolling Spartan bravery and Athenian refinement. "All were dear lovers of liberty and country," he wrote. "And what nobler virtues can be found in a man?" In deference to his oratorical skills, he won a prize in declamation.

The following fall, Terrell enrolled at Harvard, where students donned tweed suits and center-parted their hair, affecting mannerisms acquired during British travels. With loans from friends and his own earnings, some of which he netted during summer vacations, Terrell paid the annual $400 tuition bill. He also preserved his appointment cards from the registrar's office, each serving to reinforce his inclusion in the community of scholars and to remind him of his journey from menial laborer to gentleman. By February 1884, the Committee on the Academic Council on Commencement Parts had tapped him as a speaker, suggesting that he, and every orator at the ceremony, take elocution lessons. In late May, a news item about his graduation role surfaced in the *Washington Post*.

Now, ten years after he had worked in the dining room at the opposite end of the building, a score of years after President Abraham Lincoln issued the Emancipation Proclamation, Terrell faced his classmates. Media outlets from the *Hartford Daily Courant* to the *Saturday Evening Post* had trumpeted the "Virginia-born negro" who had gone from waiting tables at Harvard to speaking at its commencement. The twelve-page program, printed in Latin, listed him on page 4, in an alphabetical roster of candidates for a bachelor of arts degree, sandwiched between Rogervs Faxton Stvrgis and Avgvstvs Thorndike. On the last page, his name surfaced again, the first of the orators, speakers selected from more than two hundred seniors. The president's son, Samvel Atkins Eliot, was slated to speak after Terrell, with a talk on undergraduate life.

In a measured tone, Terrell began his address. "Twenty one years ago[,] four million negroes, subjected to the most degrading and abject servitude, were dragging their chains over the fields of the South." Silence blanketed the auditorium. With his broad forehead, trim beard, and long nose, Terrell's appearance and voice conveyed academic solemnity, like the Greek scholar he had become. Yet as one of at least two African American diploma candidates—one other, Benjamin M. Campbell, had earned a law degree—his language smoldered, at least when he spoke of slavery, that "direful evil" that was "obnoxious to every manly and generous sentiment." Invoking the abolitionists who had fought it, though, his tone softened. Those "noble men and women lived beyond the narrow limits of their time." And the Emancipation Proclamation ranked as the "great historic event of the period." Freed black men had defended the Union, performing "deeds of valor such as the proudest veterans might emulate" in a country besmirched by a history of bondage, a legacy that had "instilled itself in the very marrow of society." However, emancipation and the right to vote had served as the "salvation" of blacks, elevating them in their own regard and in the eyes of whites, bringing both groups closer to parity.

On the subject of voting, Terrell spoke from personal experience. Four years earlier, during the 1880 presidential election, he had voted for Republicans James A. Garfield, an Ohio congressman and former Union general, and his running mate Chester A. Arthur, a Vermont native. Afterward, Terrell saved a paper ticket, emblazoned with their names, and wrote along the margin: "My First Ballot." Whatever pride he felt about voting, though, whatever gratitude to the party of Abraham Lincoln, race relations in the country were deteriorating. In 1877, under Republican president Rutherford B. Hayes, federal troops had withdrawn from the South, where they had been in place since the Reconstruction Acts a decade earlier—a move essentially marking the end of Reconstruction itself. And in 1883, during the fall of Terrell's senior year at Harvard, the Supreme Court signaled its retrenchment as well. In a decision known as the *Civil Rights Cases*, an eight-justice majority invalidated the Civil Rights Act of 1875, a federal law—enacted in apparent posthumous tribute to Senator Sumner—which banned racial discrimination in public transportation and accommodations, including hotels and theaters. In finding Congress had gone too far, the Court reasoned that the Fourteenth Amendment only authorized federal lawmakers to remedy due process and equal protection violations wrought by state laws and state officials; it did not empower Congress to prohibit individuals and private corporations from discriminating. (The Court also noted, in a nonbinding comment known as "dicta," that it did not address whether Congress might validly enact a similar law for Washington, for which it had "plenary" legislative authority.)

With the tone and tenor of their analysis, the justices heralded a retreat from radical Republicanism and renewed deference to private industry and private choices. "It would be running the slavery argument into the ground to make it apply to every act of discrimination which a person may see fit to make as to the guests he will entertain, or as to the people he will take into his coach or cab or car, or admit to his concert or theatre, or deal with in other matters of intercourse or business," the Court's majority opinion read. "When a man has emerged from slavery, and by the aid of beneficent legislation has shaken off the inseparable concomitants of that state, there must be some stage in the progress of his elevation when he takes the rank of a mere citizen, and ceases to be the special favorite of the laws, and when his rights as a citizen, or a man, are to be protected in the ordinary modes by which other men's rights are protected."

Despite this, Terrell stood before his Harvard peers and projected optimism. It would have been better—"a matter of the greatest good," he conceded—had freed slaves received a few acres of land along with voting rights, since, as property owners, "not mere hirelings," they would have become "more desirable citizens." Yet on balance, surveying the previous two decades, he hailed the progress as "wonderful." African Americans had flocked to schools, he said, and educated black men were finding work and earning wages. "Freedom has called forth his intellectual powers, and the world wonders how such talents could so long have been shrouded in darkness."

Still, even Terrell's sanguinity had limits. More than a year earlier, during an incident in the adjacent dining hall, a law student identified in the press as J. H. Atwood had attacked a waiter with a chair. Afterward, Atwood was quoted in the *Boston Daily Globe*, referring to the waiter twice as a "darkey." By way of explanation, Atwood offered the employee's insolence. He had, among other offenses, refused to serve a plate of rolls, a provocation Atwood deemed "unendurable." Yet at these graduation ceremonies, John Harrison Atwood ranked among the law school's L.L.B. degree recipients, with his name etched into the program three spots above Campbell's.

While Atwood may have been on his mind, Terrell hewed to the plane of abstraction, not personal narrative. His point was to emphasize forward movement, the gradual betterment and development of the race. And, in a gesture of solidarity, he used the opportunity to impart an implicit defense of African Americans consigned to toil, as he once had, in the dining hall. When the war ended in 1865, African Americans owned a "few scattered acres" of property, he said. Now they paid taxes on real estate valued at more than $100 million. With their labor, they helped restore the South's economy, building railroads and digging canals. "These are not the deeds of lazy men."

Looking back once more to the end of the war, Terrell forged another comparison. In 1865, he said, slaves huddled in cabins, without education, legal recognition, or rights. Two decades later, African Americans were culti-vating their intellects, fostering "richness of song and warmth of eloquence." Then with his own powers of reason and persuasion, the faculties that had helped propel him to the stage, he imparted a final insight. "When we reflect that he is denied an equality of rights and hopes, that he is forced to battle with the demon caste which shuts up for him the avenues to trades and professions, and which gives a decided vantage ground to the white man— the negro's rapid progress both materially and intellectually stands as the wonder of the age." The audience, once again, rewarded him with applause.

★ ★ ★ ★ ★

After commencement, Terrell scouted for a teaching job, armed with a rec-ommendation from his Greek professor, John Williams White. Terrell had earned an "honourable record of scholarship," overcoming obstacles from the outset, including "peculiar difficulties" because of his race, wrote White, without providing specifics. "He has comported himself with quiet dignity, and leaves us with the respect alike of his instructors & his classmates."

In September, Terrell began as an instructor in Washington's secondary school for African Americans, known as the Preparatory High School and located on Seventeenth Street, NW, between P and Q Streets. He taught French, Latin, and geometry. He and Richard T. Greener—who was, in 1870, Harvard College's first black A.B. degree recipient, and who had gone on to become a principal at the Preparatory High School and a law dean at

Howard University—applied for admission to Washington's Harvard Club. They were rejected. Senator George Frisbie Hoar, a Republican senator from Massachusetts who held degrees from Harvard College and Harvard Law, protested the decision to refuse the application, as did Congressman John Davis Long, a former Massachusetts governor who had graduated in 1857. When their intercession proved fruitless, both resigned from the club.

In New England, where Terrell had cultivated a wide circle of supporters and friends, newspapers lambasted Harvard's Washington alumni. "There was nothing whatever against them, so far as appears, except the color of their skin," ran an article in the *Hartford Courant*. In Boston, Terrell's hometown for a decade, another commenter noted that Washington's Yale and Dartmouth alumni associations had several African American members. "This sort of stupidity appears to be a monopoly of Harvard among New England colleges," the *Boston Record* opined.

From temporary digs on New York's West 33rd Street, near Herald Square, Mary Church composed a letter to a friend dated July 19, 1888. Church, a twenty-four-year-old teacher, had long, dark hair and a complexion sometimes described as "Andalusian," meaning Mediterranean. In photographs, with her thick, dark eyebrows and prominent ears and chin, hers was the mien of a schoolmarm, evincing a severity that bordered on masculinity. In private, though, especially in letters to Memphis chums or relatives, she revealed a streak of girlishness.

"This is a most dismal day," she wrote, "but I shall not allow the gloom and rain to deter me from writing a few lines to you." In a series of sentences, she recapped her recent engagements: stockpiling provisions for her upcoming voyage to Europe; socializing with her mother, whom she found as vivacious as ever; and seeing her father, who had arrived in New York a day earlier. Still, for a woman about to embark on an extended European tour, she weighted her prose with melancholy. Except, that is, on the topic of shopping. She had ordered a traveling dress, she said, a "very neat suit" from Lord & Taylor. And, to ward off the chill on board the *City of Berlin*, a trans-Atlantic steamer, she had settled on a wrap, which she described to her friend as "very pretty." Bidding farewell, she promised to write soon. "It is not so easy to go as I had expected, but one must be brave to accomplish anything," she wrote.

Church's parents divorced when she was about four, and even as an adult, scars remained, fueling in her a need for recognition. Her father, Robert R. Church, was born in Holly Springs, Mississippi, in 1839, the son of Captain

Charles Beckwith Church, a white steamboat magnate, and a woman—purportedly the descendant of a Malayan princess—who was his slave and concubine. After his mother died in 1851, Robert toiled—as a slave—as a dishwasher and steward on his father's vessels, plying the Mississippi River between Memphis and New Orleans. As an adult, he opened a Memphis saloon and billiard hall, located at South Second Street and Gayoso Avenue, and brothels that employed white women. He also won a landmark civil rights victory in 1866, when he faced criminal sanctions for operating a pool hall without a billiard license; his attorney argued successfully that the county clerk had refused to issue him a license because he was black, thereby violating the newly enacted federal Civil Rights Act of 1866, which granted citizenship and equal rights to all persons born in the United States, regardless of race. Reputedly a millionaire and the South's wealthiest African American, he amassed a fortune from his various enterprises, including real estate speculation, and surrounded himself and his family with the trappings of luxury: horses, carriages, domestic help. But his father, whom Mary, as a young girl, knew as "Captain Church," did not recognize him as his son. And beneath his aura of success—his white-collar shirts and dark suits, his light complexion—lay a reservoir of turmoil, and, as the survivor of several gunshot wounds, including more than one to the head, a history of chronic headaches.

Mary Church guarded details about her childhood, including when and where her parents married and where in Memphis they lived, disclosing only hints about their relationship. She maintained that her mother, Louisa Ayers Church, learned how to read and write from her master, who was apparently her father. He also tutored her in French, allowed his white daughter, "Miss Laura," to purchase Louisa's trousseau in New York, and subsidized her wedding. In Memphis, where Louisa operated a hair salon catering to white customers, she was known as "Lou." With her soft features and ample girth, she projected maternal warmth and grace. Mary's father, Robert, on the other hand, with his mustache and jutting chin, had the tenacity and grit of a boxer.

For whatever reason, their alliance did not last. According to Mary, her father had a "violent temper"; she also stated that when Louisa was pregnant with her, she tried to commit suicide. Beyond that disclosure, Mary Church did not discuss the matter. At the time, in the mid- to late 1860s, divorce was a rarity, with blame usually fixed on the woman. But Louisa prevailed in her request for custody, and Mary—now known to her family as "Mollie"—and her younger brother, Thomas, who inherited his father's air of polish and confidence, lived with their mother, who eventually moved to New York. Robert, meanwhile, kept the Memphis real estate, since women had no legal right to own property.

When Mary was about six, Louisa sent her to Yellow Springs, Ohio, about seventy miles northeast of Cincinnati, to attend a school affiliated with Antioch College. For several years, she lived with an African American couple, whom she called "Ma" and "Pa." She received a $5 monthly candy allowance from her father—a generous sum—and rarely went home, even for holidays and vacations. Christmas presents arrived by mail. During the summer, she mostly entertained herself, reading, memorizing poetry, and playing in the woods. Later, when she was around ten, Mary was transferred to a public school in Oberlin, a town located about twelve miles from Lake Erie, where freed slaves settled and thrived, living amid white residents.

Geographically, Oberlin sat in Ohio's Western Reserve, a northeastern wedge of the state earmarked after the American Revolution as the province of the Connecticut Land Company. With its New England antecedents, its Congregational church and settlers who migrated from the east, Oberlin emerged as a hotbed of abolitionist sentiment. Before the Civil War, when the community functioned as a station on the Underground Railroad, anti-slavery loyalists smuggled fugitive slaves to freedom across the lake, in Canada. In 1858, about twenty Oberlin residents, white and black, landed in jail after rescuing a runaway, who had been captured by slave catchers. The following year, three black Oberlin residents—John A. Copeland, Lewis Sheridan Leary, and Shields Green, a fugitive slave—joined John Brown, the abolitionist son of an Oberlin College trustee, for an ill-fated raid on Harpers Ferry, West Virginia, where they hoped to seize the federal arsenal and incite a slave rebellion. More than a decade later—after Leary died during the attack on Harpers Ferry, and Brown, Green, and Copeland were captured and hanged for their roles in the insurrection—Mary lived in a rented room on an Oberlin side street, almost a mile from the center of town.

In 1880, Mary enrolled at Oberlin College, a coeducational institution established in 1833. Among its early precepts, the school pledged to foster piety and physical labor, and, beginning in 1835, to accept African American students. Well before she arrived, the founders had earned a reputation for "the reformer's aggressive spirit," marked by breadth and independence. To detractors they were radicals and fanatics. By 1880, when Mary moved into Ladies' Hall, sixty-three African Americans numbered among the college's alumni, including thirty women.

As an undergraduate, Mary socialized with whites and African Americans and, when she did not live off-campus or alone, roomed with another African American student. She took algebra and trigonometry, botany and zoology, Latin, German, and Greek. She studied the British and American canon: Charles Dickens, Lord Alfred Tennyson, and Henry Wadsworth Longfellow. She sat on the editorial board of the *Oberlin Review*, wrote poetry and penned essays about the urban poor and prejudice, filling the lined pages of composition books with thoughts that seemed to pour from her pen.

During her freshman year, Mary traveled to Washington, D.C., at the behest of Josephine Bruce, the wife of Senator Blanche K. Bruce, a Mississippi Republican. A former slave and friend of Mary's father, Senator Bruce was the first African American to serve a full term in the US Senate. The Bruces, prominent figures among Washington's black social elites, lived at 909 M Street, NW, a four-story brick townhouse with ten rooms and a Mansard roof. During her visit, they squired Mary to dances and receptions, including President James A. Garfield's inaugural ball, where she met senators and representatives and judges. On the street one day, Mary also met Frederick Douglass, the former slave and writer, who impressed her with his majestic comportment.

At Oberlin, Mary's written assignments often rippled with defiance. Black Americans were once deemed innately incapable of learning, she wrote, and that bias spurred their "struggles to resist the oppressor." So, too, for women: male contempt of their intellect and male prejudice against their efforts to study had inspired women "to improve their minds."

Still, in the world beyond Oberlin, an African American collegiate woman remained a rarity, and Mary found herself an outlier with a suitor-deflating interest in philosophy and mathematics. Even within her family, acknowledgment of her accomplishments fell short, as if her parents—both self-made entrepreneurs and extroverts—could not understand their daughter, with her intensity and reserve, her determination to master Horace and the *Odyssey*. Mary knew the stereotypes that dogged educated women—their alleged neglect of appearances, their inattentiveness to hems and heels—but she didn't quite deflect them. In an Oberlin studio, she posed for a portrait, clad in a high-necked, lace-trimmed dress. She wore her hair pulled straight back, tucked out of sight, with bangs coating the top half of her forehead, like a valance. Set against a plain backdrop, she looked into the distance, lips closed, with her almond-shaped eyes telegraphing a combination of sadness and determination.

When Mary Church graduated on June 25, 1884—the same day as Terrell—she and two of her classmates joined the ranks of college-educated African American women. As a tribute, Mollie's mother shipped her two gifts: a black dress intended as attire for the occasion and a pair of opera glasses. Both parents skipped the ceremony.

In Paris, in 1888, as late August faded into September, Mary poured her frustrations into a handwritten journal. She had taken a semester of French at Oberlin but still struggled with basics: verb tense, vocabulary, and sentence structure. She translated her thoughts literally from English, without much command for idiom or a feel for subtlety. When Parisians spoke to her with their rapid-fire certitude, meaning eluded her. Yet if they switched into English, her annoyance spiked.

Aside from the language barrier, Paris overwhelmed and unnerved Mary, with its noise and confusion, its high prices and decorum. Madame Schmitt, the widow who ran her pension, chastised her for exploring the capital by herself, telling her it wasn't "proper." Even excursions to Notre Dame and the Tuileries brought little satisfaction. In Père-Lachaise Cemetery, where she visited the graves of Molière and Jean de La Fontaine, the fabulist, she despaired at the presence of American tourists.

Worse still, to Mary's thinking, Robert Terrell kept bombarding her with letters. They had met a year earlier, when she had taught in the Preparatory High School, alongside one of her black Oberlin classmates, Anna J. Cooper. Three years into his own teaching career, Terrell was a subject of local pride, a native son who had attended Harvard. As the school year progressed, Mary worked as Terrell's assistant in the Latin department, which he chaired, and from time to time taught his senior class in Virgil.

At first, Terrell's Paris-bound correspondence seemed innocuous, involving tidbits about their peers: a female instructor's request for a one-year sabbatical, citing ill health; troubles between the principal, Francis L. Cardozo, and a colleague. Mary replied by return mail, disclosing in her diary the fact of her response though not the contents. Terrell persisted, peppering her with updates, which she logged in her journal, referring to him as "R.H.T." By September 10, she betrayed a hint of alarm. Terrell had written asking for a photograph. "What do I have to do?" she wondered.

On her journal's lined pages, Mary also ruminated about her future. She lamented the paucity of career options available to her, even with her college degree. She throbbed with impatience: to write; to become an author; to set herself apart. "I wish I could rid myself of my ambition, of my grand desire to achieve something before I die." In one entry she admitted she was afraid that she wouldn't accomplish anything.

In late September, she left Paris for Lausanne, Switzerland, where she boarded with a married couple and their two daughters. Her bedroom window overlooked the Jura Mountains. After Paris, the tranquility was welcome, as were the chocolate, country bread, and warm milk. She joined a gymnasium and hiked the surrounding countryside. She enrolled in a private girls' school, took courses in French literature, and recited her lessons in French. "God guided me," she wrote in her journal. "What happiness for me."

By late October, everything seemed to point to writing as her vocation, she penned. But R.H.T. had not relented. If anything, he had honed his technique, praising her in the area that mattered most to her: her ability with pen and paper. She composed, he said, such interesting letters—better than any other woman he knew—it astonished him she did not wish to write for newspapers. "We shall see," she told her diary.

Mary inscribed her last journal entry from Lausanne on February 11, 1889. Her father had given her permission to stay in Europe for two years, freeing her to study in Germany and Italy. Her mother, who had just won $15,000 in a lottery, planned a summer excursion to Paris and promised, in deference to her daughter's Swiss locale, to buy her a watch. After mulling logistics, Mary indulged in a bit of introspection. She had studied well and made enormous progress, but she was not at all satisfied, she wrote. She felt she must accomplish something solid to deserve everything God had given her. *Que deviendrai-je?* "What will I become?"

"R.H.T." may have wondered the same thing. In the late spring of 1889, Robert Terrell faced an audience of honorees and their guests inside First Congregational Church, a Byzantine-designed structure at 10th and G Streets, NW. Overhead, above the wooden balconies, windows soared along both sides, with pointed tips and paneled expanses of glass. The platform, raised a few stairs above the floor, looked out onto the center of the congregation, a three-story space with two side aisles and rows of curved oak pews.

While Mary roamed across Europe, honing her command of French, German, and Italian, Terrell had weathered two years of legal studies in Washington, slogging through equity jurisprudence at Howard University and churning out a thesis on testamentary capacity, a concept delineating the ability to make a valid will. On May 27, 1889, he stood before his classmates as valedictorian. Degree recipients were grouped on the left of the dais, and faculty members on the right. In the center sat Frederick Douglass, who was no stranger to First Congregational, an integrated house of worship founded by New Englanders.

A few months earlier, as Washington had girded for the inauguration of President Benjamin Harrison, an Ohio-born Republican and Civil War veteran, Douglass came to First Congregational with his white wife, Helen Pitts Douglass, to attend the twenty-first annual convention of the National Woman Suffrage Association. During the opening session, he had sat on the platform with Susan B. Anthony.

For a role model and mentor, Terrell need look no farther than Douglass. More than a decade earlier, President Hayes, another Ohioan, had appointed Douglass to two positions: United States Marshall of the District of Columbia in 1877; and three years later, the capital's recorder of deeds. More recently, Douglass had retreated across the Anacostia River, where he wrote and entertained at Cedar Hill, a brick home with a front porch ringed by cedars. Among friends, fortified by the sanctuary of his hilltop setting, Douglass spoke openly, recounting the challenges of his work and projecting serenity and optimism. For Terrell, a frequent guest, an hour of conversation with Douglass at Cedar Hill was like "a week's reading of books."

Douglass had also delivered a series of speeches commemorating emancipation in Washington. In 1885, on the twenty-third anniversary of the outlawing of slavery in the capital, he called the milestone a "comprehensive" moral victory, which elevated the country to "a higher and happier plane of civilization," enabling the American people, for the first time, to "preach liberty to all the nations of the world." The following year, a Washington publisher bound and printed his remarks, along with two other addresses, in a book titled *On the Relations Subsisting Between the White and Colored People of the United States.* On the cover page of Terrell's copy of the volume, just above the title, the author inked an inscription. "With the respect and esteem of Frederick Douglass."

Three years after that, in January 1889, Douglass spoke at another anniversary gathering, this time celebrating the twenty-sixth anniversary of Lincoln's Emancipation Proclamation. Though Douglass commended the "vast change" in the status of African Americans since the Civil War, he also lamented the state of race relations and questioned whether Americans had sufficient "virtue" to guarantee African American males their constitutional rights of free citizenship. "I only ask that the black man be treated as you treat the people who fought against us," he said. "We love our country, and only ask to be treated as those who hated it."

At the time of Terrell's graduation speech, there was speculation in Washington about patronage for blacks in Harrison's administration, with some reports even floating the prospect of an African American cabinet pick. Harrison, an Indianapolis-based lawyer who lost the popular vote by a margin of 100,000 ballots but carried the Electoral College, pled for patience. "It is quite possible the high expectations of our friends may not at once be realized, but we can at least keep things moving in the right direction."

Terrell, nevertheless, kept his aspirations unchecked. He wanted a position at the Treasury Department and, with the finesse of a Washington insider, he enlisted Harvard alumni to boost his chances. On the day of his graduation from Howard, Massachusetts congressman Henry Cabot Lodge lobbied on Terrell's behalf, sending a letter to Treasury Secretary William Windom, a former US senator from Minnesota. Terrell had performed well at Harvard, Lodge wrote, and was "a good representative of the race which the Republican party is always ready to recognize."

Not surprising, given his ambitions, Terrell's remarks to his law school classmates stressed the importance of rectitude. Only character could mediate thought and action, he said, and only "men of character" would stir others from complacency. As for the idea that he and his classmates would act and inspire as Douglass had, Terrell brooked little doubt. "We represent a young generation marching on to the battlefield of action to take the place of those whose limbs are already growing weary and whose eyes already feel the twilight. What is our duty but to make the world a little better, if we can, for those who are to follow us than we ourselves shall find it?"

In Berlin, meanwhile, Mary Church had become proficient in German. She had also won the regard of a white admirer, who she referred to in her diary as "von D." In January 1890, he proposed marriage. Her father refused to consent. Without addressing von D. by name, Robert Church explained, in a letter dated February 24, 1890, that he did not want Mary to live in Europe permanently; he also cited the abundance and ease she had known as his daughter. "Mary has been indulged all her life," he wrote. In Florence, where Mary had gone to live—and where she still composed her diary entries in German—she reacted to news of her father's "nein" with something like relief. People from different races should not marry, she wrote in her journal on March 8, 1890. She might not share that view with "the world," she added, but she agreed "in this case."

Later that year, with her sabbatical in Europe over, Mary went back to Washington, back to the Preparatory High School, and back to teaching

German and Latin. She also went back, apparently, to R. H. T. Terrell, ensconced at Treasury as a division chief (of the Fourth Auditor's Office), renewed his attentions. He approached Mary's father on January 6, 1891, with a note on Treasury Department letterhead.

"My dear Sir," he began. "The privilege I take in sending you this letter is warranted by such a sacred relationship between your daughter and myself that I do not feel that it is necessary for me to apologize for it." With Mary's consent and approval, he continued, he was writing to request her hand in marriage. This was "no hasty step." We are well acquainted, "and loving each other as we do," we look forward to a union based on happiness and contentment. Confident though he was, Terrell knew that Robert Church, who had already rejected one suitor with a reference to the extravagance Mary had known growing up, might disfavor a proposal from a mere government servant. From a financial standpoint, Terrell said, his position was "fairly good" and he had no reason to fear he would not do well in the future. He had saved about $2,000, an amount equal to his annual salary. With prudent management, he said, he would support Mary—Mollie—and supplement his savings. If the presidential administration changed in 1893 and he lost his patronage job, he could always practice law.

I trust you will consent, he wrote in the final paragraph, but added that Mollie would not contravene you if he opposed the engagement. For her, there could be "no satisfaction" without her father's approval.

★ ★ ★ ★ ★

On October 28, 1891, guests assembled inside Robert Church's home, a wood-frame Queen Anne–style mansion at 362 Lauderdale Street in Memphis. Summoned by engraved invitations, they reflected a cross section of the African American political and social elite, including friends of the host, who had remarried after Mary graduated from Oberlin. Former senator Bruce was there, as was Josiah T. Settle, a Howard alumnus, attorney, and former Mississippi legislator. To the strains of "The Wedding March," Terrell entered the parlor at 6:00 p.m., attired in a suit. Church emerged next, with Mary, who wore a white French silk gown, a white tulle veil, and an orange-blossom wreath. Her four-year-old half-sister, Annette, tended the train of the dress. From a recess near a bay window, Robert and Mary faced their relatives and friends. Potted palms, cut flowers, and vines festooned the room. The Very Reverend William Klein, dean of St. Mary's Episcopal Cathedral, performed the rites. When Mary and Robert exchanged vows, Annette proffered the wedding ring, resting on a silver tray.

After the ceremony, guests sipped Piper-Heidsieck champagne. A small band, featuring two violins, a trombone, a coronet, and a flute, played. Caterers served turkey and roast pig, along with salads, ice cream, wine, and punch. For dessert, they offered fruits, nuts, candies, and three wedding cakes, decorated with flowers. After a string of toasts, Robert Terrell confessed he had arrived in Memphis as an interloper, "with malice aforethought," to abscond with one of the city's most prized laurels.

Around 10 p.m., Mary and Robert slipped away to board a Louisville & Nashville train to New York, where they planned to visit Mary's mother, who had not attended the wedding. Afterward, to Boston and a round of parties. Back on Lauderdale Street, guests lingered after their departure, dancing until midnight.

For the next few weeks, details about the Terrells' marriage and honeymoon were featured in newspaper columns east of the Mississippi, from Boston to New Orleans. The *Washington Post* chronicled the nuptials on its front page, with a headline reading "Robert Terrell Weds." In black southern social circles, the *Post* said, it was "the most notable event" in years. The *New York Age*, a journal of African American news and opinion, logged each of their wedding presents, with the names and hometowns of the gift givers. Line by line, the list read like the inventory of a British country estate: silver butter knives, a silver oyster fork, silver tea services, a silver water pitcher.

Beneath the veneer of refinement, though, Mary radiated tension. According to several news accounts, her father had given her a diamond ring worth $1,000 as a wedding gift. Robert's parents gave the couple a washstand set. Before the ceremony, because of her impending marriage, Mary had resigned from her teaching position. She had also broken off the engagement, reconciled with Robert, and rebuffed an overture from Oberlin to work as its registrar. In a portrait, alone in her wedding dress with a fur rug at her feet, she telegraphed anxiety, as if she wondered whether she made the wrong choice.

As a newlywed, with no work outside the home, Mary Church Terrell looked to fill her days, the hours she had previously spent in a classroom. She arranged to contribute to *Ringwood's Afro-American Journal of Fashion*, a women's magazine that combined Paris couture, biographical sketches, and love stories. She gave a speech about her European travels at Bethel Literary and Historical Association, an African American discussion forum. Bethel's advisory board included her husband, whom she called "Berto"—presumably to distinguish him from her father and half-brother, also named Robert.

Yet her ostensible goal as a married woman—motherhood—proved elusive. Eight months after the wedding, Mary had a miscarriage, sparking fear within her family. Her brother, Thomas, cabled Terrell on June 11, 1892, saying if the outcome were "at all doubtful," he wanted to "come over right away." In a letter to Terrell, three weeks later, her father expressed relief that Mollie had regained her appetite.

But the miscarriage was only part of the problem. Mary left Washington and her husband in late July, first for New York, where she stayed with her mother, and then for Saratoga Springs, where she remained through mid-September. Week after week, she tended to her health and well-being, scheduling doctors' visits and spending time outdoors. In frequent letters to Robert, she assured him of her affection, but she alluded to other issues as well. When she came back to Washington, she wrote in a letter dated September 5, 1892, she wanted him to remain as near to her as he could in the evenings. She reminded him, in a letter dated September 7, 1892, that she had long wanted to achieve some recognition as a writer, but she had deferred that ambition for the time being. She also urged him to reform: to watch his diet, to exercise every day, and to abstain from drinking alcohol.

Terrell had a different agenda. Though Mary thought politics was beneath him, he stumped for the Republican Party during the 1892 presidential campaign, a rematch between Grover Cleveland and Harrison. Out on the trail, Democrats vilified proposed Republican legislation—introduced by Congressman Henry Cabot Lodge and Senator George Hoar, both of Massachusetts—to mandate federal election supervision. Known among Democrats as "the Force Bill," the measure sought to protect blacks' voting rights, responding to concerns about fraud and violence in the South, where Democrats had seized control of all-white state governments. Democrats engineered a Senate filibuster and, after ensuring the bill's demise on the Hill, conjured its memory during the campaign, inflaming their southern base with rhetoric about states' rights and the specter of Negro supremacy. Terrell, the president of the Henry Cabot Lodge Campaign Club, countered by telling Republicans that suffrage was "the chief attribute of American manhood." He also reminded them Democrats had seen no inequity in slavery.

In November, Grover Cleveland won, the first president to serve a nonconsecutive second term. His vice president, Adlai E. Stevenson, had campaigned against the Force Bill in the South. Six months after the election, as the new Democratic administration encamped in the capital, Terrell lost his Treasury post.

Exiled from government service, Terrell opened a law and real estate office at 609 F Street, NW, with John R. Lynch, his former boss at the Treasury Department. Their office building, a four-story brick edifice in the downtown business district, also housed the Capital Savings Bank, an African American institution, founded in 1888, as a source of financing for black businessmen. Lynch, an ex-slave, had served Reconstruction-era stints in the Mississippi state house and the US Congress, where he supported the Civil Rights Act of 1875. During the 1884 Republican National Convention, Henry Cabot Lodge and Theodore Roosevelt, then a twenty-five-year-old New York delegate and state assemblyman, maneuvered to anoint Lynch as temporary chairman of the gathering. A decade later, when Terrell marked his ten-year reunion from Harvard, the class secretary noted that he and Lynch specialized in appearing before government departments and the US Court of Claims.

When Terrell wasn't practicing law and real estate, he opined about race relations, including "Southern Mob Rule." In an 1893 speech about lynching and disfranchisement of southern blacks, he called for "persistent and systemic agitation" to combat indifference among the country's "best citizens," meaning, of course, northern whites. He filed dispatches to the African American press about a variety of subjects: a Frederick Douglass speech; a music recital at Bethel; a US Supreme Court oral argument by two black attorneys, who said Mississippi's exclusion of African Americans from juries violated the Fourteenth Amendment.

Not surprising, though, given his dismissal from Treasury, Terrell returned to one subject: patronage, the distribution of government jobs to reward political supporters. He spotlighted alleged Civil Service violations by African American Democrats in the Cleveland administration; he bemoaned the intrusion of politics into federal service, where, in his view, competence rather than connections had once dictated tenure. "What a miserable existence a government employee must lead!" he wrote in the *New York Age* on November 29, 1894.

After Frederick Douglass died in February 1895, Terrell identified another potential patron: Theodore Roosevelt, a Harrison and Cleveland appointee to the US Civil Service Commission. In a bylined column for the *New York Age* in May, Terrell praised Roosevelt for pushing for competency examinations and merit-based appointments; he had acted with "iron impartiality and absolute fairness." He had also appointed roughly one hundred African American clerks in Washington's government departments, and, with his reforms, opened the civil service to college-educated men and women of both races in the South. No one had done more than Roosevelt for the cause of improving government, wrote Terrell.

Mary, meanwhile, endured more loss. During the five years after her marriage, she gave birth to two girls and a boy, each of whom died at birth or not long after. As a respite from grief and malaise, she bolted for the public realm, at the nexus of service and advocacy. Along with Anna J. Cooper, she helped charter the Colored Woman's League, a Washington-based club with an educational and industrial focus, including free kindergarten and instruction for girls in sewing, gardening, and housekeeping. As overall objectives, codified in 1894, the league endorsed promoting the moral, intellectual, and social accomplishments of African Americans and fostering "the best interests of the colored people." Mary won a school-board appointment in the capital a year later, making her among the first black women to hold such a post.

Elsewhere, though, the outlook for African Americans was increasingly bleak. On May 18, 1896, the Supreme Court upheld segregated railway seating in *Plessy v. Ferguson*. The case had arisen four years earlier, when Homer Adolph Plessy, a passenger who was seven-eighths white, refused to vacate a whites-only car after boarding in New Orleans. Plessy, an envoy from a local citizens' committee intent on engineering a legal challenge to Jim Crow, was ejected from the train and thrown in jail. A criminal court put him on trial for violating a Louisiana law that required "equal but separate" railway accommodations for blacks and whites, either through segregated coaches or the use of a partition. He countered, questioning the statute's constitutionality. By a 7 to 1 vote, the Supreme Court ruled that segregated rail cars—like congressionally mandated school segregation in Washington, D.C.—were a reasonable exercise of the state's police power, the authority to ensure "public peace and good order." So long as railway segregation was reasonable under the "established usages, customs and traditions" of a particular community, the justices reasoned, its existence did not violate the Fourteenth Amendment's equal protection and due process guarantees.

The *Plessy* decision, which press accounts dubbed "the 'Jim Crow' car case," resonated far beyond the matter at hand. In a wide-ranging opinion that relied on the *Civil Rights Cases*, the majority placed its imprimatur on the mechanics and rationale of white supremacy, saying the Fourteenth

Amendment only mandated political equality, not social equality. The justices also rejected Plessy's view that "enforced separation of the two races" stamped African Americans with "a badge of inferiority." "If this be so, it is not by reason of anything found in the act, but solely because the colored race chooses to put that construction upon it," the court wrote in its decision. "If one race be inferior to the other socially, the Constitution of the United States cannot put them upon the same plane."

Justice John Marshall Harlan, a former slaveholder from Kentucky who served as a Union officer during the Civil War, filed a dissent, spurning his colleagues' conclusion and, in a strikingly blunt assessment, their premise. "Every one knows," he said, the goal of the law was to banish blacks from white coaches under the pretext of providing equal accommodations for both. As for racial supremacy, Harlan wrote, whites consider themselves "the dominant race." But the Constitution recognized no such elites, he said. "There is no caste here," he added. "In respect of civil rights, all citizens are equal before the law." One day, Harlan predicted, *Plessy* would prove as "pernicious" as *Dred Scott*—the 1857 decision that held that persons of African descent were not citizens and had no right to seek redress in federal court.

Harlan, who had also cast the only dissenting vote in the *Civil Rights Cases*, went on to condemn the majority opinion in *Plessy*, saying it would stimulate hatred and mutual distrust, precluding racial peace. As for "social equality," Harlan argued, it was "scarcely worthy of consideration." He added that African Americans "ought never to cease objecting" to their designation as criminals for sitting, or asserting the right to sit, in the same coach as whites on a public road; such a scheme, based on race, was a "badge of servitude" that violated constitutional guarantees of freedom and equality. "It cannot be justified upon any legal grounds," he wrote. "The thin disguise of 'equal' accommodations for passengers in railroad coaches will not mislead any one, nor atone for the wrong this day done."

The decision galvanized the black community. In mid-July, African American women from around the country converged in Washington for a three-day national convention, featuring a tribute to Frederick Douglass and speeches about "the Negro Problem" and the duty of Negro women. By the end of the conference, Mary was elected the first president of the National Association of Colored Women, a new organization born of a merger among the various entities, including the National League of Colored Women and the National Federation of Afro-American Women. The combined mission was, with God's intercession, to elevate home, moral, and civil life to "the highest plane."

The day after the convention, on July 17, about two dozen participants (and a few men) embarked on a "pilgrimage" to Harpers Ferry, where almost thirty-seven years earlier John Brown had staged his raid. On a sun-drenched expanse of grass, outside the brick engine house where Brown had been captured, the women posed for a photograph. Clad in floor-length skirts and bonnets, they stared into the camera, holding parasols aloft.

During her first official speech as the NACW's president in September 1897, Mary embraced a broad agenda steeped in race unity and pride. African American women had banded together, she said, to thwart customs that sabotaged their vitality. No one who knows "our peculiar trials and perplexities" would question the need for this organization or our resolve to show that we are "partners" in "progress and reform," she said. For the betterment of the race, for the betterment of their families, the National Association of Colored Women would "inculcate right principles of living and correct false views of life," promoting good manners and good morals. Mary also called for free kindergartens, and lessons in the "science of house-keeping": mending garments, saving money, purchasing nutritious food. As the product of divorced parents, as someone who had grown up isolated from her own family and from her father's business enterprises—which depended, in part, on the exploitation of women—she advanced an ideal-ized vision of domestic life, one that fostered wholesome, collective uplift. "Let us purify the atmosphere of our homes till it becomes so sweet that those who dwell in them will have a heritage more precious than great riches, more to be desired than silver or gold."

At first, Terrell hailed his wife's efforts, touting her work in the press. We have vanquished man's "savage instinct," eradicated gender discrimination, and seen the rise of the "new woman," he wrote in a letter to the editor of the *Colored American*. The National Association of Colored Women would "teach men how to live." In a bylined piece for the *New York Age* on July 30, 1896, he extolled "these splendid women" for confronting the "race prob-lem" with unprecedented determination and ability. "Women in profes-sional and commercial life find no opposition nowadays," he said.

Emboldened, Mary began lecturing. In February 1898, while seven months pregnant, she spoke to a convention of the National American Woman Suffrage Association about African American women and their efforts to foster racial progress, or as she said: "lifting as we climb, onward and upward."

As her daughter Phyllis approached her first birthday, Mary drew on her experience as a parent. In a speech to the National Congress of Mothers in February 1899, she urged her listeners to tackle the needs of African American children, making their futures "as bright and promising" as that of "every child born on this free American soil."

Eventually, Mary's lecture engagements took her away from Washington. Terrell's friends apparently warned him, predicting domestic turmoil with a wife leading a public life. But Terrell knew Mary regretted the Oberlin job, the career she thought she had forsaken. In any case, Terrell had remorse of his own, even after the 1896 presidential election, when Governor William McKinley, an Ohio Republican, defeated William Jennings Bryan, a populist Democrat who ran against the gold standard. With Republicans returning to the White House, Terrell should have been well positioned for a new appointment. But one month after the Republican convention, he had vented to the *Washington Post*, chastising the party for ignoring African American voters, many of whom ran businesses, understood currency and tariff issues, and had fielded entreaties from "Populists and silverites," who were trawling for their support. McKinley, a Civil War veteran, acknowledged Terrell's concerns from the city of Canton, where he repaired to greet well-wishers and supplicants from his front porch. In a letter dated July 25, 1896, McKinley wrote Terrell that he was "in cordial sympathy with all efforts to elevate the status of our colored citizens."

Separately, though, Terrell had also criticized Marcus Alonzo Hanna, a Cleveland-based coal and iron ore magnate who had masterminded McKinley's White House bid, financing it with $100,000 of his own money and with contributions from industrialists such as John D. Rockefeller and James J. Hill. In the *Washington Post*, Terrell rapped "party managers" for failing to appoint African Americans to a campaign-advisory panel. Blacks had earned a spot, even an "ornamental" one, with their loyalty. Terrell added a little ominously that Republicans could not "begin too soon" to reassure "this large class of voters" that they would be "treated with exact impartiality."

In his response to Terrell, Hanna bristled with hauteur. The advisory committee, Hanna wrote on July 30, remained an "open question." Should such a panel form, he continued, switching from the passive to the active voice, "I will give your communication such attention as it deserves."

Terrell had made a costly blunder. After McKinley's victory, Hanna ranked as the country's preeminent political operator, a powerbroker who prized commitment and dedication. And, through his combined roles as Republican National Committee chair and McKinley advisor, Hanna also controlled patronage, the calculus—notwithstanding reformers' pleas to the contrary—of rewarding the faithful, including southerners whose defection from the Bryan camp hinged on a promise of future employment. While the black press swirled with speculation about Terrell's prospects—the State Department, Treasury, the Justice Department—inaugural planners relegated him to a less exalted role: the Committee on Public Comfort.

In mid-June, three and a half months after the swearing-in, Terrell received a note from Theodore Roosevelt, recently installed as assistant navy secretary, the position Roosevelt coveted. Roosevelt owed his situation, in part, to Hanna, whom he had wooed in person, and to his own campaign-trail prowess as a McKinley surrogate. In his letter, Roosevelt did little more than telegraph sympathy for his fellow Harvard alumnus, alluding to his tenure at the Civil Service Commission. "You, I know, remember the interest I took in getting the young colored people of education their rights in the Government service."

Still, Terrell held out hope for a job as a local prosecutor and enlisted support from Lodge, now a US senator. With Hanna vying for an open US Senate seat, Terrell shifted tactics, opting for flattery. In an unbylined editorial for the *Colored American* on August 22, 1897, he called Hanna a "politician of consummate skill" and urged Ohio's African Americans to elect him. His efforts proved unavailing. The following year, after the United States declared war on Spain, McKinley tapped Lynch to serve as an army paymaster, leaving Terrell to manage their law and real estate firm alone.

With a wife and child to support, he lowered his expectations. "Any good paying place will suit me," he confided to a friend on August 27, 1898, almost five months after Phyllis was born. "Of course I am out for money." That fall, after dissolving his law practice and saddled with debt, he returned to teaching at the Preparatory High School, now known as the M Street High School and located at M Street and New Jersey Avenue, NW. At the end of the school year, he was promoted to principal.

While her husband's professional and financial status had declined, Mary's profile had risen, in front of both white and black audiences. On February 17, 1900, after she spoke again to the National American Woman Suffrage Association, the *Colored American* praised her "grace of bearing" and "ineffable charm," saying she delivered her remarks without notes. When she gave a commencement address in Greensboro, North Carolina, the *Colored American*, in an article dated June 9, 1900, hailed "her rare ability as an orator and race leader." And, after she registered with a speaker's bureau, she surfaced on the Chautauqua circuit in August as "the 'female Booker T. Washington,'" a reference to the founder of Alabama's Tuskegee Normal and Industrial Institute, whose appearances before white audiences helped generate support for his mission of manual and vocational training. One of her speeches was titled "Progress of the Colored Woman." Another was about Harriet Beecher Stowe, the author of *Uncle Tom's Cabin*.

In a letter to Robert from Danville, Illinois, dated August 12, 1900, Mary referred to the extensive travels of her youth, saying she derived little pleasure from roaming now, when her husband and her "dear little sweetheart of a baby" remained at home. (Her mother was taking care of Phyllis.) Yet altruism impelled her to quit the domestic sphere, "a sense of duty" to her race, she added. "I enjoy very much doing this kind of work, because I really feel that I am putting the colored woman in a favorable light at least every time I address an audience of white people," she wrote, "and every little bit helps!"

It helped in more than one way. Several sentences later, Mary acknowledged other motives, including their shortage of money, a condition she labeled "thrift." As a high school principal, Terrell's salary had stalled at $1,800—10 percent less than when they became engaged. "Then too," she wrote, "it would seem almost reckless in people of our circumstances to deliberately throw one hundred dollars into the fire, when it can be made in three weeks very easily."

2

The Greatest Woman
That We Have

From Tuskegee, Booker T. Washington routed a telegram to Robert Terrell. Washington's one-sentence directive, dated 8:27 p.m. on November 4, 1901, conjured an aura of gravitas. "Please call and see the attorney general stating that you called at my request[,]" he wrote, "confidential and private."

Washington, who was born into slavery in Virginia in 1856, had emerged as a spokesman for black Americans in the wake of Frederick Douglass's death in February 1895. In September of that year, Washington appeared at the Cotton States and International Exposition in Atlanta, Georgia, a congressionally sanctioned festival of trade, technology, and commerce. Across the fairgrounds, workers installed a midway and a Ferris wheel (the first such contraption had been constructed only three years earlier, for the Chicago World Fair), and one display featured the Liberty Bell, on loan from Philadelphia. Pavilions celebrated economic development, machinery, electricity, and the Southern Railway. A separate structure charted the postemancipation narrative of the black race, with American flags and a statue of a nude male wearing a wrist iron. The exposition's photographer, who circulated among the halls, capturing images of Native Americans and Eskimos, recorded both the "Negro building"—which had been built by African Americans—and barefoot African American boys, huddled outside at an undisclosed site called "Coonville," playing "Craps."

As a gesture of racial amity, organizers invited Washington, the head of the Tuskegee Normal and Industrial Institute, to speak on behalf of African Americans, and to do so, remarkably, from the same dais as whites. Attuned to his milieu, Washington hailed "a new era of industrial progress." He urged African Americans to befriend white neighbors, eschew "ornamental gewgaws," and gravitate toward "common occupations," such as farming and domestic service. "Cast down your bucket where you are," he said. "No race can prosper till it learns that there is as much dignity in tilling a field as in writing a poem."

Unlike Douglass, who championed assertiveness, Washington paired his self-improvement message with an ethos of submissiveness, a disinclination to fixate on "grievances" at the expense of "opportunities." He thanked "northern philanthropists" for supporting African American education—their munificence had endowed the Tuskegee Institute—calling such contributions "a constant stream of blessing and encouragement." Eight months before the Supreme Court's separate-but-equal decision in *Plessy*, Washington sanctioned compliance with Jim Crow, not defiance. "The wisest among my race understand that the agitation of questions of social equality is the extremest folly, and that progress in the enjoyment of all privileges that will come to us must be the result of severe and constant struggle rather than of artificial forcing," he said. "No race that has anything to contribute to the markets of the world is long in any degree ostracized."

Over the years, Robert Terrell and Washington, with their shared roots in antebellum Virginia, had formed a relationship premised on mutual esteem. Six months after the Atlanta exposition, Washington raised similar themes at Bethel Literary and Historical Association. In response, Terrell filed a dispatch for the *New York Age*, hailing vocational education as practiced at Tuskegee and Virginia's Hampton Institute, where Washington had received his training. "The man who teaches the greatest number of boys how to make two blades of grass grow where one grew before is doing the best work for humanity," he wrote, acknowledging, with candor forged in personal experience, that a four-year university degree was expensive and hence beyond the grasp of the working poor. Later that year, after Washington received an honorary master's degree from Harvard, he returned Terrell's compliment. As an alumnus yourself, he wrote in a handwritten note dated July 19, 1896, you know "what a blessed privilege it is" to be affiliated with its graduates. "This action of Harvard gives me new strength and courage for the work."

By November 1901, with a Harvard alumnus occupying the White House, Washington cemented his status as a powerbroker. Earlier that fall, after an assassin shot President McKinley in Buffalo, Vice President Theodore Roosevelt had become, at forty-two, the youngest president in history, heralding a series of shifts. A New York City native, Roosevelt was the first president born in a big city. Alone among his predecessors, he claimed heritage linking him both to the Union cause, embraced by his father, a Republican who backed Lincoln, and to the Confederacy, supported by his mother, who was raised on a Georgia plantation. Roosevelt was also a progressive reformer, a contrast to the conservative McKinley, who stood for postwar laissez-faire, deference to industry, and, in racial matters, deference to the South.

As the son of a patrician mother and a wealthy mercantile father, Roosevelt had grown up protected by nineteenth-century privilege: private tutors, foreign travels, and domestic help. Throughout childhood, though often sick with asthma and other ailments, he had nurtured an interest in science and an affinity for classifying birds, insects, and animals. At Harvard, he belonged to Porcellian, the most selective of the undergraduate social fraternities known as final clubs. In public life, including his previous stints as civil service commissioner and New York City police commissioner, Roosevelt revealed a sensibility that was keyed to the emerging century. Unfettered by experience or service in the Civil War, he saw reform as a safeguard, a corrective that protected institutions and countered radicalism. True to his class and his pedigree, Roosevelt viewed African Americans as inferior to whites. Still, in the long run, he felt that with increased opportunity, future generations would earn equality. In the interim, worthy blacks deserved to be recognized.

Still, Roosevelt was as yet unelected, having ascended to the presidency from the number 2 spot. Earlier in his career, as a New York assemblyman and governor, he had surmounted impressions of insubstantiality, stemming, in part, from his upper-crust and intellectual bona fides, his center-parted hair, his predilection for monocles, pink shirts, and English boaters, his summer home in Oyster Bay, Long Island. But by 1901 he was a seasoned politician, intent on winning the White House outright in 1904, and to do that Roosevelt knew he had to neutralize Senator Mark Hanna, a possible rival for the GOP nomination. This in turn required cultivating support among southerners—including African Americans—with his own spoils system, independent of Hanna's machine.

For Roosevelt, whose career stood as testament to his ambition and savvy, Booker T. Washington was a natural ally: an educator who was revered as a hero and who cultivated the black press and northern whites. Like Roosevelt, Washington relegated African Americans, at least for the foreseeable future, to a subordinate role (where as a matter of biology and culture, most of them belonged, Roosevelt believed). In January, in a column for the *New York Age*, Washington had written that most whites rarely encountered "the higher and better" class of African Americans, while the "Negro loafer, drunkard and gambler can be seen without social contact."

At the White House on September 29, 1901, nine days after McKinley's funeral, Roosevelt met with Washington and outlined his plan for improving conditions for black Americans. In deference to southern racial sentiments, he would not appoint significant numbers of African Americans in the South, where such a move would aggravate racism. Instead, as a northern Republican eyeing his prospects—no longer a Republican holdover in a Democratic administration, doling out federal largesse—he would limit such appointments to only a few "superior" African Americans.

Washington dined at the White House with the president and First Lady Edith Roosevelt two and a half weeks later, on October 16. Previous administrations, of course, had entertained nonwhite Americans at the executive mansion. President Grover Cleveland, for example, invited Frederick Douglass to a congressional reception—which the southern delegations boycotted—and hosted a dinner with Queen Liliuokalani, the Hawaiian monarch. But when news of Roosevelt's engagement surfaced in the press, southern politicians erupted, spewing venom from Alabama to Tennessee. "The president's attempt to make the Negro equal to the white man socially is an insult to the Southern people," said an ex-mayor of Charlotte, North Carolina, one of several officials who aired his grievances in the press. Others forecast Republican doom below the Mason-Dixon line. "No self-respecting Southern man can ally himself with the President after what has occurred," said Georgia's Democratic governor Allen D. Candler, a Confederate veteran who had lost an eye during the Battle of Jonesboro.

Meanwhile, as Terrell curated newspaper coverage of the imbroglio for his files, Washington lobbied Roosevelt to pick Terrell for a local judgeship, arguing that his fellow Harvard alumnus embodied the highest achievements of his race. On November 12, eight days after Washington had cabled Terrell, Roosevelt nominated Terrell to one of ten justice of the peace vacancies in the capital. A second nominee, Emanuel M. Hewlett, was the son of a Harvard gymnastics instructor, the university's first African American staff member. Roosevelt's eight remaining candidates were white.

With near unanimity, the white and black presses hailed Terrell's selection. Among whites who cared about the capital's African American students, Terrell would be "particularly acceptable," said the *Washington Evening Star*. Similarly, the *New York Evening Post* lauded Roosevelt's "common-sense" approach, opining on November 13, 1901, that Roosevelt's selective method of appointing blacks should have been implemented earlier. "Fewer negroes will be appointed under the new rules," the editors wrote, "but the colored people will be much better off with only the right sort of men representing them in office, and the relations between the two races in the South will be relieved from a needless strain."

Five months later, Terrell began arranging with his father-in-law, Robert R. Church, for a loan to help him repay about $2,000 that he owed to Capital Savings Bank. As Terrell explained in a letter to Church dated April 23, 1902, the debt stemmed from his own personal borrowings, about which he did not elaborate, and from transactions dating back to his law and real estate firm, Lynch & Terrell. The commercial ventures, which he did not describe, had turned out poorly, he and Lynch were personally liable on the debt, and neither of them had the ability to repay. As he pointed out, he was a director of the bank and he and a few other directors—he did not identify them—were significantly indebted to the institution; if it should ever fail, his borrowing could raise questions and, given his standing as a judge, he needed to remain beyond reproach.

★ ★ ★ ★ ★

Inside Metropolitan AME Church, on M Street, NW, Mary Church Terrell braved a rostrum where Frederick Douglass had once spoken. It was August 10, 1904, and an assemblage of African American elites had convened, about six blocks north of the White House, in her honor: ministers and doctors, lawyers and professors. For an *Evening Star* reporter, assigned to cover the evening, the names alone furnished copy: Robert Terrell's colleague, Judge Hewlett; Douglass's son, Charles, who had fought with the 54th Massachusetts Infantry during the Civil War. Booker T. Washington had sent his regrets, praising Terrell's "notable success abroad in behalf of our race."

Less than three months earlier, on May 25, 1904, Mary had sailed from Baltimore on a Wednesday afternoon, leaving her husband and six-year-old Phyllis, who pleaded, without success, to tag along. In June, Mary appeared before the International Congress of Women, a two-week convocation in Berlin whose planners had asked her to share her views about African American women. Terrell delivered her address in English and in German. During a separate appearance, she spoke in French. A month later, based on input from its special Berlin correspondent, the suffragist Ida Husted Harper, the *Washington Post* ran an editorial saying that Terrell had emerged as "the hit of the congress," at least among American participants, because of her proficiency in French and the host country's native tongue. A French reporter told the *Independent* that Terrell had surpassed other speakers with her "ease of manner, gracefulness and force of gesture and naturalness of expression."

Even before the Berlin engagements, Mary Church Terrell had enjoyed a spike of recognition. In mid-May, while lecturing at Oberlin, she received news from her husband, who tended to her correspondence in Washington, that the *North American Review* had decided to publish her essay, "Lynching from a Negro's Point of View." "Darling wife," he had written in a note on his judicial letterhead, "A thousand congratulations on your success with [the] Review." After her bylined piece ran in the June issue—netting her a $75.00 payment—she vaulted to international renown, sparking a rebuttal in *Harper's Weekly*, which called her article "wrong-headed" and "morbid." Lewis H. Douglass, Frederick Douglass's oldest son, and also a veteran of the 54th Massachusetts Infantry, sent her a letter of praise. In a postscript to Robert, he called her "the greatest woman that we have." "Tell her that her article is a masterpiece," he added.

Robert, meanwhile, had retreated into what he referred to as "the cold neutrality of the impartial judge," though he still managed occasional commentary, including a recent magazine piece calling Roosevelt "one of the great 'Men of Our Times.'" As a writer, Robert had a gift for grace and clarity, honed over years of contributing to the African American press. And, notwithstanding her solo credit, Mary's lynching article bore traces of his influence: a twelve-word lede, flawless typing, straightforward logic, lawyerlike marshaling of facts. But in private, at least in a communiqué from one of Robert's journalism contacts, Mary's Berlin performance sparked a hint of wonderment. "Think we can look at Mollie when she gets back?" asked a scribe from the *New York Age*.

Inside the congregation where mourners had once gathered for Douglass's funeral, the audience applauded Terrell, delaying her, for several moments, from plunging into her prepared text. On the first page of her remarks, which she had drafted for the occasion, she invoked the first-person forty-one times: "I," "me," "my," and, in one instance, "I myself." Still, from the opening sentence of her speech, she endeavored to set a tone of modesty. "The sound of my own voice has fallen upon my ears so often during the past two months, my friends," she said, "that it would be far pleasanter for me personally if I were permitted to be a spectator [rather] than a participant tonight, I assure you."

Mary thanked her supporters for their "great kindness of heart." She saluted her father and her husband, saying they had enabled her to venture abroad, and her mother, for taking care of Phyllis. And, as if addressing off-stage skeptics, Mary paused to acknowledge Robert at length. He supported her, read drafts of her articles, listened to her speeches, and served as her "confidant," "assistant," and "friend," she said. In fact, she added, he "insisted so forcibly" on her career, she felt compelled to accept speaking invitations or risk a divorce. Mary also acknowledged that a wife could not excel in literary work, on the lecture platform, or in any other field, unless her husband "thoroughly approves," and for that, he must be broad-minded, with generosity of spirit and heart.

Mary then transitioned to a broader point. During her two-month interlude in Europe, she said, she had dined with conference participants and mingled with the aristocracy on terms of "perfect social equality." In Berlin, she stayed with a German family, who settled her into a suite of rooms and assigned a maid to tend to her needs. She and the other American delegates, including the suffragist Susan B. Anthony, attended a garden party hosted by a German count and a reception held by the American ambassador and his wife. In London, two days before sailing from Liverpool, Mary had called on the Countess of Warwick.

Back in the United States, though, Mary encountered the vagaries of racial prejudice. On a train between Wilmington, Delaware, and Washington, she told the audience, she witnessed "the working of the Jim Crow car." Whatever she saw, whether she had been humiliated or someone else, she didn't say. The next day, in its coverage of the speech, the *Post* reported that every speaker inside the church, including "the guest of honor herself," viewed Mary's feats in Berlin as "a triumph for the entire negro race."

Mary left for a speaking tour in Atlanta on February 18, 1905, toting a new journal, a gift from Robert. For the next few days, she wrote about her engagements, transcribing impressions by hand on the unlined white pages. At a Congregational church, she spoke to a modest but respectful audience. In a whites-only elevator, which she rode because the freight lift was busy, a white man mistook her for a white woman. Later, though, during an evening trip to Savannah, she found herself relegated to the Jim Crow coach. "Had a restful night considering the kind of car in which I rode," she wrote.

As an inveterate newspaper reader, Mary Church Terrell knew blacks faced increasing hostility in the South, where Booker T. Washington's dinner with the Roosevelts had fueled recriminations. In recent months alone, family and peers had funneled intelligence to Mary and Robert, like battlefield correspondents filing updates from the front. A ticket agent in New

Orleans rebuffed Robert's sister Laura, who had attempted to secure a berth in a sleeper car to Tuskegee. The agent, who said the berths were sold out, told her "it was time to go back to Washington." And, as a childhood friend informed Mary in a letter dated September 15, 1904, "a very fine café" in St. Louis, where the NACW gathered for its convention, refused to serve two African Americans.

Still, even with her awareness of discrimination endured by others, Mary hadn't braced for the possibility that she, too, might face restrictions. On February 25, when she left Athens, Georgia, and found herself consigned to the Jim Crow car, she vented to her diary. The coach had no ventilation, she wrote, and a "dirty" floor, until she complained to the conductor, who had the surface cleaned. If she hadn't packed a lunch, she added, she would have starved, since the railway offered no provisions for black passengers.

That spring, on another lecture tour, Mary boarded a train in Huntington, West Virginia. At the end of her journey lay Covington, Virginia, where state law mandated separate coaches for whites and blacks. Near the border between the jurisdictions, the conductor insisted Mary move to the Jim Crow car. When she refused, he threatened to have her arrested. Concerned about missing her next engagement Mary eventually relented. But the next day, she ruminated about the incident, recalling the pleasure white passengers had derived from her degradation. In a journal entry for May 3, she grappled with shame and regret, fearing she had made a mistake. "Some of us must be martyrs for the sake of the rest."

★ ★ ★ ★ ★

On July 10, 1905, almost three dozen intellectuals converged on a hotel in Ontario, Canada, summoned by W. E. B. Du Bois, who had received a PhD from Harvard a decade earlier. Du Bois, a New England native, also wrote the 1903 treatise, *The Souls of Black Folk*, challenging Booker T. Washington's creed and preeminence. Invoking the legacy of Douglass, Du Bois rejected Washington's "attitude of adjustment and submission," his "gospel of Work and Money." Black American men had a duty to "insist" on full citizenship, as envisioned by the Declaration of Independence, he wrote.

Before disbanding the Canadian summit, attendees voted to call themselves the Niagara Movement, from the nearby falls, and endorsed principles Du Bois had articulated in his book: voting rights; equal citizenship, with desegregation; and equal educational opportunities, not just vocational training. Unlike Washington, Niagara disciples embraced protest, not capitulation, in the face of discrimination. "Persistent manly agitation is the way to liberty," they affirmed.

Du Bois's sense of impatience resonated with Mary, and, in spite of her husband's allegiance to Washington, her conduct began to betray hints of her sympathies. In the early morning hours of October 28, she entered Virginia on a Washington-bound train, bearing her home from St. Louis. At the commonwealth's border, a porter ordered her to move to the Jim Crow car. She refused. In Charlottesville, a female cousin of Robert's boarded and, together, she and Mary went to the segregated coach. "The conductor did not like it, I think," she wrote in her journal.

Mary heard Du Bois speak at Metropolitan AME Church two months later, on December 29, 1905. The US Senate had recently confirmed Robert for a second four-year term. Mary's eleven-year-old niece, also named Mary, had, only a few days earlier, come to live with her, Robert, and Phyllis. "So that is settled," the elder Mary had confided in her journal on December 23, 1905. "Whether or not it is for the best remains to be seen." On this particular evening, though, Terrell's thoughts lay with Du Bois. "I enjoyed it very much," she wrote in her diary.

★ ★ ★ ★ ★

Mary Church Terrell's personal frustrations echoed similar ones felt by black Americans on a national level, not just in Washington and not just on southern trains. Around midnight on August 13, 1906, violence erupted in Brownsville, Texas, near Fort Brown, where the Twenty-Fifth Infantry had stationed African American soldiers. A haze of ambiguity cloaked the underlying events, but in the ensuing unrest, allegedly instigated by armed black troops, a white bartender died and a police official was seriously injured. On August 16, the *Washington Post* quoted a Houston paper that referred to the soldiers as "black ruffians" and "brutes." The next day, in its lead story, the *Post* said Brownsville residents had purchased more than four hundred rifles and erected a "citizens guard" between the city and the fort, where even the officers feared the black battalion.

The War Department promised a full investigation. The inspector general, Major Augustus Blocksom, wired his initial report to President Roosevelt less than ten days after the disturbance. Blocksom's findings echoed theories—if not fabrications—floated by white residents, setting a tone and template from which the army did not deviate: a band of nine to fifteen black soldiers had staged a midnight raid, firing 75 to 150 shots; women and children had narrowly escaped harm. Even Blocksom's explanations hinted at his partiality. Whites had resented the presence of black troops, whom they deemed socially inferior, he said. Black soldiers had bristled at "slights," including their exclusion from area saloons. Unofficially, not for publication, some army officers cited Roosevelt's Booker T. Washington dinner, saying it sparked a change in attitude among the African American regiments, conferring a measure of "cockiness."

Still, even within the military, exculpatory evidence surfaced. The commander of the army's southwestern division, Brigadier General William S. McCaskey, had relayed a telegram to the War Department in August, warning that Brownsville citizens harbored "race hatred to an extreme degree." The troops' white commanding officer vouched for their whereabouts, saying he had tallied them, in their barracks, at the time of the disorder. Spent army rifle shells—proffered as proof of guilt—could have been planted.

Roosevelt meted out his punishment four weeks later: he discharged "without honor" 167 African American soldiers, stemming from allegations that they "participated in" the unrest. His mandate barred the troops—companies B, C, and D of the Twenty-Fifth Infantry—from future service in any branch of the military. And, with severity and breadth that puzzled major metropolitan dailies, he impeded them from ever working for the government, even as civilian messengers or mail carriers. In the end, Roosevelt opted to avoid alienating the South, whose trust he had labored to regain. He sided with Brownsville's whites, and in an effort to forestall adverse publicity and hold onto the black vote, didn't release his order discharging the troops until after the midterm congressional election.

The army had never granted the black soldiers a hearing, a trial, or a court-martial proceeding. The troops were given no opportunity to defend themselves, cross-examine witnesses, or test the reliability of the evidence allegedly amassed against them. Military investigators cited, as proof of the soldiers' culpability, their failure to implicate colleagues. On the basis of this alleged conspiracy to remain silent and obstruct justice, the army deemed the men unfit for service, saying they were a menace to their country.

Like legions of African Americans, Mary had revered Roosevelt for his hospitality to Booker T. Washington. When Roosevelt received an honorary degree from Harvard in 1902, she wrote to Robert from Cambridge, saying she waved to "Teddy" and that he "returned the salute." When Roosevelt had won his 1904 election bid, with African American support, Mary, Robert, and Phyllis had filed into a lunchroom on Pennsylvania Avenue and watched the inaugural parade. On September 30, 1905, when Roosevelt returned to Washington with his children, Mary and Phyllis joined a scrum of supporters to welcome the First Family back to the capital. But, as even Booker T. Washington acknowledged, with the Brownsville decision Roosevelt had squandered his support among black Americans, who consigned him to the oblivion of an outcast.

On November 17, 1906, the day after the first black troops received discharge papers, Mary descended on the State, War, and Navy Building, located just west of the White House. Unlike much of official Washington, where neoclassicism prevailed, the State, War, and Navy Building looked like a Second Empire wedding cake, fashioned from granite and cast iron. Since the late-nineteenth century, the ten-acre facility had yoked together, under one Mansard roof, three departments consecrated to diplomacy and military aggression. Adornments befitting a chateau lined the interior: gaslight chandeliers, carved mantels, floors inlaid with black slate and white marble, eight spiral granite staircases, accented with bronze balustrades and mahogany handrails.

Inside, Mary presented herself to Fred W. Carpenter, the personal secretary to William Howard Taft, Roosevelt's War Department chief. Carpenter, who projected an aura of piety, with dark, center-parted hair, and a cleft chin, informed Mary Taft had just returned from a western tour, would embark on another trip the following day, and already had more matters vying for his attention than he could resolve.

In fact, Mary did not know what she would have said to Taft had she seen him. She had no idea whether Taft, a Yale-educated former federal judge and former governor of the Philippines, had authority to countermand a directive by the commander-in-chief. But John Milholland, a New York–based member of the Constitution League, which was devoted to combating discrimination and disfranchisement, had telephoned her that morning at home and asked her to appeal to Taft directly. So she installed herself outside Taft's inner sanctum and waited.

Late that afternoon, Taft summoned Mary to his office, a space equipped with a fireplace and heavy drapes. He asked Mary what she expected him to do. At best, his options were limited. The president was traveling to Puerto Rico from Panama, where he had inspected progress on a canal that would link the Atlantic and Pacific Oceans. And Roosevelt had already decreed the soldiers' removal. Mary pressed her case, saying she merely wanted Secretary Taft to suspend Roosevelt's mandate until the troops could stand trial.

Taft repeated her request, like a jurist sparring with an advocate. All you want me to do is withhold the order, he said. Is that *all* you want me to do? he added, with gentle sarcasm and a smile. Shifting her emphasis, like a lawyer saddled with adverse facts, Mary appealed to fairness. As she no doubt knew, Taft, a Cincinnati, Ohio, native with a broad forehead, a handlebar mustache, and a frame that hovered around three hundred pounds, was the son of Alphonso Taft, an abolitionist judge who had served as President Ulysses S. Grant's attorney general and secretary of war. And Alphonso's son, renowned for his administrative prowess, had long aspired to one position, as had his father before him: chief justice of the US Supreme Court.

At 4:25 p.m. that same afternoon, Taft dispatched an eighty-word cable to Roosevelt, sent through the American legation in Panama. Roosevelt knew Mary and her husband, of course, as well as her brother Thomas. But in his communiqué, Taft did not refer to them by name, or mention his meeting with Mary. His message bore traces of the concerns she raised, though he did not attribute them to her or the Constitution League. Given the president's reputation for impulsivity—his tendency to make snap judgments—Taft couched his appeal about the Fort Brown soldiers in pragmatism. In Roosevelt's home turf, the New York Republican Club had adopted resolutions blasting the president's Brownsville edict and demanding its reversal.

"New York Repub. Club & many others," Taft wrote, had clamored for abeyance of the Brownsville directive. The army had partially complied, he continued, meaning some of the soldiers had fielded dismissal papers. And in the netherworld of partial compliance, Taft navigated with aplomb, mapping a route that would enable him to forestall additional dismissals and, perhaps, increase pressure on the president to convene a tribunal.

Taft offered to wire again the following day with an update, indicating how many troops, if any, had not yet received official notices. If the army had "fully complied" with Roosevelt's directions, he added, the status quo would be "the same" when the president returned, "without further action." In other words, Taft would not reverse the discharges if all of the soldiers had already received termination papers. But without saying so directly, he hinted at one option he retained: if only some of the soldiers had been notified, he could block the entire order.

And with the delicacy of a cabinet officer seeking subtle ways of countermanding the president who appointed him, he nudged Roosevelt to reconsider. "Much agitation on the subject[,] and it may be well to convince people of fairness of hearing by granting rehearing," he cabled.

The next day, from Atlanta to Providence, newspapers trumpeted Mary Church Terrell and her session with Taft. In Washington alone, her name landed in three papers—the *Post*, the *Herald*, and the *Evening Star*. The *New York Times* called her "one of the leading colored educators of the country." Like an avid student, she marked her copies of the articles, underlining her name and portions of the text. "At her request," the *Post* noted, Secretary Taft had cabled the president. Mary bracketed that entire sentence.

For several years, Mary had been collecting news articles about herself, pasting them into a scrapbook. For thoroughness, and a compendium of nonlocal coverage, she subscribed to a New York–based press-clipping service, Henry Romeike, Inc., which billed itself as "The First Established and Most Complete Newspaper Cutting Bureau in the World." In her journal, in which she lamented the tedium of preserving her own archives, she said her comments should be safeguarded for their historical import, as a record of black American women of her era. "I get no special satisfaction out of seeing my name in print," she wrote.

Her attentiveness to her press coverage suggested otherwise. In this case, she pored over the *Times*'s account, which reported that Roosevelt was unlikely to reverse himself. Nonetheless, the *Times* also noted that he appeared to have "exceeded"—Mary underscored that word—his "presidential authority." In particular, the *Times* said, Roosevelt might have lacked power to sanction the troops without a hearing and ban them from future nonmilitary government jobs.

Taft froze Roosevelt's decree the next day, on November 19, directing a halt to any further discharges. The president had not yet responded to his cable. But as the *Post* pointed out, if Roosevelt wished to change his mind, his war secretary had just created the opportunity.

A member of New York's Republican Club penned a letter to Mary on November 20, congratulating her on her service to humanity. "You have not lived in vain!" he wrote, adding a Latin phrase: "*Esto Perpetua*" (*May she endure forever*).

When Roosevelt finally caught up with Taft's cable, he fired off a response. "Discharge is not to be suspended unless there are new facts of such importance as to warrant your cabling me," he said. "I care nothing whatever for the yelling of either the politicians or the sentimentalists." In private, Booker T. Washington and Charles W. Anderson, a tax collector at the Internal Revenue Service's New York office, urged the administration to reconsider. Roosevelt also received letters commending his action, including one from the Harvard history professor Albert Bushnell Hart, who said that the president had given black Americans "a very necessary lesson" about justice and responsibility. Still, when Senator Joseph B. Foraker, an Ohio Republican and Civil War veteran, began calling for an inquiry, the president revealed a trace of uncertainty, asking Taft, in confidence, to probe the Brownsville matter.

Mary and Du Bois, on the other hand, telegraphed conviction and solidarity, broadcasting their dissatisfaction with Roosevelt from the December issue of the *Voice*, a Chicago-based monthly magazine. The president had "earned the distrust and disapprobation of the best class of black men," wrote Du Bois, urging all black males to "insist" upon justice for the Brownsville troops. Terrell used her piece to convey optimism, noting the incident had united American blacks. "And so for the time being, at least, let us regard the terrible catastrophe which h[a]s filled the whole race with grief as an evil out of which good will eventually come."

Meanwhile, in early December, confidential telegrams streamed into the White House from Norway. In a decision to be announced to the public the following week, the Norwegian Parliament's Nobel Committee had tapped Roosevelt for its 1906 Peace Prize, the sixth time the award had been given. Official confirmation came nine days later. Roosevelt had received the accolade for his efforts to broker a peace between Japan and Russia during the Russo-Japanese War of 1904 and 1905. The cash value of the prize was an estimated $37,000—almost 75 percent of his presidential salary. After conferring with his wife, Roosevelt donated the money to a foundation, earmarking it for creation of a "permanent Industrial Peace Committee."

That same day, December 10, Mary composed a letter to Gilchrist Stewart, a black Republican leader in New York who was spearheading the bid to denounce the president over Brownsville, and, more recently, had undertaken a Brownsville investigation for the Constitution League, the fruits of which he shared with Senator Foraker. In her note to Stewart, Mary said that she had spoken with one of the discharged soldiers, Sergeant Mingo Sanders, a veteran with more than two decades of service. Given the atmosphere in Washington, though, she did not sound optimistic about Sanders's prospects, or those of the other troops. "I hope the soldiers will be reinstated, but the road seems a bit rough just now."

To the public, Roosevelt did not equivocate. In a special message to the Senate, dated December 19, he defended his action, condemning the black soldiers as "lawless and murderous." Evidence of their guilt was "conclusive," he added, lamenting only the punishment of dishonorable discharge, and not for its severity. As a response, he said, it was "utterly inadequate." The Senate, after its own examination, would later agree with him.

★ ★ ★ ★ ★

Five months after Brownsville, on January 24, 1907, Mary Church Terrell turned to the magazine world again, this time anonymously, to confront racism in Washington. In an uncredited essay titled "What It Means to Be Colored in the Capital of the United States," Mary—without disclosing her identity—told readers of the *Independent*, a New York–based weekly, that she had lived in Washington for fifteen years and the capital had done its best to make conditions "intolerable" for blacks. From hotels and restaurants to theaters and department stores, she chronicled the city's Jim Crow restrictions, as well as the dearth of nonmenial jobs for African Americans. "And surely nowhere in the world do oppression and persecution based solely on the color of the skin appear more hateful and hideous than in the capital of the United States, because the chasm between the principles upon which this Government was founded, in which it still professes to believe, and those which are daily practiced under the protection of the flag, yawns so wide and deep," she wrote. In a comment at the top of her piece, the editor described the writer as "a colored woman of much culture and recognized standing"; he also observed that Congress controlled Washington's affairs.

Mary dealt with the South more broadly, and without the cloak of anonymity, a few months later. In August 1907, she placed an article about involuntary servitude and convict labor in the *Nineteenth Century and After*, a British magazine. She had remarked upon the phenomena before, including a year earlier in the same magazine, as part of an extended essay on the South, lawlessness, lynching, and prejudice. Now, though, she explained chain gangs in detail to her British audience. Throughout the South, she wrote, thousands of African American men, women, and children suffered a form of enslavement more oppressive than any they had known before emancipation. They were detained on "trumped-up charges," she said, were confined to cells, malnourished, overworked, and "only partially covered with vermin-infested rags."

Several weeks later, Mary received a letter from Oswald Garrison Villard, a grandson of the abolitionist William Lloyd Garrison. Villard, who soured on Booker T. Washington after Brownsville, wrote that he had railed against peonage—as the practice was called—almost weekly in the *New York*

Evening Post, where he served as publisher. "But there should be national agitation."

Mary's husband, meanwhile, defended his patron. In a bylined article for the *New York Age*, Robert hailed Booker T. Washington as "the great leader of his race," praising a recent mid-September speech to several thousand admirers at the Negro Baptist Convention. Washington, in turn, defended himself, telling the audience he never suggested that black Americans should surrender their rights. "We should do our utmost in every part of the country to prove to the world that we are worthy of the same protection of the law that is guaranteed to any other class of citizens," he said. But for Mary, who was more inclined than Robert toward Villard's call for resistance, Washington's implicit embrace of patience—his plea for blacks to demonstrate their worthiness as a condition of equality—had lost its appeal, suffering along with Roosevelt in Brownsville's aftermath.

Her own status as a race spokesperson, on the other hand, kept improving, especially among progressive whites who paid to hear her on the lecture circuit. On October 14, 1907, she appeared at Pilgrim Church in Cleveland, Ohio, her first stop on a three-week midwestern tour. As a booking, it was an auspicious start. Her speech coincided with a day-long meeting of the American Missionary Association, and brought her face-to-face with Supreme Court Justice David J. Brewer, who was also one of the speakers.

Brewer, the son of a Congregationalist minister, had abstained from the Court's *Plessy* decision, making him the only jurist, other than Justice John Marshall Harlan, not to vote with the majority. Justice Harlan, of course, had dissented on legal grounds. Brewer, an appointee of President Harrison, opted out for personal ones: his daughter had died of tuberculosis, and, on the day of the *Plessy* oral argument, he was absent from court. Still, as a member of the Supreme Court, with his New England roots, he had earned a reputation for defending individual liberties against incursions by the state. Through frequent dissents and liberal stances, including support of women's suffrage and world peace, he reflected the reform-minded, abolitionist culture in which he was raised. More than a decade earlier, Brewer had told a gathering of missionaries the United States was not "a Caucasian nation." When he introduced Terrell that morning, he called her the "leading woman" of her race.

Mary, whose black hair now bore flecks of gray, attended Congregationalist services in Washington. In Oberlin, she had sung in the choir at First Congregational Church, located about thirty miles from her venue in Cleveland.

With Congregationalists in the audience and a Congregationalist Supreme Court justice seated nearby, she was at home.

In her remarks, titled "The Strongest for the Weakest," Terrell announced that the black race was in a moment of crisis, one that called for a new commitment to federal intervention. More than four decades after the end of the Civil War, the rupture between North and South had "practically healed," she said, because northern industrialists, who owned extensive commercial enterprises in the South, had, in deference to their economic interests, capitulated to southern racism. Then she transitioned to a theme she had pressed in writing before Brownsville, including articles for the *Voice of the Negro* in March 1905 and the *Nineteenth Century* in July 1906. Southerners, she said, had manipulated racial stereotypes, exaggerating the "vices" of black people, suppressing evidence of their achievement, and deploying the "scare crow of social equality" and the "bugaboo of negro domination." In the process, southerners had "poison[ed] the public mind" against African Americans, nearly convincing the world of southern martyrdom and black brutality.

Terrell did not refer to Roosevelt by name but she left little doubt about the scope of the federal abdication she had witnessed, at the very top, culminating in Brownsville. For the previous twenty to thirty years, she said, public opinion had shifted against black Americans, and former supporters among northern whites had deserted them. "Those who were once our strongest advocates now have almost nothing to say in our behalf or to our credit."

That afternoon, when he spoke to the assembly, Justice Brewer pushed for a more conventional approach, meaning paternalistic and condescending. Some immigrants had arrived in this country bent on anarchy and destruction, he said; African Americans, on the other hand, were "grateful" for their liberty. "And while the colored brothers may be too fond of the chicken coop and the watermelon patch, they are firm believers in social order," he added, with an apparent attempt at humor. In the long run, Brewer predicted, blacks would enjoy equal citizenship, including voting rights. In the interim, they needed Christian uplift and vocational training. "It is one thing to pick cotton or hoe potatoes and something more valuable to make a watch or run an engine."

At first, Terrell's comments at the convention barely registered in the press. Washington's *Evening Star* mentioned her name and topic, as did the *New York Times*, but the *Times* concentrated far more on Justice Brewer's speech. The *Cleveland Plain Dealer*, though, led with Terrell, quoting her at length. "Colored Woman Raps the South," read the headline. Still, she had blasted the Roosevelt administration, not just southern whites, and, before long, word filtered back to Washington.

Three days after her address, Taft's War Department released a report ascribing the violence in Brownsville to the African American troops, whose cause, of course, she had championed. That evening, the *Washington Times* splashed Mary's speech—now more than seventy-two-hours old—on its front page. "South Poisons Mind of Public Against Negro," ran the headline, with her name printed just underneath. Citing the newly released findings, the *Times* also ran a Brownsville update as its lead story, saying the army's chief of ordnance, Brigadier General William Crozier, had affixed responsibility to Company B's soldiers. In three words, the headline distilled his conclusion: "Colored Troops Blamed."

★ ★ ★ ★ ★

Practically overnight, Mary Church Terrell found herself marginalized by Booker T. Washington's supporters, including those in the black press. In an interview with the *Washington Herald*, a white daily, Howard University's president, Wilbur P. Thirkield, pointedly declined to comment on her speech. So did Roscoe Conkling Bruce, the former senator's son, who had graduated from Harvard, worked at Tuskegee, and served as principal of the capital's Armstrong Manual Training High School. A health department official who did speak for attribution, Dr. F. T. Childs, said black Americans were hopeful about the future and that "worthy" members of the race, who focused on "uplift" and proved their "merit," had many friends.

The *Washington Bee*, an African American paper, went even further. Mary Church Terrell always made such "hot air" speeches far from the action, the editors said. Citing intimate details from her private life, they leveled strikingly personal critiques, noting her ability to ride in whites-only train cars and her use of a skin lightener. They went on to question her credibility. "There is as much prejudice in the North as there is in the South, and if these bleached colored Americans who are roaming all over the country would cease attempting to pass for white and get down to their naturals[,] there would not be any excuse for this tirade against the South."

The *New York Age*, so often the platform for Robert Terrell and Booker T. Washington, also dismissed Mary's Cleveland speech, deeming it "ill-advised, ill-tempered and uncalled for." If anyone should "agitate" against the South, the editors wrote, it should be southern African Americans. Like the *Bee*, the *Age* questioned her motives, noting her financial stake, as a paid lecturer, in inciting her audience. "If some of our people would just stop talking so much about the Negro problem (at so much per speech, and do more real pushing and boosting), there would be less of this alleged 'poisoning sentiment.'"

Undeterred, Mary capped her tour with a stint in Battle Creek, Michigan. Her appearance, slated for November 1, came at the behest of Dr. John H. Kellogg, a physician and holistic health practitioner who invited her to the Battle Creek Sanitarium, a health spa dedicated to well-being and temperance—tenets of its founders, who were Seventh-day Adventists. Two days earlier, scores of delegates had converged from as far west as California, descending for the National Purity Congress, a week-long event hosted by the National Purity Federation and geared toward combating vice. From Tuskegee, Washington said he hoped to attend, but asked planners to refrain from including him in the program.

At 9 a.m. on All Souls' Day, participants assembled for devotional exercises in the sanitarium's tabernacle, which had a seating capacity of 3,500. Among them were doctors, authors, ministers and educators, social hygienists and temperance activists, and most hailed from the Northeast and the Midwest— representatives of organizations that promoted chasteness. That afternoon, the itinerary featured topics such as "Purity Instruction in the Home" and "The Medical Profession and Purity." The evening session, slated for 7:30 p.m., began with remarks from John H. Roberts, a delegate from the Alliance of Honour, which the program touted as Britain's largest "purity organization"—as they were called—for young men. Roberts, an ex-actor with a handlebar mustache, urged men and women to submit to mental, intellectual, and physical examinations before marriage. He also targeted his former profession. "The theater is a menace to the home, and if we do not fight it, it will engulf the Anglo-Saxon race in a sea of lust and infamy."

Mary spoke after Roberts. She rehashed what were now recurring themes in her speeches: northern abdication; southern oppression, including peonage; and the paucity of educational opportunities for African American children. But to a reporter for the *Battle Creek Enquirer*, who had slogged through a day of "Purity!" she made irresistible copy.

In deference to her audience's mission, Terrell focused on "the condition of the colored woman." It was a topic that she had explored several times in recent years: in her article for the *North American Review*; at the 1905 national purity conference in La Crosse, Wisconsin; and, even more recently, during a February speech, when she was quoted by the *Topeka Daily Journal*. Now, in Battle Creek, Terrell said "relations" between Romans and their slaves paled in comparison to those between "many supposedly respectable" southern white men and "some" African American women. To raise an African American girl into "a pure life" is virtually impossible, she continued, saying "constant temptations" beset her. "The only servant problem the South has today, is the problem that springs out of the relations between a colored serving girl and her white employer." A mother who valued her daughter's purity would never allow her to work for whites. "The lives of some white men are such that they cannot walk the streets without meeting their unlawful children on the way to school."

The next day, the *Enquirer* plundered Terrell's comments for headlines. "Negro Speaker Assails White Women of South," read one. The reporter noted her "sarcasm" and "scornful curl of the lip," her complexion so fair she could "easily pass" for white.

The AP proclaimed that Mary had delivered a "furious invective" against southerners. The AP, which paraphrased but did not quote her, claimed she said no servant girl was safe in a white residence. From Boston to New Orleans, newspapers tracked the AP's version—though often neglecting to credit it as the source. In Washington, the *Post* followed suit, reporting, in the second paragraph of its account, that Terrell had said, "no servant girl is safe in the home of the white people."

For readers below the Mason-Dixon line, her remarks crackled with heresy. Segregationists and white supremacists had touted their roles as guardians of virtue, shielding white women from black men. Terrell, of course, had suggested just the opposite: girls of color needed protection from white men and from white women who looked the other way. Five days later, after the *Nashville American* had reported the negative reaction from a statewide conference of the African Methodist Episcopal Church, Terrell issued a clarification. Her remarks about black girls indicated they were unsafe in many white homes, she said, but she had not meant to suggest they were at risk in all of them. The next day, another Nashville newspaper said "the majority of right-thinking negroes" disagreed with Terrell.

Back in Washington, Mary tried again to clarify her position. In twin letters to the editors of the *Nashville American* and the *Charleston News and Courier*—a typed draft of her missive spanned almost five pages of text—she urged the papers to correct their stories, insofar as they suggested she had proclaimed "no servant girl" safe in a white household. I made "no such statement," she wrote, and "I have never made any such wild, sweeping and false statement anywhere in my life."

★ ★ ★ ★ ★

On George Washington's birthday, February 22, 1908, Congressman James T. Heflin angled to revise a Washington streetcar bill, an oversight measure regulating fares to Union Station, the capital's recently opened railway hub. Heflin, a Democrat, represented Alabama's Fifth Congressional District, which included the Tuskegee Institute. Out on the campaign trail, Heflin, who was known as "Cotton Tom," once reportedly said he wished someone had detonated a dynamite charge under Roosevelt and Booker T. Washington during their White House dinner. Now, almost four months after Terrell's servant-girl speech, Heflin floated an amendment calling for segregated Washington streetcars. Separate coaches for whites and blacks had fixed the race problem in Alabama, he said, and Jim Crow would have the same effect in the capital.

Several northern and midwestern congressmen balked, even denouncing the proposal as "un-American" and "evil." Representative Philip P. Campbell, a Kansas Republican, said he had never seen any offensive conduct by black streetcar passengers in Washington. Heflin retaliated with a series of questions aimed at Campbell. Do you believe black and white children should attend the same school? Would you worship with a nigger? Do you believe in racial intermarriage? Campbell, an attorney, shouted back, answering each in turn. His children attended an integrated school in his hometown, he said; he attended services with a black American the previous Sunday. And no, he would not allow his daughter to marry a black man, he said, invoking the gulf between political equality and social equality. "I would not permit my daughter to marry some white men," he added. Heflin's amendment went down in defeat.

On February 27, Mary brought Phyllis and Mary—the niece Terrell was raising—to a White House reception for visiting school superintendents. Roosevelt, who hosted the gathering, spoke about the necessity of requiring children to work. In her journal, Terrell sniffed at the president's hypocrisy. "I dare say Alice hasn't made many beds nor washed many dishes," she said, referring to Roosevelt's oldest child. "And Theodore, Jr. hasn't split much kindling."

Congressman Heflin boarded a Pennsylvania Avenue streetcar a month later, on March 27, 1908, bound for Capitol Hill. Inside the coach, he spotted an African American passenger, Lewis Lundy, drinking from a whiskey bottle.

Heflin, en route to making a temperance speech, told Lundy not to imbibe in front of female passengers. Lundy's response allegedly included epithets. They scuffled; Heflin pushed Lundy off the train. From the street, Lundy allegedly cursed at the congressman again. Heflin pulled out a .38-caliber revolver and started firing through a window. One bullet, discharged before the congressman took aim, wounded a fleeing passenger, embedding in either his ankle, his foot, or his leg—news accounts differed. Another bullet struck Lundy, either grazing his head above the right ear, or lodging in his skull or his arm—press coverage varied on this score as well. Both victims landed in the hospital.

The police arrested Heflin. According to one news outlet, he refused to ride in the patrol wagon because he was a congressman. Inside the station, Heflin entertained visits from House colleagues, including fellow members of Alabama's delegation. Speaker Joseph G. Cannon, an Illinois Republican and former prosecutor, dispatched Andrew Neal, a black messenger, who relayed information from the precinct to the House leader at home.

Heflin, an attorney, released a statement offering several justifications for his conduct: Lundy had insulted a lady by swearing and drinking in her presence; he had insulted the congressman, by subjecting him to epithets; and he acted in self-defense, drawing his weapon when Lundy gestured toward his hip pocket, as if indicating he had a firearm. As for his own gun, Heflin said the police had given him permission to carry a concealed weapon because he received threatening letters about the streetcar proposal. The next day, after Heflin was released on bail, the *Baltimore Sun* recounted, without attribution, details allegedly stemming from Lundy's medical treatment. "It is said," the *Sun* reported, that Lundy was intoxicated and demonstrated "supernatural strength," as well as symptoms of a cocaine habit.

Mary and the girls fled Washington in mid-July for a vacation in the mountains, dividing their time between Cumberland, Maryland, and Opequon, Virginia, an eighteenth-century village located in the Shenandoah Valley, about five miles southwest of Winchester. At the end of the month, during a brief trip home, Mary boarded a streetcar, juggling leisure essentials: a suitcase, a hammock, a tennis racket. On board, she asked a white man to make room for her. When he refused, she sat down anyway, prompting a comment from him. "When I tell you to move, you move," she replied. He erupted, saying, "I won't be sassed by a nigger."

Terrell slapped him. Another white passenger heckled, You're not going to let a "nigger" hit you, are you? The victim brandished his umbrella, as if he were about to strike her. "Hit me," she told him. "Just hit me, if you think [it] best." The man backed down. If he hadn't, not a single white passenger would have helped her, she wrote in her journal.

★ ★ ★ ★ ★

As a public servant, beholden to the appointment process and the politicians who controlled it, Robert was not in a position to indulge his wife. For years, they had bickered—mostly about money, especially when she bolted Washington during the summer and he remained in the capital, fielding her long-distance entreaties for cash. Now, the rift between them seemed to harden by the month.

In August, Robert joined his family on vacation for part of one Sunday. After dinner, Mary and Phyllis reclined on the hammock, clad in white dresses. In a portrait, when they once posed side-by-side, they looked like sisters, with their matching dresses and light complexions, emanating refinement and ease. Yet Robert failed to notice that Phyllis, now ten, had shorn off her braids. "He is the most unobservant man I ever saw," Mary wrote in her diary.

Later that month, a race riot erupted in Springfield, Illinois, the home of Abraham Lincoln. With its railroads, coal mines, and brickyards, Springfield had seen an influx of southern workers, black and white, drawn by the prospect of jobs. On August 14, 1908, a white woman, Mabel Hallam, accused a black man, George Richardson, of raping her. Police brought Richardson to jail, where they had detained a black murder suspect for allegedly killing a white man. When a mob converged outside the building, the sheriff shipped both black men by rail to the nearby town of Bloomington, hoping to thwart potential vigilantes. White rioters attacked black citizens instead, including an elderly black man, who was lynched. When the National Guard quashed the unrest a day later, six people had died—including four whites—dozens had sustained injuries, and an estimated 2,000 blacks had left the city.

Meanwhile, in early September, Robert fled to Boston by himself. When he returned after a twelve-day absence, Mary noted in her journal that it had been "unusual for him to stay away." On the 23rd, her birthday passed unheralded, except in her diary, where she memorialized its occurrence. Two weeks later, she wrote, she dragged her husband to stores to look at "the new Fall gowns." He bought her a pound of candy.

By virtually every measure other than intellect, the Terrells had forged an alliance of opposites. As a child she had known wealth, privilege, and separation from her family; as an adult, she had a flair for self-promotion, a memory for slights, and a habit of losing things at home and on the road. He had grown up in poverty, knowing hard work and academic success; but as an adult he struggled professionally, at least until he became a judge. Financially, he apparently relied on his father-in-law and possibly his wife for help. Robert nurtured ties to fraternal organizations, including the Masons, and relished cigars and social drinking—a source of friction with his wife. Mary, a product of protemperance Oberlin, as well as her own upbringing and beliefs about well-being, mostly abstained from alcohol. Once, in a letter, she pleaded with him to stay away from his club. "It is all bad and no good, I fear. I wish you could get recreation in some other way."

Fundamentally, they diverged about how best to advance racial equality. Unlike his wife, a political outsider by race and gender and temperament, Robert had a toehold in official Washington, leaving him no leeway for jeremiads and little margin for controversy. With the 1908 presidential election underway and Taft vying to win as Theodore Roosevelt's heir apparent, Robert's fate as a jurist, for the first time, would be decided by someone other than Roosevelt. Unlike federal judges, whose appointments came with life tenure, guaranteed by Article III of the Constitution, Robert held his post only for four years, after which his term expired. To retain his title and position, not to mention his standing in the community, he remained at the mercy of the president in office when his term ended and the Senate, which would have to reconfirm him in 1909, as it did in 1905. He had already withstood political exile, and unless he wanted to return to banishment—which he did not—he could not afford to alienate anyone who might dictate his future, including southerners in Congress—who no doubt knew of his wife's remarks on the lecture trail, since they had ricocheted across newspapers from Washington to New Orleans.

Within the political system, Robert contented himself, where possible, with lobbying for incremental reform and, above all, his own self-preservation. On the subject of Congressman Heflin and the Lundy shooting, Robert said simply that he was unaware of any history of racial strife on Washington's integrated streetcars. When the Republican National Committee inquired about his availability as a speaker, he offered a modest recommendation: creation of a Negro Bureau, which presumably would have coordinated efforts by black party loyalists. The committee rebuffed his suggestion. "On this matter I am afraid that I cannot do anything for you," wrote its secretary.

After Taft defeated William Jennings Bryan, the Democratic candidate, Terrell resorted to flattery. On November 4, the day after voters went to the polls, he wrote the president-elect a congratulatory letter, suggesting that Brownsville—such a preoccupation for his wife—had been all but forgotten: "I know that the colored people of the country are happy over your election." And with Alphonso Taft's son in the White House, dictating executive action, he added, "they need have no fear as to their rights." One month later, Terrell received a letter informing him of his appointment to the Inaugural Committee.

Meanwhile, Mary's speeches had left her defiant and isolated—not just among Washington's supporters, but within her marriage. Off the lecture circuit, she had long hurled herself into cleaning and decorating, as if they were penance for her absences. The Terrell house, a four-story red brick duplex with a pitched roof and bay windows located at 326 T Street, NW, sat back from the curb, surrounded by the row homes and single-family dwellings of LeDroit Park, a once all-white community, lined with decorative trees and shrubs, about a half-mile from Howard University. Inside, during layovers at home, Mary scrubbed and varnished floors and furniture, hung curtains and shades, rummaged through drawers, and discarded clutter. But the hours she lost to such pursuits only fanned her resentments. She employed household help, especially for cooking, yet still bemoaned the absence of anyone to assist her—an allusion to her husband's salaried existence and the domestic servants she had known as a child in her father's household, but could not afford as an adult. "I am caught in a vise of petty, harrowing domestic duties which must be done by somebody and there is no somebody but myself to do it," she wrote in her diary on March 16, 1908.

In her journal, Mary had also long despaired of her inability to write. Several years earlier, as she approached her forty-second birthday, she had vowed to author a treatise about African American women, spanning slavery to the present. When she discussed books and race with an acquaintance named Mrs. Stephen Van Rensselaer Cruger, a grandniece of Washington Irving who published "society" novels under the pen name "Julien Gordon," the response was not encouraging. The racial problem called for "a great novel," Cruger said, and given Terrell's cushions of income and education, her life did not lend itself to fiction. She suggested that her friend read Edith Wharton's novel *The House of Mirth*, with its depiction of Lily Bart, banished by scandal from New York's Gilded Age elites. Still, Mary pined for literary acclaim, wishing she could dedicate herself "exclusively" to craft and composition. Later that fall, when Robert sent her a desk from his office, she effused to her journal, conceding a moment of happiness.

Instead of writing, she shopped. In Washington's downtown department stores, such as Kann's and The Palais Royal, Mary's retail expenditures ballooned. Month after month, she lined her diary with finds, listing them by price and provenance, from suits and dresses to hats and shoes, even the occasional ball gown. She frequented a dressmaker and fielded appointments with a seamstress, who met her at home. She scheduled fittings and refittings, remade old frocks and commandeered new ones. She also outfitted Phyllis and Mary, whom she referred to her as her daughter, with summer dresses and winter coats, patent-leather shoes, satin collars, and parasols.

Six months after her streetcar incident, Mary's spending bordered on compulsion, like her mother, who had exhausted her lottery winnings while visiting her daughter in Europe. In early January 1909, two months before Taft's inauguration, Mary confided in her journal that she had ventured downtown and, inside one of the stores, found a tailored, three-piece suit for $48.75 and a blue broadcloth directoire, with a white lace front and hint of black, for $39.75. "Nearly ninety dollars is a great deal to spend for clothes[,] and yet I must have something I can wear."

At the end of January, after a morning in the stores, Mary etched a similar lament. "Spending money all the time, but the children must appear well and so must I," she wrote. A few days later, she confessed she had spent more than $300 in less than a year—roughly 10 percent of Robert's salary.

3

They Come Standing Erect

Inside the Tokes' Inn, a two-story wood-frame and log structure, erected in the 1880s and operated by former slaves, Mary Church Terrell sorted newspaper clippings about herself, arranging them in chronological order. The next day, the second of her vacation in Opequon, Virginia, she shifted her focus to Phyllis, an eleven-year-old prospective seventh grader who loved horses. As a mother, Mary admired her daughter's sweet nature, as well as her self-possession and physical endurance, but as a college graduate and school-board member, she worried about Phyllis's academic shortcomings, including even her penmanship. In her diary entry for July 28, 1909, Mary vowed to spend an hour with Phyllis every day devoted to reading, writing, and spelling.

On August 15, eight days after extending her vacation, Mary wrote a letter to her husband, bemoaning the breadth of Phyllis's deficiencies. "I try to be as calm as I can when I give her her reading lesson, but she is enough to try the patience of Job." As a former teacher who took great pride in her academic accomplishments and those of her husband, she marveled at her daughter's inability to spell a word, or sound it out, so she could try to pronounce it. "I feel like a criminal, when I think how I allowed her to run wild nearly six weeks last summer[,] without requiring her, forcing her[,] to read every day[,] as I am doing now," she said. Phyllis disliked reading, Mary realized, "because she actually doesn't know how."

After thanking Robert for sending a money order—and requesting another—Mary chose her regrets with care. She was sorry, she told her husband, that he could not spend some of his vacation with them, but she understood his aversion to the country and forgave him. They would see each other soon, she added, before signing off, with "kisses and hugs from your devoted wife."

★ ★ ★ ★ ★

As the summer of 1909 faded into fall, Mary's father, who owned the T Street duplex, deeded her half of the dwelling to her. In early September, she acknowledged a sense of gratitude and financial security. Two weeks later, on her forty-sixth birthday, she wrote an elegy for the book she yearned to write, a feat that receded further away than ever. Duties and cares surrounded her, a prison of affairs large and small, she wrote in her diary. "I am bound hand and foot," she said. "I hope I shall be able to devote some of my time and strength to literary work before I die."

In public and within her family, Mary adhered to regimen: tennis games, the Matron's Whist Club, school-board functions, a picnic with Robert and the girls. For tea with Pinckney B. S. Pinchback, a Reconstruction-era governor and lieutenant governor of Louisiana, she served crab salad and tongue. For a Booker T. Washington speech, she and her husband stationed themselves on the platform, like royalty. In the seclusion of her journal, though, she complained of exhaustion and plotted escapes. She fantasized about moving to New York with the girls and settling in the suburbs, away from Washington's oppressive, southern-style discrimination. She tallied the funds in her bank accounts, a total of $1,218, and mulled a trip to Europe. She thought about writing a book anonymously, melding her articles into a race-relations treatise.

Still, as much as Mary weighed the concept of leaving her husband, she resisted actually doing so. In part, she understood firsthand the implications, both for Phyllis and Mary and for herself. As a young girl, she had withstood the trauma of her parents' divorce and seen her mother attempt to start over in New York. As an adult, she had spent years cultivating an image of success and refinement, a public persona, shared with her husband, of membership in the black political and social elites, making them an early twentieth-century Washington power couple. Robert Terrell, with his Harvard pedigree and his professional stature, stood at the center of that realm, a linchpin to her access, just as her father's wealth had conferred status and privilege on Robert. As husband and wife, their symbiosis, however fraught with complexity and discord, continued to reap rewards. He now sat, after a congressional reorganization of the capital's judiciary, as a judge on the Municipal Court of the District of Columbia.

Instead of ending her marriage, Mary channeled her energy elsewhere. She wrote overdue replies to letters, sparred with the cook Eva, and fretted about the delay-plagued installation of a hot water heater. "House-keeping is a regular sepulcher in which a woman who wants to accomplish something buries her talent and time," she wrote in her diary on November 20.

★ ★ ★ ★ ★

Ten days before Christmas, Mary went to the Justice Department, then a five-story brownstone at 1435 K Street, NW, overlooking McPherson Square. From the exterior, with its bay windows and balconies, the headquarters building radiated discretion and inscrutability, like a private club. Inside, President Taft's attorney general, George W. Wickersham, presided over the department's antitrust prosecutions, including lawsuits against American Tobacco Company, E. I. du Pont de Nemours and Company, and Standard Oil Company.

That morning, with his reappointment in limbo, Robert had confided in his wife. Someone had sent an anonymous letter to the White House, claiming Terrell knew or should have known about the insolvency of the Capital Savings Bank. As Terrell had feared, the bank had collapsed in November 1902 and gone into receivership in early 1903, leaving a trail of litigation in its wake. To honor such a man with a judgeship would be to reward "rascality," the complainant said. Robert had denied the allegations in a written reply to Wickersham, saying similar charges had materialized in 1905, during his first reconfirmation, and the Senate Committee on the District of Columbia, which had jurisdiction over the capital, had unearthed no evidence of wrongdoing. In fact, the bank receivers had sent letters to the panel exonerating him, he said, and other knowledgeable citizens had chimed in as well, confirming he had done everything possible to salvage the institution.

Four years earlier, when antagonists vied to derail her husband's reconfirmation, Mary had withdrawn into herself. Since then, though, the landscape had shifted, as had her sense of authority within official Washington. Three weeks before Taft's inaugural, on February 12, 1909, Du Bois and Villard had formed the National Association for the Advancement of Colored People, a coalition of African American and white leaders who built upon the model of the Niagara Movement. Spurred in part by the Springfield riot the previous summer, they timed their announcement, at least initially, to coincide with the centennial of Abraham Lincoln's birth. And despite her marriage to a Booker T. Washington supporter, and her history of monopolizing headlines, Du Bois recognized Mary as a charter member.

On the other hand, the NAACP also offered her little role or recognition—no official function speaking on behalf of the organization—a snub to which she professed indifference, especially after the NAACP passed resolutions criticizing President Taft, to whom, as the wife of a Republican appointee, she felt some allegiance. She would not allow Du Bois and the others to deter her from laboring to eradicate "the awful conditions" under which we live, she told Robert, in a letter dated June 4, 1909. "I don't care how they dislike me, how nasty, mean and small they are, they shall not stand between me and the principle in which I believe with all my heart and for which I am willing to suffer, if need be, and work."

In any case, Mary didn't need the NAACP. She knew Fred Carpenter, who had followed Taft from the War Department to the executive mansion, where he functioned as a kind of chief of staff. That spring, Carpenter had rescued her from embarrassment by orchestrating Taft's presence at the M Street High School's graduation. Taft had initially accepted Mary's personal invitation to attend the ceremony—and she had boasted of her feat—but in his official reply to the school board, the president had informed them that he would have to decline.

At the commencement ceremony, where Taft sat next to Mary on the platform, he used a portion of his remarks to set the record straight. He had attended the graduation after all at the insistence of his "official assistant," Major Arthur Brooks, he said. Brooks, who was black, served as his valet. Mary Church Terrell had "seconded" the request, Taft said, adding—with a hint of exasperation—she had "great influence down at the White House." Mary knew Brooks and noted in her journal that Taft had flattered him, by referring to him in such a capacity. She also finessed Taft's comment about her role as "seconder," focusing instead on his reference to her alleged clout. Taft had paid her a "*great compliment,*" she wrote, calling it "one of the red letter days" of her life.

Now, with her husband's tenure and livelihood in peril, Mary installed herself in Wickersham's office, seeking an appointment. His private assistant fended her off, informing her that the attorney general was unavailable. If the charges against her husband were false, added the secretary, Attorney General Wickersham would disprove them and behave fairly; if they were true, nothing she could say would help. Mary marched over to the White House five blocks away and buttonholed Carpenter, who crafted a letter of introduction. Back at the Justice Department, armed with her White House correspondence, she got Wickersham's assistant to relent.

Later that day from home, Mary pulled out a sheet of board-of-education stationery and dashed off a note to Carpenter. After bringing him up to date on her second foray to the attorney general's office, she asked Carpenter to speak with Taft and Wickersham about Robert's role at Capital Savings. Her husband's political foes had manufactured the allegations in order to retaliate against Booker T. Washington, sabotaging an appointment he had endorsed, she wrote. "I feel sure you will use your influence in my behalf," she added.

Even with Robert's confirmation no longer in doubt, their estrangement deepened. In her diary, Mary offered little insight into developments in the White House or on the Hill, no hint about whether her intervention had helped her husband or whether he resented her for trying. She did, however, chronicle evidence of the chill between them. On Christmas, a year after giving her husband fur-lined gloves and a topaz pin, she gave him a pair of slippers. His mother-in-law gave him three pairs of socks—which, Mary noted in her journal, she had paid for, not her mother. Robert presented his wife with a teaspoon, notched with teeth, for eating citrus (nine months earlier she had taken a lecture tour in Florida). The previous Christmas, he had given her a sapphire and diamond ring.

At the top of her journal entry, just above December 25, 1909, Mollie wrote: "Berto gives me an orange spoon."

Robert retained his judgeship—surviving for another four-year term in early January, when Taft reappointed him, and a few days later, on January 11, when the Senate confirmed him. But the Taft administration proved far less progressive about race relations than Terrell and some of his peers had hoped. At the one-year mark of his presidency, in March 1910, Taft sent Robert a note in which he conceded as much but also deflected blame. "I have not done all I ought to do or all I hope to do in the matter of the recognition of colored men, but positions are very hard to find," Taft wrote. "Nobody resigns and nobody dies."

As Robert and others knew, though, Taft bore more responsibility than he allowed, since he had set a tone of retrenchment within moments of assuming office. In his inaugural address, Taft had pledged to continue Roosevelt's reforms and initiatives: suppressing abuse by railroads and industrial combinations, promoting peace abroad, constructing the Panama Canal. Taft also promised to increase harmony, "the already good feeling" between the North and South. African American men must pin their hopes on "industry, self-restraint, thrift and business success," he had said. But when it came to patronage, Taft parsed his language carefully, as if he were drafting a contract. "Distinguished" black men would receive official appointments "when suitable occasion offers," he said. Yet he elaborated a narrow vision of suitability, invoking a calculus familiar to any lawyer: a balancing of interests. Where a community's "race feeling" is so widespread that an African American appointment could hinder local government and aggravate racial tension—an obvious reference to the South—the damage inflicted by such a move might outweigh its benefit, and the president must exercise his discretion carefully, so as not to create "more harm than good."

Twelve days after the inauguration, Taft interpreted his new standard. He nominated a white man to serve as the collector of the port of Charleston, South Carolina—a position previously occupied by a black. Later that month, the *Chicago Tribune* reported, the new administration would spurn "professional politicians and dangerous agitators" in favor of "constantly conservative negroes."

A few days after Robert heard from Taft, he also received an update from his former law partner, Major John R. Lynch, an army paymaster in San Francisco. He and Lynch numbered among a handful of African American beneficiaries of Taft's patronage, most of whom were in Washington. According to Lynch, he had heard that the Taft administration would not appoint or retain any African American men in the South.

Nationwide, backlash against blacks manifested itself in other ways. Later that spring, a group of Galveston, Texas, residents unveiled plans for a publicly financed $500,000 memorial to "mammy," the archetypal southern black woman who managed to combine servitude with dignity. Resolutions in support of the undertaking hailed "mammy" as "one of the grandest characters" in world history, known for her "pure, unselfish and unfaltering devotion." Less than two weeks later, the *Washington Post* ran an editorial—reprinted from the *New York Sun*—calling for the monument's construction in the nation's capital. Not every hero or patriot deserves an edifice, the editorial said, but everyone, North and South, could unite around "the old black mammy": the millions who "enjoyed her kindly ministrations," and those who had merely heard of them. "To Southerners, whether we refer to those still living [in the] South, or to the countless thousands who are now distributed all over the North, the East, and the West, hers is a name to conjure with. White aproned, turbaned, always devoted and alert, she nursed a strenuous and proud race through the ailments and vicissitudes of childhood."

For Mary, a shrine to a subservient, enslaved black woman countered everything for which she had struggled since *Plessy*, when she gravitated toward club work and the NACW. As an activist and commentator, though, she had her own insights into the phenomenon. Six years earlier, in her *North*

American Review article, she had written that southerners revered illiterate African Americans, including "a dear old 'mammy' or a faithful old 'uncle,'" and repudiated those who were educated and cultured and allegedly wanted "social equality."

During the summer of 1910, the Terrells responded with a blend of flight, public bullishness, and private alarm. In late July, Mary and the girls decamped for Oak Bluffs, Massachusetts, a resort community on Martha's Vineyard with roots as a destination for Methodist revival meetings and a history of openness toward black domestic servants, whose white employers owned summer homes on the island. On Commercial Avenue, a ribbon of road stretching from the edge of downtown to East Chop, Mary, Phyllis, and Mary settled into the Wyoming House, a private home where the front window overlooked an expanse of sand, and just beyond, the ocean. In a letter to Robert, Mary poured out plans and directives: swimming lessons for the girls; an urgent need for money; a request for a box of "Palmer's Skin Success," a lightening cream designed to help reverse sun-induced darkening. "If I had searched the whole country over[,] I could not have found a more beautiful spot than this," she wrote.

Robert, meanwhile, embarked on a lecture tour in the Midwest, where he spoke to the Cleveland Association of Colored Men. In his remarks, he sounded his usual themes: thrift, hard work, frugality. "Optimism has been the saving grace of the black man in this country." In a letter to Booker T. Washington, though, he admitted that Taft's inaugural address still rankled African American leaders in Cleveland and Detroit. And, looking ahead to the next election, he warned that Ohio's black voters might protest by defecting to the Democrats, or boycotting the polls altogether. He had defended the president in his speeches, explaining that he was misunderstood and remained a friend of African Americans. "I am frank to confess that I did not make a very deep impression," he wrote Washington.

★ ★ ★ ★ ★

Twenty-three years after his own valedictory address, Robert Terrell prepared to speak to another graduating class of law students. He had won a spot on Howard University Law School's faculty the previous June, appointed by the board in 1911 to teach domestic relations, the doctrines governing divorce, alimony, child support, and custody. (An exam question for one of his classes hinted that he, too, had pondered a separation: he asked whether a husband bore responsibility for his wife's "necessaries," her essential expenses, if they did not live together.) Meanwhile, with Taft struggling to justify a second term, Robert knew that he and his generation had failed. Instead of vanquishing racial injustice, they had settled for tenure in the so-called Black Cabinet, as the *Afro-American* newspaper dubbed Taft's black loyalists. To the next generation, they had bequeathed the burden of racial inequality, the still-unfulfilled promise of the Thirteenth, Fourteenth, and Fifteenth Amendments.

Still, in his remarks to the Howard Law Class of 1912, Robert imparted a message of hope. The sun was rising and would continue to rise "until it reaches the fullness of noon," he said. But as a loyal Republican, who tethered his career to the party of Lincoln, Roosevelt, and Taft, privately he feared for their collective fate, and for a future characterized by marginalization and irrelevance, including his own. "I believe our race will one day produce the lawyer who, by his ability and his eloquence will win from our highest courts an opinion establishing us in our full rights as American citizens," he said. Such a man, perhaps even a Howard alumnus, would succeed because he wouldn't just argue his case as an attorney. He would appeal for justice as "a sufferer—the man who feels the iron in his own soul."

★ ★ ★ ★ ★

On September 25, 1913, the year of the Emancipation Proclamation's fiftieth anniversary, Robert composed a letter to Mary, whose father had died a year earlier, leaving her an inheritance reportedly worth $250,000. The appraised value of her portion of the bequest—a portfolio of Memphis real estate, improved and unimproved, which she held jointly with her brother Thomas—was considerably lower, a total of roughly $112,000 for the interest she and Thomas shared, which was still enough, of course, to leave Mary comfortable. Her half-siblings, Robert and Annette, and their mother, Anna, had inherited the brothels and the home on Lauderdale Street where Mary and her husband had held their wedding—a combined bequest with an appraised value of about $193,000. Regardless of whether Mary knew about what happened inside her father's commercial enterprises, she knew that, compared to her father's second family, she and Thomas had inherited the less desirable assets: vacant lots and substandard structures.

More recently, at the start of the school year, Mary and the girls had decamped to Oberlin, where Mary, a college freshman, was grappling with chemistry and French; Phyllis, who had completed two years of high school in Washington, had enrolled in Oberlin Academy, the college's preparatory school, and was studying violin and piano at the Oberlin Conservatory of Music. Before she left, Mary had leased the T Street home to tenants and dispatched her daughters to inform their father of their imminent departure for Ohio.

Six months earlier, Woodrow Wilson, a Virginia native, had installed himself in the White House—the first Democrat in twenty years and the first southerner since the Civil War. As Robert had foreseen, Wilson had mined anti-Taft backlash among African Americans, siphoning more black votes from Republicans than any previous Democrat. Even Du Bois, in the August 1912 issue of the *Crisis*, the NAACP's magazine, had endorsed Wilson, citing a record of indifference to blacks compiled by Roosevelt and Taft, dating back to Brownsville. Within days of the election, Robert predicted he would lose his judgeship in January 1914, when his term expired.

Wilson, a former Princeton University president, telegraphed gentility, with a thin face and a prominent chin, a long nose and pince-nez glasses. But as a presidential hopeful, he positioned himself as a man of the people, a progressive alternative to Teddy Roosevelt, who ran on a third-party ticket, and Taft, the Republican standard-bearer. Buttressed by his record as New Jersey governor, where he had combated trusts and monopolies, Wilson pledged "new freedom" and "fair and just treatment" for all. And, as a congressional scholar-turned-president, he nurtured ambitions of legislative overhaul, such as a ban on child labor and a graduated income tax—measures designed to safeguard rank-and-file citizens.

With Democrats in control of both houses of Congress, though, southerners harbored an agenda of their own: segregate Washington's streetcars, prohibit interracial marriage in the capital, and terminate all black appointees, especially those who supervised white women. Southerners also dominated Wilson's cabinet, including several key posts: James Clark McReynolds, who was born in Kentucky, as attorney general; William G. McAdoo, who was born in Georgia, as Treasury secretary; and Albert S. Burleson, a Texan, as postmaster general. Their combined influence, coupled with Wilson's reluctance to antagonize the southern Democrats who ran Congress, gave African American government workers little confidence in the security of their positions.

At a cabinet meeting in April 1913, a month after Wilson's inauguration, Burleson denounced integration in the federal workforce. By July, the post office had segregated its ranks. Treasury followed suit that fall, consigning blacks to separate offices, restrooms, and dining tables. Wilson, who had inherited and actively preserved an institutional bias that excluded black students from Princeton, unseated all but two of Taft's black appointees in Washington and installed white men in their places.

Robert, one of the two holdovers, remained at home in the T Street duplex, supervising the dispersal of belongings to storage. He remained circumspect about his living situation—even with an old friend. In his spare time, he stopped by his new quarters, apparently a rented space at 421 T Street, NW, vying for a glimpse of the paperhanger. Under the circumstances, he hoped for the best: that his room would be ready within a day; that the wallpaper wouldn't be too terrible. For all their discord over the years, Mary's decision to leave had surprised him, sparking remorse and contrition.

"My dear, dear Wife," he wrote. You deserve peace, calm and contentment, and "in spite of your pessimism," you will receive your just desserts some day, he said. He recounted his efforts to vacate the house—"your home," as he called it—including an eggnog set and a soup tureen he rescued from next door, where her bother Thomas once lived. "This will be our last night in the old homestead," he said, referring to himself and Nagi, the family bulldog. Without elaborating, Robert apologized for the "turmoil" before she left. He regretted, too, that they had not held "a family council[,] behind closed doors for several hours," to give the children a sense of what it meant to "break up a home."

Meanwhile, from lodgings on North Professor Street in Oberlin, Mary battled college officials, from the dean of women to the president. She had brought Phyllis and Mary to Oberlin, in part, to give them a chance to socialize with white students. She also hoped the girls, and fifteen-year-old Phyllis in particular, would benefit from a climate of intellectual and moral development, qualities she associated with her own college experience and friendships. Citing a shortage of on-campus housing for underclass students, however, her alma mater had relegated her daughters to a boarding house, where they lived with other African American girls. Mary believed, in spite of denials and explanations to the contrary, Oberlin had done so to avoid offending white students.

Now parted all but officially, Mary and Robert still corresponded on a regular basis. Week after week, he wrote her—once in pencil, because he couldn't find a pen. Though she stood to inherit a portion of her father's real estate fortune, Robert quibbled about expenses, agreeing to a $50 monthly allowance for her, challenging her suggestion that he could survive on a mere $35, when his room alone cost $18. In a letter to him dated October 24, 1913, she vented about racial bias she perceived at Oberlin: an

American history professor who criticized radical Republicans in Congress for their alleged failure to consider southern views during Reconstruction; the exclusion of most black students (but not, for the most part, her daughters) from college social life, especially in dormitories; a white girl who objected when a white boy invited Mary to a reception. Robert in turn shared gossip about friends and acquaintances: a woman Mary knew whose husband had gone to Europe with the children; the academic brilliance revealed by the daughter of Kelly Miller, who himself was a Howard University professor; John Milholland, the former Constitution League member who had phoned Mary about Brownsville, had gone on to serve as NAACP treasurer and, more recently, had banned his son from Harvard's football team. Robert reminded her they would be apart on their wedding anniversary and angled for her to visit him, in his renovated living space, with freshly stained floors and new bedroom shades. He even fantasized, or professed to, about living in a college town.

Throughout the fall, Robert also gave Mary updates about efforts, spearheaded by Villard, the NAACP, and others, to contest Wilson's segregationist policies. In mid-October, the Mu-So-Lit Club, a literary society for the capital's African American men, raised $100 for the NAACP. Later that month, roughly 2,500 people crammed into Metropolitan AME Church to hear Villard, while an overflow audience, which Robert estimated at 2,000 persons, congregated outside. When Villard mentioned President Wilson's name, the crowd hissed—an outburst Robert told Mary he deemed "a wrong thing at the nation's capital," though he understood the animosity that spawned it.

By mid-November, Robert landed in bed with food poisoning. In a letter to Mary, he blamed a tainted meal at "some hashery," since he no longer dined at home. On the cusp of his fifty-sixth birthday, he was betraying a sense of mortality, fretting about his pulse and his diet, professing the need for moderation and restraint. And, nearing the end of his term as a judge, he ruminated about whether Wilson would reappoint him. He had earned plaudits across the legal community, from white and black lawyers alike. But with race hatred inflaming Capitol Hill and much of the country, his letter conveyed a sense of unease. "You are never sure of it until you have been confirmed after appointment and have your commission in your hand," he wrote Mary. To a friend, he conceded far less equipoise. "I am still here, but sitting on a can of nitro-glycerine, likely to be exploded in a week or two," he wrote, adding as an aside, this might be my last chance to write you on my judicial stationery.

★ ★ ★ ★ ★

On January 22, 1914, Mississippi's senator James K. Vardaman—known for his beliefs in white supremacy—vowed to resist the confirmation of any black American. "I am sorry to differ with the President with regard to the Terrell case," Vardaman said, "but I do not believe the negro and the white man can live together on terms of political equality in this country." Wilson sent Terrell's name to the Senate anyway, in mid-February, prompting relief from Robert's family and friends. "It is a[n] honor well-deserved," cabled Booker T. Washington from Tuskegee on February 19. But with Vardaman spearheading opposition in the Senate and her husband's judgeship once again in peril, Mary returned to Washington, settling into 421 T Street while Robert appeared to bunk, at least initially, at the YMCA, located at 1816 12th St., NW. In an appeal to Senator Theodore E. Burton, an Ohio Republican and Oberlin alumnus, she said she feared Robert might collapse under the strain. "After struggling for years to excel in his chosen profession," she wrote on March 20, 1914, "after receiving indisputable proof of the fact that he has achieved brilliant success, he now feels the ground slipping from under his feet, and sees failure staring him in the face."

Fourteen months later, after the Senate confirmed Terrell for the fourth time, he filed for bankruptcy. In court documents, he disclosed assets of $62.50 and $13,492 in liabilities, including debts dating back to his law practice with Lynch and his tenure with Capital Savings Bank. After Robert's insolvency landed in the local black press, which sympathized with him, Mary retreated to the West Coast. In San Francisco, she gave a lecture in lieu of attending Phyllis's graduation from St. Johnsbury Academy, a private school in Vermont.

That summer of 1915, presumably using money of her own, Mary supervised completion of a wooden bungalow in Highland Beach, Maryland, an African American resort located about five miles south of Annapolis. Founded by Charles Douglass in 1893—after a nearby resort's restaurant refused to serve him and his wife, Laura, because they were black—the community overlooked the Chesapeake Bay, with a stretch of beach and a handful of streets lined with cottages; Mary, who knew Frederick Douglass, of course, had purchased a lot there two decades earlier, apparently using funds she had earned as a substitute teacher. Summer residents, including doctors and lawyers from Washington and Baltimore, fished and swam, went crabbing, and collected their mail at the post office. Mary relished the simplicity and the restorative setting, the isolation from telegram and train service, the proximity to other accomplished African Americans.

Next door to Mary's bungalow stood Twin Oaks, a two-story home erected for Frederick Douglass in 1895, with a wraparound veranda and large windows facing the bay. Douglass, who died before the structure was finished, had designed a porch upstairs, just off a front bedroom. There, from a space barely large enough for a chair, the vista opened to the Eastern Shore, where he had been born in slavery.

In Washington, meanwhile, the horizon for African Americans kept shrinking. President Wilson tapped Attorney General McReynolds to fill a Supreme Court vacancy. During his stint at the Justice Department, McReynolds had forced the resignation of William H. Lewis, a black assistant attorney general and Taft appointee who offended southern whites by joining the American Bar Association.

By 1916, effects of the new segregation reverberated in the capital and across the nation. In June, with Europe consumed by war, a "national preparedness" parade in Washington confined African American participants to a Jim Crow section. The War Department issued a directive two days later, segregating troops by race. Mary felt the impact, too. That summer, she entered People's Drug Store, a local chain known for discount pricing and a name that conjured egalitarianism. Situated on the ground floor of a commercial building at the corner of Fourteenth and U Streets, NW, next door to a bank, the pharmacy had opened a year earlier, in August 1915. When Mary ordered a glass of soda water, the clerk refused to serve her. Afterward, she called Malcolm G. Gibbs, the chain's founder and proprietor. Gibbs, a Tennessee native, asked her to come see him in person. He promised to investigate.

For Robert, what had happened to Mary at People's served as a jolt and a turning point. During a lecture tour in Texas nine months earlier, in the immediate aftermath of Booker T. Washington's death in November 1915, he said that he believed southern men "generally are fair-minded and willing to help" blacks. Now, in a letter to Gibbs, dated August 10, 1916, he voiced his objections. My wife, a thirty-year resident of Washington, has never before been refused service at any soda fountain or any place of public accommodation in the city, he wrote. She is a woman of national reputation who studied in this country and abroad, he added. "I can't see how any clerk or salesman could ever have thought of refusing accommodation to a woman of my wife's appearance and demeanor."

Robert didn't just chastise Gibbs for his wife's sake, though, he personalized the incident. I have a right to complain about this discrimination against a race from which you draw your customers, he wrote, couching his grievance in economic terms, raising the specter of a boycott. This branch of People's is located in a predominantly black neighborhood, he said, and he had patronized the outpost, the chain's third in Washington, since it opened. And, he added, he had spoken with neighbors, who shared his views. "For fourteen years and more I have served on the bench, as a judge in this City, and this is the first time that I have ever had to resort to a thing of this kind, and I hope it will be the last."

Gibbs responded two days later, in a letter delivered by messenger. Personally, he said, he deplored the incident. "We do not care to serve people of any race at our fountain who are not genteel, but such objection could certainly not obtain against your wife, yourself or any high class colored person," he wrote. The employee had been reprimanded, and he was certain it would not happen again, Gibbs added, thanking Terrell for the opportunity to clarify his store's policy for him and his friends. "We appreciate your business and will do everything humanly possible to merit it."

Both Terrells, apparently reconciled as a couple, fled for the foothills of the Berkshires, near Amenia, New York, less than two weeks later. While President Wilson was running for reelection, they and more than four dozen other men and women converged on Troutbeck, Joel Elias Spingarn's Dutchess County estate. Spingarn, the son of an Austrian Jewish tobacco merchant and a former chairman of Columbia University's comparative literature department, had studied at Columbia and Harvard and, more recently, emerged as one of the NAACP's white leaders. After Booker T. Washington's death, Spingarn agreed to host a conference of African American leaders at Troutbeck, where the previous owners had launched the local literary and historical societies, and forged connections to Ralph Waldo Emerson and Henry David Thoreau. In this setting, with participants bound by a pledge of confidentiality, the planners hoped to bridge the chasm between Booker T. Washington's supporters and the NAACP. Some, including Du Bois, hoped to take things a step further, anointing the NAACP as heir apparent to Washington's movement, aligning behind its goals: freedom from the constraints of previous slavery and peonage; freedom from ignorance and disfranchisement; and social freedom from insult. Invitations to the gathering, extended by Spingarn personally, netted luminaries ranging from Villard and Du Bois to Major Robert R. Moton, Washington's successor at Tuskegee.

And, in a rare double billing, both Terrells were on the program. For Friday, August 25, the first full day, the organizers enlisted Mary as an evening speaker, to talk about "Social Discrimination." Earlier, they tapped Robert to preside over a two-hour session devoted to "The Negro in Politics." William H. Lewis, the ex-assistant attorney general whom McReynolds had fired, opened the panel.

During breaks from the proceedings, the conferees repaired to the surrounding wilderness. They swam in a lake and hiked in the woods; they reclined on hillsides and gathered flowers. Under a tent, they ate communal meals. By the end of the third day, they vowed to forge ahead together, transcending old wounds and antagonisms. They adopted resolutions, pledging their commitment to political freedom and education of all kinds for African Americans. On the Troutbeck lawn, thirty of them posed for a photograph, with a striped tent in the background. Arranged in three rows, seated in front and standing in back, they stared into the camera, black and white, male and female, aligned shoulder to shoulder. Mary sat in the second row, with her hands in her lap, wearing an open-necked white blouse, hatless and smiling. Robert did not appear among them.

Meanwhile, a political cartoon surfaced in Georgia, depicting Robert on the bench, smoking a cigar and holding a gavel, inside a courtroom packed with white spectators. President Wilson—who had declined an invitation to attend the Amenia Conference—stood before Robert in the image, bowing slightly, saying he was delighted to appoint him as a Washington city judge. A dialogue balloon over Terrell's head read, "Dis cote come to order, you white folks stan' up an' receive yo' sentence!"

★ ★ ★ ★ ★

After the United States declared war on Germany in April 1917, some 370,000 African Americans served in the military, more than half of them in France. Yet as it had during the Civil War, the army mustered black troops into segregated regiments. Black soldiers, shipped in Jim Crow railway cars to southern training camps, were barred from the Army Air Corps and the Marines. In France, Washington's segregated army unit, the 1st Separate Battalion, vied for the right to face combat as soldiers, not as menial laborers. Twenty-five of the battalion's 480 troops—more than 5 percent—received the Croix de Guerre, in recognition of their valor.

Mary spent much of the war in Washington, where the Chamber of Commerce reserved 2,000 rooms for out-of-town war workers and temporary housing sprouted in the Union Station plaza, a few blocks from the Capitol. Howard University appointed her as a temporary French instructor, citing "the present emergency." Robert served on a board of instruction for African American servicemen and a Washington, D.C., Liberty Loan Committee, which generated publicity for US Treasury bonds to help finance the war.

In the spring of 1918, after surviving his fifth Senate confirmation, Robert relayed a batch of newspaper clippings highlighting his career to former president Teddy Roosevelt, whose four sons were serving in the military. "Since you gave me my start as a judge," he wrote, "I thought that the articles enclosed herewith might be of interest to you." Roosevelt responded four days later with a note, typed on letterhead from the *Kansas City Star*'s Madison Avenue office in New York. "That's mighty nice."

The following fall, toward the end of the war, Robert spoke to a crowd of more than 1,400 people at a Baptist church in Newport News, Virginia. He believed, as did Mary, the contest against German aggression and oppression would yield dividends at home, including freedom for all, irrespective of race or color. African Americans were not just fighting to make the world safe for democracy, he said in late September, echoing Wilson's 1917 speech asking for a declaration of war. They were fighting to make the United States a safe place for African Americans.

In November, Robert received a letter from Sgt. Bernard G. Cooper, a Washington native who had served in France, braving chemical gas. In Lakewood, New Jersey, where Cooper was convalescing, the hospital relegated African American patients to separate tables in the dining room, as if they were contagious, he said, and required them to carry their own food from the kitchen because attendants refused to wait on them. I didn't think we'd be treated like this after risking our lives abroad and our people bought liberty bonds at home, wrote Cooper. "We were all Americans in the field[,] fighting for the great cause for the World."

Meanwhile, the War Camp Community Service, an agent of the War and Navy Departments that deployed a network of operatives, mostly in the South, to monitor recreational conditions at war training facilities, braced for racial tension. African American soldiers had tasted freedom and equality during the conflict, especially in France, where they enjoyed the same civic privileges as whites, an official wrote, but many southern whites would expect a restoration of prewar race relations. "The Negroes will never again submit quietly and without protest to such an arrangement," he said.

Eleven days later, two weeks after the war had ended, the service offered Mary a job, starting immediately, at an annual salary of $2,000, plus travel expenses. As a condition of employment, with fear of Bolshevism mounting in the Russian Revolution's aftermath, she had to sign a declaration of loyalty to the US government. Mary accepted the position, which was based out of the War Camp Community Service's headquarters in the Metropolitan Life Tower in New York. From her new workspace on the thirty-ninth floor, she wrote Phyllis and Mary, who were now both in their twenties, struggling to build relationships and careers. In a letter, sprinkled with exclamation points, Mary gushed about her responsibilities, including her authority to screen and recommend other African American women, who would report to her. "I shall be a Supervisor with a capital S!"

With only office work to fill her days, and no domestic chores, Terrell rejoiced in her independence. "Believe me," men who sit at a desk and earn a salary, without the annoyances that "worry a poor housekeeper to death," go to Heaven on a bed of flowery ease, she wrote, paraphrasing Frederick Douglass. "Home Ain't Nothin' Like This!"

★ ★ ★ ★ ★

The mob amassed after nightfall, near the White House, on July 19, 1919. Wilson, who had returned from the Paris peace conference eleven days earlier, had retired to the *Mayflower*, the presidential yacht, seeking refuge from exhaustion and ill health. White servicemen, including some in uniform, convened on Pennsylvania Avenue. Around them alongside the National Mall, lay a neighborhood known as "Murder Bay," an area renowned since before the Civil War for its gambling dens, brothels, and its allure to servicemen on leave.

Even before temperatures soared into the mid-80s, war veterans and residents had roamed a capital stewing in misery: Prohibition; job and housing shortages; an onslaught of seventeen-year locusts, winged insects also known as cicadas. In June, fears of Bolshevik insurrection surged after a bomb exploded outside the four-story townhouse of Attorney General A. Mitchell Palmer, a Quaker ex-congressman from Pennsylvania. And, for several weeks, Washington's white newspapers had featured stories about a series of attacks on women, blaming the incidents on blacks, even though one alleged victim who had accused two African American men of sexually assaulting her recanted two weeks later. On July 9, the NAACP warned the white dailies they were "sowing the seeds of a race riot." Two days later, as if heedless of the admonition, the *Afro-American* referred to a "colored maniac" who had attacked six girls, five of whom were white.

On July 19, a police detective questioned a black man in the alleged assault of a white woman, a serviceman's wife, after she left work at the Bureau of Engraving and Printing. As word of the incident circulated, servicemen, bent on vengeance, vowed to "clean up" Southwest Washington, where the Bureau of Engraving and Printing had its headquarters. Southwest, the smallest of Washington's quadrants, stretched along the south side of the Mall, from the Capitol to the Lincoln Memorial's construction site, where former president Taft, who headed the memorial commission, had unearthed the first shovel of dirt in 1914, on Lincoln's birthday.

Late in the evening of July 19, a throng of more than one hundred soldiers, marines, and sailors fanned across the Mall, sweeping about three hundred civilians into their ranks. About two blocks from the Bureau of Engraving and Printing, they attacked Charles Ralls—the suspect the police had questioned—and threatened to lynch him. Ralls escaped and sealed himself inside his house. Nearby, a black man, George Montgomery, was returning home from a store when a mob bashed his skull with a brick, leaving him in a heap on the street until the police intervened and had him sent to the hospital. Later, on the other side of the Mall, at Seventh and Pennsylvania, police arrested two alleged ringleaders: Private E. H. Moore, who was stationed at Bolling Field in Anacostia and who had bragged about getting "three of them," and Eugene Paul Shafer, a naval reserve petty officer also stationed in Anacostia.

The next day, Major Raymond W. Pullman, the police chief, dismissed the melee as the handiwork of "a few hotheads." But after darkness that evening, white servicemen and civilians stormed Pennsylvania Avenue, armed with clubs. At Fourteenth Street, two Marines leaped into a streetcar and assaulted an African American passenger. At Fifteenth Street, a crowd attacked a black man outside the Treasury Department; a block away, two others were assaulted outside the White House. Soldiers stormed another streetcar, pummeled an African American passenger, hauled him from the coach, and kept pounding him. The police department's headquarters sent two black chauffeurs home, fearing for their safety.

On Monday morning, July 21, the *Washington Post*'s lead story opened with the scene on Pennsylvania Avenue. Long the setting of inaugural parades and celebratory processions, the thoroughfare had served as the "arena" for a race riot. Farther down, the article said—erroneously—that all available servicemen in the area had been directed to assemble at 9 p.m. that evening, between Seventh and Eighth Streets, on Pennsylvania. From there, the *Post* reported, they would embark on a "clean-up" that would cause the previous evenings "to pale into insignificance."

At the White House, Wilson returned from his river cruise on the yacht, unrested and unwell, complaining of pain. His physician, Rear Admiral Cary T. Grayson, ordered him to bed, telling the press the president was suffering from dysentery. Wilson's staff canceled his appointments. Throughout the day, gun dealers reportedly sold more than five hundred revolvers and hundreds of rounds of ammunition.

After 10 p.m., a new wave of violence rocked the capital. Inside a streetcar at Ninth and G Streets, behind the Rialto Theater, an African American man pulled out a revolver and started shooting, wounding two soldiers and a civilian. Two blocks away, on a streetcar near Seventh and G Streets, a black passenger aimed through a window and emptied his firearm into a cluster of jeering whites, wounding four in a spray of bullets and shattered glass. On New York Avenue, between Sixth and Seventh Streets, an African American man leaned out of a window and shot at a group of soldiers, wounding one. A seventeen-year-old African American girl allegedly shot and killed a police detective. Sharpshooters commandeered the Howard Theater's roof, a few blocks from Mary's duplex.

By the next morning, Tuesday, July 22, the fatalities included the police detective, a Marine private, and a twenty-two-year-old black navy veteran named Randall Neal, whose father had toiled as a messenger to nine House speakers—and tended to Congressman Heflin after his arrest in 1908. In its lead story, wrapped by a banner headline, the *New York Times* registered alarm. "Many of the negroes are defiant and do not hesitate to insult and attack white men and women," it wrote.

Up on Capitol Hill, Congress rushed to condemn the carnage. In the House, Representative Frank Clark, a Florida Democrat, pressed for an investigation, saying lawmakers had a duty to secure Washington's streets for "the good women of the land" and ensure that the "rape demons" were brought to justice. Representative Henry I. Emerson, an Ohio Republican, denounced the bloodshed as "a national scandal" and called for martial law to protect the capital's citizens, regardless of race or color. Massachusetts Democrat James A. Gallivan blamed Prohibition and bootlegging, saying home-distilled "green whisky" had incited the rioters. On the opposite end of the Capitol, Senator Byron P. Harrison of Mississippi introduced a bill once again calling to segregate Washington's streetcars.

Late Tuesday, Wilson summoned his War Department secretary, Newton D. Baker, to the White House. Baker, a former Cleveland mayor, had spent much of the morning on the Hill and some of the afternoon with the police chief. Off the record, officials knew the unrest, now almost seventy-two-hours old, had to be quashed.

That evening, at the behest of the War Department, an estimated 2,000 federal troops descended on Washington, including Marines from a base in Quantico, Virginia, and cavalry from Arlington's Fort Meyer. Sailors from the *Mayflower* strode ashore bearing nightsticks and automatic pistols strapped to their thighs. Army soldiers from Camp Meade, near Baltimore, marched in columns, with rifles slung over their shoulders. Major General William G. Haan, the commanding officer of the 32nd Division in France, oversaw the operation from a temporary post in police headquarters, where a makeshift arsenal arose, stocked with more than 1,000 army-issue Colt .45 revolvers and more than 20,000 rounds of ammunition. Soldiers and cavalry patrolled the streets and streetcars, enforcing orders to arrest anyone who disturbed the peace. Movie theaters and poolrooms shut their doors, as did near-beer saloons, with their nonalcoholic brews. Just before midnight, Haan said he had toured the city without spotting any trouble.

With the violence quelled, the editorial pages now weighed in. "What a spectacle it is when the civic safeguards provided by Congress break down, and the very lawmakers themselves and the representatives of foreign governments must seek protection from the military power!" wrote the *Washington Post*, warning about possible calls for withdrawal of the diplomatic corps. The *New York Times* bemoaned the demise of prewar Washington, with its small-town placidity and well-behaved, law-abiding African Americans. "Most of them admitted the superiority of the white race, and troubles between the two races were undreamed of," the editors claimed.

A week after the riot began, Robert issued a statement with Emmett J. Scott, an Amenia conferee and former Booker T. Washington aide. Culpability rested primarily with white servicemen who "ran amuck [*sic*] through the streets of the National Capital," they said, provoking retaliation by African Americans. The NAACP, meanwhile, lobbied Attorney General Palmer to prosecute the *Washington Post* for inciting a riot with its story about the alleged "mobilization."

Two days later, after racial unrest rocked Chicago—sparked when a white man killed a black swimmer for encroaching on the white section of a local beach—the *Washington Evening Star* reprinted two letters, allegedly written from jail by a Washington-riot suspect, who addressed the governors of Mississippi and Georgia. The sender identified himself as "S.S. of the United States," which stood for "sharpshooter," according to the police. "We went and killed Germans for your rights, and we can also kill Americans for our rights, and if I hear any more of lynching in the state of Georgia, I will come quickly, and the people will weep after I leave, because I sweep from the cradle up," the letter read.

On August 8, the *Afro-American* ran a dispatch about an evening meeting of the National Race Congress, headed by Reverend William H. Jernagin, who had arrived in Washington several years earlier and, as pastor of Mount Carmel Baptist Church, established himself as an activist and community leader. Inside John Wesley AME Zion Church on Fourteenth Street, NW, a speaker urged African American men to bar their daughters and wives from entering the white man's kitchen. The pastor, Reverend Dr. M. Brown, said that black Americans needed their own hardware stores to facilitate gun sales. "This is a radical age, and the old leaders must go," he maintained.

The following day, on August 9, the Treasury Department relayed a letter to Mary in Washington, typed on the agency's letterhead. At the secretary's direction, the missive heralded her appointment as a clerk in the Bureau of War Risk Insurance, with an annual salary of $1,100. A handwritten date directed her to appear for the oath of office on September 1.

★ ★ ★ ★ ★

Throughout the summer and into the fall of 1919, racial violence exploded in more than two dozen cities, from Elaine, Arkansas, to Longview, Texas. More than one hundred people died and thousands more sustained injuries, mainly African Americans. James Weldon Johnson, the NAACP field secretary who probed Washington's unrest, dubbed the collective tumult, when blood flowed in the streets, the "Red Summer."

Robert, meanwhile, shelved concerns about his high blood pressure and diet and juggled a series of lecture engagements. By May 1920, six months before the presidential election, he was finalizing a much-revised speech, titled "The Negro Today." For Terrell, the war had done more than Taft's capitulation to southern racism, more than Booker T. Washington's death, more than Wilson's segregationism. The war had radicalized him, and, in the aftermath of nationwide racial upheaval, he filled his remarks with a sense of immediacy. War and revolution had forged a new world, he said, and African Americans, who had proven their loyalty on and off the battlefield, expected to reap the new regime's dividends on equal terms with whites. "The Negro problem will never be settled right until our white brother accepts, without reservation, those eternal truths enunciated by the Declaration of Independence and legalized in the Constitution."

Until then, he said, it was "our duty to contend and contend, to protest and protest" until lawmakers, judges, and other authorities recognize "equal and exact Justice." This is "our fight in the new Reconstruction for a fair and square deal," he added. "Black men do not come begging: they come standing erect, demanding their just share of the fruits of war as American citizens."

4

An Example for All the World

Before leaving for Ohio, Mary Church Terrell dashed off a note to Phyllis and Mary. Her letter, composed on September 30, 1920, ran on the official stationery of the Republican National Committee in New York, with an engraved image of an elephant holding its trunk aloft. Five weeks earlier, ratification of the Nineteenth Amendment had enfranchised women across the country, capping a seventy-two-year quest for suffrage. Robert, charting developments that summer from Washington, had written to Mary, who was in Highland Beach, that no one would understand "the full import" of the change until after the presidential election in November. Then, with both parties scrambling to boost turnout, the RNC had enlisted Mary for outreach among African American women on the East Coast, making speeches and recruiting party backers.

The real battleground, though, lay roughly five hundred miles west of Manhattan, between Lake Erie and the Ohio River. Long a Republican stronghold—cradle of abolitionists, John D. Rockefeller's Standard Oil Company, and six GOP presidents—Ohio had tilted to the Democrats in the previous two elections, embracing Wilson's progressivism. During the war, as southern blacks migrated to northern industrial centers, Ohio's African American population surged; the *New York Times* predicted more than 80,000 black Ohioans would cast ballots on November 2. At nominating conventions that summer, roughly three months after the Senate blocked America's participation in the Treaty of Versailles by seven votes, both parties tapped Ohioans as their presidential standard-bearers: Warren G. Harding, a first-term Republican senator, and James M. Cox, the Democratic governor, who enlisted the thirty-eight-year-old Franklin D. Roosevelt as a running mate. That fall, in a bid to counter perceived Republican loyalties among blacks, Ohio's Democratic state committee raised the specter of "negro domination," urging voters to defend the honor of white women and children and banish from the state the "menace" of blacks.

Harding was born near Blooming Grove, in central Ohio's Morrow County, on November 2, 1865, almost seven months after the Civil War ended. The eldest of eight children, he grew up on a family farm; later, when his father established a medical practice, he lived in Caledonia, Ohio, surrounded by rural mainstays, including *McGuffey's Readers* and a one-room schoolhouse. Harding also played in the Caledonia Silver Cornet Band, whose members rehearsed in a barbershop. After graduating from Ohio Central College, Harding dabbled in law and teaching, salvaged the *Marion Star* from bankruptcy, and married Florence Kling DeWolfe, the daughter of a wealthy Marion businessman. It was not a happy union. He nicknamed his spouse "the Duchess," carried on an extended extramarital affair with the wife of a Marion friend, and gravitated toward politics. In Columbus and Washington—as state senator, lieutenant governor, and then US senator—with his bent for poker and cigars, he sparked few antagonisms, standing out, if at all, for affability and party loyalty, not legislative acumen. In the Senate, he dodged controversial issues, such as radicalism and labor unrest, but endorsed Prohibition and women's suffrage. He supported the war but opposed the Treaty of Versailles, saying he was "old-fashioned."

As a newspaper publisher, a party stalwart who relished golf and glad-handing, Harding proved adept as a presidential candidate, peddling himself to a broad swath of outlets: film, radio, magazines, and, of course, newspapers, which reprinted his campaign photographs. Days after the Republican convention, on June 15, 1920, a Washington-based public relations agency circulated a black-and-white image of Inez P. McWhorter, Harding's African American cook, clad in a long-sleeve white dress. Facing the camera, she posed in front of a bank of kitchen cupboards, near a loaf of bread and a tray of rolls. The caption described her as the Aunt Jemima of the senator's household.

Less than three weeks later, Harding and his wife left for Marion, where he planned to campaign from his front porch. In doing so, he was echoing the strategies of three fellow Ohioans who had won the presidency: James A. Garfield, who greeted supporters from the veranda of his Mentor abode; William McKinley; and William Henry Harrison, a Virginia-born aristocrat whose North Bend farm spawned his hard cider, log-cabin, and common-man imagery. The RNC even maneuvered to erect McKinley's Canton flagpole in the Hardings' front yard.

Before Harding fled the capital—with a chauffeur, a box lunch packed by McWhorter, and a retinue of newspaper reporters trailing in two separate cars—a camera crew documented his departure. Harding's Washington home was in the Kalorama neighborhood, a leafy enclave lined with mansions and embassies, near Rock Creek Park. In the backyard, where he mingled with reporters and handed out stogies, photographers perched on a garage wall, filming him from multiple angles, as if, one reporter noted, he were matinee idol Douglas Fairbanks.

Later that month, in a July 22 speech from Marion formally accepting the nomination, Harding pledged to return the country to "normalcy." Seeking to distance himself from Wilson and Theodore Roosevelt, with their progressivism and intellectual heft, Harding espoused "party government," not autocracy—a swipe at Wilson and his failed treaty-making. "No man is big enough to run this great Republic," he said. To a nation cleaved by foreign war and domestic violence, he extolled midwestern virtues: thrift, prudence, simplicity, steadiness, and common sense.

For black Americans, Harding's message seemed to offer promise, particularly in phrasing that echoed Justice Harlan's *Plessy* dissent. "The Constitution contemplates no class and recognizes no group," Harding said in his acceptance speech. He embraced antilynching legislation, saying the federal government should "remove that stain from the fair name of America." He also articulated a broad statement of equality. With their battlefield sacrifices, he said, African Americans had earned the "full measure of citizenship," and "should be guaranteed the enjoyment of all their rights," as required by "the American spirit of fairness and justice."

In late September, after the RNC beckoned, Terrell headed to New York, where she plunged into campaign work and related travel. While she searched for temporary lodgings in a boarding house, she kept her trunk, stocked with corset covers and a blue chiffon frock, warehoused in train-station storage. Even fellow activists had trouble tracking her down. Mrs. Richard Edwards, the Peru, Indiana–based treasurer of the League of Women Voters, which had been founded that year to educate the new female electorate, wired Mary on September 26, inviting her to an event dubbed "Social Justice Day"; the telegram bounced from her duplex at 326 T Street, where tenants paid her a monthly rent of $50, to yet another rented space at 1323 T Street, NW, where Robert scrawled a handwritten note to his wife along the bottom margin. "I did not arrange this," read the note. "You had better attend at [the] Committee's expense."

In her letter from headquarters, Mary told her daughters that she was leaving on an RNC-financed trip to Marion, where Harding would deliver "strong utterances" on social justice. She floated the notion of a Washington visit, before saying she could only come home if they were ill, and, in that event, she'd "jump into an airplane and fly." "Look after Papa," she added.

★ ★ ★ ★ ★

From her vantage point near Florence Harding, on a tree-lined thoroughfare in Marion, Mary spotted Senator Harding, attired in a pinstripe suit, white shirt, and dark tie. With his white hair and dark bushy eyebrows, Harding looked like a local bank president, master of the links and boardroom. As an orator, a craft he had honed on the Chautauqua circuit, he betrayed the flat consonants and vowels of his origins. But today, following a campaign swing through Maryland, West Virginia, and Kentucky, his voice sounded hoarse.

Harding's Marion home, with its gabled roof, dark green wooden facade, and white trim, projected stability. The front porch spanned the width of the abode, culminating in a rounded section, like a gazebo, with Ionic columns girding the balustrade. Out back, reporters encamped in a newly constructed wooden shed, nicknamed "the shack." Harding dropped by often, primed to chat, field questions, chew tobacco, and pitch horseshoes.

In addition to Terrell, roughly five thousand women descended on Marion for Social Justice Day. Some had arrived by rail, in sleeper cars from Chicago and specially commissioned trains from Dayton and Columbus. They had traveled from as far away as Texas, Colorado, and Washington State. Many of the town's stores had shuttered for the occasion—billed as one of the "front-porch campaign's" largest events—meaning that retail clerks from Marion joined in as well, melding with politicians' wives and notable figures, including Alice Roosevelt Longworth, the late president's daughter (Roosevelt had died in January 1919, at the age of sixty) and Corinne Roosevelt Robinson, his sister.

Under gray skies, the women fell in behind their marshal, Marie Edwards, who draped herself in a fur stole. Delegation by delegation, they paraded up Mount Vernon Avenue, a pageant of newly enfranchised voters, with flags and banners marking their hometowns and employee organizations. African Americans participated as well, led by Lethia C. Fleming, the Republican national director for work among black women. Social workers and suffragettes, educators and homemakers, they all spilled into the Hardings' yard, where a layer of gravel coated the grass and immigrant women in costumes from their native lands knotted near the front steps.

From his porch, Harding gave a speech that embraced a litany of causes, invoking motherhood, clean living, honest labor, and the sanctity of hearth and family. He extolled respect for law and order and called for creation of a federal department of public welfare to protect working women—"an army of potential maternity"—through measures such as an eight-hour day and "equal pay for equal work." At the end of his remarks, he condemned violence and lynching. Afterward, women in fitted gowns and hats bedecked with feathers swarmed around the candidate, trying to shake his hand. Florence Harding, who wore her gray hair coiled into a cap of curls, hovered at his side.

In interviews with a *New York Times* reporter, delegates hailed the speech. "There is nothing equivocal about the promises made by Senator Harding," said Mary Roberts Rinehart, a writer who helped organize the event. The *Washington Post*, in its front-page account, said Harding had suggested he might appoint a woman to run the new "public welfare" agency.

Afterward, Mary went back to New York, where Robert wrote to her on October 6. It is well for the Hardings to meet you and gain insight into the caliber of our women, Robert Terrell said. Before the campaign, they knew nothing about African Americans, so let their knowledge flow though "the best channel," he added. Like other prominent black figures, he hoped that women's suffrage would help African Americans. Ambitious whites who needed votes would court educated African American women, who organize into groups, and the association will benefit our race, he wrote. He predicted Harding would win in "a walkover."

Before closing, Robert pivoted to family matters, griping about Billie Goines, a pharmacist who had married Phyllis in early 1919. When Phyllis and Billie were newlyweds, Robert had adopted a tone of bemusement, dubbing them "theater fiends" who ventured to Baltimore for a show. (In the same letter to Mary, on February 24, 1919, Robert wrote that with a husband who looked like he did—Goines apparently had a light complexion—Phyllis could "travel anywhere.") In the intervening months, though, Mary had backed her son-in-law financially, presumably with her own money, staking him in his own business, and Goines, who was unpacking and arranging chemicals and drugs in his soon-to-be-opened shop, had exhausted Robert's patience. "He must begin to pay for his bread and butter and keep, too," he wrote. "I am too far along in life to carry young people."

Three days before the presidential election, Mary's secretary in New York typed a letter to Harding. (She had tutored herself in dictating, a skill her husband confessed he had never perfected.) "This time next week," she told the senator, "you will be president of the United States." For five weeks, she wrote, she had toiled night and day, exhorting African American women to vote for Harding. She had made speeches from Wilmington, Delaware, to Newport, Rhode Island. She had forged a network of Republican loyalists and ridden midnight trains back to New York, so she could report to her office the next morning. Practically every black woman in her territory would vote for him, she said, and the night before, in Baltimore, she had told her audience that they could trust him completely. She had looked at him on Social Justice Day and heard his noble and eloquent sentiments, his indictment of mob violence, and felt he meant every word, she added. "I know you will give every racial group in this country a square deal," she wrote. "That is all we want."

Before signing off, Mary tacked on a paragraph highlighting her Republican bona fides. She was, she said, the wife of Judge Robert H. Terrell and she had lived in Washington under the Wilson administration—and, she added, she knew what that had entailed. On the campaign trail, Mary had spoken more bluntly. "Every colored man outside of a lunatic asylum knows that if he votes for a Democrat instead of a Republican president he is giving his enemy a stick to break his own head," she had told her Newport audience on October 12. In her letter to Harding, she only alluded to the electoral stakes for blacks, to still-smoldering resentments fueled by Wilson's segregationist policies. "It will be a tragedy, if the Democratic Party is continued in power," she wrote. "It will be a fatal blow to law, order, justice, prosperity, and peace. God grant the country will be spared such an affliction."

When the results started to trickle in, Terrell was at headquarters. As a Washington resident, she still had no local, congressional, or presidential voting rights, no basis to log in her journal when and where she cast a ballot. Instead, in a half-page entry devoted to November 2, 1920, she fumed about a story in an Atlantic City newspaper, which said she had delivered a lengthy address the previous evening. The paper had "a grudge against us," she wrote. Though she left her meaning unclear—whether the perceived animus extended to Harding supporters in general or to black women in particular—she noted that her remarks had consumed forty-five minutes, fifteen fewer than another recitation. "I will not speak again at such a meeting," she added.

Meanwhile, in Marion, the Hardings stood in line and voted, with a film crew in tow. That evening, after Harding celebrated his fifty-fifth birthday, listeners tuned, for the first time, to radio coverage of presidential election results. Buoyed by the imagery of the "front porch campaign"—including Inez McWhorter slicing a watermelon on the steps—Harding had earned more than 60 percent of the popular vote, the most commanding margin ever recorded.

"Landslide for the Rep[ublican] Party," Terrell noted in her journal.

★ ★ ★ ★ ★

In early January 1921, while Mollie's Memphis relatives slipped inquiries and concerns about Berto's health and blood pressure into their Christmas-gift thank-you notes, Harding's inaugural committee tapped Mary for a panel charged with disseminating information about the ceremony. A few days later, around January 12, Harding relayed a telegram to the committee chairman in Washington, directing him, as a matter of fiscal prudence, to dispense with all celebrations surrounding the event, including the parade and inaugural ball. The president-elect went to St. Augustine, Florida, where he golfed (using an African American as a caddy). In early February, McWhorter appeared before a film crew, mixing dough for the strawberry shortcake recipe she planned to bring to the White House. A nonpartisan citizens union urged Harding to appoint an African American cabinet member.

On Inauguration Day, March 4, 1921, the *Afro-American* reminded readers about Wilson's failures, his silence on "fairplay" for blacks, his tacit complicity with racist congressional Democrats. "Woodrow Wilson leaves the White House today, with the praise of his successor ringing in his ears, and with the ill-will and disfavor of his colored fellow countrymen," the *Afro* said. "No President of the United States has been so unpopular and so thoroly [*sic*] hated in the history of the nation." Inside, on page 12, the "Big Inauguration Contest" featured a two-sentence puzzle, which, unscrambled, indicated that Harding had won after vowing to stop lynching.

Just before 11 a.m., Wilson, nearly blind and partially paralyzed by a stroke he had suffered in early October 1919, filed through the White House's front door. Film crews poised nearby, heeding an injunction against shooting footage of the president until he had installed himself in a waiting convertible. Limping and leaning on a cane, Wilson was helped into the back seat by his valet, Arthur Brooks. Then Wilson, who had spent much of the previous seventeen months in bed, doffed his top hat to Harding, who bowed and sat down next to him. Embargo lifted, motion-picture cameras whirred.

★ ★ ★ ★ ★

At 1:18 p.m., under clear, blue skies, Harding stood bare-headed and sun-tanned, clad in a morning coat and striped pants, on the Capitol's east portico, where tens of thousands of spectators had convened. Inspired by the ancients, the Capitol hugged a bluff almost nine stories above the Potomac River. Around the Capitol's periphery, unfolding across fifty-eight acres, lay the gardens conceived by Frederick Law Olmstead, who designed New York's Central Park. For lawmakers, Olmstead had created an oasis of green-ery, with fountains, benches, and curved walkways, dotted with magnolias and sweet gum trees—a sort of Americanized Tuileries. But Olmstead's landscape also buffeted Congress from the rest of the city. Senators and con-gressmen did their work behind a stone fence, enhancing their isolation and boosting the Capitol's aura of Olympian majesty—an effect magnified by the hilltop setting.

On a platform girded by four Corinthian columns, Florence Harding perched near her husband, wearing a chinchilla-trimmed coat and a straw hat spiked with feathers. Chief Justice Edward D. White, a Louisiana native and Confederate Army veteran who had spent two years as a Union prisoner of war, had Harding place his hand on the Bible used by George Washington. And with the bound volume open to Micah 6:8—a verse extolling justice, kindness, and walking humbly with God—he recited the oath of office.

Just below the rostrum, members of the Marine Band had amassed, near war veterans on leave from Walter Reed Hospital, including some confined to wheelchairs. On the plaza beyond them, uniformed troops enforced a perimeter, herding a sea of bystanders into reserved areas. In the tickets-only section at Harding's back, dignitaries clustered in rows: men in top hats, Supreme Court justices, members of the diplomatic corps in military rega-lia, a gentleman with white plumes tufting from his headgear.

In his inaugural address, the first one amplified by an electronic loud-speaker, Harding pledged to initiate "an era of good feeling." "Our supreme task is the resumption of our onward, normal way," he said. In deference to the Nineteenth Amendment, he lauded women for uplifting political dis-course, for their intuition, refinement, and intelligence. But his speech—a paean to his campaign themes of isolationism, convention, and thrift—con-tained no reference to a federal public welfare department, no promise to appoint a woman to his cabinet. Nor did it mention antilynching legislation or equal rights for African Americans.

Later that afternoon, as one of his first official acts, Harding issued an order granting public access to the White House, which had been off-limits—by decree of First Lady Edith Wilson—since Wilson's stroke. Around 5 p.m., after the president's family gathered for a luncheon, the mansion's iron gates swung open. Crowds poured through the entrance as if they were in Marion, roaming the lawn, massing on the front portico, peering through windows.

A week after the inauguration, the *Chicago Defender* reported that Harding had promised—to an unidentified source described as "one of our influential men"—that he would integrate federal office buildings, removing all signs of segregation and banishing discrimination. Three months later, the Associated Negro Press, a news service for black publications, grilled a Justice Department official about placards, located in the building, denoting whites-only men's rooms. The official feigned ignorance, saying he knew nothing about them. But even if they existed, he added, he saw no basis for an objection, since whites hadn't complained. "It seems all right to me," he said.

It was not an auspicious start to an era of good feeling, as least as far as black Americans were concerned. For Mary, the betrayal was even more profound. Her half-brother Robert—a Republican voting rights activist who, in 1918, founded the NAACP's Memphis branch—had shuttered their father's brothels and waded into national politics. During the 1920 presidential campaign, he spearheaded black voting efforts in Kentucky, Illinois, and Indiana. After the election, when Tennessee backed a Republican candidate for the first time in fifty years, Robert assumed control of federal party patronage for blacks nationwide. Yet even he was unable to help her land a position in the new administration.

Mary had other disappointments, too. At some point after she returned from Oberlin in 1914—she remained, as ever, circumspect—she and her husband had reconciled. They apparently kept separate bank accounts, though, and, at least during the summer, when she took up residence in Highland Beach, separate schedules. In Washington, they projected togetherness, showing up for church or the theater as a couple. On January 25, 1915, when she gave a speech at a meeting about the Belgian Relief Fund, he introduced her as "the Chairman of the Chairman"—an honorific she had inscribed, with evident approval, into her diary. Their letters to each other evinced warmth and affection; her journals reflected difficulties, familiar frustrations, and regrets. She wrote on January 4, 1921, for example, about finding two hundred whiskey bottles in the basement of her rental home at 1323 T Street, where she had lived for roughly five years; she did not say who was responsible for leaving them there. She confided on February 23, 1921, that she had told Robert she was unhappy about his priorities and his failure to make more time for social events with Phyllis. And on June 27, 1921, she wrote that she would refuse to pay the outstanding $200 balance on a debt he had incurred to her Memphis real estate broker.

Still, after almost four decades in Washington, Robert Terrell retained his sense of official correctness, his instinct for acknowledging and praising his patrons. On August 13, he composed a letter to William Howard Taft, directing it to the Supreme Court. Chief Justice White had died in May, and Harding, who had delivered the speech nominating Taft at the 1912 Republican convention, chose the former president as White's replacement, handing his fellow Ohioan the job he had long coveted. The Senate confirmed Taft later that day, making him the first person to sit atop the executive and judicial branches in the republic's 145-year-history.

In one paragraph, typed on municipal court stationery, Terrell congratulated Taft on his new post, voicing optimism and gratitude. "I believe that matters touching the interests of the people, regardless of race or color, will find fair and just treatment when they are brought before you for determination and settlement. I am glad that it has been my good fortune to serve as a Judge under a commission issued by you when you were President."

Taft replied from his summer home in Murray Bay, roughly one hundred miles north of Quebec. He thanked Terrell for his note and his sentiments. "I am glad to have an expression of confidence from you in my desire to act in matters which may come before me, without regard to race or color," he said.

Unofficially, though, in letters to friends and Mary, Terrell's health diverted and rattled him. He had suffered from high blood pressure for several years, and during the spring of 1922, his condition—however ill-defined in correspondence with his wife—triggered absences from work. Even after returning to the bench on March 18, 1922, he feared a possible reversal, worrying that rainy weather might undermine his recovery. "I am far from well," he wrote the next day, in the postscript to a note to Mary, who was in Memphis monitoring the real estate, improved and unimproved, she and her brother Thomas had inherited from their father. Earlier that month, Thomas had urged her to sell "some of the idle stuff"—meaning, presumably, empty lots without income-generating rental houses or buildings—so he could pursue a potentially more lucrative investment opportunity in Manhattan: yellow taxicabs. "New York is wild about them," he wrote. Mary reported back to Thomas on March 21, with a letter touching on affairs ranging from her husband, who was "sick," to the "ignorant," low-income whites who refused to treat her with respect, including one who had bowed to her without removing his hat.

★ ★ ★ ★ ★

In mid-May 1922, more than a year into the Harding presidency, Robert received a formal invitation from the Lincoln Memorial Commission, whose provenance dated to Taft's presidency. Under the auspices of Chief Justice Taft, who still chaired the commission, it bid Terrell to a ceremony, on May 30, 1922, dedicating the monument to the sixteenth president. A separate enclosure, engraved on a smaller card, directed guests to mail their acceptances to Lieutenant Colonel Clarence O. Sherrill, a North Carolina native who served as Harding's military aide and the commission's executive officer. Sherrill, a West Point–trained engineer who wore his army uniform with knee-high leather boots, was "in charge of the ceremonies."

Meanwhile, there would be speeches, and Robert R. Moton, the Amenia conferee and Tuskegee principal, was slated to give one of them. Like Booker T. Washington, Moton was a Virginia native and Hampton graduate, a voice of conservatism, not conflict. Moton also boasted access to white powerbrokers, Washington officials, and corporate chieftains, including Julius Rosenwald, the president of Sears, Roebuck and Co., who sat on Tuskegee's board. They all surely expected accommodationist remarks. Three years after the "Red Summer" and six years after Amenia, however, Moton intended to capitalize on the dedication and its nationwide broadcast—aired over naval radio stations—with a civil rights message.

Seven days before the ceremony, on May 23, 1922, Taft routed a telegram to Tuskegee, charged to his personal account. He and Colonel Sherrill had spent much of the past week or so wrestling with details: acceptances and regrets from state governors; a substitution in the program's paper stock, swapping the architect's Italian selection for a less-expensive American linen; seating arrangements for Robert T. Lincoln, the former president's seventy-eight-year-old son, who planned to attend with his wife and his physician. Taft had also read Moton's draft speech and, four days after receiving it, issued his response. "Shall have to ask you to cut five hundred words," he wrote. Beneath the veneer of geniality, though, Taft's main concern was content, not length. He suggested Moton give the address "more unity and symmetry" by stressing "tribute" and deemphasizing "appeal." "I am sure you wish to avoid any insinuation of attempt to make the occasion one for propaganda."

The next morning, Moton wired Taft back a telegram from Tuskegee. He was in the midst of commencement activities, he wrote, but he had already revised his speech to conform to the chief justice's suggestions and he planned additional changes and cuts.

★ ★ ★ ★ ★

Hours before the ceremony, crowds streamed onto reclaimed swampland at the Mall's western edge, along the banks of the Potomac. They arrived by the thousands, in cars, on foot, and by streetcar. Near the end of 23rd Street, while some two hundred members of the Grand Army of the Republic and one Confederate veteran marched on Pennsylvania Avenue, spectators converged along the Reflecting Pool, about 2,000 feet long and 200 feet wide. That morning, for the first time, the public saw the basin filled with water. At the head of the Reflecting Pool, aligned on an axis with the Capitol and the Washington Monument, rose the profile of the Lincoln Memorial: a Doric temple, carved from Colorado marble. Unlike the Capitol, the Lincoln Memorial deflected attention, orienting visitors toward the Reflecting Pool and the Mall, fostering meditation. Conceived as a tribute to the fallen president, the memorial also served notice of Washington's transformation from a backwater—just another southern town—to a global capital, with public spaces rivaling the Arc de Triomphe and the Place de l'Étoile in Paris.

About a block away from the memorial, a military sentry directed black guests to an enclosure, dubbed Section Five. As invitees, summoned by Taft's commission, they reflected status and accomplishment, including several friends of the Terrells, such as Emmett Scott, the Amenia conferee with whom Robert had issued his postriot statement in 1919, and Perry W. Howard, president of the National Negro Bar Association. Their green tickets gained them admission to a roped-off enclave, separated from the rest of the audience. Unlike other guests, whose passes conferred access to individual wooden chairs, they found benches, surrounded by grass and weeds.

After Harding's inauguration, Colonel Sherrill had banished African Americans from East Potomac Park Golf Course, a public facility adjacent to the Jefferson Memorial, saying they could only play on Tuesdays. By the one-year anniversary of Social Justice Day, Henry Lincoln Johnson, a

Washington-based former Taft appointee, privately denounced Harding as "that lying nigger in the White House," a reference to a rumor, fanned by opponents, that Harding's abolitionist forebears had produced mixed-race children. Lincoln Johnson, known to the *Chicago Defender* as "Linc," had opted out of the dedication altogether, sensing a likelihood of trouble.

In Section Five, Whitefield McKinlay realized what was happening and hesitated about how to react. McKinlay, a local real estate magnate, had amassed a record of Republican loyalty, dating back several decades. Like Robert, he supported Lodge in 1892; like Robert, he had served as a director of Capital Savings Bank and, at one point, declared bankruptcy over debts stemming from its insolvency, after a court ruled that shareholders could be held liable as partners for depositors' claims. In 1910, when Taft appointed McKinlay to serve as the customs collector for Georgetown's port, a neighborhood-citizens group objected, saying the president should have tapped a white person, or at least a "coal black" African American—an apparent reference to McKinlay's light complexion. Now, faced with his seating assignment, McKinlay told his military escort he'd think about taking it. "Well[,] think damned quick," the guard said. Others in the vicinity objected, calling for the soldier's reassignment. His commanding officer defended him, saying it was the only way to keep colored people in their place.

McKinlay walked out. Twenty African American ticketholders joined him, including Scott and Howard, taking their guests and wives with them. Only a handful stayed behind.

★ ★ ★ ★ ★

Moton stood just underneath the top step of the monument. Overhead, amplifiers and loudspeakers lined the roof, transmitting sound across the plaza. At Moton's back, on the shrine's threshold, sat an assemblage of dignitaries, including Robert Lincoln and the president and First Lady. Behind them was the two-story statue of Lincoln, sculpted from Georgia marble by Daniel Chester French, who depicted the former president with his gaze to the east, toward the Reflecting Pool. On the wall above Lincoln's head, carved into the Indiana limestone, an inscription read: "In this temple as in the hearts of the people for whom he saved the union the memory of Abraham Lincoln is enshrined forever."

★ ★ ★ ★ ★

From the opening sentence of the speech Moton originally drafted, he invoked the theme of liberty and keyed it to the second-class citizenship of

African Americans. He alluded to the Gettysburg Address, a speech delivered at the dedication of a cemetery for Union soldiers, where Lincoln pledged to bring to completion the unfinished work for which so many had perished. The "great task remaining before us," Lincoln stated, was "a new birth of freedom." Since 1620, Moton proclaimed, freedom has been our national heritage, "the battle-cry" of a unified people from the Revolution to the recent world war, a legacy "bequeathed to all her sons." Still, he continued, a nation dedicated to freedom had, from the outset, subjected African Americans to bondage, unleashing the twin forces of slavery and liberty, which "developed side-by-side." God had "thrust" the black race into "the path of the onward-marching white race," leaving blacks to prove, to America and the entire world, whether the rights to life, liberty, and the pursuit of happiness applied equally "to all mankind."

Moton also hailed the Lincoln Memorial as a "symbol of our gratitude." And none were more thankful for Lincoln's sacrifice than the twelve million African Americans whose emancipation he had ensured. In a nod to Taft, who viewed the dedication as an opportunity for sectional healing, Moton conceded that Lincoln had died to save the Union. But he also pressed further, implicitly rebuking the midwestern amiability and racial relativism of Taft and Harding, saying that Lincoln's claim to greatness lay in his role as emancipator. Amid uncertainty, against the guidance of his advisors, he had liberated a race, vindicating "the honor of a nation conceived in liberty" and "dedicated to the proposition that all men are created equal."

Had African Americans proven worthy of Lincoln's sacrifice? Moton asked. "No group has been more loyal," he said. "Whether bond or free, he has served alike his country's need." African Americans understood their "incongruous position in the great American republic," he continued, but to their "everlasting credit," and in spite of the nation's failure "to deal fairly" with them, their loyalty remained beyond question. Based on statistics— from land, home, and business ownership to professional achievements and literacy rates—blacks had proven their worth in peacetime as well. In any case, Lincoln had not died only for African Americans; he had sacrificed his life to vindicate the nation's honor, to ensure, as he said at Gettysburg, that government of, by, and for the people "should not perish from the earth."

With conviction that resonated from the hills of Amenia and the battlefields of France to the streets of downtown Washington, Moton posed another question: "What nobler thing can the nation do as it dedicates this shrine for him whose deed has made his name immortal—what nobler thing can the nation do than here about this shrine to dedicate itself by its

own determined will to fulfill to the last letter the lofty task imposed upon
it by the sacred dead?" The Lincoln Memorial, he said, this emblem of our
reverence, was "but a hollow mockery, a symbol of hypocrisy," unless they
brought to fruition everywhere the principles for which Lincoln died. The
federal government has not always provided "the best example" to the states,
he continued, but any government that can suppress injustice and mob rule
abroad can do so on its own terrain. Black and white, North and South, we
must find a path out of these hardships together, and "square ourselves with
the enlightened conscience and public opinion of all mankind." Otherwise,
they would "stand convicted not only of inconsistency and hypocrisy, but of
the deepest ingratitude that could stain the nation's honor."

Had he given that speech, it might have been Moton's finest moment.
And, at first, his remarks—now one page shorter than his original composition, in deference to Taft's suggestion—hewed closely to his initial draft. But
when Moton reached what had been the emotional high point of his speech,
with statistical evidence of African American achievement, he punted. Gone
was any overt reference to the Gettysburg Address—inscribed, in its entirety,
on a limestone wall inside the memorial. Gone were Moton's demands for
accountability, for freedom for "*all* the people," and his repeated references
to "unfinished" business. Excised, too, were his indignation and sense of
hypocrisy, his plea, on behalf of African Americans everywhere, for full and
equal citizenship.

Instead, when Moton broached the subject of race relations, he inserted
a reference to the country's global stature. The entire world was watching
America—"with anxious heart and eager eyes"—to see whether different
races could "live together in peace." In deference to Taft and the commission, he framed his references to the South in terms of reconciliation, saying
blacks and whites were toiling together for their mutual progress and afflu-
ence, proving that a nation dedicated to equality for all "*can*" endure." While
he spoke, about a half dozen Confederate veterans, clad in gray uniforms,
massed at the base of the steps next to an American flag. A handful of
Union soldiers, frail and unsteady, clumped on the other side of them. "As
we gather on this consecrated spot," Moton added, "his spirit must rejoice
that sectional rancours and racial antagonisms are softening more and more
into mutual understanding and effective cooperation."

Still, Moton did not capitulate entirely. He embraced the legacy of "the
martyred dead": a renewed dedication to "equal opportunity and unham-
pered freedom" for all citizens, no matter how humble, regardless of race or

creed. He referred to Lincoln as "the great Emancipator." He invoked an aura of shared commitment, saying blacks would devote their ongoing loyalty and cooperation to realizing "the lofty principles established by his martyrdom." Then, summoning Lincoln's Second Inaugural Address, he looked again to the forum of global opinion. "With malice toward none, with charity for all," he said, "we dedicate ourselves and our posterity, with *you* and *yours*, to finish the work which he so nobly began, to make America an example for all the world of equal justice and equal opportunity for all."

For his own speech, Taft stood atop the stairs, surveying the crowd before him. His arrival had been preceded by a cavalcade of Washington officialdom: Secretary of State Charles Evans Hughes; the French and British ambassadors; cabinet officers; US senators; and, filing in two-by-two, members of the House. Taft radiated proprietary dignity, like a father of the bride. Shifting his gaze between his remarks, etched on paper he held in his hands, and his audience, he rocked back and forth on his feet as he spoke, like a lawyer arguing a case to a jury.

A decade earlier, during his unsuccessful bid for reelection in 1912, Taft had trawled for African American support with speeches at Metropolitan AME Church. In one, he had denounced lynching, calling it "a disgraceful page in our social history." In another, he had touted the Emancipation Proclamation as Lincoln's "greatest act," a move that extinguished the "living lie" of slavery, which had nullified the Declaration of Independence. Now, though, Taft hailed Lincoln not as the president who freed the slaves but as a "Christ-like character" who had saved the Union. With a nod to the monument's riverbank setting, on the border between North and South, Taft said the ceremony marked the return of "brotherly love" between the regions. He invoked Reconstruction, conveying empathy for southerners, saying that their wounds would have healed more easily had Lincoln survived. "Here is a shrine at which all can worship."

Harding's speech followed Taft's, both in the program and in content as a tribute. Emancipation, he said, was a means to the end of maintaining the union and preserving nationality. How Lincoln would have "rejoiced," he added at one point, departing from his prepared remarks, to see the image now before him, with veterans of the blue flanking the flag on one side, and veterans in gray on the other. Beneath him, a cheer rose from the ex-combatants.

After the ceremony, Harding paused to chat with Robert Lincoln, while film cameras and still photographers recorded their conversation. Visitors climbed up the white marble stairs and spilled into the chamber, where, across the pink marble floor, they beheld the statue of Lincoln. In an open alcove to Lincoln's left, above the Second Inaugural Address, a sixty-foot mural, titled *Unification*, depicted the Angel of Truth: a bare-breasted white woman, rendered in jewel tones, joining the hands of two female figures representing North and South. Inside the alcove on Lincoln's right, a twin mural by the same artist, Jules Guerin, hung over the Gettysburg Address. In the second painting, titled *Emancipation*, the Angel of Truth hovered in the center, with her arms outstretched over her head, liberating a cluster of slaves.

Two days after the ceremony, one of the Section Five ticketholders filed a grievance with Taft. Most of the African American guests had felt compelled to leave to avoid the humiliation of sitting in a Jim Crow section, wrote George Murray. Such segregation stemmed from "a concession to Southern social sentiment" and was "entirely out of place on a public occasion."

Taft replied on June 4, two days after the *Afro* ran a story about the walk-out. Murray's letter surprised him, he wrote, since he had directed Colonel Sherrill that "no such *segregation*"—which he underlined—should occur. "If colored people did sit in a particular place, it must have been accidental, for certainly nobody having authority connected with the dedication was authorized to bring it about." The NAACP's Washington branch demanded Sherrill's removal. Segregated seating at the memorial's dedication was "most shocking and atrocious," the NAACP said, especially since the sitting president shared Lincoln's party affiliation.

Meanwhile, on June 9, Princeton University bestowed an honorary degree on Harding. The next day, the *Chicago Defender* urged readers to boycott the Lincoln Memorial. Officials had opened the shrine, the editors said, but it remained unconsecrated. "When juster and more grateful men come to power and history shall have rebuked offenders against the name of Abraham Lincoln, those set free in his death and glory will gather with their children and their benefactors to dedicate the memorial."

★ ★ ★ ★ ★

Robert Terrell's health continued to deteriorate, so much so, apparently, that when the black press chronicled the Lincoln Memorial ceremony, his name did not appear among the guests—either those who walked out or those who remained. Then, in early June, he had an asthma attack, followed by a prolonged case of hiccups, the resolution of which defied medical treatment for days. When the *Chicago Defender* ran a story about his predicament, saying his friends had grown "alarmed" and "worried" over his well-being, handwritten notes and typed letters trickled into 1615 S Street, NW, a three-story row house Mary had purchased about a year-and-a-half earlier. While he lay in bed in her home, plagued by insomnia and unable to eat, correspondents proffered remedies: prune juice, damson preserves, a drop of turpentine placed in the navel, a grain of cocaine, coupled with an ice bag on the pit of the stomach.

On June 12, two weeks after the Lincoln Memorial ceremony, Harding nominated Terrell to a sixth four-year term. The Senate confirmed him ten days later. That day, Harding and Attorney General Harry M. Daugherty inked their signatures on his commission, touting his "Wisdom, Uprightness and Learning." His friends in Washington and the African American press hailed his reappointment, much as they regretted his frailty. The *Washington Eagle*, noting his two decades on the bench, argued that Terrell reflected honor on the entire race. Emmett Scott, in a congratulatory letter, called Harding's move "about the only decent thing of his administration, so far as we are concerned."

★ ★ ★ ★ ★

Robert, who had suffered an apparent stroke, complained to Mary about his regimen of inactivity. Physically unable to return to work, he doted on and walked the dog. He commended Congressman Hamilton Fish, the New York Republican, for objecting to the banishment of African American undergraduates from Harvard's freshman dormitories. He lent his name to an organization, alongside that of Moton's and Reverend Jernagin's, dedicated to erecting a Washington-based monument to African American war veterans. The project, first proposed in Congress in 1919, resurfaced four years later as an antidote to the "Black Mammy" statue, whose adherents in the Daughters of the Confederacy had revived that cause, with the Senate's blessing.

Mary, meanwhile, pressed on, juggling engagements, "as if," a relative noted, "nothing had happened." She joined black leaders for a meeting with the War Department secretary to decry a segregated bathing area at the tidal basin, near the Lincoln Memorial. She canvassed, without success, for a magazine to publish her short stories. She drafted a letter to the editor, which ran in the *Washington Evening Star* on February 10, 1923, and in the *Washington Herald* a few days later, about the "Black Mammy" memorial. Enslaved black women, she pointed out, had no homes of their own, no legal rights to marriage, and their own children were often sold away, not to be seen again, while they raised the offspring of their white mistresses. "Colored women all over the United States stand aghast at the idea of erecting a black mammy monument in the capital of the United States," she said. "Surely in their zeal to pay tribute to the faithful services rendered by the black mammy the descendants of slaveholding ancestors have forgotten the atrocities and cruelties incident to the institution of slavery itself." Saying she needed "a change and a rest," she escaped to Florida about two weeks later for a midwinter lecture tour.

In private, Mary bemoaned her husband's resistance, his lack of concern about diet and relaxation. He, in turn, betrayed a sense of vulnerability, expressing relief when she decided to come home from yet another trip, this time to Boston. "I miss you so much," he wrote, in a letter dated March 26, 1923. His wife was right to worry. Robert's second stroke hit later that spring, impairing his speech and leaving him paralyzed on one side. For several months, he languished at Freedman's Hospital, while relatives urged Mary not to despair. In October, Howard Law School canceled his salary and transferred his classes to another professor. After the Christmas holidays, the Mu-So-Lit Club suspended his dues and arranged for a monthly floral arrangement, delivered to his room, as a gesture of its respect and admiration.

Mary herself was recovering from a car accident and planning Mary's wedding to Leon A. Tancil, a physician and "fine catch," as the elder Mary had once described him in a letter to Robert encouraging the match. She was showing signs of strain as well. On April 14, 1924—eleven days after robed white men, reputedly affiliated with the Ku Klux Klan, staged a cross burning at Columbia University, seeking to oust a black law student from his Furnald Hall dorm room—she spoke at an antisegregation meeting in Washington. Over in the local trial court, the NAACP was challenging Washington's racial restrictive covenants, which barred property owners from selling to African Americans. In one of the cases, NAACP lawyers were defending a purchase by Emmett Scott, who had already moved into his dwelling.

As a prospective homebuyer, Mary had already experienced real estate discrimination. Whites had attempted to thwart her, too, both before she moved to S Street and, decades earlier, in LeDroit Park, where a white homeowner once refused to sell to her and Robert after learning they were black. In the intervening years, when Mary again considered buying a home to take the place of the still-rented T Street duplex, she realized that real estate agents only showed her rundown properties. At one point, not long after

Harding was elected, Mary sought to enlist Harriot Stanton Blatch, the daughter of suffragist Elizabeth Cady Stanton, to purchase a house and flip the property to her. But Blatch lived in New York and, though sympathetic, advised Mary to find a white friend in Washington to effectuate the transaction. Eventually, in order to buy her S Street row house, which the agent initially refused to sell to her because she was black, Mary agreed to pay several thousand dollars more than the asking price and make a larger down payment (though, when she later wrote about the incident, she did not disclose the specifics).

Now, inside John Wesley AME Zion Church, Mary vented to an audience convened by Kelly Miller, the Howard University professor and Amenia conferee. The trouble with some of us is that we protest too much in secret, behind closed doors, she said. Some of us will not speak out in tones "the whole civilized world" will hear, but if we want to accomplish anything in this country, if we want to defeat segregation, we will have to agitate. "Our chief duty," she added, "to our white brother is to try to save him from himself."

★ ★ ★ ★ ★

Robert left the hospital during the summer of 1924, not long after Mary returned to Oberlin for her fortieth reunion. With another presidential election looming that fall, both parties assembled for political conventions, dominated by fallout from Washington scandals and a resurgent Ku Klux Klan, whose membership had soared. Harding had died of a heart attack a year earlier, in August 1923, tainted by corruption among his inner cabinet members. Republicans, who convened in Cleveland in mid-June 1924, coalesced around Harding's successor and former vice president, Calvin Coolidge, a probusiness conservative. Democrats gathered in New York two weeks later, fractured by race, Prohibition, and the Klan.

Against this backdrop, the NAACP assembled in Philadelphia on June 25 for its fifteenth-annual conference, an event consumed by frustration with two successive administrations: Wilson, the Democrat, and Harding, the Republican. In a public statement, the NAACP denounced the Republican Party for failing to abolish segregated federal offices in Washington, failing to pass anti-lynching legislation, and failing to eliminate Jim Crow interstate railway cars. Democrats, the NAACP added, were beholden to the South, with its Jim Crow laws, mob rule, lynching, and inferior schools for black children. With both parties pandering to the Klan, the NAACP said, African Americans should step up their "agitation," seek relief in court, and wield the ballot "to reward our friends and to punish our enemies." In November, Coolidge defeated John W. Davis of West Virginia, the Democratic nominee, in part because the candidacy of Robert M. La Follette, a Wisconsin progressive, had split the Democratic vote, siphoning support from disaffected liberals.

Back on S Street, still barred from working, Robert listened to the radio and indulged regrets, mourning his dependency, knowing he was a burden to his wife. After the election, Mary, who had just turned sixty-one, lobbied the Coolidge administration for an appointment at the Labor Department. Even after the agency rejected her bid, saying she was a lecturer, who lacked the training and expertise to conduct investigations, she kept prodding, peppering Coolidge's secretary with letters. In a post-Christmas note to her brother Thomas, she fretted about cash flow—the nonliquidity of their father's real estate holdings, and expenses—even though Robert still drew a salary from the court.

Meanwhile, the NAACP sent her a copy of its 1924 annual report, a sixty--eight-page, single-spaced document chronicling its efforts to combat segregation, disfranchisement, and lynching. During the calendar year, the association said, it had fielded 476 requests for assistance, hailing from all regions of the United States; for meritorious grievances alone, cases with the potential to create nationwide precedent, its annual legal defense budget could exceed $50,000. Near the end of the report, in a section devoted to finances, the NAACP acknowledged the newly formed women's auxiliary, a New York–based entity whose members had, with a pair of benefits, netted more than $1,900 for the national office. Two separate groups, the Women's Defense Fund, based in Kansas City, and the Ladies' Service Group of Washington, D.C., had together raised an additional $1,600. Mary Church Terrell's name did not number among those mentioned. But her half-brother, Robert, had earned a spot on page 1, alongside luminaries such as Du Bois and Spingarn, as a member of the board of directors.

Mary received a check for $1,180 from D. S. Van Court, her Memphis real estate agent, two months later, reflecting half the proceeds, less taxes and commission, from the sale of a Camilla Street lot she owned with Thomas. Inside her S Street home, she tuned into a radio-fitness class, sponsored by Metropolitan Life Insurance Company. When she had trouble keeping up, she complained to Met Life's health broadcasting bureau, saying portions of the program, which included push-ups, moved too quickly.

Two weeks before Christmas, Robert suffered an asthma attack. He retreated to his bed a week later and died on December 20, 1925, at the age of sixty-eight, after a cerebral hemorrhage. Mary had understood, and con-fided to her family, that Robert would never recover from his second stroke, the one that had debilitated him in 1923. Still, his death provoked a sense of shock, one she managed, at least at the outset, by concentrating on the mun-dane, scrambling to file a life-insurance claim.

Meanwhile, condolence notes and telegrams flooded her dwelling, bearing addresses from Cleveland to Tuskegee. Robert had known three generations of African Americans, from Frederick Douglass and Booker T. Washington to a younger cadre, just emerging. "It is impossible now to estimate the great loss that has befallen us," wrote Arthur G. Froe, Washington's recorder of deeds. Inside the judiciary, colleagues and members of the bar paused to pay tribute. Charles Hamilton Houston, the first African American editor of the *Harvard Law Review*, announced Robert's death during proceedings in the local trial venue. From the bench, Chief Justice Walter I. McCoy man-dated the entry of an order, logged into the tribunal's records, registering sorrow over Terrell's demise. McCoy, the president of the Harvard Club of Washington—whose members had blackballed Robert four decades ear-lier—said Terrell's career had honored the university. The next day, the mu-nicipal court adjourned for five days, until after the burial.

On Christmas Eve, mourners filed into Metropolitan AME Church, where floral arrangements from around the country lined the sanctuary. Robert's pastor, the Reverend Robert W. Brooks, extolled his rise from anonymity to distinction. Whitefield McKinlay, who spawned the Lincoln Memorial walkout, served as an honorary pallbearer. So did Perry Howard, who had strode out of the dedication ceremony with him, and William L. Houston, the father and law partner of the attorney who eulogized Terrell in court.

News accounts of his death and funeral, splashed across the front pages of the African American press, reverberated with tribute. "During his long and brilliant career here in the District, he stood out as a man who was [a] good conscientious Christian, and loved as he lived," said one. The *Washington Eagle* ran a photograph of the Terrells together, with Robert seated in a high-backed chair next to a window, clad in a suit and tie. Mary stood next to and slightly behind him, a seeming tableau of deference.

5

The Radicalization of
Mary Church Terrell

After Robert's death, Mary started composing her memoirs, beginning a draft in longhand. She had, of course, yearned to write for decades, dating back at least to Paris, and widowhood seemed to liberate her. Alone at sixty-two, she also battled grief and anxiety, especially about her prospects. Almost three weeks after Robert's funeral, she wrote her brother, Thomas, confiding that she hadn't had the energy, physical or mental, to collect her husband's obituaries from the black press. She had, however, visited Congressman Martin B. Madden, an Illinois Republican, to inquire about seeking Robert's salary for the remainder of his unexpired term. And, in her note to Thomas, she lamented her lack of influence within the NAACP. "Dubois [sic] doesn't hate me and he certainly doesn't *love* me," she wrote.

In early March, Thomas furnished Mary with a manual titled *Help for Student Writers*. She dashed off a note thanking him, promising to share her first $1,000 check. "Don't laugh!" she wrote.

On June 29, 1926, six months after Robert died, Terrell received a letter from the editorial department of Little, Brown & Company, the Boston publisher, expressing interest in her autobiography. The editor, Herbert F. Jenkins, did not offer her a contract, or set a word limit, or impose a deadline. Instead, he conveyed a series of suggestions. He recommended that she read a few examples of the genre, including *The Story of My Life* by Helen Keller, which had been published in 1903. He steered her toward magazines, including the *Atlantic Monthly*, which often featured prepublication excerpts from memoirs. He advised her to send him a few early chapters, rather than waiting until she had finished the entire manuscript. And he encouraged her to push ahead with the work, saying that her story, told simply, honestly, and in chronological order, might have broad appeal. "It seems to us that you have an excellent opportunity of presenting a penetrating and truthful picture of the experiences of a colored girl who achieved success despite many obstacles."

A little more than a year after she began writing, in early 1927, Mary finished typing her first four chapters. When she read the pages in succession for the first time, she had to stop. "It is so disappointing!" she wrote in her diary. As a tonic, she fled to the department stores, where she bought a $25 black satin dress and a pair of shoes. Jenkins, who reviewed the chapters a few weeks later, prodded her toward candor and disclosure. Not long after that, in April, he shared a confidential reader's report, suggesting she needed to focus on brevity. She responded with a seven-page letter.

Mary mailed her final manuscript to Jenkins eight years later, in March 1935. Almost a full decade had elapsed since she first contacted Little, Brown about the project and Jenkins had responded with suggestions. On March 22, she received a letter from an employee, not Jenkins, thanking her for her submission and promising to respond with a decision. "I pray they will publish it," she wrote in her diary. Over the years, though, she had succumbed to despair.

Mary's literary aspirations had long hinged on the feat of publishing her life story, not the rigor of narrating it, in all its complexity. She had thought that, with relative ease, she could generate a publishable manuscript. As a writer, though, let alone as a memoirist, she faced several hurdles. Self-scrutiny and openness did not come easily to her, in matters large and small, even—perhaps especially—among friends. In 1915, for example, when she went to the Mayo Clinic for two months and withstood three operations, including one to remove her gallbladder and another to remove a goiter, Robert covered for her, telling friends that she was on a speaking tour. On a car-insurance application in 1924, she appeared to indicate that she was fifty, a decade shy of her actual age, and in response to a question about her race, she said she was white. Even more important, she resisted transparency about her encounters with racism. In part, as she would later write, as an African American woman she was reluctant to reveal "the 'WHOLE' truth." If she did, she said, whites would accuse her of bitterness.

Even before starting her autobiography, Mary finessed personal facts that had the potential to contradict her image as a race spokesperson and crusader. Almost three decades earlier, when she pondered writing about her travels in the Jim Crow South, she had contemplated writing anonymously or concealing her identity, either to mask the extent to which whites had subjected her to the humiliation of segregation, or the degree to which she had foiled the system by passing for white, about which she was understand-ably sensitive—or perhaps both. Similarly, in her memoirs, Terrell tended to focus on her achievements, from Oberlin to Berlin, omitting or glossing over incidents that exposed her hardships as a daughter, mother, wife, and activist, including her mother's suicide attempt and tensions in her relation-ship with Robert.

In an undated handwritten draft, for example, presumably early in the process, Mary wondered what some of her white friends would think of her if they could read her mind. "Shall I or shall I not reveal the secrets of my heart?" she wrote. In a typed draft, also undated, she noted that she had in-tentionally decided not to explore in depth the "obstacles" and "barriers" she had encountered because of her race, opting instead to focus on "oppor-tunities" she had enjoyed to showcase her talent. Over time, as she revised the manuscript, she excised potentially telling details she had included in various drafts, including one Oberlin incident. A teacher, she wrote, had advised her to decline an invitation from a white male student and to go to a reception instead with her black classmate, Ida Gibbs.

From a technical standpoint, Terrell struggled with fundamentals. Her prose sagged under the weight of repetition and cliché. Over the years, even before tackling her memoir, she had accrued a slew of rejections. One editor, who dismissed her short stories as "unconvincing" and "uninterest-ing," conceded the sincerity of her motives, but said she needed to dedicate more effort to "the art of expression and presentation." Another said her work, like most propaganda fiction, lacked subtlety and "story interest." Joel Spingarn, a founder of Harcourt, Brace and Co., Inc., also believed that her literary work fell short. "I can't say exactly why this is so," he wrote, "but perhaps it is because you are more intent on reforming this world than on creating an imaginary world of your own, after the artist's fashion."

During her autobiography's nine-year gestation period, moreover, Mary faced a welter of demands on her time and psyche, especially during the Depression. When real estate values plummeted, so did her income from her inheritance, which was tied up in the Memphis properties left to her by her father. In 1931, she divided up her S Street home into apartments and installed herself on the ground floor with Phyllis, who had separated from her husband in 1923 and who slept on a daybed in the library. Throughout the early 1930s, Mary's journals resounded with references to card parties, shopping, and debt.

Around the same time, Mary became involved with Representative Oscar S. DePriest, a Chicago Republican who, in 1928, was the first African

American congressman elected in the twentieth century, and the first elected in the North. He was also married and seven years her junior. In her diary, she dubbed him "DeP." Like a much-younger woman afflicted with a crush, she kept track of when he called on her to say goodbye and when he had admired her appearance at a reception. She fumed when he misled her about his whereabouts on Christmas, and, on New Year's Eve, prayed the relationship would continue. When the liaison ended two years later, Mary expressed relief. Months after that, she bristled at his refusal to lend her a typewriter.

Other diversions drained her, too. In 1934, she filled her journal with grievances about her tenants. One complained about a lack of heat and hot water and didn't pay rent. At the end of the month, he moved out and took the lightbulbs. Meanwhile, she angled to be given an honorary degree from Oberlin; found a lump under her arm—which the doctor dismissed as no cause for concern; stewed about Phyllis's impending second marriage; and toiled at a succession of administrative and clerical jobs, before being laid off. In late August, as she approached her seventy-first birthday, a doctor checked her heart and blood pressure, and, though they were fine, referred her to a specialist. In her journal, next to the date and time of her pending appointment, she inscribed the word *Psychoneurosis.*

During moments of seclusion, she tried to focus on her manuscript. In late November 1934, when she ate Thanksgiving dinner alone in a cafeteria, she reread her journals from the 1920s. Parsing events—such as Phyllis's separation from her first husband—she weighed whether or not to include them in her memoir's account. "At my wit's end," she wrote in her diary on December 9. At one point, on February 28, 1935, she confided to her journal that she should have started rewriting sooner.

With others, Mary hedged about her prospects, often deflecting responsibility. In a letter to Mary Roberts Rinehart, the writer who helped spearhead Social Justice Day in 1920, she said she didn't know how to make her writing acceptable to white people. Rinehart responded a few weeks later, saying her manuscript was "greatly improved" and even "fascinating," but expressing reservations about its prospects. The next day, at the Mayflower Hotel, Mary met with the British author H. G. Wells, who had entertained her at his home in 1919 after she gave a lecture abroad. In her journal the following day, March 17, 1935, Mary noted that Wells furnished her with his London agent's address. (She didn't say whether or not she sent a query.)

Inside S Street, on April 11, 1935, Mary noticed a letter from Jenkins. She had spent much of the day focused on urgencies outside the realm of memoir, at home and abroad. At the Cosmos Club, the famous literary salon on H Street, she attended a luncheon on behalf of the Community Chest, a privately financed fund for aiding charities. Afterward, she watched a screening of *Road to Life*, a Russian film, dating back to 1931, about homeless children who lived on the streets.

Jenkins, now a vice president at Little, Brown, with his name appearing just underneath the president's on the letterhead, had bad news: after careful consideration, Little, Brown had resolved not to publish her. He denied a suggestion by Mary, in previous correspondence with him, that publishers would reject her manuscript because she was a black woman. Publishers had acquired memoirs by Booker T. Washington and James Weldon Johnson— and might also acquire hers—precisely because they were African American, he said. As for differences between those autobiographies, published some years earlier, and Mary's, Jenkins offered no analysis. Instead, he quoted from the reader's report, which deemed her material "interesting" but "far too long." In the end, Jenkins wrote, Mary had simply failed to tell her story in a manner that would captivate readers and ensure its commercial viability. Hard times had something to do with this. In the years since she first contacted him and he reviewed her initial chapters, he pointed out, book sales had plummeted by 40 to 60 percent.

★ ★ ★ ★ ★

Later that same day, April 11, Mary typed a letter to her brother, Thomas. In her S Street apartment, where she stashed her correspondence and brochures in a window seat, she didn't refer to her letter from Jenkins. Instead, she thanked Thomas for sending her a list of literary agents, recounted her experience with one who sought a $10 fee for simply reading her manuscript, and told him she had landed an article in the *Washington Sunday Star* about the Julius Rosenwald Fund, named for the head of Sears, Roebuck & Co.

Still, her failure weighed on her. "I fear I am beginning to be a bit discouraged," she wrote. I might have succeeded as a writer if I had tackled a noncontroversial subject, she added. If she had lived in New York, she continued, she could have associated, as James Weldon Johnson did, with men like Brander Matthews, a Columbia professor of dramatic literature, and Nicholas Murray Butler, the president of Columbia University. "You have let the pesky race question alone and have written the most interesting stories," she told Thomas, who was also a writer; and as "an artist," not "a missionary" or "a reformer," you should succeed in selling your work. Before signing off, she inserted a few lines of advice, telling him to keep his sentences short and clear. "It is quite the vogue, I hear."

In the days that followed, Terrell sought consolation outside the home: a card party; an outing to Hahn's, a department store, to exchange a pair of shoes; a screening of *Don Q, Son of Zorro*, starring Douglas Fairbanks. Inside Metropolitan AME Church, she listened to a speech by First Lady Eleanor Roosevelt, who urged African Americans to pursue their goals through politics. "I love her," Mary jotted in her diary, on April 14. Still, she swung from shame—saying she didn't want anyone to know she had written her autobiography—to resilience, saying she would never be satisfied until she saw it published.

A week after fielding Little, Brown's rejection, on April 18, Mary composed an eight-line prayer at the front of her journal, in the space allotted for New Year's Day. "Banish my unpleasant thoughts. From worry set me free."

★ ★ ★ ★ ★

On Easter Sunday, 1939, near the base of the Lincoln Memorial, Mary spotted a black limousine. A motorcycle escort flanked the car, as if shepherding a head of state. Across the plaza and around the Reflecting Pool, thousands of spectators had gathered—white and black Americans—braving the rawness of early April, with wind gusting off the Potomac. Men, women, and children had converged for a free twilight concert given by Marian Anderson, the African American contralto hailed by Arturo Toscanini, the Italian conductor, as a voice heard once in a century.

Terrell had no entrée to the memorial's stairs, where workers had installed a temporary stage, draped in green carpeting and wired with about half a dozen microphones. Earlier in the day, when she went to the YWCA after church, Reverend Robert W. Brooks, Robert's pastor, informed her that he had a platform pass for the performance and offered to give her a ride. Mary replied that she would tell the usher she had neglected to bring her ticket. Now, as she and Brooks broached a walkway leading to the rostrum, Anderson emerged from her limousine, clad in a mink coat and a mink-trimmed hat. When Mary and Brooks fell in behind, no one questioned their credentials.

Buoyed by her good fortune, Mary settled into the province of dignitaries. Arrayed in rows, on either side of a Steinway piano, they sat facing the Reflecting Pool, with the Lincoln Memorial at their backs. Seventeen years after the dedication ceremony, on April 9, 1939, blacks and whites aligned in chairs together: Walter White, the NAACP's secretary, Charles Hamilton

Houston, the NAACP's special counsel, and Senator Robert A. Taft, a first-term Ohio Republican and the son of the former chief justice.

Harold L. Ickes, Roosevelt's interior secretary, stood at the podium, prepared to deliver remarks that the White House had vetted. In front of him, an estimated 75,000 people had congregated, making it one of the capital's largest assemblages since admirers greeted Charles Lindbergh in 1927, after his transatlantic flight. Just behind Ickes sat Kosti Vehanen, a Finnish pianist who toured with Anderson. When Vehanen first glimpsed the crowd—which stretched across the plaza in a semicircle, trailing halfway around the Reflecting Pool—he despaired; he thought no one would hear the piano.

Ickes, a sixty-five-year-old New Deal veteran and Roosevelt administration insider, presided over the National Parks and the Public Works Administration, which, in the six years since its inception, had funded more than 34,000 construction projects, ranging from battleships to municipal sewers. He also numbered among a handful of New Dealers, including the First Lady, who were attuned to the welfare of American blacks. In Chicago, during the 1920s, Ickes had briefly served as president of the local NAACP; as interior secretary, he banned racial discrimination in public-works employment, spoke to black audiences, and, in 1937, lobbied FDR to tap William H. Hastie, Charles Hamilton Houston's cousin, for a federal district judgeship in the Virgin Islands, making Hastie the first black federal judge—a distinction even Robert Terrell, with his successive four-year presidential appointments, had not achieved.

Now, though, the plight of American blacks, and Washington's culture of subjugating them, had sparked a national moment of reckoning. Two months earlier, the Daughters of the American Revolution had denied Anderson access to Constitution Hall, which they owned, citing a policy against African American performers. Washington's school board banished Anderson, too, refusing her permission to use an all-white public high school auditorium, invoking a similar rationale: in a segregated system, a black singer could not perform from a white stage. Walter White denounced the board's decision, blasting the hypocrisy of American outrage over Nazi Germany, where, on November 10, 1938, during a rampage known as *Kristallnacht*, Storm Troopers had torched almost 200 synagogues and sent 20,000 Jews to concentration camps. At the end of February, Eleanor Roosevelt dispatched a telegram to a mass meeting at Brooks's church, voicing her regret over Anderson's travails. The next day, in her syndicated newspaper column, the First Lady announced her resignation from the DAR, saying that to remain as a member of the organization, which she did not identify by name, would imply her approval of its actions.

Even in the South, editorials lambasted the DAR. Refusing Anderson was "an act of insanity almost impossible to believe," said Jackson, Mississippi's *Daily News*. "We love our colored singers and listen to them with the keenest appreciation." In Columbia, South Carolina, the *State* warned that the incident had shifted public opinion, creating opposition to segregation.

When Anderson's manager, Sol Hurok, proposed an outdoor concert, Walter White suggested the Lincoln Memorial. Ickes agreed, with Roosevelt's consent. But neither the First Lady, who spent the holiday in Hyde Park, New York, nor the president, who spent it in Warm Springs, Georgia, appeared in person for the occasion. So it fell to Ickes to juggle the roles of emcee and ethicist, introducing Anderson to the masses before him and to radio listeners around the country, tuned to NBC's live broadcast. "In this great auditorium under the sky," Ickes said, "all of us are free." The spectators burst into applause.

Unlike Chief Justice Taft's speech seventeen years earlier, with its reunification narrative, Ickes reclaimed the shrine as a symbol of freedom. We gather today, at this monument to "the great emancipator," Ickes said. He also lauded the symmetry: a tribute concert at the Lincoln Memorial by "a daughter of the race" Lincoln liberated.

Still, with southern Democrats in command of both houses of Congress, Ickes trod carefully. In an oblique reference to Roosevelt, then in his second term as president, Ickes referred to Thomas Jefferson as "that other great Democrat in our short history," one who professed a belief in equality. Even in our era, he said, some pay "lip service" to equality and freedom, the "twin planets" in the democratic constellation. Ickes attached the nation's founding principles—which the DAR was presumed to embody—to Anderson's artistry. "Genius, like justice, is blind," he said. "For genius has touched with the tip of her wing this woman, who, if it had not been for the great mind of Jefferson, if it had not been for the great heart of Lincoln, would not be able to stand among us today a free individual in a free land."

Finally came Anderson's performance. Bare-headed, with her chin-length hair framing her face and her mink warding off the chill, she scanned the horizon. In front of her, atop a raised platform, an encampment of news gatherers huddled, wielding tripods and headsets: sound crews, photographers, cameramen. To her left, a flank of men in overcoats and fedoras arrayed in a line, next to a scrum of uniformed police officers. In the distance lay the expanse of the Reflecting Pool, the parallel lines of its surface pointing toward the Washington Monument.

Anderson squared her shoulders. Vehanen played the opening of "America." Amplified through loud speakers, it sounded to him as if he had marshaled the power of ten organs. "My country 'tis of thee," she sang, standing almost motionless, her eyes clamped shut. Her voice—renowned for its range, warmth, and emotional resonance—floated across the plaza, carrying for blocks. When latecomers heard her, they stopped and doffed their hats. As she trilled the last note, a wave of sound washed over the crowd, like a collective sigh.

For her second selection, Anderson opted for an aria, "O, Mio, Fernando," from the third act of *La Favorita*, an opera by the nineteenth-century composer Gaetano Donizetti. While she sang, the Lincoln statue glowed in the background behind her, bathed in specially installed floodlights. Supreme Court Justice Hugo L. Black, an FDR appointee and former Alabama senator, arrived during the third number, Franz Schubert's "Ave Maria," which was followed by a trio of spirituals: "Gospel Train," "Trampin'," and "My Soul Is Anchored in the Lord." Anderson closed with an encore: "Nobody Knows the Trouble I've Seen," a lament, tethered to the hope of future deliverance.

Instead of a second encore, Anderson returned to the microphones and made a brief statement. "You don't know what you've done for me," she told the crowd. "The immensity of this affair has had such an effect on me that I'm not up to a speech."

After the concert, Mary donned a black velvet and violet hat and filed into a reception at Howard University's Frazier Hall, a women's dormitory erected a decade earlier. Inside, Anderson anchored a receiving line with her mother, university officials, and Charles Hamilton Houston, who had represented her before the school board and orchestrated a grassroots protest, the Marian Anderson Citizens' Committee. Later that evening, Terrell turned to her journal. "The Lord certainly gave his angels charge concerning me today."

Since Little, Brown had finally rejected her memoirs, Mary had undergone a spiritual awakening, marked by a struggle for acceptance and efforts to pray. In late May 1936, she had traveled to Stockbridge, Massachusetts, for a retreat sponsored by the Oxford Group, an evangelical Christian movement founded by Frank Buchman, a Lutheran minister who stressed personal and spiritual renewal through veracity, disclosure, and selflessness. Before setting out, in a letter to Phyllis, she admitted to feeling some uncertainty. "I shall tell you what it is all about when I know myself," she had written.

At the end of 1936, Mary and a group of women from the Nineteenth Street Baptist Church had visited a Washington-area home for the elderly, armed with apples, oranges, and boxes of candy. Mary, then seventy-three, had made her own concessions to aging: false teeth, eyeglasses, hearing tests. Inside the facility, Mary recognized a woman she knew. Later, in her journal, she suggested how the visit had upset her. "God forbid I sh[ould] be so situated." The following month, as publicity chairman of a new committee dedicated to combating delinquency and crime, Mary circulated minutes from the first meeting. We are living in an age of moral decay, her report said, citing the comments of an anonymous speaker, and only religious revival can lead to change.

While she explored her spirituality, she remained pragmatic—even cautious—about social protest. Then again, her wariness may have had a nonspiritual component, too. In Memphis, the city had seized her half-brother Robert's real estate holdings—including their father's former home and the buildings that once housed his brothels—and auctioned them off on March 15, 1939. Robert Church Jr. had owed $89,000 in unpaid city, county, and state fees.

Three days after Anderson's performance, Terrell met with an Oberlin peer, Nettie Swift, who had recently moved to Washington and, after an almost-six decade lapse, renewed their friendship. Over lunch, they discussed Mary's memoirs, which a Christian publisher had just rejected. Later, Mary attended two meetings, including one of the Marian Anderson Citizens' Committee, where a discussion ensued about picketing the DAR's upcoming convention. In her journal, Terrell confided her misgivings, her concern that any such protest would be "an anticlimax," doing "more harm than good."

★ ★ ★ ★ ★

Inside the Supreme Court's marbled chamber, on April 17, 1939, William O. Douglas sat next to Charles Elmore Cropley, the clerk. Just after noon, Chief Justice Charles Evans Hughes proceeded with the matter at hand. Hughes, who replaced William Howard Taft, who had died in 1930, read Roosevelt's commission of Douglas, the president's fourth appointment to the Court. Douglas's wife, Mildred, sat in the gallery, with Douglas's sister, brother, and sister-in-law. Eight justices rose to their feet. Douglas, with his thatch of sandy-colored hair and Boy Scout mien, raised his right hand and faced Cropley, who held a Bible.

Outside, the Supreme Court's West Portico towered over First Street, facing the Capitol. Masterminded by Taft, and completed in 1935, the tribunal's relatively new headquarters filled an operational and symbolic void: for the first 146 years of its existence, the nation's highest court operated in leftover space, including the Capitol basement. Even before Congress financed construction, Taft began planning with Cass Gilbert, the architect who designed New York's Woolworth Building. For the Supreme Court, Gilbert envisioned a temple of justice, inspired by ancient Rome, radiating the dignity of the Lincoln Memorial. Not everyone cheered the result of Taft's vision, with its Vermont-marble exterior and Alabama-marble corridors, its oak paneling and twin, five-story spiral staircases. In fact, in May 1935, roughly five months before the Court held its first session there, Justice Harlan Fiske Stone had denounced the edifice as "almost bombastically pretentious."

Elsewhere in the capital on that rainy Monday, officials at Griffith Stadium postponed the Washington Nationals' sold-out season opener against the New York Yankees, at which President Roosevelt had agreed to toss out the first pitch. Delegates rallied for the DAR's forty-eighth continental congress, to be kicked off that evening in Constitution Hall. An AP preview, centered above the fold on the *New York Times*'s front page, referred to Douglas as "unconventional."

Inside the Court's chamber, Douglas recited the judicial oath, pledging to administer justice to everyone, to "do equal right to the poor and to the rich," and to discharge his duties faithfully and impartially. With that, he became the youngest member of the Court in 127 years. As the justice with the least seniority, he assumed his station at the end of the raised mahogany bench, next to Stanley F. Reed, a fifty-four-year-old Kentucky native whom Roosevelt had appointed to the Court a year earlier.

From a black leather chair, Douglas watched as his colleagues released opinions, including one in which they ruled, by a 6-to-2 margin, that the Labor Department could not deport an Austrian immigrant who had allowed his Communist Party membership to lapse. Only "present" or active Communist Party affiliation warranted deportation, the majority ruled. In dissent were Justices Pierce Butler, a Harding pick, and James C. McReynolds, the Wilson appointee, who, during his almost twenty-five-year stretch on the Court, had indulged his bigotries with virtual impunity. He had refused to speak to his Jewish colleagues, Louis D. Brandeis, who had just retired, and Benjamin N. Cardozo, who died in 1938, or pose in photographs standing next to them. Now, in his dissent, McReynolds championed the immigrant's repatriation. "That he is an undesirable is made manifest."

Elsewhere in the courtroom, a reporter for the *New York Times* monitored Douglas, logging his reaction for the next day's paper. "During the rest of the day, Mr. Douglas watched the proceedings intently, a faint smile playing now and then over his quizzical face," the *Times* said in its account.

★ ★ ★ ★ ★

Mary Church Terrell had finally found a way to publish her memoir. After a string of disappointments in New York, she had settled for releasing it on her own, through Ransdell, Inc., a publisher and printer of books, magazines, and catalogs in Northeast Washington whose other titles included scholarly, legal, and medical treatises and *Who's Who in the Nation's Capital*. She had also convinced H. G. Wells to write a preface to the book, which was to be titled *A Colored Woman in a White World*. On April 18, 1940, she telegraphed him, letting him know his ten-page essay had arrived, sent along by Marjorie Wells, the author's daughter-in-law and secretary.

Mary's return cable, an exemplar of concision, did not betray any emotion, let alone disappointment. "Many thanks," she wrote.

But, in fact, in his contribution, which was called "Introduction," followed by an earlier version of her title, Wells had not raved about her effort. As much as he liked her, he wrote, her book was "artless," a "loose and ample assemblage of reminiscences of very unequal value." (Her publisher was in favor of deleting those assessments.) Wells also wrote that her memoir suffered from "a discreet faltering from explicitness." Still, he added, he would not edit or reorganize the text, which reflected the author and her milieu: her personality and patterns of thought; her flaws and talents; the evolving social environment she inhabited. "When, as my reward for this Introduction, I get the book nicely printed and inscribed, I shall put it on my shelves not among the masterpieces of art, but as the living Mary Church Terrell, the most subtle, almost inadvertent, rendering of the stresses and views and impulses that characterise [*sic*] the race conflict as it appears in America."

For the next few months, while Terrell reviewed early proofs of her book, a younger generation of activists, steeped in labor unrest, nonviolent civil disobedience, and grassroots organizing, pressured Roosevelt on civil rights. In Washington, much of the ferment traced to Charles Hamilton Houston, the attorney who eulogized Robert in court. Houston, who served as an army officer in a segregated unit during World War I, earned a bachelor of laws degree from Harvard in 1922 and a doctorate of juridical science, the equivalent of a PhD, a year later. After a fellowship in Spain, secured with the help of Professor Felix Frankfurter, Houston, a handsome man with patrician bearing, returned to Washington. With his intellect and Harvard credentials, his aura of polish and confidence, he could have emulated Robert Terrell's career, pursuing a federal judgeship. Instead, he practiced law with his father, William L. Houston, and, from their F Street office, dedicated himself to fighting racism and discrimination.

Houston also spent eleven years at Howard Law School and, as a teacher and dean, he overhauled the curriculum, steeling and grooming a cadre of future civil rights lawyers. Among them was Thurgood Marshall, who graduated as valedictorian in 1933. During the Depression, when white Washington businesses prospered under the New Deal, Houston gravitated toward the New Negro Alliance, a coalition of attorneys and NAACP stalwarts who spearheaded boycotts and pickets against businesses that refused to hire African American employees. Their targets ranged from a U Street hot dog stand to People's Drug Store, including the outlet at 14th and U Streets that once refused to serve Mary.

As much as Houston embraced street protests, he also believed in attacking discrimination in court. During a three-year stint as the NAACP's special counsel in New York, from 1935 to 1938, he conceived and implemented a program to undermine segregation, focusing on *Plessy*'s separate-but-equal legacy. By contesting deficiencies in publicly funded graduate schools, he knew, the NAACP could force southern states to choose: either construct equal facilities for African Americans, which was economically infeasible, or integrate all-white ones. Under his stewardship, the NAACP challenged the University of Missouri Law School, which paid African Americans to undergo legal training in an adjacent state. Houston, who argued the case in the Supreme Court, said Missouri had to build a law school for blacks that equaled the existing program for whites. Justice McReynolds swiveled around in his chair, keeping his back to Houston for his entire argument. On December 12, 1938, in *Missouri ex rel. Gaines v. Canada*, the Supreme Court agreed with Houston, over McReynolds's dissent, laying the groundwork for future challenges. Two days later, Mary sent a $5 donation to the New Negro Alliance to help subsidize the People's Drug boycott.

Even after returning to private practice in Washington and leaving Marshall, his former student and assistant, in charge of the NAACP's legal strategy in

New York, Houston concentrated on civil rights. Independent of the NAACP, which focused on soliciting donors and attacking segregated schools, he pursued a broader agenda, reflecting his interests in economic justice and ending discrimination by the military. As a Washingtonian, moreover, he understood, better than NAACP officials in New York, how to operate in the capital, including when and where to pursue issues that mattered to ordinary blacks. In June 1940, just three months before Congress imposed the first peacetime draft, he sent a letter to Roosevelt, urging him to integrate the armed forces. Roosevelt's only reply came from his secretary, James Rowe Jr., who wrote in a two-line note that the president thanked him for his letter. Undeterred, in January 1941, Houston joined an emergency committee objecting to segregated festivities during Roosevelt's third inaugural, slated for the twentieth of that month.

With Europe again consumed by war, Houston's efforts were starting to pay off. Five days after FDR's swearing-in, A. Philip Randolph, the fifty-one-year-old president of the Brotherhood of Sleeping Car Porters, called for a march on Washington, mobilizing as many as 10,000 African Americans—laborers, professionals, soldiers, women, and children—to protest racial discrimination in the military and the national defense program. Like Houston, Randolph believed black Americans could not secure "first-class citizenship" without jobs, especially for men. Since Roosevelt had, earlier that month, in his annual State of the Union address on January 6, rallied Congress and the nation for war with his "four freedoms" speech, Randolph announced that his march "would wake up and shock official Washington as it has never been shocked before."

★ ★ ★ ★ ★

Inside Frazier Hall, on January 25, 1941, Mary attended a reception in her honor, heralding publication of her memoirs. Roughly five hundred invitees convened, with a leather-bound guest book and a punch bowl, to fête her publishing success. But Mary, who tracked sales and reviews, increasingly knew otherwise. She had incorporated Wells's essay—trimmed of some of his most negative comments—into the published volume, using it as a preface. The *Afro-American*'s favorable review echoed some of his critiques, noting details she had omitted. Even First Lady Eleanor Roosevelt, Mary's idol, conceded she had not read it. In a letter dated March 24, 1941, she apologized, invoking her workload and lack of reading time, and promised to keep a copy of the book "on hand."

Frustrated as a memoirist, Mary reoriented back to her roots in protest. On April 11, her name appeared on a four-page document titled *A Statement on the Position of the Negro People in America*. Essentially a declaration, the statement demanded Jim Crow's eradication from the armed forces and civilian life, and bore the names of twenty-one other advocates, including Paul Robeson, who had emerged as one of the most heralded actors, musicians, and activists of his era. After a brief legal career in New York, Robeson had earned acclaim on stage and screen, including a London performance of *Othello* in 1930, the first time a black man had played the lead in a major production of Shakespeare's play in roughly seventy years. Eight days after the joint statement, on April 19, the *Chicago Defender* reported that the First Lady had withdrawn her sponsorship of Robeson's upcoming Washington concert, a benefit for Chinese war orphans and a job drive by the National Negro Congress, a labor and civil rights coalition.

In the meantime, Randolph homed in on the administration, coordinating and publicizing his demonstration. His office assembled a "Dear Friend" missive, on letterhead emblazoned with a Pullman-car image and a dedicated phone number for evenings, Sundays, and holidays. In the letter, dated April 26, Randolph invited a few prominent black Washingtonians, including Terrell, to convene at the YMCA on April 30, for a discussion of his march. His hope, he wrote, was to force Roosevelt to issue an executive order that would ban discrimination against African Americans in government departments and the defense industry. "It is the growing opinion of the colored man today that he must fight for his rightful place in national defense with everything he has got," he had written earlier that month, in a bylined column for the *Afro-American*.

The Roosevelt administration, in turn, lobbied Randolph to cancel. In June, after Randolph refused to alter plans and urged blacks "to gird for an epoch-making" assemblage, FDR summoned him to the White House. During a conference with Walter White, New York mayor Fiorello H. LaGuardia, War Secretary Henry L. Stimson, and Navy Secretary Frank Knox, Randolph, who had scheduled the march for July 1, asked the president to sign an executive order requiring defense contractors to hire African Americans. Roosevelt balked, wary of alienating southerners and exposing himself to future claims from other interest groups. But with Randolph calling for a silent processional of blacks, filing en masse from Gettysburg to the Lincoln Memorial, government officials harbored more pressing concerns: how such a mobilization, with a segregated capital besieged by African

American dissenters, would be viewed by the Nazi government and used for propaganda.

Under questioning from FDR, Randolph predicted a turnout of 100,000 supporters. White confirmed the projection. Roosevelt, who had experienced Washington's 1919 riot as an assistant navy secretary, capitulated. A week later, on June 25, 1941, he issued an executive order barring the defense industry and the federal government from discriminating by "race, creed, color or national origin." His directive also established a Committee on Fair Employment Practice, an executive-branch entity charged with overseeing compliance with the order and investigating discrimination complaints. That evening, Randolph called off the protest.

Roosevelt's mandate, however, did not prohibit segregation by the military. During World War II, as in previous conflicts, black troops mustered into black regiments, where most were relegated to menial roles, toiling as cooks and ditch diggers or working in motor pools. Still, there were signs of progress. For the first time, in 1942, the Marines accepted blacks. African American pilots, known as the Tuskegee Airmen, flew combat missions in North Africa and Italy. Roughly five hundred black soldiers took part in the invasion of Normandy on D-Day.

In Washington, though, resentments over discrimination festered, with the city's integrated streetcar system serving as flashpoint. In July 1942, the Committee on Fair Employment Practices, known as the FEPC, fielded complaints about Capital Transit Company's refusal to hire black streetcar operators and bus drivers. Although Roosevelt's executive order did not extend to private employers, Capital Transit, a privately owned public utility chartered by Congress, fell within the FEPC's jurisdiction. When Capital Transit hired one black trainee, sixteen white drivers strode out. A few dozen white and black Washington residents formed a coalition, picketed, and organized a mass demonstration in May 1943, seeking to draw attention to the controversy. But the FEPC had no power to subpoena witnesses, no meaningful way to enforce compliance with Roosevelt's directive. Capital Transit retained its all-white pool of conductors and drivers, triggering a prolonged standoff.

That summer, Randolph revived the notion of a march on Washington. In a four-column manifesto published under his byline in the *Chicago Defender* on July 3, 1943, he said a nonviolent mass mobilization of African Americans— from the working classes to the educated elites—should remain an option, albeit one of "last resort." Washington did not just exist as the nation's capital, he wrote; it functioned as democracy's global headquarters and as well as Dixie's capital, where southern Democrats blocked civil rights measures, such as antilynching legislation, and banished African Americans from the Capitol's restaurant. Washington had emerged as the world's "nerve center," its "financial and economic powerhouse." If African Americans caved now, yielding to Washington's Jim Crow, colored citizens everywhere would view them as "the classic second-class citizens of all times."

★ ★ ★ ★ ★

Mary had begun emerging from isolation and retreat, responding to the exigencies of war. In May 1943, she lent her name to a letter urging the Senate Judiciary Committee to approve the Equal Rights Amendment, which would have prohibited discrimination on the basis of sex. She extolled the Tuskegee Airmen. At Houston's behest, she wrote a letter defending Mary McLeod Bethune, an African American educator and Roosevelt advisor charged with subversiveness by Representative Martin Dies Jr., a Texas Democrat who chaired the Special Committee to Investigate Un-American Activities. Still, on the brink of her eightieth birthday, in August 1943, Mary indulged an old regret, her lack of success as a short-story writer, and aired a new one: her failure to train as a lawyer when Robert taught at Howard.

As an octogenarian, her restlessness proved short-lived. More than a year after V-J Day, Mary applied for membership in the American Association of University Women's Washington branch. Technically, she claimed, she had belonged in the past—she did not say when—and was seeking reinstatement. As Mary knew, however, she was also mounting a deliberate effort to test the branch's admission policy, a decision she had made in alliance with Nettie Swift, her Oberlin friend. Nettie, who was white, had joined the Washington branch in 1939 and wanted to enjoy the club's amenities—including dinners—with Mary. But when Nettie asked about proposing an African American member, officers spurned her inquiries. On paper, Terrell satisfied the lone admission criterion, which was that she hold a degree from an accredited institution. Still, on October 9, 1946, the branch's eight-member executive committee voted unanimously to reject her. The following day, the membership chairman, Maude Spier Brubaker, notified her of the decision by letter, refunding the dues payment she had enclosed with her application. With that move, the branch's Washington-based, college-educated white women had encapsulated racial dynamics in the capital.

Before the war, with little fanfare, the Roosevelt administration had desegregated the federal workforce. Starting with the Interior Department, most government cafeterias integrated, offering workers the opportunity to dine alongside one another, regardless of race. Jim Crow restrictions, dating back to the Harding administration, also disappeared from the capital's federally controlled parks and recreation areas, including picnic grounds in Rock Creek Park and golf and tennis facilities in West Potomac Park.

But three months after V-E Day, Senator Theodore G. Bilbo, a Mississippi Democrat who was running for reelection in 1946, called for construction of a Washington stadium with Jim Crow seating. As chairman of the Senate's Committee on the District of Columbia, which approved actions taken by the city's presidentially appointed commissioners, Bilbo functioned as Washington's unelected mayor, dictating everything from dance-hall regulations to weed disposal. By trawling for votes at home based on his white supremacist credentials—including a vow, during a speech in Meridian, Mississippi, to keep Washington segregated—he set the tone for the capital's postwar race relations, one of increasing polarization. He targeted federal contributions to Howard University, saying they were unconstitutional. He reputedly complained to the D.C. police chief about black motorcycle police who detained white drivers. On September 4, 1946, three months after the Supreme Court invalidated segregated seating on interstate buses in *Morgan v. Virginia*, an *Evening Star* editorial noted a historical irony: the Confederacy, which failed to capture Washington during the Civil War, now held the city "as a helpless pawn."

Elsewhere on the campaign trail that fall, less than a year after Joseph Stalin said Communism and capitalism could not coexist and that war was unavoidable, Republicans exploited fear of Communism at home and abroad. In November, the GOP seized control of the House and the Senate for the first time since the Depression, spawning a crop of freshman legislators such as Representative Richard M. Nixon of California and Senator Joseph R. McCarthy, a local judge and former Marine from Wisconsin. Five months later, on March 21, 1947, President Harry S. Truman—elevated to the presidency after FDR's death in April 1945—issued an executive order, purging the executive branch of disloyal and subversive employees. Truman also directed Attorney General Tom C. Clark to create a register of entities bent on overthrowing the government.

For progressives, postwar Washington, with its race-baiting southerners, anti-Communist Republicans, and presidentially sanctioned crackdown on disloyalty, yielded opportunity and risk: a chance to highlight, to a world audience, the hypocrisy of segregation; the specter of being tainted as "subversive" for doing so. Within months of Truman's loyalty order, Houston and

Randolph intensified their efforts, lashing out at Jim Crow in the symbolic core of postwar American dominance—Washington and the military.

They were not alone. In Chicago that June, the Congress of Racial Equality launched a plan to saturate Washington with protests against segregation. Founded in 1942 by James Farmer, a seminary student, and Bayard Rustin, who had been raised by Quaker grandparents, CORE, as it was known, had labored for more than two years to interest the NAACP in its agenda of nonviolent direct action, inspired by Indian independence leader Mahatma Gandhi. (During the war, Howard students, emulating Gandhi, had staged restaurant sit-ins to protest the capital's segregated dining facilities.) With the NAACP committed to a courtroom strategy, CORE announced an Interracial Workshop in July 1947, when participants would stage nonviolent demonstrations across Washington, targeting venues such as restaurants and recreational facilities.

Like previous black leaders, including Booker T. Washington, Randolph and Houston cultivated the black press. Six days after CORE unveiled its Washington project, with Randolph serving on an advisory committee and Houston slated to train participants—presumably in nonviolence—a *Chicago Defender* columnist blasted the House Committee on Un-American Activities (HUAC) for its crackdown on those it perceived as radicals. The opinion piece, published on June 21, 1947, ended with a quote from Mary. "Suspected of 'Communist' is every colored person in America who believes in civil and political rights and proposes to get them, and every white person who thinks he ought to," she said.

On June 24, Terrell spoke at the opening session of the NAACP's thirty-eighth annual convention, a six-day affair with a legal-department update from Thurgood Marshall. Inside the conference headquarters, at John Wesley AME Zion Church, Mary welcomed the attendees, apologizing for any inconveniences they might suffer, including refusals to be allowed into hotels, restaurants, and theaters. She urged the delegates, having experienced Washington's conditions directly, to engage in "holy warfare" on segregation and discrimination. Toward the end of the convention, after five days of proceedings, President Truman stood before a podium at the Lincoln Memorial, the first president to address the NAACP. On a blistering afternoon, flanked by a pair of American flags, he said the country had "reached a turning point" on race. As if summoning Robert Moton's undelivered speech, he stressed the importance of ensuring freedom and equality to all Americans. "And when I say all Americans—I mean all Americans."

CORE volunteers began fanning out across Washington a week later. At the National Zoo's cafe, the manager locked himself inside, rather than serve a delegation of black and white patrons. A white woman chastised a similar party at the National Gallery of Art, unable to conceal her distress at the sight of African Americans and whites eating together. At the YMCA coffee shop, located at 1736 G Street, NW, workshop members waited four hours for service. The next day, a larger delegation sat for eight hours. On the third day, July 18, officials barred them from entering and threatened to have them arrested.

Mary granted an interview to the *Afro-American*, in which she bemoaned that Washington, the nation's capital, was still mired in race bias. Recently, she told the reporter, a nearby pharmacy, which she had long patronized, had refused to serve her a cold drink. She also sensed a hardening of attitudes among clerks in downtown department stores. A photograph accompanying the story, which ran on August 2, 1947, depicted her seated in an armchair inside her S Street apartment, clad in a short-sleeve dress and lace-up oxfords, squinting through spectacles at a book.

The *Evening Star* ran an AP story two and a half weeks later, saying a Russian newspaper, *Trud*, had opined about Washington's treatment of African Americans. Under a Moscow dateline, the AP said, *Trud* reported that African Americans were barred from restaurants, movie theaters, barbershops, and beaches when whites were present. "Let us remember," *Trud* reportedly wrote, "this is all taking place in the city which, according to the reference books, has the residence of the President and the Capitol building in which Congress sits."

Before long, in September 1947, HUAC released a list of more than thirty African Americans it claimed to have identified as "Communists" or "Communist sympathizers." Under the tutelage of J. Parnell Thomas of New Jersey and Mississippi's John E. Rankin, the panel flagged a range of educators, artists, and activists, including Robeson, Du Bois, and Langston Hughes. At the center, benefiting from their alleged sponsorship, was the Civil Rights Congress, a recent outgrowth of the International Labor Defense (ILD), which, according to HUAC, served as the Communist Party's legal arm.

Since CRC's inception in the spring of 1946, when Robeson and Mary McLeod Bethune lent their names to the letterhead, the organization had articulated a mission much like that of the NAACP: establishing nationwide branches and defending civil and democratic rights. As a newcomer, though, the CRC threatened the NAACP's fundraising prowess, including contributions that subsidized its legal department. From the outset, when Thurgood Marshall said the NAACP would send an observer, not a delegate, to the

CRC's organizational assembly, the NAACP eyed the CRC with caution. Within days of CRC's creation, the NAACP's observer dismissed it as a "nuisance," not a "front" for the Communist Party—though, the observer noted, a small Communist Party faction had asserted control over the organization along the way. Within a month, Roy Wilkins, an assistant secretary for the NAACP, denounced the CRC as "a CP outfit" and warned an NAACP branch in New Orleans to steer clear. The CRC, meanwhile, called for Attorney General Tom Clark's removal from office and launched a national campaign to oust Senator Bilbo, sponsored, in part, by Robeson.

Later that fall, on October 29, 1947, Truman's Committee on Civil Rights, a fifteen-member panel first assembled almost a year earlier, released a 176-page report urging federal action to eliminate segregation and racial discrimination. In a separate section, the committee denounced the capital's treatment of African Americans, calling the status quo "intolerable," shameful, and a "failure of democracy." The panel recommended congressional initiatives to transform Washington into "a symbol of democracy to the entire world": abolition of segregated public schools and racially restrictive covenants; equal access to public accommodations, including restaurants; and self-government for residents. Truman announced that the report would serve as a testament, to the entire globe, of the country's "renewed faith" in government based on freedom and just laws.

Pockets of Washington rippled with defiance. The same day that Truman's civil rights panel unveiled its report, the YMCA updated the Interracial Workshop and its attorney, Belford V. Lawson Jr., about the G Street coffee shop: the metropolitan Washington board of directors had adopted a resolution endorsing segregated seating. Rayford Ellis, the Interracial Workshop's chairman, sent Mary a one-page memorandum on October 31, bemoaning the coffee shop's recalcitrance. In a handwritten note at the bottom of the page, Mary lambasted the Y's so-called Christians for their "brutal anti-Christian policy," which flouted teachings promulgated by Jesus Christ. "God have mercy on you!"

In official Washington circles, Truman's executive order on loyalty had refined a tool, admittedly one not new to his administration or limited to the executive branch, for discrediting resistance, including civil rights activism by blacks. That December the attorney general unveiled his debut list of "subversive" groups. Clark's pronouncement featured more than five dozen organizations, ranging from American Youth for Democracy to the Washington Book Shop Association. Like HUAC—and notwithstanding

Truman's speech at the Lincoln Memorial—Clark also highlighted several interracial organizations devoted to securing minority rights, including the National Negro Congress, the partial beneficiary of Robeson's Washington 1941 concert; and the Civil Rights Congress.

Truman, preoccupied with the upcoming presidential election, continued to endorse civil rights. Hoping to appeal to northern black voters, he dispatched his civil rights message to Congress on February 2, asking lawmakers to make lynching a federal crime. He also sought measures to ban discrimination at the polls, in employment, and in interstate travel.

Randolph, Houston, and other African American leaders met with the president in March. Randolph, imbued with a sense of urgency, pressed Truman to integrate the armed forces. Black Americans in the Midwest were unwilling to fight for democracy overseas until they realized its benefits at home, he said. Truman bristled, saying it was their country as much as his. Houston, who memorialized the session in an April 3 column for the *Afro-American*, detected that Truman was afraid to act. "We have lots of work to do before we achieve the recognition of first-class citizens in the armed forces, and we had better get busy because we do not have much time," Houston wrote. Segregation in the capital reemerged as national news later that spring. On May 13, 1948, New York City's school superintendent canceled a Washington sightseeing visit for fifty-one students between the ages of eight and fourteen, who had won recognition as outstanding school-crossing guards. The Supreme Court had, only ten days earlier, in *Hurd v. Hodge*, barred federal courts in Washington from enforcing restrictive covenants that prohibited the sale of real estate to blacks in the capital. But Washington's hotels, citing local custom, still refused to accommodate the New York students, whose ranks included four African Americans. When school officials learned blacks might also be banned from eating alongside and entering public buildings with whites, they withdrew altogether. The next day, the crossing-guard story landed on the front pages of the *New York Times*, the *New York Herald Tribune*, and Washington's *Evening Star*. That afternoon, Randolph led seven protestors, both whites and African Americans, in a picket line outside the White House. As Secret Service agents watched, Randolph passed out lapel buttons that read "Don't Join Jim Crow Army."

Congress, meanwhile, debated punitive measures for alleged subversives. On May 31, the Senate Judiciary Committee convened a hearing on a bill, introduced by Congressmen Karl E. Mundt, a South Dakota Republican, and Richard Nixon, that would require Communists to register with the government. Robeson, who appeared before the panel to testify against the bill, refused to answer a question about whether he belonged to the Communist Party. Several thousand protestors picketed outside the White House alongside Robeson two days later, calling for civil rights legislation and defeat of the Mundt-Nixon Bill. During a rally at the Washington Monument, Robeson likened Washington's segregation to "terrorism." "The struggle for peace and the kind of America we want has reached another level," he said. "We will take the power from their hands and, through our representatives we will direct the future destiny of the nation."

Houston defended Robeson. Walter White had recently warned Houston he might be attacked by an anti-Communist newsletter, but Houston, whose name graced a CRC advertisement opposing the Mundt-Nixon Bill, had no patience for caution, from White or anyone else. In a column for the *Afro-American*, published on June 12, 1948, he said all blacks resented segregation and African American men had no interest in fighting in "a jim-crow" military. "We have no desire to be martyrs; we are not seeking publicity or striking a pose. But some of us have made up our minds we are willing to pay whatever price is necessary to make democracy work."

In Washington a week later, CORE endorsed Randolph's plan to target military segregation with a campaign of nonviolent civil disobedience. At a street meeting on Harlem's West 125th Street not long after that, Randolph advised a white, draft-age youth not to register to be drafted into the segregated army. "If, as the result of your insistence upon freedom, you face arrest," Randolph said, "I hope that you will go quietly with the police, firm in the knowledge that millions of freedom-loving people throughout the world stand behind you." On July 26, Truman issued an executive order mandating equal treatment and opportunity, without regard to race, for all persons in the armed services. He also established a fair-employment policy for the federal civil service.

★ ★ ★ ★ ★

In November, Truman edged Thomas E. Dewey, a law-school classmate of Justice Douglas, by a margin of roughly two million popular votes. With military integration decreed by executive mandate and Truman in the White House for four more years, Houston, along with other white and black progressives, renewed the push to integrate Washington. Five weeks after the election, the National Committee on Segregation in the Nation's Capital released its ninety-one-page report, subsidized by the Rosenwald

Fund. The report, unveiled on December 10, called Washington's racial separatism a "blot on our nation," which undermined America's moral leadership in world affairs. At the beginning of one chapter, titled "Symbol of Democracy," the authors spotlighted the observation of a visitor from India: "I would rather be an Untouchable in the Hindu caste system than a Negro in Washington."

Packed with graphics and anecdotes, photographs and charts, the study also reflected the influence of Houston, who sat on the research committee. In a chapter devoted to the growth of prejudice, a three-paragraph primer traced the evolution of Washington's 1872 antidiscrimination law—banning racial discrimination in public restaurants—pointing out that it had "mysteriously disappeared" from the capital's codified statutes near the turn of the century. Absent evidence of a repeal, the report said, "some lawyers" speculated the law might still be binding. Within that one reference, an almost throw away observation about one of Washington's Reconstruction-era civil rights laws, lay the basis for upheaval—a fulcrum, more than five decades after *Plessy*, for attacking segregation in the capital and beyond. Truman's civil rights study—generated for a president from Missouri, whose belief in legal equality for African Americans stopped short of endorsing social equality—had not mentioned the Reconstruction-era ordinances. At a luncheon heralding the report's issuance, Senator Wayne L. Morse, an Oregon Republican, urged Truman to integrate dining facilities at National Airport, which hugged the Potomac in Arlington, Virginia.

The next day, the *Evening Star*'s editorial page dismissed the study as propaganda. Houston countered with a publicity drive, responding to critics while simultaneously suing a National Airport restaurant and soda fountain for refusing to serve two blacks. In an *Afro-American* column published on December 18, he said Washington belonged to the entire country and should embody democracy's best, including the Reconstruction-era civil rights laws, not its worst. "No self-respecting colored citizen wants any favors," he wrote. "All he asks is to be judged on his individual merit and conduct as a human being. We had that right in 1872 and when we ask for full civil rights in the District, we are not asking for anything revolutionary; but merely to go back to the standards set over 75 years ago."

On Christmas Day, the *Chicago Defender* said Houston was "rubbing his hands and grinning" and "planning a trick or so." In the meantime, his courtroom strategy generated another victory and another round of backlash. The Civil Aeronautics Association issued a regulation, on December 27,

1948, prohibiting segregation by National Airport's concessionaires. In an interview with the *Washington Post*, an attorney for the restaurants stonewalled. "As far as we're concerned right now, we're going to maintain the status quo," he said.

That same day, Thomas G. Buchanan Jr., the CRC's executive secretary in Washington, sent a letter to Mary; in it, he lay the foundation for a new legal challenge—one with the potential to link the Rosenwald-funded committee's research, Houston, the Reconstruction-era civil rights laws, Terrell, and the entire edifice of legalized segregation, in the capital and across the South. The Civil Rights Congress had reviewed the Rosenwald-financed report, particularly the section about Washington's antidiscrimination ordinance, Buchanan said. "If such a law could be restored to full validity, it would mean a new Declaration of Rights for our colored population," he wrote. "Once the wall of segregation is shattered, the road that leads to equal opportunity in schools, housing, hospitals, jobs and recreation will stretch before us."

Mary had known the CRC's national executive secretary, William L. Patterson, for almost fourteen years. In May 1934, she had joined him for a Mothers' Day delegation to meet with FDR about the Scottsboro boys, nine African Americans falsely accused and convicted of raping two white women in Alabama. White House aides told them Roosevelt was out of town. Patterson, a lawyer and Robeson friend whose career included stints in the NAACP and as vice chair of the Communist Party of Illinois, had written Mary afterward, in his capacity as the ILD's national secretary, thanking her for taking part. More recently, during a pre-Christmas conference with administration officials and CRC delegates, including Patterson, Mary had voiced her agreement with the Rosenwald study. Her support was meaningful to Patterson and others, in part because Mary had received in 1948 her long-sought honorary doctorate from Oberlin, as well as an honorary doctorate from Howard. She was beginning to be celebrated as one of the movement's grande dames.

Now, Buchanan asked Mary to participate, along with a cadre of "responsible" Washingtonians, in a test case designed to resuscitate the Reconstruction-era ordinances. The proposed challenge would emanate from a designated group of white and black Americans, who would seek service in a public dining area, he said. They must behave in a "serious and dignified manner," he added, and possess such standing in the community that no one would question their account, which might provide the basis for a lawsuit. The CRC hoped Terrell would participate, he continued, given her prominence in Washington's civic life and in the nation as a whole. "We ask you to do so as a public service, in full consciousness of the far-reaching significance your action may have."

Mary hesitated after the CRC—which had earned a slot on the attorney general's "subversives" list—approached her about a test case of the Reconstruction-era laws, wavering in her commitment. Initially, in February, she said she had ignored warnings to shun Communists because she didn't believe they could overthrow the government of the United States, which after all had developed the atomic bomb. In mid-April, though, she backed out of attending the World Peace Congress in Paris, where Robeson numbered among the speakers. Not long after that, on April 21, several news outlets, starting with the AP, reported that Robeson, in remarks at the conference, had said African Americans would refuse to fight Russia on behalf of a regime—the United States—that had oppressed generations of blacks. That day, the NAACP issued a statement saying Robeson did not speak for African Americans, who would defend their country in the event of war. Even Houston distanced himself, telling the *Post* African Americans "would fight any enemy" of the United States.

In a story published by the *Atlanta Daily World* on April 22, Mary told Alice Dunnigan, a reporter for the Associated Negro Press, the truth: that she had canceled her Paris travel arrangements after reading about the summit's alleged Communist ties. She could not afford to link her name to Communism, she said. The next day, on April 23, the *Afro-American* surfaced with a different explanation: Terrell failed to find a travel companion for the journey, which would have strained her health. From Copenhagen, Robeson defended himself, saying, in an interview in early May, his remarks had been "distorted out of all recognition."

Within the span of less than two months, though, Terrell overcame her doubts. The final indignity emanated from the American Association of University Women, whose obstructionist local faction had contested her membership bid for almost three years. On June 13, 1949, a three-judge panel of the federal appeals court in Washington upheld the local branch's right to exclude African Americans. For Mary, now eighty-five, the court's decision instilled clarity, impelling her toward the broader struggle. She had had enough.

Mary appeared at the Hotel Theresa in New York on June 22, to speak to the National Committee to Free the Ingram Family. Named for a Georgia woman, Rosa Lee Ingram, who had been convicted of killing a white man, the organization listed Terrell on its letterhead as chairman. Her remarks, crafted for the occasion, resounded with defiance. "A time comes in the life of a human being and in the life of a group of human beings when patience ceases to be a virtue and becomes an ugly, disgraceful vice," she said. Many of us fail to protest discrimination because "we are afraid of being called agitators," she added, noting that people had also called William Lloyd Garrison and Frederick Douglass "agitators."

Rather than distance herself from radicalism, however, as she had earlier that spring, Mary embraced it. "Most of the injustices have been wiped out because there were people called Agitators [sic]," she said. Then, as if to dispel any doubt about her resolve, she crystallized her position. It is our duty to avail ourselves of every legal means—"every LEGAL means"—at our disposal to deliver a message to the world and the country, she said: "we are tired of being patient with being pushed around."

Back in Washington, Mary attended a meeting at the Phyllis Wheatley YWCA to discuss the antidiscrimination laws. About two dozen persons gathered with her, drawn by an entreaty from Buchanan, the CRC's executive secretary; the Progressive Party; and Therese L. Robinson, who served as national executive secretary of the National Committee to Free the Ingram Family. After deliberations, they organized a steering committee and selected temporary officers, including a temporary chairman.

Elsewhere, Washington remained fractured by race, anti-Communism, and Robeson. On June 23, the American Association of University Women's Washington branch seceded from the national organization, which had voted to accept qualified members regardless of color. In an editorial, the New York Times chastised the D.C. affiliate, saying college-educated women should know better, and "women representing the capital of this democracy ought at the least to act as though they believed in democracy." Not long after that, in July, HUAC called Jackie Robinson, the first African American major-league baseball player, to refute the comments attributed to Robeson in Paris. Robinson dismissed as "silly" the notion that African Americans would not defend their country. "We can win our fight without the Communists and we don't want their help."

Undeterred, Mary aligned publicly with fellow activists. In mid-September, she petitioned the United Nations about discrimination in the United States, saying, in prepared remarks, African Americans in Washington fared "no better" than blacks in Georgia and Mississippi. On her eighty-sixth birthday, she lent her name to a statement, along with Houston and E. Franklin Frazier, a Howard University sociology professor, defending Robeson's right to speak and sing at a Negro Freedom Rally in Washington. When Robeson appeared at the event in October, he told his audience he would keep fighting until black children could walk the capital's streets "with the same human dignity as any other citizen."

Later that month, while Mary agreed to serve as permanent chairman of the committee to revive the Reconstruction antidiscrimination laws, Houston's health collapsed. By mid-November, he lay confined to bed, felled by a heart attack. Houston's father, who took over his correspondence, told the NAACP's Roy Wilkins that his son could not handle any business. Houston's incapacitation—like Robert Terrell's more than two decades earlier—left a psychic and symbolic void, a three-generational continuum stretching back, through Robert, to Frederick Douglass. Mary Church Terrell, of course, had known all three of them. On November 19, the *Afro-American*, whose Baltimore-based president, Carl Murphy, chaired the NAACP's legal redress committee, reported that Du Bois and Patterson had attended a Soviet Embassy party in Washington, marking the anniversary of the Russian Revolution.

Meanwhile, attorneys for the Justice Department and the NAACP, including Thurgood Marshall, girded for a trio of civil rights cases slated for argument in the Supreme Court the following spring, when Justice Douglas returned from convalescence: *Henderson v. United States*, which challenged segregated railway-dining cars; *McLaurin v. Oklahoma State Regents for Higher Education*, which contested Jim Crow restrictions imposed on an African American graduate student; and *Sweatt v. Painter*, which sought to topple whites-only admissions to the University of Texas Law School. Justice Felix Frankfurter had already solicited *Sweatt* and *McLaurin* analyses from William T. Coleman Jr., a Harvard Law School graduate whose selection as the first African American law clerk in the Court's history had spurred articles in the *Washington Post* and the *New York Times*. In his memo to Justice Frankfurter, dated August 5, 1949, Coleman had inserted a personal observation: "Segregation is always a humiliating experience."

Given the stakes, the NAACP left little doubt about its loyalties and its goals, which did not include challenging Washington's segregated restaurants—even though the cause had mattered to Houston, whose young son had once been upbraided and called a racial epithet for climbing onto a stool at a drugstore soda fountain near his father's office. Instead, the NAACP's New York leadership distilled another lesson from Washington: an aversion to radical blacks. Just before Christmas, on December 21, 1949, Roy Wilkins, now the NAACP's chairman, issued a decree barring Communist-front entities, such as the Civil Rights Congress, from its upcoming civil rights mobilization, set to convene in Washington in mid-January. "We shall see to it that representatives of irresponsible organizations are kept out of the Conference."

Mary Church Terrell had gone from Oberlin to Battle Creek, from NAACP charter member to NAACP outsider. Now, at the age of eighty-six, at the center of anti-Communist politics, world affairs, and the evolution of *Plessy*'s separate-but-equal doctrine, Mary Church Terrell—agent provocateur—braced for one more fight.

6

Segregation Will Go

On Monday, the first business day after Thompson's Restaurant refused to serve her, Mary Church Terrell filed into the municipal court building on Fifth Street, NW, the same institution over which her husband had once presided. Inside, on January 30, 1950, she and her compatriots—Reverend William Jernagin, Geneva Brown, and David Scull—urged Clark F. King, an assistant corporation counsel assigned to the criminal division, to prosecute the restaurant for violating the Reconstruction-era antidiscrimination ordinances. They—three blacks committed to civil rights and one like-minded white—had sought out Thompson's three days earlier and courted its rebuff for the very reason of depositing the issue before local prosecutors, appealing to them to bring a criminal case. Without the cooperation of King's office, they had no recourse against Thompson's under the laws they hoped to revive. The statutes did not empower them, as individual citizens, to press charges on their own. King dialed his boss, Vernon E. West, the corporation counsel, whose title denoted his role as the District's chief legal officer, and for violations of local ordinances, its top prosecutor. West told King to do nothing. Washington's commissioners were mulling the laws' validity.

That afternoon, two of Mary's pro bono attorneys, David Rein and Margaret A. Haywood, staged a press conference. Haywood, a thirty-seven-year-old former housewife, had worked as a secretary at Houston & Houston while attending Robert H. Terrell Law School, a segregated—meaning all-black—program founded in 1930, when Howard shuttered its night school. With its evening classes, Terrell Law School catered to students with full-time jobs, such as Haywood, enabling them to pursue degrees at night. Rein, a New York City native, graduated from Columbia College and Columbia Law School and, in the 1930s, moved to Washington, where he worked at the National Labor Relations Board and the Office of Price Administration; during the war, he enlisted in the marines and served in the

Pacific. Afterward, he opened a firm with Joseph Forer, a graduate of Rutgers and the University of Pennsylvania Law School who had also worked at the National Labor Relations Board and the Office of Price Administration.

In the late 1940s, while Congress and the executive branch trawled for evidence of disloyalty and subversion, Rein and Forer immersed themselves in difficult and disfavored causes: opposing the Mundt-Nixon Bill; defending labor unions and alleged Communists; upholding the Bill of Rights. Rein, who received a $300 legal fee from the Civil Rights Congress in June 1947, represented Gerhart Eisler, a German refugee whom HUAC denounced as "the No. 1 Communist in the United States." And on behalf of the National Council of American-Soviet Friendship, Inc., one of three organizations contesting their inclusion on the attorney general's "subversives list," Rein and Forer had just filed in the Supreme Court a petition for certiorari—the formal means of seeking review of a lower court's ruling—asking the justices to decide the constitutionality of the subversiveness designation. If they won, their case had the potential to upend Truman's loyalty program.

As progressives and New Deal veterans, Forer and Rein also nurtured ties to the National Lawyers Guild, which HUAC had branded a Communist front in 1944. In May 1949, the guild's Washington chapter issued a legal opinion, which Charles Hamilton Houston, Forer, and Haywood signed, saying the antidiscrimination ordinances remained "in effect as binding and enforceable law in the District of Columbia." And on January 22, 1950, a week after Congressman Nixon urged HUAC to investigate the guild, Forer endorsed a special report, prepared by a guild panel and delivered to Truman, accusing the Federal Bureau of Investigation, directed by J. Edgar Hoover, of illegally probing the political views of thousands of private citizens, amassing information through illegal wiretaps and warrantless searches of private mail and private homes.

Now, on January 30, 1950, while Rein and Haywood spoke, a reporter for the African American press culled material for a story. Reasonably soon, the attorneys said, they anticipated a decision from the corporation counsel's office. Beyond that, they declined to speculate about future moves if the prosecutors failed to act.

The *Washington Post* ran a six-inch story on page B-8 the following day, with the headline "Case Filed to Test Old Racial Law." By name and race, the article identified the four individuals who objected to Thompson's failure to serve them, including Mary. When the *Post* referred to their allegations, it bracketed the word "*complaint*" with quotation marks. Relying on King, the *Post* said the corporation counsel's office had declined to prosecute, pending a decision by the capital's commissioners.

On February 21—which happened to be twelve days after Senator Joseph R. McCarthy surfaced in Wheeling, West Virginia, and brandished an alleged list of 205 "known Communists" in the State Department—the commissioners broke their silence. They said they would prosecute the next restaurant-discrimination complaint they received, using the incident to assess the soundness of the Reconstruction-era laws. From the editorial page, the *Post* appealed to reason and principle. "If the laws are determined to be valid, let no one fear that the community will be rent asunder by them," the editors said; rather, their recognition would spur more widespread acceptance of integration. "How this community ever lost the sense of common humanity that prompted it to adopt the civil rights acts of 1872 and 1873 is not easy to explain. But it is a sense that needs to be regained." The Washington Restaurant Association, a trade group, directed members to keep segregating until a court ruled otherwise.

A week after the commissioners announced their decision, Mary returned to Thompson's, with a different coterie of supporters. Inside, she selected a bowl of soup. The Reverend Arthur Fletcher Elmes, a pastor at People's Congregational Church, and Essie Thompson, a member of the cafeteria workers' union, placed pie and donuts on their trays. At 11:30 a.m., they edged down the line together, with David Scull rounding out their ranks, tapped once more to participate as the sole white.

At the cashier's stand, a man introduced himself as Sylvester W. Becker, a vice president and superintendent of the chain's Washington division. As if following a script, he proceeded to implement corporate policy. Only Scull could purchase something to eat, he said. The other three could not.

★ ★ ★ ★ ★

Justice Douglas landed back in Washington from Arizona on March 25, almost two weeks later than anticipated, after a flu outbreak prompted doctors to delay his return. In letters, he trumpeted his health and fitness, regaling friends and acquaintances with his exploits: a mountain lion hunt; expeditions into Mexico's San Juan Mountains; a three-and-a-half-hour ascent of Baboquivari, a 7,700-foot peak about fifty miles southwest of Tucson. On his third day back, his secretary sent rock samples to the Interior Department, explaining that the justice had collected the specimens in Arizona and would appreciate guidance in classifying them.

When Douglas wasn't otherwise engaged—informing his wife, Mildred, he intended to move out, accepting an invitation to the Gridiron Dinner, orchestrating a stag book-release party in Yakima for *Of Men and Mountains*—Court business awaited. During his absence, the Justice Department had weighed in on the civil rights cases, *Henderson*, *Sweatt*, and *McLaurin*, now slotted for argument in early April. Before advocates appeared in person in the courtroom, both sides submitted written briefs, explaining the factual and legal issues and why they thought they were entitled to win. In this trio of appeals, the Justice Department's submissions bore the imprimatur of the solicitor general's office, a unit headed by Philip B. Perlman and staffed in part by Philip Elman, a former law clerk to Justice Felix Frankfurter. Perlman, who oversaw the federal government's Supreme Court litigation, had also filed a friend-of-the-court brief in *Shelley v. Kraemer*, a 1948 decision, issued the same day as *Hurd v. Hodge*, invalidating enforcement of racial restrictive covenants by state courts. In *Henderson*, Perlman and his team amassed a sixty-six-page tome urging the Court—for the first time—to jettison *Plessy v. Ferguson*'s "separate-but-equal" doctrine, which, they argued, was "wrong as a matter of law, history and policy."

On the surface, *Henderson* resonated with *Plessy* parallels, arising from Jim Crow restrictions on southern trains. On May 17, 1942, Elmer W. Henderson, an African American field representative for President Roosevelt's Committee on Fair Employment Practices, boarded a Southern Railway train from Washington, D.C., to Birmingham, Alabama, where he was assigned to investigate alleged violations of the executive order, issued by FDR on June 25, 1941, banning race discrimination by defense contractors. That evening, beginning around 5:30 p.m., Henderson made three separate visits to the dining car. Each time, in the Jim Crow section near the kitchen, white passengers partially occupied two tables the railroad had reserved for African Americans. Rather than place Henderson in an empty seat alongside whites, the steward turned him away. When the railroad detached the dining car around 9 p.m., Henderson still hadn't eaten.

Henderson filed a complaint with the Interstate Commerce Commission five months later, saying Southern Railway's refusal to serve him violated Section 3 of the Interstate Commerce Act, which barred subjecting passengers to "any undue or unreasonable prejudice or disadvantage." In testimony, he said the entire episode had embarrassed him, shaming him in front of the waiters and other passengers. Initially, his case went before the commission and a three-judge federal district court in Maryland, which ruled

that the railway had violated the Act's Section 3 ban on unreasonable prejudice. The railroad then modified the dining car rules, establishing ten tables
for white patrons and one table for blacks—with a curtain separating the
blacks-only table from the whites-only tables. The commission and the district court upheld the modified rules, persuaded that the railway had,
through the revised regulations, tailored its accommodations to reflect demand:
it set aside four of its forty-four seats—or roughly 9 percent—for African
American patrons, who composed only about 4 percent of its dining-car
business.

Seizing on *Henderson*'s facts, Perlman's brief waged an assault on *Plessy*. As
a matter of law, he argued, the ICC's order upholding the dining-car regulations violated the Interstate Commerce Act and the Fifth Amendment's
due process clause, which bars the federal government and its agencies from
discriminating, in an arbitrary and capricious manner, solely based on racial
distinctions or classifications. Specifically, he said, the directive imposed,
with a government agency's sanction, a regime of mandatory race discrimination on interstate passengers, depriving them of the right to equal treatment, to which they were entitled under the Interstate Commerce Act and
the Fifth Amendment. As Perlman recognized, *Plessy*, which arose under the
Fourteenth Amendment's equal protection clause, did not control the resolution of *Henderson*, which could rely simply on the antidiscrimination pro-
vision in Section 3 of the Interstate Commerce Act. Still, Perlman urged the
Court to reexamine and reverse *Plessy*'s separate-but-equal mandate, saying
its legal and factual assumptions were "erroneous" and "obsolete." Perlman
anchored his point in common sense, saying equal treatment meant "the
same treatment." "The phrase 'equal rights' means the same rights," he wrote.

In a wide-ranging argument, citing authorities ranging from Booker T.
Washington to Richard Wright, the author of *Native Son*, Perlman dismantled *Plessy*'s logic. To the extent the Court's majority held that segregation
did not stigmatize African Americans as inferior, he wrote, abundant evidence demonstrated otherwise. And to the extent *Plessy* assumed segregation
infringed only "social" rights, which fell outside the Fourteenth Amendment's
equal protection clause, he also disagreed. "The Amendment strikes at inequality without qualification."

After dissecting precedent and the history of the Fourteenth Amendment,
Perlman turned to policy, tracing the public interest in eradicating Jim
Crow. With footnotes citing academic and medical journals, he recited a
litany of segregation's detrimental effects, including a "master-race psychology"

among whites and feelings of inferiority, frustration, and aggression among African Americans. Quoting Jackie Robinson's HUAC testimony, he alluded to the prospect of black radicalism. And in foreign affairs, he wrote, segregation had long posed an embarrassment, citing instances in which Soviet diplomats and media outlets had criticized the United States for its treatment of African Americans.

Perlman, who quoted several times from the *Plessy* dissent, invoked Justice Harlan's warning that the "thin disguise" of separate but equal would not mislead anyone. Emancipation had proven "a most complicated task," Perlman wrote, given the "subterfuges" devised to thwart the Thirteenth and Fourteenth Amendments. "'Separate but equal' is a constitutional anachronism, which no longer deserves a place in our law."

★ ★ ★ ★ ★

On March 31, at 1:30 p.m., Municipal Court judge Frank H. Myers convened a hearing in Mary's case against Thompson's. Inside a second-floor courtroom, a throng had gathered, an audience, according to one reporter, of about two hundred spectators. The day before, a press release had emanated from an entity called the Coordinating Committee for the Enforcement of the D.C. Anti-Discrimination Laws, targeting the evening papers. The Coordinating Committee, the informal name for the coalition seeking to revive the eighty-year-old antidiscrimination laws, operated under Mary's stewardship; its members, as a matter of respect, referred to her as "Mrs. Terrell." Annie Stein, Rein's neighbor in Southeast Washington, served as the committee's secretary and workhorse, commanding the business and strategy and tactics of day-to-day operations: mailings, press relations, volunteer recruitment.

Stein, a thirty-seven-year-old Brooklyn native, had grown up in a Williamsburg tenement, the youngest of three sisters. Her father, a pushcart peddler, emigrated from the Ukraine in 1904. At Hunter College in the early 1930s, Stein gravitated toward activism, including the National Student League, an antiwar, prolabor organization that she helped found with some peers from City College. She marched in May Day parades, joined the Young Communist League in 1933, and, later that year, during a conference at Howard University, staged visits to Jim Crow restaurants, demanding equal service. When she graduated from Hunter the following spring with a mathematics degree, she had already attracted the scrutiny of the Federal Bureau of Investigation, which had placed her under surveillance.

That fall, as the New Deal fueled an employment boom, Stein and her husband, Arthur, moved to Washington. Arthur Stein, a Columbia University–trained mathematician, found work as a statistician at the National Recovery Administration. In their spare time, the Steins joined the Marian Anderson Citizens' Committee, picketed the DAR, and attended the Marian Anderson concert. In 1941, after Arthur Stein became active in the United Federal Workers of America, a radical union for government employees, the FBI investigated him as a potential subversive, interviewing his former neighbors and college professors. Despite a year-long probe, the bureau unearthed no conclusive evidence, and, in an interview, Stein—who was a Communist—denied any affiliation with the party. Several years later, between December 1946 and September 1947, the FBI tapped Arthur's phone, monitoring and transcribing the calls he and his wife placed.

As a preview to the proceedings before Judge Myers, the Coordinating Committee's press release summarized the allegations against Thompson's, with the names and backgrounds of the four complaining witnesses: Scull, Elmes, Thompson, and Mary. It also contained a statement from Mary, linking her Washington-based activism to a broader national and international context, and implicitly defending her own patriotism. "Those who are trying to enforce the anti-discrimination laws here in Washington are rendering their country a great service," the release quoted Mary as saying. "They are trying to stop it from being disgraced any longer by preventing hotels and restaurants from refusing to serve colored people in the capital of what is called the greatest democracy on earth."

In a written court filing, Ringgold Hart, a local lawyer who represented Thompson's Restaurant, and King, the prosecutor, stipulated to the essentials: three well-behaved and respectable African Americans had entered Thompson's on February 28 and requested service; the restaurant had refused to accommodate them solely because of their race. Moreover, official records contained no evidence of any attempted prosecutions under either Reconstruction-era antidiscrimination law, the 1872 ordinance, or its 1873 successor, with their collective ban on race discrimination by restaurants—despite the passage of almost eight decades since their enactment. In theory, this simplified Judge Myers's task, leaving him only one issue to resolve: the laws' validity. After almost three hours of argument, he took the matter under advisement.

Up on Capitol Hill, Congressman John S. Wood, a Georgia Democrat, wrote a letter to Mary, declining her entreaty to testify about the Mundt-Nixon

Bill. Wood, a former judge who chaired HUAC, cited the panel's workload. However, he offered to insert her statement into the record.

★ ★ ★ ★ ★

The first spectators arrived at the Supreme Court at 8 a.m. on April 3, three hours before the chamber opened. That afternoon, as daffodils bloomed outside, the justices presided over oral argument in *Henderson*, the first of the three civil rights cases slated for consideration in a two-day stretch. About five hundred observers watched at least part of the proceedings, including visiting high-school students, and, as a testament to interest in the cases amid Washington's overlapping political and social circles, Mrs. Alben W. Barkley, the vice president's wife, and Gwendolyn Cafritz, the wife of a Washington real estate developer. The eight jurists—their ranks thinned by the recusal of Justice Tom C. Clark, Truman's former attorney general— heard from lawyers for the principles, including Southern Railway and the Interstate Commerce Commission. (Clark's previous tenure at the Justice Department created potential conflicts of interest for him on the Court when, as in *Henderson*, the federal government was a party.) In a last-minute addition to the Justice Department's team, they also heard from J. Howard McGrath, marking his first appearance before the Court as Truman's attorney general.

McGrath, a former US senator from Rhode Island, lacked Perlman's intellectual sophistication and facility for constitutional analysis. But, as the *Post*'s Supreme Court reporter, Chalmers M. Roberts, noted over the weekend, the Truman administration had deposited its civil rights agenda before the Court, asking the justices to discard separate but equal. And the presence of McGrath, who chaired the Democratic National Committee in 1948, when Truman won his party's nomination for president, telegraphed the administration's political calculus. Still, Roberts radiated skepticism, alluding to the judgment of unnamed sources. "The betting around town, however, is that the court majority will find a way to duck the red-hot issue."

One by one, the various attorneys advanced their theories, urging the justices either to look ahead, to a more egalitarian future, or backward, preserving the racial status quo. Henderson's lawyer, Belford V. Lawson Jr., invoked the symbolism of the Court's main entrance, with its engraved bronze doors, commemorating the evolution of Western law, from King John and the Magna Carta to Chief Justice John Marshall. Overhead, the building's sixteen marble Corinthian columns supported the triangular wedge of the architrave whose base read, "EQUAL JUSTICE UNDER LAW." Lawson, who had represented the Interracial Workshop during its YMCA coffee-shop protests, asked the Court to repudiate *Plessy*, so "Equal Justice Under Law" would become "a reality."

A railroad attorney, meanwhile, said the steward had denied Henderson a seat to preserve "peace and order," not because of his race. Laughter rippled from the audience and the bench. Justice Frankfurter, renowned for grilling lawyers during oral argument, asked, "Then the way to keep peace and order is to keep empty seats at tables?"

Finally, the justices heard from Samuel F. Hobbs, a sixty-two-year-old Democratic congressman and former state judge from Alabama—and an elder in Selma's First Presbyterian Church—who appeared at the behest of fellow members of the House Judiciary Committee. In December, Hobbs had filed a ten-page *Henderson* friend-of-the-court brief, saying integrated dining would be "the kiss of death" for Southern Railway, rendering its operations "absurd" and "impossible." Besides, he added, the Constitution gave Congress the power to regulate interstate travel and, by voting down integration proposals—fourteen times—by his reckoning, at least in the House—Congress had exercised its trust "for the best interests of all!"

In his plea to the jurists, Hobbs, acting as an emissary from Dixie and a co-equal branch of government, echoed his brief, which cited Scripture for the proposition that divine will compelled the existence of Jim Crow dining cars, to avoid offending white passengers. God was "the first author of seg-regation," he told the Court, and God made mankind with different color and facial characteristics. If his Tuskegee friends, Booker T. Washington and George Washington Carver, were alive today, he said, "they would echo my sentiments." To those watching his performance from the press section, Hobbs, born ten years after federal troops had withdrawn from the South, conjured another era.

On April 8, 1950, Douglas and his fellow jurists sequestered themselves in their oak-paneled conference room, with its fireplace and floor-to-ceiling bookshelves. Around a rectangular walnut table, seated in order of seniority, they shared their preliminary judgments on the civil rights cases. To preserve confidentiality, they met without staff or law clerks, like a secular College of Cardinals, huddled inside the Sistine Chapel to elect a new pope.

As each justice spoke, starting with the chief, Justice Douglas memorialized his colleagues' thoughts with handwritten notes on small sheets of white paper. At the top lay the typewritten purpose of the meeting, "Conference," and the date. Just underneath, centered at the top of the paper, were the case names: *Henderson, Sweatt,* and *McLaurin.*

As a group, the justices embodied a number of divisions and contrasts—with the obvious exceptions of race and gender. During his five years in office, Truman had appointed four of the nine, padding the Court with two of his cabinet members and two of his Senate colleagues: Chief Justice Fred M. Vinson, his ex-Treasury secretary, Tom Clark, his former attorney general, Harold H. Burton, a former Republican senator from Ohio whose work ethic he admired, and Sherman Minton, a former federal appeals court judge and US senator from Indiana with a predilection for chewing tobacco and ribald humor. The remaining jurists owed their tenure to FDR: Frankfurter, Douglas, Stanley F. Reed, Hugo Black, and Robert Jackson. Geographically, they split almost evenly, with four justices claiming southern roots: Clark from Texas; Black from Alabama; Vinson and Reed both from Kentucky. The remainder hailed from virtually everywhere else: Douglas from the West; Frankfurter and Jackson from New York; and Minton and Burton from the Midwest.

Each of the justices had worked in the federal government before landing on the tribunal and collectively their background spanned all three branches. Most had weathered official Washington in some capacity, and several boasted cabinet-level experience. Black, Burton, and Minton had represented their home states in the Senate; Vinson had spent several terms in the House. Jackson and Clark had served as US attorneys general, Reed and Jackson as solicitor general. Douglas, of course, headed the Securities and Exchange Commission, after launching himself, like Frankfurter, as a law professor. Frankfurter had also served in Washington over the years, including a stint as chairman of the War Labor Policies Board during World War I. And Robert Jackson, as a detour from the Court after World War II, had shouldered the role of chief US prosecutor during the war-crimes trials in Nuremberg, Germany.

In short, they had won elections and responded to constituents, earned appointments and counseled presidents, run government agencies and endured media scrutiny. When they spoke in conference, they drew on decades of knowledge and wisdom, much of it accrued outside the federal judiciary. When they shared their impressions about *Henderson, Sweatt,* and *McLaurin,* proceeding through each case in sequence, their comments reflected a range of concerns, tinged with pragmatism, unease, and instinct.

In *Henderson,* a consensus emerged from the outset, a narrow, statutory approach that skirted *Plessy* and the Constitution. Vinson, Black, and Reed said the railroad's Jim Crow dining tables violated the Interstate Commerce Act—its Section 3 ban on "any undue or unreasonable prejudice or disadvantage." Frankfurter, who apparently agreed, nevertheless expounded on the futility of seeking to decode congressional intent in adopting the Fourteenth Amendment—a matter of profound concern to him since, he believed, no one knew the underlying purpose of its framers. Jackson warned that *Henderson*, *Sweatt*, and *McLaurin* were fraught with peril for the Court and the country, especially since he could find no constitutional basis for distinguishing between graduate and elementary schools.

It was a crucial point, enmeshed in the law and culture of separate but equal. Segregated elementary schools, of course, were not before the justices, since *Henderson* arose in train travel, and *Sweatt* and *McLaurin* in graduate schools. But, as Jackson's query suggested, several broad issues hovered over the conference: whether to overturn *Plessy*, as Perlman had exhorted them to do; the implications for segregated education if they did; and the potential repercussions if, instead, they struck down *Plessy* for graduate schools and left it intact in segregated elementary and high schools. For segregation opponents, such as the Truman administration, *Henderson*, *Sweatt*, and *McLaurin* presented the opportunity to abandon *Plessy*. For segregationists, they stoked fears of that very outcome—integrated public-school classrooms, with black and white children seated side by side—anathema to the South. Even narrow decisions would resonate, a point illustrated by the oral arguments: the appearances of McGrath and Hobbs, the tenor of Hobbs's assertions, the throng of spectators.

Jackson weighed the policy implications. Is it "wise" for us to ban segregation? he wondered. Would we be doing "more harm than good[?]" He was, he said, "fluid enough to join any theory." Burton and Minton echoed their most senior colleagues, saying they would reverse *Henderson* on statutory grounds.

The two remaining cases, *Sweatt* and *McLaurin*, hinged on alleged constitutional infirmities under the Fourteenth Amendment's equal protection clause. As the justices discussed them, complexities surfaced, especially among the southerners. The most senior justices—Vinson, Black, and Reed—all of whom hailed from the South, aired their views first.

In *Sweatt*, the University of Texas Law School had denied an African American student admission to its all-white facility, creating instead an unaccredited, segregated law school for blacks with five full-time professors and twenty-three students, compared to sixteen full-time professors and 850 students in the program for whites. A Texas trial court upheld the dual in-stitutions, ruling them substantially equivalent, a finding upheld by the state's appellate tribunal. In *McLaurin*, the University of Oklahoma admitted an African American doctoral candidate to its graduate education program, but required him to sit apart from white students: at a desk in an antecham-ber outside the classroom; at a designated desk in the library's mezzanine, not in the reading room; at a separate table in the cafeteria, where he and white students ate at different times. A federal district court upheld the restrictions, ruling that Oklahoma officials had not violated the equal pro-tection clause.

For Vinson, *McLaurin* offered a straightforward path to resolution: the uni-versity had admitted an African American and treated him differently than whites, an equal protection violation. Black echoed Vinson, saying he would require southern states to demonstrate compliance with the separate-but-equal requirement, a burden they had not met in *McLaurin* or *Sweatt*. As for the distinction between elementary and graduate schools, Black said, the South had a custom, dating back to the Civil War, of segregating elementary and high schools, but no such tradition for law and graduate programs.

Still, Black, a former Alabama judge, knew that southerners harbored en-trenched hostility for racial "commingling." Segregation could be construed to encompass, as Adolf Hitler had, racial hatred and superiority, he said. But southerners would shutter elementary and high schools rather than mix races, he warned. In the end, he seemed inclined toward preserving *Plessy* for the time being—criticizing the decision, but retaining separate but equal.

The other southern justices struggled, too, especially with *Sweatt*. Vinson, at one point, inclined toward expansiveness, saying, as a matter of policy, no harm would result from mingling races. Like Jackson, he had difficulty dis-tinguishing between professional and elementary schools. But on the merits, whether the Texas law schools were equal, he was inclined to affirm. Clark, on the other hand, deemed the law schools unequal. Like Vinson, he balked at saying the equal protection clause only applied to graduate programs, not schools for children. Perhaps we should overrule *Plessy*, he said—before retreating, unwilling to upend separate but equal beyond the facts of *Sweatt* and *McLaurin*. Reed carved out a third approach, saying the Texas law schools were equal, but he would remand for further fact-finding.

For the remaining justices, unfettered by regional predilections, both cases warranted the same result: reversal, primarily because the states had failed to provide the same opportunities for African American students and whites. In *Sweatt*, Frankfurter invoked his Harvard experience, citing the importance of interaction among students.

Douglas did not log his own comments into his notes, but Justice Reed captured them in his, and Douglas did not hedge or qualify his position. In *Henderson*, he said, he would confront *Plessy* directly and overturn it.

★ ★ ★ ★ ★

In her text, addressed to Congressman Wood and published in HUAC's hearing record with a date of May 5, 1950, Mary Church Terrell invoked her title as honorary president of the National Association of Colored Women, the organization she had founded in *Plessy*'s aftermath, more than half a century earlier. Throughout, she drew on insights dating back to the suffrage movement, when, she said, courts and legislatures vied to obstruct full citizenship and equality for women.

In the present, the movement for civil rights absorbed a setback of its own, the recent death of Charles Hamilton Houston. Before he died, on April 22 at the age of fifty-four, Houston had called for one of his clients, Gardner Bishop, a barber on whose behalf he had struggled to secure parity between black and white Washington schools. Houston told Bishop to keep fighting. When Reverend Elmes had eulogized Houston in Howard's Alfred Rankin Memorial Chapel, Justices Black and Clark numbered among the mourners. In her written salvo to HUAC, which had gone through several drafts dating back at least to early April, when Houston was incapacitated, Terrell summoned Houston's sense of self-possession. Without saying so directly, she also betrayed her own concerns. She chaired a coalition sprinkled with progressives, including Forer and Rein, and at least one Communist, Annie Stein. And with her test case, Mary had aligned, though not overtly, with the Civil Rights Congress, one of then–Attorney General Clark's subversive organizations.

Her statement invoked these considerations in the abstract, separate from her battle against Thompson's. Given the climate in Washington, though, the issues melded, especially since Houston's illness and death had left Terrell to finish the struggle—not quite alone, since she had the Coordinating Committee, but without his gravitational, moral, and intellectual force at the movement's helm. Many whites believe African Americans deserve full citizenship, Mary wrote, but the Mundt-Nixon Bill would impede interracial reform initiatives, deeming them subversive, and preserve the status quo—which was precisely the authors' intent, she said. "The real subversives," she added, were the Klan and similar entities who would rather "murder" African Americans than see them win first-class citizenship.

★ ★ ★ ★ ★

Justice Burton circulated a draft of *Henderson* at the end of May. As crafted for the majority, Burton's opinion reflected the consensus at conference: avoiding *Plessy* and the Constitution, holding that the railroad had violated Section 3 of the Interstate Commerce Act, subjecting black passengers to unreasonable "prejudice" or "disadvantage," in violation of the statute, by confining them to a designated table and denying them service at vacant seats elsewhere in the dining car. Still, for Burton, *Henderson*—and his having been selected by Vinson to draft the opinion—heralded something of a vindication.

Burton, a World War I veteran and former Cleveland mayor with no experience as a judge, had struggled to adapt to the Court's workload, flashing doubts even before his swearing-in. When court was in session, he routinely toiled six days a week from early in the morning until late in the evening. At the end of his workday, on the way home, he often stopped at the Senate gym for a swim and a steam. Yet his productivity, as gauged by written output, languished behind the other justices; he had generated only a handful of opinions each term. The first Ohio justice since Taft, Burton also evinced a sense of humility, as if awed by his proximity to history. During oral arguments, more senior colleagues routed him handwritten notes, like students confined to study hall. Douglas sent jokes; Frankfurter—drawing on their shared affiliation as graduates of Harvard Law—identified Harvard alumni among the advocates. Burton annotated each slip of paper in his minuscule print, adding the case number and context, enshrining them in his files.

As the Court's only Republican, a moderate who, as a politician, had sympathized with the NAACP, Burton grappled with substance. Sometimes he lost his bearings in an institution, which, by the time of his arrival in late 1945, was dominated by FDR's band of intellects and personalities. Frankfurter, alert to a potential ally, coached Burton about his opinions, highlighting points that troubled him. Still, less than a year after joining the Court, Burton filed the only dissent in *Morgan v. Virginia*, which struck down segregated seating on interstate buses. Three years later, Drew Pearson, a syndicated columnist who chatted with Douglas, dismissed Burton as a Truman and Vinson loyalist, a drudge ill-equipped to stand out on his own. Burton saved the column and added it to his collection of press clippings: election returns from Cuyahoga County, Ohio, as tabulated by the *Cleveland Plain Dealer*; a story, also from the *Plain Dealer*, about his emergence as a dark-horse Republican presidential candidate; a photograph of him, from the *Christian Science Monitor*, donning his black robe.

★ ★ ★ ★ ★

At first, Douglas composed his conference memo in longhand. Echoing Perlman's brief, he wrote at length, filling thirteen pages with his insights and rhetorical questions, eschewing the conservatism of Justice Burton's approach. After revisions, Douglas added the *Henderson* caption on the first page. Unlike a majority, dissenting, or concurring opinion, destined for publication in the *United States Supreme Court Reports*, a memo to the conference served as a snapshot of a justice's thinking, which generally remains shrouded in obscurity at least until his files have been made available to archivists. After oral argument in *Henderson*, *Sweatt*, and *McLaurin*, Justice Clark circulated a conference memo about his opposition to overruling *Plessy*. Since the controversies originated in his region, he said, he hoped his views might be of assistance to his colleagues.

Douglas betrayed no such civility. The *Henderson* opinion proceeded on untenable grounds, compounding the problem of segregation, he wrote. He disputed Burton's interpretation of the statute. He seized on a line from Burton's draft, referring to the "at most symbolic" division of dining-car tables. "But what segregation is not symbolic?" Douglas asked. He referred to Justice Harlan's *Plessy* dissent, noting the Court had never repudiated *Plessy*, which stood, even to that day, as "a constitutional sanction for the practice of segregating the races." And, he added, in a feint to proponents of judicial restraint, he believed the Court should avoid constitutional adjudication where possible, including cases such as this one, which raised a divisive and significant issue. "But I see no other alternative," he wrote. "This case squarely raises the issues of *Plessy v. Ferguson*, which I think should be met."

Douglas circulated his *Henderson* memo on May 31, prompting Burton to note in his diary that Douglas had floated "a dissent." That same day, Justice Frankfurter issued a conference memorandum of his own, a three-page statement with six numbered paragraphs. From his introductory phrase, summoning the pedantry of "it will be recalled," to his opening and closing references to "Brother Burton," Frankfurter donned the mantle of collegiality, as if admonishing a captive audience of first-year law students, some of whom needed his tutelage more than others.

In their previous careers, Douglas and Frankfurter had cultivated a friend-ship based on mutual admiration, swapping letters and praise. As colleagues on the Court, though, their relations curdled into animosity. "As you know, I am no poker player," Frankfurter once told Douglas, in a note criticizing an opinion, "and, naturally, therefore, I do not believe in poker playing in the disposition of cases." Character and temperament drove them apart as well. Frankfurter, a constitutional scholar, relished the Court and its routines and devoted himself to their mastery. Early in Vinson's tenure as chief justice, Frankfurter furnished him with a "tabular analysis" of the Court's search-and-seizure cases. He chided Vinson about the need to clarify the order in which justices read oral opinions from the bench—Frankfurter suggested seniority. He wrote Vinson three days in a row about proposed amendments to the Federal Rules of Civil Procedure.

Douglas, by contrast, fled the Court as often as he could, finding sanctu-ary elsewhere: out West; at Joseph P. Kennedy's Palm Beach estate; and, when-ever possible, outdoors. He hunted mallards in Arkansas and gazelles in Persia. He angled for trout in Maryland, Idaho, and Washington State. He col-lected wildflowers and displayed pressed grasses under a glass tabletop. He gathered lichen in Goose Prairie, Washington, and diverted samples to the Smithsonian Institution for identification.

Still, for all his restlessness and range, Douglas rebuffed invitations to serve elsewhere. He rejected an offer to serve as Truman's running mate in 1948, telling the president he wished to remain on the Court. In private, to others, he reputedly said he didn't want to be the "number two man to a number two man."

Douglas and Frankfurter clashed on substance, too, each bearing traces of the law schools that trained them. Frankfurter, a disciple of Harvard's Oliver Wendell Holmes Jr., revered judicial restraint. Douglas, shaped by Columbia in the 1920s, viewed the courts as a bulwark against governmental excess, especially in the arenas of civil rights, civil liberties, and protecting minori-ties. In 1949, he wrote the opinion in *Terminiello v. City of Chicago*, reversing, on First Amendment grounds, a disorderly conduct conviction for a speaker who incited a mob with political and racist diatribes. Frankfurter dissented, saying the majority had, for the first time in 130 years, reversed a state tribu-nal's sentence on grounds not raised at trial or on appeal, the Holmesian equivalent of blasphemy.

In *Henderson*, Frankfurter had already pled for moderation in private, asking Burton, in a letter dated May 26, to trim a discussion that cataloged the "unreasonable discriminations" endured by black dining-car patrons, including the "at most symbolic" partition between customers of both races, who otherwise had "identical tickets." This was, of course, the phrase cited by Douglas in his memo—but in Douglas's case with the hope of spurring his colleagues to a bolder result. Toward the end of his missive, Frankfurter said he doubted any member of the Court opposed racial inequality more than he. But he also felt strongly, he added, about how the Court exercised its jurisdiction. "No one single cause has got this Court into more needless trouble than needlessly deciding issues not before the Court or going needlessly beyond an adequate ground of disposing of a controversy, particularly when popular passion is involved."

Now, wading into *Henderson* with his colleagues, Frankfurter defended Burton's approach and opined about judicial overreach. Burton's opinion went too far in one respect, he said, by referring to the division between the dining-car tables as "symbolic." By doing so, he added, the Court embraced an antisegregation slogan, a word associated with the belief that segregation stigmatized African Americans with the taint of inferiority. We should not adopt that term, he wrote, and if we do, we broach the very topic that, at least for now, we have agreed to evade: segregation itself, including Jim Crow primary schools.

Around the same time—presumably in response to Frankfurter—Douglas revised his approach, converting his *Henderson* memo into a concurring opinion. The difference transcended mere formalism. A separate concurrence, slated for publication, would telegraph his position to an audience beyond the justices, including the attorneys, professors, and journalists who combed the Court's decisions, scouring the text and footnotes for clues about its possible future direction. Such a move would also contravene Justice Black's sense of propriety, his belief in not venting intramural grievances in published opinions.

Through drafts and revisions, however, Douglas had amplified his *Henderson* views, honing his constitutional analysis. In *Plessy*, the Court had justified its decision upholding segregated railway cars in part by looking to Washington, D.C., where Congress had mandated a separate system for black children—"the constitutionality of which does not seem to have been questioned," the majority had written. In other words, the justices had suggested, because Congress had sanctioned segregated schools for Washington's black students, the Court could (and did) uphold—and the Fourteenth Amendment did not prohibit—segregated seating for black train passengers in Louisiana. With his *Henderson* draft concurrence, Douglas confronted that legacy at its base: to overturn

Plessy and Jim Crow across the South, the Court had to start by upending government-sanctioned segregation in Washington.

Adopting Perlman's logic, Douglas noted that the segregated dining cars at issue in *Henderson* bore the imprimatur of the Interstate Commerce Commission, an agency of the federal government. As a result, he said, the railway's government-approved segregation violated the Fifth Amendment's due process clause by discriminating against blacks, treating them unequally by making them wait when the blacks-only seats were filled, even if the white section had vacant seats. To illustrate his point, he looked to Washington, and drew an analogy. Invoking the specter of the Holocaust and the recent history of World War II, he likened the dining car's federally sanctioned Jim Crow to an act of Congress banishing Jewish or Irish residents to a confined section of the capital, denying them access to some streets, and segregating them in public transportation. Such a law would discriminate by race, treating the targeted groups unequally, relegating them to second-class citizenship, much as Adolf Hitler's "yellow Star of David" had with Jews in Nazi Germany, he said.

Douglas did not mention segregated restaurants in his Washington hypothetical. Nor did his draft opinion embrace "social equality" for blacks. Instead, he limited his support to "legal equality." Still, he had, in broad terms, anticipated *Thompson*, repudiating—albeit on Fifth Amendment grounds, not under the Reconstruction-era civil rights laws—racial segregation in the federal capital. Quoting Harlan's *Plessy* dissent, he staked out a rationale, endorsing the notion of a "color-blind" Constitution, a society without a "ruling class" or "caste," where segregation on public vehicles and streets violated "our standards of equality under the law." "There can be no legal equality when racism becomes the way of life."

On June 3, Douglas scrawled a message to Burton on Supreme Court letterhead. If he filed a separate *Henderson* opinion, he wrote, only "the attached pages"—he enclosed the first three, which focused on the Interstate Commerce Act—would bear on anything Burton had written. Douglas's chambers annotated his concurrence again two days later, saying he "never circulated or filed" it. Perhaps he hadn't intended to file the concurrence, notwithstanding his note to Burton. Perhaps, as a writer and author, Douglas sharpened his thoughts by committing them to paper. Or perhaps he realized that *Thompson*—still pending before Judge Myers—could land before the Court eventually, and decided not to comment on segregation in Washington before the justices had taken up the issue. Other than his drafts,

and the annotations his staff made on them, he left little by way of explanation for his decision not to make his opinion known. And he apparently
waited until the last minute to commit himself.

Justice Burton, meanwhile, read from the bench on June 5, reciting the
opinion he had crafted for the Court. After announcing the *Henderson*
ruling, keyed to Section 3 of the Interstate Commerce Act, he explained its
rationale: the railway unreasonably disadvantaged African American passengers by denying them service because they could only sit in seats reserved
for them, even if other places—reserved for whites—remained vacant.
Contrary to his law clerks' advice, he had etched a line through an entire
sentence, heeding Frankfurter's admonition. "~~The division between these
tables is at most symbolic~~," it read. In the end, the jurists had all aligned
behind Burton, except Clark, who recused himself, and Douglas, who concurred in the result and kept his reservations to himself.

Later that day the Court unveiled unanimous decisions in *Sweatt* and
McLaurin, invalidating, on equal protection grounds, the segregated regimes
at issue in each case. Both opinions, authored by Vinson, dodged *Plessy*, with
holdings pegged to their graduate-school settings. Removal of these state-
imposed requirements would not necessarily ameliorate prejudice, or prevent students from choosing not to "commingle" with a black peer, Vinson
wrote in *McLaurin*, but at least the state would not be depriving him the
opportunity to win approval "on his own merits."

Later still, while the *Evening Star* splashed *Henderson* atop its front page,
Burton received a telegram from Lancaster, Pennsylvania, from one H. C.
Valentine. "I hope you are happy with this decision," wrote Valentine. "I also
hope they share your personal table next to you." Even Valentine's own
grandfather, he said, who fought in Gettysburg with a New York regiment,
would not have extended the struggle this far. "Are these United States
becoming a second Africa with a future quadroon Supreme Court[?]"

A naval architect from the capital's Northwest quadrant sent a postcard to
Burton as well, identifying himself as J. S. Shelton, a "U.S. Taxpayer." Which
Supreme Court decision, Shelton wanted to know, stood for the proposition that train passengers with "identical tickets" should receive "identical
accommodations"? He had been forced to stand while African Americans—
he used a racial slur—received preferential seating, and he wanted to raise "a
big fuss about it," he said.

Within hours, reaction to *Henderson*, *Sweatt*, and *McLaurin* engulfed the
AP wire. From New York, the NAACP released a statement hailing the

decisions, saying the nation's courts had recognized, long before Congress, the government's legal and moral obligations to grant civil rights to all citizens, regardless of race. In Georgia, Governor Herman Eugene Talmadge, a Democrat, vowed defiance. "As long as I am governor, Negroes will not be admitted to white schools."

Mary composed a statement for *Our World Magazine*, a New York–based publication for African Americans. The Supreme Court's decisions, she wrote, had opened a door of educational opportunity, one that could never be closed again. Hopefully, she added, similar progress would follow in elementary and secondary schools, including those in Washington.

As letters and postcards trickled into Burton's chambers—like the one from Valentine and Shelton—from around the country, with several expressing anxiety and ill will, the *Star* ran an editorial cartoon on its front page, above the fold. In the image, Chief Justice Vinson stood outside the main portico, clad in his judicial robe, holding a sign saying the Court was closed until October. "We gave them enough in one day to last all summer," his dialogue balloon read. The black-and-white ink drawing found its way into Justice Burton's files, as did a *Los Angeles Times* article reporting that Douglas had been named Father of the Year.

Two days later, on June 9, Thurgood Marshall responded to the Civil Rights Congress, spurning a bid at cooperation. In a letter to William Patterson, Marshall declined to mount a joint defense of African American men accused of raping a white woman in Martinsville, Virginia. "We have never been convinced that the Civil Rights Congress is primarily interested in the protection of the rights of Negroes," Marshall wrote.

Meanwhile, in light of *Henderson*, *Sweatt*, and *McLaurin*, the NAACP began recalibrating its legal strategy. "The complete destruction of all enforced segregation is now in sight," Marshall told a reporter for the *Atlanta Daily World*. Later that month, NAACP officials converged in Boston for their forty-first annual conference. During the proceedings, while NAACP attorneys plotted an all-out focus on seeking integrated public schools, not just equal facilities within segregated systems, the delegates adopted a pair of resolutions. One authorized the board to expel Communists from the organization. The other pledged to combat segregation in Washington with "every legal and constitutional means," saying the capital's failure to embody democratic ideals had captured attention worldwide. The Washington resolution referred to the *Thompson* test case, but not to Mary Church Terrell.

★ ★ ★ ★ ★

Judge Myers released his *Thompson* decision on July 10. In a twelve-page opinion, Myers dismissed the charges against Thompson's, holding that the Reconstruction-era antidiscrimination laws had been repealed by implication. In essence, Myers ruled, the ordinances emerged from Washington's "short-lived" territorial government, which a later law, the Organic Act of 1878, had replaced, establishing the commissioners as a permanent local government and granting them broad authority to regulate restaurants. By exercising that authority, he reasoned, they displaced any previous legislation on the same subject.

As precedent, Myers cited two Supreme Court decisions, dating back to 1886 and 1891, respectively. Those opinions, which arose in the capital, rejected pleas for back pay on the grounds the Organic Act had, by implication, superseded and repealed an 1861 law governing the topic. Nowhere did Myers take into account the Supreme Court's recent shift on racial discrimination, including *Henderson*, which construed a federal statute in a way that invalidated segregated dining. He did mention, in "dicta," that well-behaved African Americans had "a real problem" finding decent restaurants in many areas of the capital. But the solution did not lie in attempting to revive "old municipal regulations," especially when later laws had replaced them, he wrote.

The next day, a *Post* reporter named Benjamin Bradlee queried the NAACP for reaction. Walter White, the executive secretary, alluded to the presence of American combat troops in Korea, a development Truman had dubbed a "police action." Two weeks before Judge Myers's decision, North Korea, headed by Communist Premier Kim Il Sung, invaded the democratic Republic of South Korea. "Radio Moscow will tell the world in the next 24 hours that the Nation's Capital is still Jim Crow by judicial decision," said White. The *Star*'s editors, meanwhile, argued that Washington's public dining options for African Americans were "disgracefully inadequate." "If the abandonment of segregation in restaurants is the only remedy for this condition, the *Star*'s belief is that segregation will go."

7

This Thing Can Be Licked

Legal technicalities drove Mary Church Terrell back to Thompson's Restaurant for a third time, a little over two weeks after Judge Myers issued his decision. In essence, by dismissing the charges, Myers had found the restaurant not guilty, an outcome prosecutors could not appeal. So on July 27, Mary returned, this time with Reverend Elmes and Joan Williams, a white woman who served as executive secretary for the Washington Fellowship—the interfaith organization of which Scull was president. Once again, the cafeteria declined to serve them.

Afterward, Mary and her colleagues huddled at the law offices of Forer and Rein, where a photographer for the *Pittsburgh Courier* snapped a portrait: David Rein standing, smoking a pipe; Joseph Forer seated at a desk, signing papers, with his back to venetian blinds. Mary, seated off to the side, wore a print dress and a small brimmed hat with a tuft of netting. When Judge Myers, citing his previous ruling, quashed a renewed new bid to prosecute the restaurant, the Corporation Counsel's office filed an appeal.

That fall of 1950, Mary and her compatriots bore down, like Houston in the 1930s, waging combat in court and on the sidewalks. On her eighty-seventh birthday, while an *Afro-American* photographer hovered in the background, she coached volunteers about contesting segregated seating at dime-store lunch counters. A month later, she sent a letter to Philip Perlman, asking him to file a *Thompson* friend-of-the-court brief.

Across much of the capital, and certainly within Congress, however, the zeitgeist hewed toward fear of nonconformity and dissent. In September, roughly three months after Truman ordered American troops into Korea, Congress passed the Internal Security Act, dubbed "the McCarran Act" for its sponsor, Senator Patrick A. McCarran, a Nevada Democrat. With the country embroiled in the Cold War's first military engagement—against a Communist aggressor the *Washington Evening Star* denounced as the "Red invasion army," with its "60-ton Russian-made tanks"—the McCarran Act targeted alleged subversion at home. Exceeding even the restrictions envisioned by the Mundt–Nixon Bill, which Congress never enacted, the McCarran Act compelled Communist and "Communist front" organizations to register with a Subversive Activities Control Board, a five-member panel appointed by the president. During a presidentially proclaimed "Internal Security Emergency," including a state of internal insurrection in support of a foreign enemy, the measure also authorized the attorney general to apprehend and detain, in places of confinement, anyone likely to engage in, or conspire to engage in, acts of espionage or sabotage.

At first, Truman balked, vetoing the McCarran Act with a 6,000-word message to lawmakers. "The course proposed by this bill would delight the communists, for it would make a mockery of the Bill of Rights and of our claims to stand for freedom in the world." In private, he deemed the measure "one of the most absurd pieces of legislation passed by any Congress." Within a little more than twenty-four hours, the House and Senate overrode his veto, ushering the act into law. Only forty-eight House members and ten senators backed the president.

China plunged into the war later that fall, unleashing an estimated 260,000 troops to counter an attack by General Douglas MacArthur, the commander of the UN forces. On December 16, 1950, Truman decreed a national emergency, citing the global "menace" of "communist aggression," calling for rapid mobilization of the defense industry, and urging "all citizens" to remain loyal to the nation's founding principles. On Christmas Eve, Mary grabbed her cane and purse and marched in a picket line outside Kresge's, a five-and-ten-cent store, as they were called, located at Seventh and E Streets, NW, where management refused to serve African Americans. After the holiday, the *Afro-American* ran a photograph of Mary, clad in a winter coat and lace-up oxford heels, holding a placard that read, "Don't Buy at Kresge's—The *only* Jim Crow Dime Store on 7th Street." The store capitulated on January 12, 1951, announcing it would serve African Americans.

But for Terrell, whose activism drew on her stature and respectability, success brought scrutiny, opportunity, and anxiety. On February 8, 1951, she typed a three-page response to an invitation from Attorney General McGrath, who had summoned her on official letterhead, embossed with his name and title, to the Annual Brotherhood Dinner, sponsored by the National Conference of Christians and Jews. The United States was waging a battle against Communism, whose adherents seek to divide Americans, according to McGrath, and she could foster unity by attending the event at the Mayflower Hotel. "The enemy is Communism!" In her reply, Mary said she had little knowledge of Communism, other than information she derived from reading newspapers. But she did know a lot about the so-called "race problem," she wrote. "I wish the conditions under which colored people live all over the United States could be improved, not only for their sake, but because I love my country."

Before long, the Brotherhood Week campaign emerged as a Rorschach test on race and patriotism. McGrath, whose office presided over the subversives list, embraced the undertaking as a Cold War imperative. Terrell, who was fighting to end the global embarrassment of a segregated capital, lent support while defending her patriotism. And Hecht's department store, a local enterprise with a Jim Crow lunch counter, underwrote a full-page public service announcement in the *Washington Post* on February 19, touting its support as well. In the center of the bulletin, underneath a caption of "Man to Man," an image depicted two males locked in a handshake. Brotherhood begins at home, it said, not overseas. "We can't afford to blind ourselves to the disturbing and undermining racial and religious antagonisms in America."

In Mary's case, though, questions about loyalty lingered, as did concerns about her alliances. Toward the end of Brotherhood Week, on February 24, Terrell met with Dorothy Swift, Nettie's daughter, who served as president of the AAUW's Washington branch. Over dinner, Dorothy urged Mary to withdraw her sponsorship of the American Peace Crusade, an antiwar initiative endorsed by W. E. B. Du Bois and Paul Robeson. The previous day, with plans underway for a rally in the capital on March 15, three Peace Crusade allies had urged Mary not to pull out.

Dorothy had known Mary for years. At Nettie's request, she had edited Mary's memoirs in 1939, when she prodded her to trim fifty pages from a 450-page manuscript. In 1940, she looked at the manuscript again before Ransdell finalized its release. Like her mother, Dorothy had defended Mary in 1946, when the AAUW's Washington membership committee rejected her application. She sided with her during the three-year skirmish that followed, when the branch asserted its right to discriminate and the national organization insisted on race-blind membership criteria. And Dorothy stood by Mary when the prosegregation camp bolted, reorganizing as the University Women's Club, Inc., and set itself up in separate headquarters, located at 1515 New Hampshire Avenue, NW.

In McCarthy-era Washington, however, even Dorothy had limits. She had read in a newspaper that the American Peace Crusade was a "Communist organization." Four days earlier, in fact, Secretary of State Acheson had denounced the Peace Crusade as a Communist propaganda tool. With Dorothy, Mary demurred, saying she had checked with McGrath's office, which deemed the Peace Crusade non-Communist. But with loyalty boards probing federal employees about their tastes in music, theater, and art, and state universities compelling employees to submit to loyalty oaths, Dorothy fretted about Terrell's allegiances, fearing she would cast disrepute on the Washington branch of the AAUW, which Mary finally had joined after the national organization intervened and the University Women's Club broke away.

For Mary, endorsement of the Peace Crusade rippled with complexities. She had criticized the war in Korea based on the military's mistreatment of African American soldiers, a concern shared by the NAACP. Over in Japan and Korea, Thurgood Marshall had undertaken a probe of military courts martial; in private, he expressed unease about black soldiers, who were facing cowardice charges more frequently than whites. Mary, the mother of two daughters and the widow of a husband who had been too old to serve in World War I, also confronted, for the first time, the fear of losing a loved one in combat: her nephew Thomas, her brother's son and namesake.

Still, Terrell had lived through the first "Red scare" three decades earlier. In the current climate, she knew, upstanding citizens were seeing their reputations and livelihoods shattered by the taint of Communism or Communist sympathies. After the strife surrounding her admission to the AAUW's Washington branch, she recoiled at the thought of alienating its members, whose tastes inclined toward discussions of "The American Way" and Marianne Moore's poetry, not civil rights and the H-bomb.

A few days later, while she was considering what to do, Mary attended a *Thompson* hearing in the Municipal Court of Appeals. She and Annie Stein watched from the front row. Before a three-judge panel, which was weighing the viability of the antidiscrimination laws, two attorneys made their arguments. Chester H. Gray, the principal assistant corporation counsel, said the eighty-year-old ordinances had been validly enacted and never repealed. Ringgold Hart, of course, as the lawyer who represented Thompson's, urged the court to affirm Judge Myers, stressing the ordinances' heritage as civil rights legislation, geared toward modulating social behavior. "Mrs. Stein thought our side strong," Mary wrote in her diary, in the entry for February 28.

Mary and Dorothy Swift met again later that day, this time over lunch at the YWCA. Afterward, Mary went to the AAUW's national headquarters, located about four blocks from the White House, in a townhouse at 1634 I Street, NW. On the second floor, a row of double windows overlooked Farragut Square, a swath of green about the size of a city block. At the center of the park stood a statue of Admiral David G. Farragut, who spearheaded Union naval victories at New Orleans and Mobile Bay. Inside the AAUW, Mary spoke to Emily Morrison, the wife of Dr. Philip Morrison, a Cornell University physics professor who sponsored the American Peace Crusade. Dr. Morrison, who once joined and later renounced the Communist Party, had worked on the Manhattan Project with his graduate-school mentor, J. Robert Oppenheimer, helping test and assemble the atomic bomb unleashed on Nagasaki. After the war, Morrison toured Japan and the experience turned him into a peace and arms-control proponent.

Emily Morrison and Mary discussed everything, as Terrell wrote in her journal, including her concerns about her nephew. Morrison gave her some literature. In the end, she said, Mary should do as she wished.

Civil rights activists had long attracted scrutiny and suspicion, of course, and the period following the Korean War's outbreak proved no exception. Even before the McCarran Act, in August 1950, the State Department revoked Paul Robeson's passport, depriving him of the opportunity to perform concerts and earn income abroad. In an editorial, the *New York Herald Tribune* hailed the move, saying Robeson had accrued a record as an "agitator," a propagandist for Russia and Communism, and a proponent of peace and disunity.

Mary Church Terrell was, of course, no Paul Robeson, a stage and screen actor of international renown. But neither was she a Communist. During the 1930s, when she had lobbied for release of the Scottsboro Boys—a cause embraced by Charles Hamilton Houston and Communists alike—her writings, speeches, letters, and diaries betrayed no evidence of enlistment in the party's fold, no endorsement of its ideology. "I am not a Communist, never was one and never will be one, and have no interest in it whatsoever," she told the Maryland Committee for Peace in October 1950, "except to ponder how in the world it ever got that way." She had aligned herself with other activists, including Du Bois, Robeson, and Patterson, whose activities triggered criticism and even alarm. In all likelihood, however, since HUAC had not subpoenaed her, and Wood rebuffed her efforts to testify before the panel, no one had denounced her as a member of the Communist Party.

Still, for the next three weeks, she filled her diary with reappraisals. Inside an African American church at Ninth and S Streets, where she and Annie Stein attended a speech by the poet Langston Hughes, Terrell noted the paucity of African Americans in the audience; black women and white women even sat on separate sides of the platform. At home, Mary pored over her files, sifting through letters. "They worry me greatly," she wrote in her journal on March 7, conveying discomfort about her correspondence, and presumably, the sympathies it revealed, including perhaps the Civil Rights Congress or the American Peace Crusade—or both. Ten days later, she ducked an invitation to a meeting about the impending execution of Willie McGee, an African American Mississippi man, convicted of raping a white woman, whose defense the Civil Rights Congress had coordinated. She feared, she wrote in her diary, she was being recruited by the American Peace Crusade. On March 19, she resigned as one of its sponsors. Even she had succumbed to the heightened sense of danger and peril.

★ ★ ★ ★ ★

On April 4, 1951, HUAC released a 166-page, single-spaced report, written under Chairman Wood's imprimatur, decrying a campaign to sabotage American morale and military superiority by undermining domestic support for nuclear weapons. Titled *Report on the Communist "Peace" Offensive: A Campaign to Disarm and Defeat the United States*, it cited sources ranging from confidential, cooperating witnesses and the Federal Bureau of Investigation to press accounts and internal documents, most of which were based on innuendo and circumstance. With their ties to "peace fronts," the individuals identified in the report were allegedly perpetuating the myths of Communist pacifism and Western aggression. This "'peace' offensive," the report announced, was "the most dangerous hoax ever devised by the international Communist conspiracy."

The committee spotlighted African American activists, denouncing Robeson as a "known" Communist and accusing Langston Hughes of allegedly supporting as many as eighty Communist-front organizations. In a three-page primer on Du Bois, HUAC said he had never, to its knowledge, declared himself a Communist, but he was "tremendously obsessed with communism," a self-described "fellow traveler," with a "distinct preference" for Communist-front entities. Paragraph by paragraph, HUAC tracked Du Bois's activities and statements: his co-chairmanship of the World Peace Congress in 1949; his association with the Civil Rights Congress; his appearance, in

November 1949, at the Soviet Embassy party marking the Russian Revolution's anniversary. Unlike the NAACP and its "outstanding leader," Walter White, the committee said, Du Bois did not speak for "the great mass of Negro people."

In text and lists scattered throughout the report, HUAC named Mary Church Terrell five times. The committee did not suggest she was a "known" Communist Party member. Rather, based on documents ostensibly generated by alleged peace-front entities, HUAC consigned her to the ranks of "fellow travelers," alongside Du Bois, Morrison, and more than fifty other individuals. These persons, HUAC reasoned, had "affiliated with such a significant number of Communist fronts that they may be said to constitute a body of reliable and consistent supporters of Communist organizations."

As evidence of such entanglements, Mary's name also appeared in appendices to the report, amid supporters of four allegedly subversive organizations. Along with Reverend William Jernagin and Geneva Brown, the original test-case participants, the panel folded Terrell into a roster of Washington residents who allegedly supported the Stockholm appeal, an initiative to ban atomic weapons. She and William Patterson, the CRC's national executive secretary, graced a separate section, based on their alleged sponsorship of the World Peace Congress in 1949. Her name emerged again, along with individuals such as Du Bois, Morrison, and Jernagin, for the Mid-Century Conference for Peace, which had convened in Chicago, Illinois, in May 1950. (A press release circulated two weeks before the meeting said that "H-Bombs" could obliterate "our country's destiny of full democracy for all.") And on page 135, HUAC identified Terrell, Du Bois, Robeson, Morrison, and more than eighty others as initial sponsors of the American Peace Crusade.

Communist subversion preoccupied the Supreme Court as well that spring, although, in a pair of decisions, the justices scrutinized activities by the executive branch, not Congress. By a 5-to-3 vote on April 30, 1951, generating a total of six opinions, including a dissent from Reed, Vinson, and Minton, the Court invalidated the attorney general's "subversives list," dating back to 1947. The case, known as *Joint Anti-Fascist Refugee Committee v. McGrath*, consolidated challenges from three organizations, including Rein's client, the National Council of American-Soviet Friendship, Inc., which professed to maintain cultural and educational ties to the Soviet Union. All three entities had landed on then–attorney general Clark's roster on November 24, 1947. In a follow-up classification on September 17, 1948, he had branded them "Communists."

During briefing and oral argument the previous fall, O. John Rogge, a Progressive Party leader and former assistant US attorney general, represented the antifascist refugees. In his brief, Rogge attacked Executive Order 9835, which had spawned the subversives list, saying Truman's directive unjustifiably curtailed freedom of thought, expression, and association protected by the First Amendment. For several years, the FBI had tracked Rogge's press coverage, lining his surveillance file with articles from outlets such as the *Daily Worker*, the *Post*, and the *Star*. HUAC had eyed Rogge as well, sprinkling his name throughout its "peace" report—including once alongside Terrell, Du Bois, and Morrison—as a "reliable and consistent" supporter of Communist entities.

During his appearance before the tribunal, Rogge denounced the subversives list as an attempt to exploit anti-Communist furor for political purposes. "Publication of this fake and libelous blacklist is part of the contest between Congress and the Administration to whip up the hysteria that is gripping this country today." Perlman, saddled with defending the loyalty program, said the roster safeguarded the Constitution and democratic government. That same day, the FBI logged both statements, typed in all capitals, into its Rogge dossier.

Justice Burton, who wrote the opinion for a divided Court in *Joint Anti-Fascist Refugee Committee*, dodged resolving whether the organizations warranted Communist labels. (Only Justice Douglas joined Justice Burton's opinion; the other non-dissenting justices concurred in the result.) Burton's plurality opinion ruled that the attorney general—Justice Clark, which is why he had of course recused himself from the case—had acted in a "patently arbitrary" manner. In particular, the nation's chief law-enforcement officer, now McGrath, had failed to show that, based on evidence, reasonable grounds existed for doubting the entity's loyalty.

The Court's FDR appointees, Black, Douglas, Frankfurter, and Jackson, filed separate concurrences, floating their own rationales. Justice Black said the First Amendment barred the executive branch, with or without a hearing, from generating and publishing a tally of "subversives." Justice Frankfurter, in a lengthy dissertation about due process, said the attorney general's "wholly summary" factual determinations contravened notions of fundamental fairness as guaranteed by the Fifth Amendment. Justice Jackson said he would reverse based on the Justice Department's failure to provide a hearing "at any stage." Douglas said the underlying constitutional inquiry was one of this generation's most critical issues. "The problems of security are real," he wrote. "So are the problems of freedom. The paramount issue of the age is to reconcile the two."

The *Atlanta Daily World* ran an Associated Negro Press story about HUAC's "peace" report two days later, on May 2. The front-page article bore the headline "Negro Leaders Accused of Having Red Affiliations." According to the article, HUAC had identified many African American religious leaders and public figures not usually tagged "pink," including Jernagin and Mary.

★ ★ ★ ★ ★

David Rein called Mary's phone, memorialized in the AAUW directory as NOrth 7–3691, to share the good news. In the Municipal Court of Appeals, on May 24, 1951, a two-judge majority had reversed Judge Myers, upholding the validity of one of the Reconstruction-era antidiscrimination laws.

Four months short of her eighty-eighth birthday, Mary walked less and napped more. In her journal, in which she still charted her travails as a landlord and mother-in-law, she logged a variety of complaints, including back pain and an inability to recall where she put things; she had, for example, forgotten to turn her clock forward in the spring. In spite of her hearing aid, she despaired over poor acoustics, especially during meetings or speeches. Over the phone, she managed to hear enough of a draft press release to approve it. In five typed paragraphs, the statement hailed the court's ruling, thanked the National Lawyers' Guild, and called on African Americans throughout the capital to insist on equal service. "This decision is a climax in our long hard fight to eliminate Jim Crow from Washington restaurants," it said, attributing Mary. "Of course," it continued, "I am overjoyed."

That evening, during a dinner at First Congregational Church, Terrell shared her triumph with Nettie Swift. She also entertained a bridge foursome in her home, where a rival player nabbed first prize. "Box of paper," she noted in her journal. "Nothing wonderful." Mary derived comfort, however, from an 11:15 p.m. broadcast, which announced her legal victory. In the upper left hand corner of her diary, she etched a note above the date: May 24, 1951. "Great Day!"

Five days later, Terrell and Annie Stein met with ministers and volunteers at Vermont Avenue Baptist Church, which was located in a residential neighborhood about a mile north of Thompson's Restaurant. Inside the library, twenty-four hours after a special session of the Coordinating Committee, Mary and her colleagues planned a mass meeting, slated for June 15, to celebrate her win. Item by item, they worked through their agenda, weighing details and forging consensus. They clarified the scope of the event, originally conceived to galvanize support for a four-week-old boycott of Hecht's, where management refused to serve African Americans at the downtown store's basement lunch counter. They tacked on a protest against Vernon West, who had announced he would not enforce the antidiscrimination laws until litigants had exhausted their appellate remedies.

When the conversation pivoted to arrangements for a speech from Terrell, presumably to energize the ranks, she balked. Mary had just spoken at a mother-daughter luncheon in Baltimore, she said, and, after more than half a century on the lecture platform, she had decided to quit. One of the ministers pressed, seeking an explanation for her reticence, as if unwilling to accept that she, after a career of embracing and sparking controversy, had silenced herself. Her doctor had forbidden her to accept any more speaking engagements, she said.

Later, after Annie Stein drove her home, Mary enlisted her son-in-law Lathall Langston, Phyllis's third husband, for help with another project. At a market, on the eve of Memorial Day, she selected pink and red peonies for the graves she planned to honor: Robert, her mother, her brother. In private, on the unlined pages of her journal, she ruminated about "that Mass Meeting." The thought of writing and delivering a speech filled her with dread, she wrote.

The next day, Mary searched for old letters, lamenting the task as a waste of her time, wondering about their value. She nursed a bout of indigestion with Wheatena, boiled eggs, and Bisodol, an antacid. She pored over recent editions of the *Afro*, meting out assessments in her diary. Over and over, the *Afro*'s coverage met with her approval: a "long account" of her *Thompson*'s rout; a photograph of her with Elmes and Williams; a picture of her, manning the Kresge's picket line. "*Afro* treats me handsomely," Mary wrote in her journal. Absent from her assessment, at least as logged into her diary, was an *Afro* article, published on April 14, about the "peace report." The story, which ran without a byline, identified several African Americans whom the panel had implicated, including Du Bois, Robeson, and Jernagin. Mary's name did not appear among them. At some point on May 30, Mary reversed herself. She decided to speak at the mass meeting after all, she wrote in her diary. In that setting, surrounded by supporters, she could express opinions she couldn't voice "anywhere else."

★ ★ ★ ★ ★

On June 4, 1951, the Supreme Court released a decision in *Dennis v. United States*, upholding the convictions of eleven American Communist Party leaders for violating the Smith Act, a federal law that barred conspiring to advocate or teach overthrowing the government by force. Chief Justice Vinson's opinion, joined by Reed, Minton, and Burton, capped an almost-two-year battle to contest the guilty verdicts, which were imposed after a nine-month trial. As in *Joint Anti-Fascist Refugee Committee*, the jurists fractured. In his opinion, Vinson said the defendants "intended to initiate a violent revolution whenever the propitious occasion appeared," and indoctrinated their members accordingly, meaning they "were properly and constitutionally convicted," whether or not they actually sparked rebellion.

Douglas (who was arranging logistics for a Himalayan expedition that summer—horses, porters, an audience with the Dalai Lama)—filed a dissent, as did Justice Black. Under the First Amendment, Douglas wrote, the government could not punish the teaching and advocacy of Marxist-Leninist doctrine, even if the ideology endorsed overthrowing the republic by force, unless prosecutors also offered evidence of imminent harm, such as acts of sabotage. To satisfy the Constitution, the government had to base speech restrictions on more than fear, opposition, or revulsion at the underlying content.

Throughout his opinion, Douglas alternated between legal analysis—the technicalities of the clear-and-present-danger doctrine—and a conversational, sweeping defense of the First Amendment, calling for broadmindedness, inclusion, pluralism, and dissent, not intolerance of nonconformists. Free expression "occupied an exalted position" in our constitutional framework, he said, safeguarding every religious, political, philosophical, economic, and racial group. "This has been the one single outstanding tenet that has made our institutions the symbol of freedom and equality," he wrote. "We have deemed it more costly to liberty to suppress a despised minority than to let them vent their spleen."

★ ★ ★ ★ ★

From the pulpit, the sanctuary of Metropolitan Baptist Church evoked the prow of a ship, a bulwark of strength and simplicity. Rows of straight wooden pews lined the floor beneath the vaulted ceiling and facing the speaker. At the opposite end, where worshippers filed through double doors, a trio of pointed-arch windows stretched skyward, topped by a small rose window, like a porthole.

Metropolitan Baptist resonated with symbolism. The church, located on R Street, owed its existence to former slaves who fled to Washington during

Figure 1. Before graduating from Oberlin College in 1884, Mary Church posed for a portrait in a local studio. Neither of her parents attended her graduation ceremony.

Photo Courtesy of the Oberlin College Archives.

Figure 2. Robert H. Terrell, who graduated from Harvard in 1884, was appointed to a serve as a justice of the peace in Washington by another Harvard alumnus, President Theodore Roosevelt, in 1901. Terrell continued as a presidentially appointed judge, reappointed and reconfirmed every four years, until his death in 1925.

Figure 3. Members of the National Association of Colored Women made a pilgrimage to Harpers Ferry, West Virginia in July 1896 and posed outside the engine house—seen in the background—where John Brown had been captured.

Harpers Ferry National Historical Park.

Figure 4. This undated photograph from the Historic American Buildings Survey shows Mary Church Terrell's home at 326 T St., NW, with an unknown woman standing atop the stairs. The other half of the duplex had been torn down after a fire.

Library of Congress, Prints & Photographs Division, HABS DC, WASH, 522–1.

Figure 5. Amenia Conference participants gathered at Joel Elias Spingarn's Dutchess County, New York estate in August 1916, attempting to repair the rift between the NAACP and Booker T. Washington supporters. Mary Church Terrell is seated in the second row, third from the left. Her husband Robert, who attended the gathering, did not appear in the photograph.

Oxford University Press wishes to thank The National Association for the Advancement of Colored People, for authorizing the use of this image.

Figure 6. Robert R. Moton, the Tuskegee principal, delivers his revised speech at the Lincoln Memorial dedication ceremony on May 30, 1922. Prominent African American guests walked out of the event, to protest segregated seating.

Library of Congress, Prints & Photographs Division, LC-USZ62-99406.

Figure 7. William O. Douglas on March 20, 1939, after President Franklin D. Roosevelt appointed him to the Supreme Court. Douglas, who was sworn in a month later at the age of 40, was Roosevelt's fourth Court appointment and the youngest justice in 127 years.

Library of Congress, Prints & Photographs Division, LC-DIG-hec-26327.

Figure 8. Justice Hugo L. Black, seated on the left, attended the Marian Anderson concert at the Lincoln Memorial on April 9, 1939. Next to him, on the right, was his future colleague on the Court, Senator Sherman Minton of Indiana. (The woman pictured is Black's wife.)

Library of Congress, Prints & Photographs Division, LC-H22-D-6299

Figure 9. This undated photograph, from the early 1950s, features members of the Coordinating Committee, including Mary Church Terrell, who was seated in the center of the front row, third from the left, and Annie Stein, who was seated in the front row, on the far left.

Photo courtesy of the Stein family.

Figure 10. Outside the Supreme Court on November 5, 1951, Justice Douglas conferred with Iranian Prime Minister Mohammed Mossadegh, who was in Washington for an extended stay.

State Department, courtesy of the Harry S. Truman Library.

Figure 11. In June 1952, Mary Church Terrell stood with African American ministers, outside Murphy's Dime Store, protesting its segregated lunch counter. She is at the center of the group, fourth from the left.

Courtesy: Moorland-Spingarn Research Center at Howard University.

Figure 12. Nine Supreme Court justices posed for a photograph with President Dwight D. Eisenhower at the White House, on February 6, 1953, four months before deciding *Thompson*. Justice Douglas stood in the front row, on the far left. The others in the front row, from left to right, are: Justice Reed and Chief Justice Vinson, President Eisenhower, and Justices Black and Frankfurter. In the back row are two unidentified officials plus, from left to right, Justices Minton, Clark, Jackson and Burton.

AP Photo/Harvey Georges.

Figure 13. After winning a unanimous opinion from the Supreme Court in *Thompson*, Mary Church Terrell posed for this portrait at Cedar Hill, Frederick Douglass's home in Anacostia, with a bust of Douglass in the background. The photo ran, along with her article about Douglass, in *Ebony* Magazine's October 1953 issue.

the Civil War and commissioned an African American architect, Calvin T. S. Brent, to design a house of worship, which parishioners erected by hand. The red brick facade, completed in 1882, hugged a residential block just north of Logan Circle, about five blocks from Mary's home. With its tower and steep, gabled roof, Metropolitan Baptist stood as a testament to pride and progress, calling the community's faithful to worship.

To the audience, Mary professed her joy and gratitude. With all her heart, she said, she congratulated them for their good citizenship and interest in community affairs, their intent to improve conditions. In a departure from previous speeches—some of which clanked with first-person references—she embraced the language of collectivity. We have gathered here tonight, she said, "to celebrate the great victory we have won." When the municipal court of appeals upheld the antidiscrimination laws, she added, it handed black Americans their greatest triumph here, in the capital, in almost one hundred years.

Picking up on a theme from the planning meeting, Mary blasted Vernon West for failing to enforce the ordinances. "We are not going to fuss and fume," she insisted. Rather, "in a dignified, disgusted way" we will say "we are shocked beyond expression" that West had, with his policy, encouraged hotels, restaurants, and other eating places to defy the law. His stance had fueled resistance from the civil rights community, too. Six days earlier, twenty volunteers—sixteen blacks and four whites—had staged a three-hour protest at the basement lunch counter of Hecht's on Seventh and F Streets, occupying stools, while management ignored their presence and directed African American waitresses not to serve them.

Mary reserved the core of her talk, however, for the House Committee on Un-American Activities, tracing the panel's hypocrisy on civil rights. For a considerable time, she said, HUAC had ordered witnesses to appear and queried them about their intentions, their alleged plot to overthrow the government by force. But all the Communists in Russia and around the world could not have devised a more effective scheme to derail the United States than West's decision not to enforce a valid ordinance, she said, especially a law that would spare thousands of Washingtonians the heartbreak and shame of discrimination, segregation, and injustice. "Will the House Un-American Activities Committee summon Mr. West before it to explain why, as a law-enforcement officer, he refuses to enforce a law?" "We here tonight have a right to ask that question and to insist upon an answer."

Paragraph by paragraph, Mary Church Terrell inverted McCarthyism's logic. West had sullied America's reputation abroad with his contempt for democratic principles, she said, and Joseph Stalin should thank him for the services he had rendered. Grave consequences would ensue, she predicted, if prosecutors elsewhere followed West's example, declining to enforce laws that fostered racial equality. West had behaved like a dictator, she added, one who could tutor Spain's General Francisco Franco in autocracy's nuances. And with his intransigence, West had flouted a court ruling, an affront to the *Thompson* judges who crafted the majority opinion.

For all her indignation, though, Mary elevated her grievances, mustering a sense of urgency. She refrained from opining about the *Dennis* defendants, whose photograph on the front page of the *Daily People's World*—the "only labor daily west of the Mississippi"—landed in Justice Burton's clippings file. Still, she knew the Supreme Court might one day consider her case, and the odyssey to that destination, with a prerequisite slog through the US Court of Appeals for the District of Columbia Circuit, would consume a commodity she did not measure in abundance: time.

Vernon West would not relent until *Thompson* landed before the Supreme Court, Mary said. She had no doubt, she added, that the justices would uphold the antidiscrimination ordinances. "But I am no longer 'Sweet Sixteen,'" she said, "and I would like to live long enough to see this law enforced."

★ ★ ★ ★ ★

For six days, from June 26 to July 1, 1951, delegates congregated in Atlanta, Georgia, for the NAACP's forty-second annual convention, its first such gathering in the Deep South in thirty-one years. They gathered inside the municipal auditorium, a Modernist structure located less than a mile from Georgia's state capitol. One year after Governor Talmadge vowed to resist the Supreme Court's decisions in *Henderson*, *Sweatt*, and *McLaurin*, Thurgood Marshall unveiled the NAACP's new legal strategy. During the opening session, before more than seven hundred conferees, Marshall pledged an immediate assault on segregation everywhere, including hotels, theaters, and restaurants. The program would target Jim Crow restrictions enforced by state and local laws, borrowing an education case theme: racial segregation fosters "psychological roadblocks," preventing African Americans from achieving equal social status, as guaranteed by the Fourteenth Amendment.

Throughout the conference, which featured a keynote speech by NAACP administrator Roy Wilkins and a Woman's Auxiliary reception with punch, cookies, and a receiving line, the NAACP bolstered its stance against dissidents. During a police-brutality panel, an NAACP attorney warned against aligning with Communists, who tried to exploit such cases for publicity. "Make no compromise with Communists, for theirs is the kiss of death," said Norman B. Johnson, chief counsel for the NAACP's Brooklyn, New York, chapter. Although delegates blocked, by a vote of 262 to 55, an initiative that would have created a roster of un-American organizations and banished their adherents from the NAACP's ranks, they did adopt a resolution reaffirming their commitment to barring Communist Party members from joining the NAACP. Separately, they expressed support for Du Bois, who had resigned from the NAACP in 1934, gravitated toward black nationalism, attended international peace congresses, including the one in Paris in 1949, and had been indicted for failing to register as a foreign agent.

Perhaps most significant, the delegates also endorsed a resolution insisting on "complete uniformity" and compliance with organizational policy in all efforts to upend separate but equal. Earlier in the month, the *Afro* and the *Chicago Defender* had reported a $40,000 fundraising drive—sponsored, in part, by Terrell and Mary McLeod Bethune—to finance litigation contesting Washington's racial segregation. As adopted by the convention, the NAACP's unity resolution barred members, officers, and attorneys from participating in any lawsuits "or other activities" that endeavored, "in any manner," to challenge Jim Crow in public schools, housing, and accommodations. It gave the board disciplinary authority over the noncompliant. And it said the NAACP constitution restricted membership to persons who behaved in accordance with the organization's policies and principles. When it came to raising money and resisting *Plessy* in or out of court, the NAACP had sent a message: the men in New York controlled strategy and fundraising; women belonged in the receiving line, presiding over cookies and punch.

★ ★ ★ ★ ★

Josephine Baker, the Paris-based African American chanteuse and dancer, swept into Hecht's on July 2, the day after the NAACP adjourned its convention. She had landed at National Airport three hours earlier, emerging from her plane in a suit, hat, and pumps, with a handbag dangling from the crook of her elbow. Baker, a St. Louis, Missouri, native and supporter of the French Resistance during World War II, only performed in venues that did not discriminate against African Americans, which excluded her hometown, and, of course, most of the capital. At the behest of Mary McLeod Bethune's National Council of Negro Women, Baker had booked a performance at the National Guard Armory, which did not observe Jim Crow. But first, on a humid Monday afternoon, she braved Hecht's basement lunch counter and ordered a soda.

With 175,000 square feet of retail space, Hecht's towered over Seventh and F Streets. A bronze canopy shielded the entrance, like the marquee of a Broadway theater. Inside, where walnut-finished escalators shuttled customers among the first three floors, there were specialty displays, from millinery and teen fashions to the Girl Scout shop. The men's store, a second-floor redoubt with pine paneling and leather furniture, boasted a stock of attire for fat men—or, in display-ad parlance, "Stouts." Employees, whom the company dubbed "associates," received gold watches after twenty-five years of service, talismans of a corporate culture steeped in paternalism, family loyalty, customer satisfaction—and exclusion, since the store did not hire black sales personnel.

Hecht's traced its roots to Baltimore, where Moses S. Hecht, the son of German immigrants, peddled cantaloupes door to door. In 1896, Hecht and his brother, Alexander, ventured south to 513–15 Seventh Street, NW, a narrow, five-story building in Washington's commercial district; inside, they stocked items ranging from blankets and boys' knee pants to men's underwear and women's batiste shirtwaists. After World War I, Hecht's expanded, erecting its $3 million flagship in 1925, down the block from the original site. After World War II, as defense spending boosted the capital's economy and customers fled to the suburbs, Hecht's launched an establishment in Silver Spring, Maryland, and, a year later, in 1948, won recognition as Brand Names Retailer of the Year. By 1950, Hecht's generated $85.3 million in annual sales and, among department stores nationwide, ranked as the fifth largest consumer of newspaper advertising, with a total of 5.6 million lines, five times more than nearby Garfinckel's.

After the Brotherhood Week ad, the Coordinating Committee, still under Mary's leadership, confronted Hecht's about the downtown flagship, with its segregated lunch counter. In mid-April, when Hecht's decided not to alter its policy, the committee authorized a boycott, urging customers to spurn both stores and cancel their charge accounts. On June 5, at a cornerstone-laying ceremony for a $6.5 million turquoise brick outpost in Arlington, Virginia, Charles B. Dulcan, a Hecht's executive vice president and general manager, signaled recalcitrance. "The men who founded this business were poor men, yet they, and hundreds and hundreds of others who joined them, made progress because they were free to serve their communities as they wished to be served."

Within days, the Coordinating Committee targeted the lunch counter. Beginning on June 9, volunteers staged Saturday "sitdowns," seeking service, fielding denials, and declining to vacate their stools. Every hour, the committee calculated, each demonstrator deprived Hecht's the patronage of six customers.

Now, on July 2, when a Hecht's ad in the *Post* touted the upcoming July Fourth fireworks on the grounds of the Washington Monument, Josephine Baker placed her order for a soda. She was refused. Baker, who was staying nearby at the Willard Hotel, complained to the manager, telling him that African American boys were dying in Korea, fighting for democracy their own people could not enjoy. Washington is the world capital and should be an example of living democracy, she said. He agreed with her, but said Hecht's would abide by its policy so long as Washington segregated its schools and other public facilities.

That evening, before a sold-out audience of 6,000 fans, Baker vowed to fight Jim Crow, especially in the capital. "I went exploring and saw some of the sore spots myself today. Once our people get together and realize their power, with the help of God, this thing can be licked."

★ ★ ★ ★ ★

In late June, while the NAACP caucused in Atlanta, the Solicitor General's office quietly filed a *Thompson* friend-of-the-court memorandum in the D.C. Circuit, the first time the Truman administration had surfaced in the litigation. The six-page brief, which bore Philip Perlman's name, said the capital's racial discrimination was "a serious flaw" in the republic, a matter of grave concern to the entire nation. "The United States is now endeavoring to prove to the entire world that democracy is the best form of government yet devised by man. It must by its own example demonstrate the superiority of the free, democratic way of life."

The Coordinating Committee inaugurated a picket line outside Hecht's three weeks later, after Bethune composed a *Defender* column, which ran on July 14, citing the Baker incident and praising Perlman and Mary. "In every field of living[,]" Bethune wrote, "we must push down the barriers of quibbling and evasion, and align ourselves solidly—in the Capital of our Nation and in the least of its hamlets—against the forces of segregation and separatism that divide and imperil our democratic way of life." Before a week had elapsed, the first wave of protestors arrived at Seventh and F Streets. At 4 p.m. on Friday, July 20, about a half-dozen volunteers descended, bearing signs urging customers to stay away. Within an hour, eighteen pick-eters had blanketed the entrances, under the gaze of store officials and police officers.

At a press conference the following week, Truman declined to comment on the antidiscrimination laws and West's decision not to enforce them, saying the matter was pending in the courts. Meanwhile, Annie Stein gave the *Afro* an initial estimate of the picket line's effectiveness. By her tally, 90 percent of Hecht's prospective African American customers—and 5 percent of whites—had honored the protest, declining to bypass the marchers and enter the store. By mid-September, roughly two weeks after Justice Douglas returned from his Himalayan trek and called for diplomatic recognition of China, saying it was "the only logical course," Congressman John E. Rankin, a Mississippi Democrat, introduced a bill to repeal the Reconstruction an-tidiscrimination laws. In an interview with the *Afro*, Rankin said they would foment racial strife in the capital if they remained "on the books."

★ ★ ★ ★ ★

On January 13, 1952, the cover of the *New York Times* magazine featured General Dwight D. Eisenhower, clad in uniform, inspecting US troops. In the week's top story, Eisenhower had decided to accept the Republican presidential nomination, were it offered to him. Over in the *Times's* Book Review, *Strange Lands and Friendly People,* Justice Douglas's account of his Asia and Middle East trips in 1949 and 1950, ranked at number 8 on the general (meaning nonfiction) bestsellers list, where it had presided for three of the previous four weeks. On the fiction list were *The Caine Mutiny* by Herman Wouk and *The Catcher in the Rye* by J. D. Salinger.

The issue also contained an essay by Douglas titled "The Black Silence of Fear," addressing the dangers of intolerance and the nation's mood, the "drift" toward repression. To the delight of some and the dismay of others, Douglas had started to do what Supreme Court justices were not supposed to do—make public pronouncements about policy matters. During an impromptu press conference at the San Francisco airport on August 31, 1951, after re-turning from his trip along the southern borders of China and Russia, he had announced that the United States should offer formal recognition of the new Communist nation. In public, the White House remained silent. But Senator Tom Connally, a Texas Democrat and Truman loyalist who chaired the Foreign Relations Committee, said Douglas was neither secre-tary of state nor president—and never would be. The United States had no intention of recognizing "Red China," Connally added, before lashing out at Douglas again. "I think he ought to stay home instead of roaming all around the world and Asia making fool statements. We're really at war—in a sense—with Red China now."

Truman dispatched a three-paragraph letter to Douglas on September 13, marked "*Personal.*" With a flash of pique, Truman thanked the jurist for his "continued interest in politics and foreign affairs," but informed him that he had been "somewhat embarrassed" by Douglas's comments on Communist China. Bluntly, he informed Douglas of his position: the United States would never recognize "that cut throat organization" so long as he could prevent it. "Since you are on the highest Court in the land[,] it seems to me that the best thing you can possibly do would be to give your best effort to that Court and let the President of the United States run the political end of foreign and domestic affairs."

Douglas sent Truman a response on September 25, a four-page, single-spaced clarification, defending his views on foreign policy, reiterating his desire to stay on the Court, and expressing his hatred of Communism. Still, he did not refrain from opining, based on his travels, about America's diminishing influence. "I have returned from Asia full of fear," he wrote. "The day may not be far distant when we are left in all our loneliness with our atomic bombs." Truman replied with a handwritten note on October 2, saying he felt "much better," conceding his own impulsivity, and offering to chat some day, so they could "clear the air."

Douglas, however, kept meddling. Later that fall, on November 5, he entertained a visit at the Court from Mohammad Mossadegh, Iran's elected prime minister. The day before their meeting, the *Times* had reviewed *Strange Lands and Friendly People*, in which Douglas wrote about having seen Mossadegh in 1950—when he was not yet prime minster—deliver a speech condemning British control of Persian oil. Mossadegh—who had in fact embarked on a plan to nationalize Iranian oil production—was in Washington seeking a settlement with the British, who effectuated control through an entity known as the Anglo-Iranian Oil Company. He arrived at the tribunal with an entourage, including Lt. Col. Vernon Walters, a military-intelligence officer and Truman confidant who spoke six Western European languages, Chinese, and Russian. Inside and outside the Court, a photographer documented the event: Douglas and Mossadegh walking together, down a corridor; Douglas and Mossadegh huddled in conversation, with the Library of Congress in the background, while Walters leaned in, listening.

Douglas wrote Truman again on November 12, directing his letter to Key West, Florida, where the president had gone for a vacation. After apologizing for the intrusion, and stressing that he wrote "only as a by-stander," Douglas asked Truman to lend or grant "the Persians" $10 million a month for a year. (Mossadegh had also asked Truman for financial assistance, in a letter dated November 9.) Such a loan, Douglas wrote, would give Mossadegh time to liquidate British control. "If Russian influence enters Persia, it will be a very dark day," Douglas warned.

Truman, who wrote Douglas a week later from Key West, did not respond to the justice's proposal, or even mention Persia. (He had responded to Mossadegh on November 14, saying he needed more time to make a decision.) Instead, Truman thanked Douglas for an inscribed copy of *Strange Lands and Friendly People*. "I'm reading it with a lot of interest," he wrote.

Now, in his January 13 *Times* essay, Douglas highlighted "an ominous trend": intolerance of unorthodoxy. In declarative sentences, he retooled a speech he had given at Brandeis University in November, a few days after his session with Mossadegh. He touted his approach as an author, venturing into the world's "back regions" on foot, on horseback, or by Jeep and talking with villagers and peasants. He criticized American foreign policy for its militaristic focus on anti-Communism and staving off Soviet domination, at the expense of promoting democratic ideals and freedom. According to the prevailing consensus, he wrote, those who disagree "must be secretly aligning with Russia." At home in the United States, fear of Communist subversion had been "magnified and exalted far beyond its realities." "Character assassination" and distrust abounded; innocent gestures were conflated into indicia of disloyalty. "Those who are unorthodox are suspect," he wrote. "Everyone who does not follow the military policymakers is suspect."

★ ★ ★ ★ ★

Mary Church Terrell perched atop a stool in Hecht's basement, at the lunch counter, a few days after Douglas's piece ran in the *Times*. Her dining companions were Alice Trigg, the boycott chairman; Helen Brown, the captain of volunteer recruits; and Annie Stein. An *Afro* reporter joined them as well, primed to chronicle their reception.

More than eight months into the boycott, the Coordinating Committee claimed to have deprived Hecht's of $6 million in business. A Hecht's spokesman denied that figure, citing quarterly financial statements. Even with associates ringing cash registers in Virginia and Maryland, though, the Washington store generated roughly 60 percent of the chain's sales. The financial impact of the boycott could not be ignored. On January 14, two weeks before the end of the fiscal year, store officials reversed the lunch-counter policy, directing workers not to discriminate. The committee issued a statement, urging supporters to reopen their charge accounts. The following day, when the *Afro* called to confirm the new stance, James Rotto, the sales and publicity director, issued a challenge. "Why don't you come down and see for yourself?"

During the first two weeks of January, Mary had written nothing in her 1952 journal (a Week-at-a-Glance calendar given to her by Annie Stein for Christmas). Day after day, as the new year unfolded, the entries remained blank: no meetings or dinners; no receptions or cocktail parties. Mary even failed to note the *Thompson* oral argument on January 7, when all nine judges of the D.C. Circuit presided en banc—a highly unusual step. In essence, as their collective presence telegraphed, the case raised issues of such importance the entire tribunal had resolved, on its own initiative, to participate, rather than delegate resolution to a three-judge panel.

Based on her calendar, one might surmise that Mary Church Terrell was not well. But on the afternoon of January 16, with the Hecht's white sale in progress in all three stores, she radiated vitality. As she chatted with a reporter and ate her lunch—ham sandwich, pie, coffee with cream and sugar—she distilled a lesson, as if reverting to her days as a teacher. "We're second-class citizens because we sit idly by."

Afterward, outside the store, Mary, Stein, and their colleagues posed for a photographer. Around them, on streets that had been overrun by rioters in 1919, stood commercial buildings that had borne witness to milestones, personal and historic. In the early 1850s, from headquarters nearby, an abolitionist newspaper serialized *Uncle Tom's Cabin*. Less than a block away, at 609 F Street, Robert Terrell and John Lynch had practiced law and real estate together, inside the Capital Savings Bank Building. A few doors farther down, at 615 F Street, Charles Hamilton Houston had worked alongside his father.

For the photograph, slated to run on the *Afro*'s front page, the activists arrayed shoulder-to-shoulder, with Hecht's bronze doors at their backs and the company's name overhead, rendered in sans-serif capital letters. Annie Stein positioned herself near the back, on the far right, clad in a hat and coat, holding a purse. On the far left stood Mary, her shoulders squared and spine erect, bedecked in a fur-trimmed coat and black hat. In her right hand, she gripped a cane, pressing it into the pavement, as if marking the spot.

Up on Capitol Hill, meanwhile, roughly a mile's distance from Hecht's, Senator James O. Eastland, a Mississippi Democrat, introduced a bill authorizing Congress to declare an internal security emergency within the meaning of the McCarran Act—a move the law itself entrusted to the president. Eastland, a plantation owner with a fondness for cigars and Chivas Regal, sat on the Judiciary Committee's Internal Security Subcommittee, the Senate's equivalent of the HUAC. Known to fellow Mississippians as "Big Jim," he had won his first full term in 1942, vowing, in campaign-trail appearances outside local courthouses, to prevent blacks and whites from dining together in Washington.

In his legislative proposal, Eastland purported to bypass the president and authorize Attorney General McGrath to start detaining anyone likely to commit sabotage or espionage during a foreign-led internal insurrection. As a *Baltimore Sun* reporter gleaned from sources, McGrath had already undertaken preliminary steps to establish such facilities, with an estimated capacity of 3,000 suspects, at three locations: a former military airport in Arizona and two World War II–era prisoner-of-war camps in Arizona and Oklahoma. But Eastland, who was up for reelection in two years, claimed to have received "reliable information" that 20,000 Kremlin agents were already in the United States, intent on its destruction. "If we are to keep faith with those of our own flesh and blood who are facing the bullets of the Communists on the battlefields of Korea, the least we can do is to promptly seize and detain under lock and key each and every one of the 20,000 identifiable, trained, hardened traitors."

★ ★ ★ ★ ★

Nettie Swift availed herself of a typewriter six weeks later. She was in New York, staying with one of her daughters on Riverside Drive. As she approached her ninetieth year, a white-haired doyenne with spectacles, Nettie had trouble seeing and reading. She nonetheless pecked out a letter to Mary, occasionally mistaking adjacent letters and numbers. (At the top of the page, she typed her address as "404 Rif3ewie3 EDrive.") "Hurrah" for the Hecht's victory, Nettie wrote. "The world does move."

Then, Nettie imagined Mary's reaction and responded to it. You will say progress is too slow, which is true, but we must be grateful and "keep pushing." After musing about her own upcoming birthday, and her inability to fathom why she had lived so long, Nettie fumed about the pace of appellate decision-making, as if it were an affront to prospective nonagenarians.

I suppose you are rushing around as usual, she wrote. She warned Mary to guard against back pain and stave off bronchitis, seeming to anticipate, though, that the woman she'd known for roughly seventy years would not slow down. "I wonder what the co-ordinating Co.*s next move will be," she wrote.

8

A Bigger Step Is in Order

On a Saturday in early June 1952, Mary Church Terrell joined the queue outside G.C. Murphy's, a five-and-ten-cent store located at Twelfth and F Streets, NW, five blocks from Hecht's. The night before, she and Nettie Swift had dined at the Water Gate Inn, a Foggy Bottom restaurant with exposed beams, brick fireplaces, views of the Potomac River, and a menu featuring popovers, prime rib, and Dutch apple-cheese pie. In her journal, she didn't mention whether the dining room had ever practiced segregation or whether, like the Mayflower, it was a venue that accepted her without question, or even what she had eaten; but she did note that "dinner was a treat." On the sidewalk near Murphy's, where commercial storefronts and cars lined the curb across the street, Mary paused for a photograph, clad in a tailored short-sleeve dress, pumps, and a brimmed hat. Six African American ministers grouped in a semicircle around her, along with the wife of one of the clergymen.

During the Coordinating Committee's two-year boycott of downtown five-and-ten-cent stores, all but one of the chains had folded, yielding to integration. Three had shifted in response to negotiations with the committee or internal deliberations: Woolworth's, Grand's, and McBride's. Kresge's, of course, had capitulated after six weeks of picketing. Neisner's folded in the summer of 1951, citing the *Thompson* decision in the Municipal Court of Appeals. By June 7, 1952, one hold-out remained: the F Street outpost of G.C. Murphy's, a McKeesport, Pennsylvania-based company with three Washington branches, only one of which still adhered to Jim Crow. The Washington-area manager had vowed to continue segregating there until the Supreme Court ordered him to stop.

After their win at Hecht's, and a brokered triumph at Lansburgh's Department Store in March, Mary and the committee had targeted Murphy's. She wrote the company's chairman on April 24, 1952, conveying her shock that a store with northern roots would number, among dime stores, as the capital's last Jim Crow adherent. When that failed, the committee launched a picket line outside the F Street establishment.

The clergymen around Mary were tall and short, young and old, attired in suits, ties, and fedoras. They held the wooden shafts of neatly lettered signs, some resting them on their shoulders, as if awaiting a turn at bat. "I FOUGHT IN KOREA but...CAN'T EAT HERE!" read one placard. "WE WANT TO SIT DOWN TO EAT" read another. Next to Mary, a man raised his sign aloft. "MINISTERS OF THE GOSPEL SAY END DISCRIMINATION." Mary anchored the group, like a hinge. Alone among the participants, she carried no sign. Instead, she balanced a purse in one hand and a cane in the other, leaning away from the camera, with her chin tilted upward.

On Monday, June 9, two days after the photograph was taken, the Supreme Court added two civil rights cases to its fall argument calendar: *Briggs v. Elliott*, which arose in Clarendon County, South Carolina, and *Brown v. Board of Education*, which originated in Topeka, Kansas. The NAACP and Thurgood Marshall had shepherded both through the lower courts. Together, they presented to the justices the very issue they had evaded in *Sweatt* and *McLaurin*: the constitutionality of segregated public elementary and high schools.

★ ★ ★ ★ ★

President Truman assumed his place at the podium on Howard University's campus around 5:45 p.m., outfitted in a cap and gown. It was June 13, 1952. Secret Service agents lingered nearby, stationed at either end of the row in which Mary sat, up front in a section for dignitaries. Nearby, in the same row, sat Mary Bethune, whose speaking engagement in Englewood, New Jersey, had been withdrawn, six weeks earlier, amid protests that HUAC had once linked her to allegedly subversive organizations. Earlier in the day, Terrell had attended a White House reception for AAUW members, hosted by First Lady Bess Truman.

Howard University was located about half a mile from the T Street home Mary once shared with Robert. The campus hugged a hilltop, dotted with red-brick buildings. At the base of a quadrangle sat the Founders Library, a federally financed tribute to intellectual inquiry—dedicated by Interior Secretary Harold Ickes in 1939—with a Georgian facade, limestone trim, and a clock tower modeled after Philadelphia's Independence Hall. Next door, set back from the street, was Andrew Rankin Memorial Chapel, where mourners had eulogized Charles Hamilton Houston. Across Howard Place, beyond a Carnegie library completed in 1910, rose Frederick Douglass Memorial Hall, an architectural soulmate of the founders' building.

Roughly 15,000 guests had congregated outside Douglass hall—graduates, parents, and alumni—for the university's eighty-fourth commencement. For Truman, the engagement came in his administration's waning months, eleven days after the Supreme Court rebuked him in a separation-of-powers showdown known as the *Steel Seizure Case*. Faced with a threatened labor strike earlier that spring, Truman had issued an executive order, directing his commerce secretary to wrest control of steel mills nationwide, citing wartime-production needs. Vinson had assured Truman, in confidence, such a course could withstand legal scrutiny. But on June 2, by a 6-to-3 margin, the justices ruled to the contrary, telling Truman that he had no authority, express or implied, as commander-in-chief or otherwise, to federalize privately owned factories. Two of Truman's appointees, Burton and Clark, sided with the majority, leaving Vinson, Reed, and Minton as the president's lone defenders.

Now, with General Dwight D. Eisenhower vying for the Republican nomination at the party's upcoming Chicago convention—and promising to appoint African Americans to diplomatic posts abroad—Truman was eying his legacy. First he saluted the institution that had invited him and the "vision" of its founders, who created a university dedicated to educating freed slaves. Talent and genius knew no boundaries of race, nationality, or creed, he said. "The United States needs the imagination, the energy, and the skills of every single one of its citizens."

Shifting to his administration's record, Truman looked back to 1946, touting his decision to create the Committee on Civil Rights. Since then, he maintained, the country had witnessed progress in every region, in all aspects of national life. Just the other day, he added, one of his southern friends told him the previous five years had been the nation's best ever for race relations. The audience applauded. Bethune nodded her head in agreement.

But with southern Democrats blocking his legislative agenda, the milestones Truman cited were due mainly either to executive order or the Supreme Court. He alluded to the decisions in *Shelley*, *Sweatt*, and *McLaurin*, hailing them for shattering racial barriers in residential neighborhoods and publicly financed graduate schools. He heralded the integration of the armed forces, now that the navy and air force had abolished racial restrictions and the army was advancing toward the same goal. And, as if addressing the justices, or anyone who feared violence would rock the South should the Court overturn *Plessy*, Truman pointed to the absence of civil unrest. "The prophets of doom have been proved wrong. The civil rights program has not weakened our country—it has made our country stronger."

Still, Truman conceded that there was unfinished business, vowing to push Congress to adopt his civil rights program. Indirectly, he also sniped at Eisenhower. "I am not one of those who feel that we can leave these matters up to the States alone, or that we can rely solely on the efforts of men of good will," he said.

Before closing, Truman returned to the Cold War. Around the world, people envied the "American way of life," he said, but Americans also had an obligation "to lift up the weak and the downtrodden" around the globe, including those who lived in former colonies or possessions. Our nation "is great because of its diversity," he added, and we must bear this in mind as we seek world peace; if we lay aside "false ideas of racial superiority," we can help others improve their lives. "If all the people of the world, including the people of the Soviet Union, could know and appreciate this fact, lasting peace and universal justice would not be a dream. It would be a reality."

Truman was not the only one thinking about the coming presidential election. During a Sunday-afternoon radio spot transmitted over WUST two days later, Mary engaged in a question-and-answer session. According to a transcription of the interview, the moderator, Revella Clay, introduced her studio guest as "a very famous woman" who had seriously considered the candidates. Washington residents still had no voting rights, no power to cast a ballot for local elected officials or for president. Nevertheless, Clay announced that Mary Church Terrell, "a loyal Republican for almost eighty-eight years," had decided to back a Democrat, and asked Mary to explain why.

I believed in the GOP "with all my heart," Mary replied. "But[,] as of a few days ago, I am a Democrat[—]an Averell Harriman Democrat," referring to Truman's former Commerce Secretary and the former ambassador to Great Britain and Russia. As a justification, Mary gave a simple one: Harriman believed in civil rights, and if elected, would recommend federal action to banish segregation in Washington. Clay quarried for more insight, asking whether Mary had qualms about forsaking a party she had supported—including her work as a speaker in 1920—since women gained the right to vote. Mary responded, that it had been an "easy" decision; she had grown disillusioned with Republicans long ago, when they aligned with "Dixiecrats," southern Democrats in Congress, and Harriman had won her by endorsing integrated public schools. Throughout her life, Mary Church Terrell had idolized public figures, ranging from John Brown to Charles Lindbergh, and once again her hero worship turned on race relations. Black children and white children would grow up attending different schools, "misunderstanding each other," and feeling, perhaps, as if they were enemies. Harriman understood that peril.

With Democrats pinning their hopes on the twenty-year legacy of FDR and Truman and their domestic agendas, Mary paid homage to the outgoing administration. Truman had earned her gratitude in 1946, for assembling his Civil Rights Committee, and she had great respect for him. "I believe he has been the greatest president this country has had since Abraham Lincoln, in so far as my racial group is concerned."

★ ★ ★ ★ ★

On a weeknight inside Murphy's, eleven days later, Terrell requested a slice of pie. Around her, roughly two dozen sit-down strikers had descended, including a Baptist minister. Men and women had lined up side by side, seated in identical swivel chairs with padded backs. On the wall facing them, a sign read, in part, "RESTAURANT." Despite the radio appearance, in recent days, Mary had retreated from public view, diverted by the plight of her nephew, Thomas, a newly sworn-in member of the Washington bar. Thomas resembled her brother in many ways, including his air of refinement, his light complexion, and, now, his professional training. After her brother died in January 1937, Mary had moved to become her nephew's guardian—and fended off, in a New York courtroom, a competing bid by her half-brother Robert, whose efforts she opposed because, she wrote in her journal, she didn't want her then-young nephew raised in Memphis, with its segregated streetcars and movie theaters. In the intervening years, Mary had doted on Thomas. She had given him an allowance and paid his rent, nagged him about finding a job, and stewed about his future, dreading his susceptibility to the draft.

Earlier in the week, she had ushered Thomas into Senator Herbert H. Lehman's office, hoping to enlist the New York Democrat in the cause of securing her nephew an air force commission. Lehman, a World War I veteran, former governor, and ex-investment banker, did not meet with them. After a two-hour wait, during which Lehman's secretary wondered aloud about the propriety of such a request, Mary and Thomas left. Lehman called Mary that evening, however, saying he wanted to see her.

Now, on Thursday, June 26, 1952, a five-and-ten-cent store with roots in Appalachian mining communities refused to accommodate her. The manager of Murphy's insisted she take her place, on foot, at the counter's Jim Crow section.

Mary turned on him. "Aren't you ashamed asking an old woman to stand up in order to get served in the nation's capital?" she said. "You know I can't stand."

★ ★ ★ ★ ★

In late July, Democrats convened in Chicago, where they nominated Adlai E. Stevenson, a first-term Illinois governor, as their presidential standard-bearer. Stevenson, whose namesake grandfather served as vice president during Grover Cleveland's second term, had been Truman's top choice all along. Stevenson, in turn, bowed to party leaders, including Truman, in selecting Senator John J. Sparkman of Alabama, a tenant farmer's son, as his running mate. Sparkman, revered in the Senate for his affability, had resisted Truman's civil rights program, calling it a "colossal blunder." More recently, he had helped broker a platform truce among northern and southern delegates. In its final iteration, the party's 1952 ticket, with its stay-the-course tributes to Truman and FDR, bore the hallmarks of sectional compromise.

In separate provisions, the platform endorsed Truman's "loyalty program," which southern congressmen had subverted to undermine civil rights activists, and home rule for the District of Columbia, which southern congressmen opposed, fearing it would enfranchise the capital's African American residents, who would vote to end segregation. A six-paragraph proviso on civil rights teemed with similar contradictions. On the one hand, it approved Truman's policies, including federal civil rights legislation and desegregating the armed forces. On the other, it embraced states' rights, with plaudits for cooperation among citizens and state and local governments. The plank, which alluded to the outcomes of *Shelley*, *Sweatt*, and *McLaurin*, said nothing about desegregating public elementary and high schools. Nor did it take a position on Washington's Jim Crow.

Eisenhower, the Republican nominee, sat down with NAACP representatives in late August, including administrator Roy Wilkins. During a forty-five-minute interview, Eisenhower refused to endorse federal fair employment legislation, saying he would enlist a commission to study workplace discrimination and fashion recommendations. He did, however, express support for abolishing segregation in Washington, though he professed a lack of clarity, given congressional oversight, about how to accomplish such a goal. The

NAACP issued a press release, saying his declaration about desegregating the capital lacked specifics.

With the onset of the back-to-school shopping season, Mary sent a letter to local ministers under the Coordinating Committee's name, urging them to remind their congregations only to patronize enterprises, such as Kresge's and Woolworth's, that did not segregate customers. "BUT DON'T BUY EVEN ONE PENCIL AT MURPHY'S DIME STORE." The next day, on August 29, a confidential informant told the Federal Bureau of Investigation's Washington field office that Communist Party members in Washington had been encouraged to participate in the Coordinating Committee's activities. Then, with a children's picket line planned for the coming Saturday, Murphy's Washington district manager, C. P. Kerley, called Annie Stein on September 3 and asked for a meeting. In his office that afternoon, at 3 p.m., he met with Annie and Mary and agreed to integrate the store, starting the next morning.

Before they left Murphy's, the lunch-counter manager escorted them to his post. From their seats, they ordered coffee and strawberry shortcake. Afterward, the committee sent another letter to supporters under Mary's signature, this time announcing victory. "Today, every dime store without exception in the city of Washington is serving everyone equally and peacefully, bringing closer the day when one third of Washington's citizens will be treated as first class citizens."

But for Mary and the committee, vindication proved short-lived. On September 13, the *Afro-American* reported that over the local NAACP's objection Truman had signed a law expanding Washington's trespass statute. The legislation, introduced by a Democratic congressman from South Carolina and a Democratic senator from West Virginia, made it a misdemeanor to enter a public or private dwelling in the capital against the will of the person in charge and remain in place after fielding an entreaty to leave. Mary had criticized the proposal as ill-conceived, warning it could be deployed against African Americans who staged sit-down protests in white elementary schools or public playgrounds. Sponsors of the bill said it would control vandalism and loitering around public schools.

★ ★ ★ ★ ★

On her eighty-ninth birthday, September 23, 1952, Mary logged one event in her journal: a visit from Annie Stein. An official celebration—a luncheon in Terrell's honor at the Hotel Washington—would take place at the end of the following week. Stein, who stayed for a few hours, gave Mary a book—a gift from her and Arthur—titled *A Documentary History of the Negro People in the United States*, edited by Herbert Aptheker, a white Marxist historian, with a preface by W. E. B. Du Bois. Another well-wisher proffered Mary a book as well, *South of Freedom*, by Carl T. Rowan, a black journalist who chronicled his rail and bus journey below the Mason-Dixon line (a project she once considered undertaking herself, under a pseudonym). In her journal, Mary noted that Rowan was "an Oberlin man."

Meanwhile, the *Afro's* front page on September 23 featured an update from Eisenhower's campaign train, alongside a story about a possible legal challenge to Washington's new trespass law. In St. Joseph, Missouri, an African American woman, clad in a red-checked dress and white apron, her head wrapped in a white bandanna, presented the candidate with a box of Aunt Jemima pancake mix. A public-relations officer for Quaker Oats claimed credit for the incident, saying Aunt Jemima was "the greatest legendary character in the world, with the exception of Santa Claus."

At 9:30 that evening, Senator Richard M. Nixon, the thirty-nine-year-old Republican vice-presidential nominee, appeared on national television after *The Milton Berle Show*. Nixon, of course, had vaulted to national prominence as a congressman with his probe of Alger Hiss, the former State Department official who was serving a five-year prison sentence. For several days Nixon had faced allegations about his own fitness for office, stemming from a claim that he siphoned money from a campaign fund, worth an estimated $16,000, to defray personal expenses.

From the outset of his thirty-minute speech—the so-called Checkers Speech, named for the family dog, which had also been a gift—Nixon trawled for sympathy. He deflected any implication of impropriety, calling the accusations an attack on his "honesty and integrity." More than once, he referred to them as a "smear." On air, he unveiled the fruits of an independent review by Price, Waterhouse & Co., the accounting firm, and Gibson, Dunn & Crutcher, a Los Angeles law firm, and proceeded to read the attorneys' conclusion, which exonerated him of wrongdoing. In defiance of a directive from Eisenhower's advisors, Nixon refused to yield his spot on the ticket, saying he was not "a quitter."

The public rallied behind Nixon. The *Afro* dredged up information about his $41,000 Washington home, disclosed as a debt during his speech. Inside the Recorder of Deeds' Office, the *Afro* learned that the deed to Nixon's center-hall colonial, located at 4801 Tilden Street, NW, contained a restrictive covenant prohibiting its sale to "persons of negro blood or extraction," including Jews, Armenians, Persians, or Syrians. As the *Afro* reported, the Nixons consented to the provision on July 5, 1951, more than three years after the Supreme Court, in *Hurd*, proclaimed such covenants judicially unenforceable in the capital. In a follow-up story a week later, the *Afro* said that the deed to Senator Sparkman's Washington home contained the same restriction, as did those of dwellings owned by his Alabama colleague, Senator Joseph Lister Hill, and Democratic senators from Tennessee, South Carolina, and West Virginia.

On October 7, three days later, the *Afro*'s front page took aim at Eisenhower, who had forged his candidacy around his popularity and war-hero status, with thirty-second televised political advertisements and a three-word slogan: "I Like Ike." Until his nomination, the *Afro* reported, Eisenhower had owned a partial stake in a Howard Johnson's restaurant, located at Fourteenth Street and New York Avenue, NW. As *Afro* readers knew, in late August—while Eisenhower professed support for ending segregation in Washington—the restaurant allegedly fired its night manager for serving two African American soldiers.

In Boston, meanwhile, an *Afro* reporter quizzed Patricia Nixon, the vice-presidential candidate's wife, who blamed the Truman administration for Washington's segregation, saying she and her husband had to sign the restrictive covenant. "We both have had to work for a living and until Mr. Nixon was elected to the Senate, had to count our pennies like every other poor couple," she said. "We know what it means all right, and what the colored people, in their struggle, have to contend with."

Outside the pages of the *Afro*—which on October 7, endorsed Stevenson—the election emerged as a referendum on Truman, including the issues of Korea and Communist subversion. During a televised speech from Detroit on October 24, Eisenhower promised his administration would focus on ending the war, and, if elected, he would travel to Korea, where American forces had suffered more than 100,000 casualties, including more than 25,000 deaths. The next day, both parties flooded the *Afro* with full-page ads. "Jim Crow Sparkman would Be One Heartbeat from the White House," warned one, authorized by the Republican National Committee. Democrats countered with a photograph of Eisenhower shaking hands with South Carolina governor James F. Byrnes, a former Supreme Court justice who had threatened to close his state's public schools, rather than integrate them.

Mary endorsed Stevenson on October 30, five days before the election, saying that she was "born a Republican" but she believed he would abolish segregation in the capital and enforce the Reconstruction-era civil rights laws. "Governor Stevenson has shown beyond a shadow of a doubt that he judges people by their ability, character and words on general principles and not by the color of their skin," she said in one of two press releases about her distributed by the Stevenson-Sparkman Club of the District of Columbia. "If Governor Stevenson is elected there is every reason to hope and believe that he will use the prestige and power which a President of the United States possesses to see that this law [*sic*], declared valid by the Municipal Court of Appeals, is enforced," she said in a separate release issued in her name. The *Star* converted her statement into a four-paragraph story, which it ran on page 4. In her journal, she inscribed the headline verbatim: "Mrs. Terrell, 89, Backs Democrats for First Time."

On November 4, voters handed Eisenhower 55 percent of the popular vote and an electoral-college landslide—thirty-nine of the forty-eight states, including Illinois and Missouri, the home turf, respectively, of Stevenson and Truman. The Democratic ticket netted only two border states, Kentucky and West Virginia, and a crescent-shaped wedge of the Deep South: Georgia, Arkansas, Alabama, Mississippi, Louisiana, and the Carolinas. On Capitol Hill, Republicans leveraged Eisenhower's appeal into a takeover, eking out a ten-seat majority in the House and a one-vote margin in the Senate.

★ ★ ★ ★ ★

By 10 a.m. on December 9, 1952, more than 250 hopefuls had assembled, including students, ministers, and government workers, in the marble corridor outside the Supreme Court's chamber. Men and women, black and white, stood in business attire and dress shoes, speaking in hushed voices, bearing thermos jars filled with coffee. As photographers and television cameramen recorded images of their vigil, they waited, hoping to land one of the roughly fifty seats available to the general public.

That afternoon, the Court would begin the first of three days of oral argument, spread over ten hours, in five school-desegregation cases. Four of the five—*Brown*, *Briggs*, and proceedings from Delaware and Virginia—had NAACP lawyers, including Thurgood Marshall, who was slated to argue *Briggs*, the South Carolina case. The Washington-based litigation, *Bolling v. Sharpe*, traced its antecedents to Charles Hamilton Houston, who, beginning in the late 1940s, had challenged the capital's segregated public schools, seeking to make them, at every stage of instruction, equal to white facilities. After Houston's death, James M. Nabrit Jr., a Howard law professor, mounted an all-out challenge to segregation, not just a quest for all-black schools that were equal to white facilities. On November 10, 1952, six days after the election, the Court had granted certiorari in *Bolling*, then pending before the US Court of Appeals for the D.C. Circuit, and bundled it for argument with the four other school cases.

A week before oral argument, on December 2, Attorney General James P. McGranery and Philip Elman had filed a thirty-two-page friend-of-the-court brief in all five cases, urging the Court to abandon the separate-but-equal doctrine. Elman, notwithstanding his role as an advocate for the federal government, saw himself as Frankfurter's honorary law clerk, a life-long subordinate and confidant. He and the justice spoke frequently by phone, often on Sunday evenings, when Frankfurter shared gossip, and, in the school-segregation cases, communiqués from within the tribunal. In his filing, Elman had led with a discussion of the capital, underscoring the importance of undoing segregation in Washington, where, he said, the issue of racial discrimination was "particularly acute."

"This city is the window through which the world looks into our house," Elman wrote. He quoted Truman's 1948 civil rights message, with its aspirational notion of making Washington "a true symbol" of freedom. He quoted the report of Truman's Civil Rights Committee, with its rebuke to Washington as "a failure of democracy." Finally, he quoted Secretary of State Acheson: "Although progress is being made, the continuance of racial discrimination in the United States remains a source of constant embarrassment to this Government in the day-to-day conduct of its foreign relations; and it jeopardizes the effective maintenance of our moral leadership of the free and democratic nations of the world."

Inside the Court, an *Afro* reporter circulated among the potential spectators. This was one of the most important cases since *Dred Scott*, said an NAACP attorney from Philadelphia. A janitor's wife from West Point, Virginia, referred to her sixteen-year-old daughter, who according to her mother, had been on a strike of some kind since early September, along with about two dozen other students, all holding classes among themselves to protest conditions at their school. A white woman who taught in a segregated Texas high school said that nothing about segregation was right.

Mary meanwhile was battling a cold. Her affliction surfaced in her journal a week earlier, the same day she learned of Annie Stein's decision to move to Brooklyn. It was a tragedy, Mary told a lunch companion at the YWCA; she'd never be able to manage without her. The next morning, her nephew Thomas came to visit, bearing news that she had been dreading: the army had drafted him and, within a week, he would be leaving for basic training. Mary stayed in bed that entire day, and in her room for the next forty-eight hours.

On December 9, while the Supreme Court contemplated the fate of segregated public schools in Washington and elsewhere, Mary spent much of the afternoon with Thomas. After they said good-bye, she turned to her diary and updated her condition: at home, in bed. She wrote of her admiration for her nephew's intellect and the breadth of his reading; she relished conversations with him about current events, more so than with anyone else. "God bless and protect my dear boy!"

The next day and into the day following, oral arguments in the school cases continued before the Supreme Court. One of them was *Bolling*, which arose when the Washington board of education refused to admit African American students to an all-white junior high school in 1950. As framed by Nabrit, the Howard law professor whose complaint the district court had dismissed for failure to state a claim upon which relief could be granted, resolution hinged on whether the capital's dual schools violated the Fifth Amendment's due process clause, since the Fourteenth Amendment only applied to the states. Nabrit argued that Washington's segregated educational system unconstitutionally deprived black students of their protected Fifth Amendment right to choose to attend nonsegregated schools—and did so arbitrarily, solely on the basis of race, a rationale that did not serve a legitimate educational purpose.

In his friend-of-the-court brief, Philip Elman had suggested an out in *Bolling*. Unlike the states involved in the four other cases, all of which had mandated segregated education, Congress had not, with "explicit and mandatory language" required racially segregated schools in Washington, D.C., he said. If lawmakers had done so, he added, "a grave and difficult question" would arise under the Fifth Amendment—meaning the Court would have to address whether Congress, by imposing segregated schools on Washington, had unreasonably or arbitrarily deprived black schoolchildren of fundamental rights or liberties. But the Court could skirt the issue altogether, he wrote, by assuming Congress had neither approved nor disapproved segregated schools in the capital and remanding the case to the district court with instructions to declare so directly. The board of education would then need to decide, as "its own independent choice," whether to abandon or preserve segregation—clarifying the situation for possible future litigation. As framed by Elman for the justices, it was a dodge.

During the *Bolling* argument, Nabrit split his allotted hour with his co-counsel and teaching colleague, George Edward Chalmers Hayes. Congress had been aware of Washington's segregated schools, he said, but it had never required the practice; instead, it had delegated decision-making to the discretion of D.C. officials—who were unconstitutionally infringing upon the Fifth Amendment liberty rights of black students by denying them access to unsegregated facilities. Hayes went further, saying only "pure racism" could explain segregation in Washington schools, suggesting lawmakers had deferred to the racial proclivities of local residents. When Chief Justice Vinson defended Congress, Hayes did not budge. Congress had acted out of expedience, he said, as "a matter of politics."

Nabrit, who went next, elaborated on governmentally imposed racial classifications, the same issue Justice Douglas had explored in his unfiled *Henderson* concurrence. When Congress or the states impinge on liberty interests, Nabrit said, the Court should be suspicious. Referring to the detention and internment of Japanese Americans during World War II (which the Court had upheld with a series of opinions, including its 1944 decision in *Korematsu v. United States*), he said the emergency wartime measures at issue in those cases, which deprived the detainees' constitutionally protected liberty rights, were nevertheless justified: the government had reason to doubt the detainees' loyalty. For black schoolchildren in Washington, he continued, liberty was "just as precious" as it had been for Japanese Americans during the war. But for segregated Washington schools, unlike the wartime detention, he could find no governmental justification. "I assert that there is absolutely no basis that can be produced that would be accepted in our country in 1952 that would justify Congress making such a racial basis for the exclusion of a student from a high school in the District of Columbia."

The attorney for Washington's schools, not surprisingly, disagreed. Congress had intended to establish racially separate facilities in the capital, said Milton Korman, who specialized in school-board matters at the corporation counsel's office. Congress did so, he added, not arbitrarily or unreasonably, but out of benevolence, to educate black children in an atmosphere devoid of hostility. To rebut Elman's brief, and the notion that a segregated capital harmed the nation in world affairs, Korman quoted from *Dred Scott*—perhaps the most reviled and controversial opinion in Supreme Court history. The tribunal's decisions, he read, should not reflect "the mere reflex of the popular opinion or passion of the day." Besides, Korman added, only Congress could prohibit school segregation in the District of Columbia, and even without congressional action, the capital had moved, on its own, toward integrating theaters, restaurants, and hotels.

On rebuttal, Nabrit pounced. "You either have liberty or you do not," he said. "We submit that in this case, in the heart of the nation's capital, in the capital of democracy, in the capital of the free world, there is no place for a segregated school system. This country cannot afford it, and the Constitution does not permit it, and the statutes of Congress do not authorize it."

Under the byline of the Coordinating Committee's executive board, with Terrell's name and title in all capital letters, the *Afro* published an editorial on December 13, titled "Segregation in D.C." Elsewhere, in news accounts and photographs, the editors flooded their Saturday issue with the school cases. From the front to page 7, sprinkled among advertisements for whiskey and bourbon, and admonishments to buy NAACP Christmas seals, the *Afro* brimmed with oral-argument summaries and dispatches, including a feature on the "Gentler Sex of Both Races" who waited in line. One article profiled the Reverend Joseph A. DeLaine, a guiding force behind *Briggs*, who arrived too late to find a spot inside.

The Coordinating Committee's piece looked ahead to January, responding to Eisenhower's inaugural committee chairman, Joseph C. McGarraghy, who prodded hotels and restaurants to honor a two-day Jim Crow hiatus during the swearing-in ceremony and related events. "I don't anticipate trouble from any of them," he said. The Coordinating Committee mocked the specter of a voluntary, temporary ban on segregation, deeming it a "hypocrisy." What would happen, it wondered, after workers removed the bunting and flags and out-of-town visitors fled? "Will we who remain in Washington be relieved of the need to be on our best behavior?"

In a few paragraphs, the Coordinating Committee also traced the history of the *Thompson* case, saying the matter remained under consideration by the US Court of Appeals for the D.C. Circuit. Regardless of the outcome there, it said, the American people had decided it was time to abolish segregation in Washington. A two- or three-day reprieve—though "long overdue"—was not enough. "A bigger step is in order."

★ ★ ★ ★ ★

As usual, Justice Douglas came to the Court's conference equipped to take notes, like a botanist logging field data (he was an active practitioner of that as well). For each of the five cases before the justices, he had his sheets of white paper, with pretyped headings, dated December 13, 1952. Under the Court's internal accounting, *Brown* ranked as number 8.

Douglas, a successful author, had a similar flair for efficiency and productivity in his writing career. In the past few days alone, he had furnished his editor, Kenneth McCormick at Doubleday, with two sections of his next nonfiction book, an account of his travels throughout Southeast Asia the previous summer. He promised—if he survived the workload—to deliver a final draft of the rest of the manuscript in early January. He arranged to discuss *Beyond the High Himalayas*, his recent book about trekking through northern India and western Tibet, with Walter Cronkite, in a televised half-hour program to be broadcast on CBS in Washington. For the *New York Times*, he agreed to review *Annapurna* by Maurice Herzog, a French alpinist's account of his 1950 Himalayan expedition. Douglas's earlier book, *Of Men and Mountains,* had made him a recognized expert on mountaineering. After the *Brown* conference, Douglas planned to attend the Gridiron Club's winter dinner as a guest of the *New York Times*.

Meanwhile, correspondence trickled into Douglas's chambers about the school-segregation cases. In a letter, W. H. Lewis, the president of the Southern Leadership Institute, urged Douglas to allow southern whites, not "outside organizations and agitators," to equalize educational facilities across the South. Another correspondent, John Kolitar from Boothwyn, Pennsylvania, wondered how "a group of Negro taxpayers" could afford such litigation. "Who is behind it?" he wrote. "Communists? Civil Rights [C]ongress?" At the top of each missive, Edith Allen, who quarantined the justice's mail on pending cases until the Court issued its decision, had written and underlined: "No answer."

More than two years had elapsed since the Court released *Henderson, Sweatt,* and *McLaurin*, and, from his spot at the head of the conference table, Vinson began the conference roughly as Elman had begun his brief, launching into a statement about Congress and segregation in the capital. Congress had passed the Civil War and post–Civil War constitutional amendments (the Thirteenth, Fourteenth, and Fifteenth) and yet also authorized, or failed to prohibit, school segregation in the capital, he said, and Washington had long accepted the practice. He seemed to signal, as he had during the *Bolling* oral argument, deference to Congress and misgivings about upending the capital's segregated schools. With respect to segregation elsewhere, though, Vinson conceded that schools had to be equal—now or in the future—and, that parity would take time. As the author of *Sweatt* and *McLaurin,* Vinson also distinguished those decisions, saying their individual litigants had won personal rights, effective immediately, against the universities. In the matters before them, by contrast, desegregation would affect many students, in several school systems. The Court could not avert its eyes to the problems in some regions, he said, but neither could he overlook potential reactions, including the possibility that some areas might abolish public schools completely if ordered to desegregate. In the end, Vinson did not indicate how he would vote. Rather, he said, the situation was "very serious and very emotional," and created "serious practical problems."

Black also started with segregation in Washington. At first, he parsed the technicalities, wondering whether Congress might enjoy greater latitude in the capital since the Fourteenth Amendment only applied to the states. Still, Black conceded it would be an anomaly if Congress could segregate— meaning in Washington schools—and the states could not.

As for the constitutionality of segregation in general, Black argued that Thurgood Marshall had overstated his case. And, like Vinson, Black foresaw the potential for obstruction and violence if the Court required integration of black and white children. South Carolina might abolish public schools, he warned, and other states would likely initiate evasive techniques and feign compliance. He had concerns, moreover, that a ruling against segregation would galvanize opposition, placing federal courts on the "battle front," slated to preside over injunction and contempt proceedings. Nevertheless, he was "driven," he said, to conclude segregation was unconstitutional, even knowing, as he did, such a stance meant "trouble."

Justice Reed, who had evaded *Plessy* when the justices pondered *Henderson*, *Sweatt*, and *McLaurin*, said he would uphold separate but equal. Like Black, though, he betrayed his southern sensibilities. State legislatures had "informed views" on segregation, he said, and they were authorized to "make up their minds on this question." He cited prosegregation sentiment in various states—presumably those below the Mason-Dixon line—and, after referring to "constant progress" in fostering the interests of African Americans, said the states should "be left to work out the problem for themselves."

Still, Reed signaled amenability to another outcome, a resolution other than the position he staked up front. The Constitution was "not fixed," he acknowledged, and the document could evolve with popular opinion. To the extent that a "body of people" deemed a practice unconstitutional, he suggested, such a change could ensue, but the requisite shift had not occurred when seventeen states practiced Jim Crow. Even so, he conceded, segregation was "gradually disappearing."

Justice Frankfurter, like Black and Vinson, focused initially on Washington. By doing so, of course, he acknowledged concerns civil rights activists had raised about the capital for years. His former student, Charles Hamilton Houston, had written him in 1925 about the all-white District of Columbia Bar Association, which denied black attorneys access to its law library. But Frankfurter, who sat on the NAACP's national legal committee as a Harvard law professor, had coexisted with, and even disregarded, Washington's Jim Crow for more than a decade. In 1940, he crossed a civil rights picket line outside a whites-only movie theater to attend the screening of a film about Abraham Lincoln, as did several other prominent New Deal–era figures, including Eleanor Roosevelt and Secretary of Agriculture Henry A. Wallace. Six years later, when protestors from a progressive veterans' group and the Southern Conference for Human Welfare swarmed outside George Washington University's Lisner Auditorium, where only white patrons could see Ingrid Bergman starring in *Joan of Lorraine*, Frankfurter breached the picket line again, as did Justice Reed. In many respects, Frankfurter reflected the realm he and his colleagues inhabited, one in which color and race denoted function and status.

On the eve of a new, Republican administration, however, Frankfurter denounced Jim Crow in Washington with the zeal of a convert. Segregation in the nation's capital was "intolerable," he said, a different issue than segregation by the states, but a due process violation under the Fifth Amendment, which applied to Congress. To reinforce his point, he—the champion of judicial restraint—invoked the experience of his former law clerk, William T. Coleman Jr., who was black. Coleman's one-year service with Frankfurter ended in 1949, after he wrote his memo analyzing *Sweatt* and *McLaurin*.

Frankfurter, of course, had long nurtured ties with many of his former students, including Houston, and his former law clerks, including Elman. And now, in the midst of the *Brown* and *Bolling* deliberations, Frankfurter invoked the memory of Coleman, who had gone on to a career in private practice, assisting Thurgood Marshall and the NAACP in the school-segregation cases. As Frankfurter knew, Coleman's stint in the Court drove home the vagaries of a segregated capital. During their year with the justice, Coleman's white co-clerk, Elliot L. Richardson, had once suggested going to lunch with other law clerks at the Mayflower Hotel—only to learn, by phone, that the restaurant would not serve an African American customer. Feigning an excuse to Coleman, Richardson opted instead for Union Station and later confided in Frankfurter and Coleman about the reason for the switch.

Still, Frankfurter lobbied to stall. All five cases should be scheduled for reargument, he said, meaning a complete do-over in the courtroom before the justices at a later date, and *Bolling* should be reargued after Eisenhower took office in January. Two-and-a-half months earlier, in a letter to Richardson, Frankfurter had professed relief that the Court would hear the school cases after the November election, and that their outcome would "not serve as campaign fodder." But now he hoped to delay a decision until the arrival of a new White House team. The incoming president had "promised to change the law" in Washington—meaning abolish Jim Crow—and Frankfurter perceived an advantage, "a gain in law administration," for such a policy shift to emanate with the help of the new executive branch leadership, rather than as a "coercive" mandate from the tribunal.

As for the merits in the remaining cases, in which the Fourteenth Amendment applied, Frankfurter struggled to justify deviating from precedent, even one as problematic as *Plessy*. He parried Vinson's concern about personal rights and picked up on a theme from Elman's brief, noting these were equity suits, which could provide some leeway in forging decrees. He spurned the NAACP's "sociological" approach—its reliance upon expert testimony purporting to show, through an experiment with white and black dolls, psychological harm wrought by segregation. He dismissed any effort to discern the purpose of the Fourteenth Amendment, saying he had read "all of its history" and could not conclude that the framers intended to abolish segregation. He wanted to know "why what has gone before is wrong" and refused to accept, as a blanket rule, that the Constitution banned treating whites and African Americans differently. In the end, having settled on no basis for invalidating segregation by the states, he said the cases should be reargued.

Douglas, who spoke next, thought resolution was easy. Under the Fourteenth Amendment and the Fifth Amendment's due process clause, Douglas said, governments could not fashion race-based classifications. He was, in essence, ready to decide all five cases, striking down segregated schools in each. Concerns about timing were irrelevant; the underlying merits beyond dispute. He did concede, however, that "application" of this simple principle could prove difficult.

Jackson, who spoke after Douglas, sounded, at first, like Frankfurter. He found nothing in the Court's opinions and nothing in the text and history of the Fourteenth Amendment to support striking down segregation; Thurgood Marshall's brief, with its reliance on sociology, provided no guidance either. But Jackson entertained doubts about invalidating Jim Crow, saying it would harm African Americans to place them in white schools. Still, he recognized the imminence of segregation's demise and said he would "go along" with a decision that, employing "equitable remedies," gave the states time to abolish the practice. *Bolling*, the Washington case, he added, should be reargued, and appropriate congressional committees should have the opportunity to submit briefs and participate in oral argument.

The least senior justices betrayed familiar allegiances. Clark, the only remaining southerner yet to speak, advocated "delay" and signaled amenability to compromise. He would "go along" with a decision giving lower courts flexibility to tailor relief to the circumstances. "Otherwise," he said, we have led the states to believe segregation is constitutional and "we should let them work it out."

Burton and Minton, on the other hand, aligned conceptually with Douglas. Education encompassed "more than buildings and faculties," said Burton; it also reflected "a habit of mind." Under the Fourteenth Amendment, he added, states had no choice: segregation violated the equal protection clause, and "separate education is not sufficient for today's problems." Touching on his experience as Cleveland's mayor, Burton said he had integrated African American nurses into white hospitals. But like Clark and Jackson, he said the Court should give the states "plenty of time" in its decree.

Minton, who spoke last, shared Douglas's preference for simplicity, repudiating separate but equal. "Classification on the basis of race does not add up," he said. "It's invidious and can't be maintained."

★ ★ ★ ★ ★

Among the *Afro* reporters who covered the Eisenhower inauguration, the president-elect had already made news. The night before, during a preinaugural concert at the Uline Arena, African American performers, such as the Nicholas Brothers and Lionel Hampton, shared billing with white entertainers, including Ethel Merman and Edgar Bergen. On the platform a few minutes earlier, Eisenhower had shaken hands with Dorothy Maynor, an African American soprano who had sung "The Star-Spangled Banner."

At 12:30 p.m., Eisenhower positioned himself on the dais. Forty years earlier, as a West Point cadet, he had marched in Woodrow Wilson's first inaugural parade. On January 20, 1953, as a sixty-two-year-old former general attired in morning coat and striped trousers, he radiated vigor and stamina, with his square jaw and broad forehead, his raised right hand pointing skyward. A few feet away, facing Eisenhower, stood Chief Justice Vinson, cloaked in a black robe and radiating weariness: shoulders slumped, under-eye circles, gray hair tousled.

Two weeks earlier, Truman had dispatched his final State of the Union message to Congress, forgoing, for the first time, an in-person appearance. In his written text, read aloud by House and Senate clerks, he invoked the pending transition and "the burdens" of the presidency: "the Communist menace," the specter of atomic warfare, the complexity of leading "the whole free world." He alluded to the hydrogen bomb, hailed the "great awakening" of the national conscience on civil rights, and lambasted the corrosiveness of fear, "hysteria," and intolerance. "The inquisition, the star chamber, have no place in a free society." Now, as Washington basked in nearly 50-degree temperatures and sunlight cast a gleam on the US Marine Band's horns, Richard M. Nixon, newly sworn-in as vice president, shared Truman's front-row spot on the inaugural platform. Behind them, Vinson's colleagues, the eight associate justices, sat in row D.

For the swearing-in ceremony, Eisenhower had selected two Bibles. One, which he received for his West Point graduation, lay open to Psalm 33:12; the other, which George Washington had used in 1789—and Harding in 1921—was open to II Chronicles 7:14, a verse about forgiveness and healing. After reciting the oath, Eisenhower shook hands with Truman and kissed his wife, Mamie (whose bangs had spawned a flurry of inquiries inside the Hecht's beauty salon). As the crowd cheered, the president smiled and hoisted his arms in a V-shaped salute, a staple of his campaign-trail appearances. In a departure from his prepared remarks, circulated in advance to the press corps, he asked his listeners to bow their heads.

A hush fell over the plaza. "Give us, we pray, the power to discern clearly right from wrong, and allow all our works and actions to be governed thereby, and by the laws of this land," said Eisenhower. "Especially we pray that our concern shall be for all the people regardless of station, race or calling."

After the benediction, Eisenhower climbed into a Cadillac Eldorado convertible and rolled down Pennsylvania Avenue with the top down, flanked by the US Army Band, an infantry battalion, and members of the Secret Service. For the next few hours, while Eisenhower stood at attention overlooking Pennsylvania Avenue, state governors and official delegations streamed by: a Kansas cowboy band, an Alaskan dog team, mounted police from Cleveland. Interspersed among the floats and gun battalions, African Americans marched as well, including cadets from Washington's Armstrong High School and Howard University's ROTC. When black units veered into camera range, viewers who were tuned to the local ABC affiliate, WMAL-TV, saw a station break or a commercial.

Meanwhile, about two miles southeast of the White House, thousands of Truman loyalists descended on Union Station. At Track 9, the *Ferdinand Magellan*, an armor-plated Pullman car consecrated to presidential travel since FDR's administration, waited to deliver the Trumans home to Missouri. Fans milled behind a roped-off area. Cameras whirred. Local attorneys numbered among the enthusiasts, including William L. Houston, Charles's father.

Porters and baggage handlers, clad in work attire, paused to offer their assessments of Truman, some gleaned from firsthand experience. "Just as nice a man as I ever met," said G. G. Parker, a Pullman porter from Norfolk, Virginia. "He'd sit and talk to you just like he'd talk to his family—about common, ordinary things."

On board, Truman greeted a crush of admirers, shaking hands with senators, generals, advisors, and ambassadors. Arthur S. Prettyman, Truman's White House valet, unpacked the former president's belongings. At 6:20 p.m., ten minutes before Truman's scheduled departure, Vinson arrived, aided by a police escort. "I just had to come and say goodbye to the old boy," he told Truman. Outside, partisans chanted, "We want Harry." Truman, outfitted in a suit and tie, emerged on the rear platform, smiling and waving. Cheers rang out; people sang "For He's a Jolly Good Fellow." Truman made a few remarks, saying he was just "a private citizen" and ducked back inside.

Moments later, the *Ferdinand Magellan* edged away from the gate, lumbering down the track, into darkness. Prettyman, who had also served as FDR's valet, lingered to watch. He had traveled to Rio de Janeiro with Truman and helped Roosevelt with the task of getting dressed. When Prettyman fought a bout of pneumonia, Truman had visited him at the Naval Hospital in Bethesda, Maryland. More recently, during Truman's final days in office, Prettyman marveled to a *Post* reporter about the president's good spirits. And now, Prettyman, too, had quit the White House, easing into retirement.

Police officers disassembled the ropes. Inside the station, passengers clumped at ticket windows and flocked to refreshment stands. Some of the travelers still wore "Ike" buttons.

Later that evening, Justice Burton donned white tie and tails and posed with his wife for a photograph at the National Guard Armory, where an estimated 10,000 revelers descended for one of two integrated inaugural balls. Until 2 a.m., Republican stalwarts—including a trainload from Cleveland—frolicked to the sounds of Guy Lombardo and William C. Handy, an African American jazz composer, heralding the Republican resurgence, the end of the New and Fair Deals.

★ ★ ★ ★ ★

Less than forty-eight hours later, on January 22, 1953, the US Court of Appeals for the D.C. Circuit released its *Thompson* decision. By a 5-to-4 vote, the majority—all of whom were appointed by FDR or Truman—sided with the restaurant, invalidating the capital's antidiscrimination laws and decreeing them unenforceable, though they did so in two separate opinions. In an opinion authored by Chief Judge Harold M. Stephens, the majority ruled that Congress, with its constitutional grant of exclusive legislative authority over the capital, had only delegated "municipal" powers to the District government, empowering it to tackle local matters, such as street repairs. But as civil rights legislation, the jurists reasoned, the Reconstruction-era ordinances trespassed into the realm of "general" legislation, where only Congress had power to act. Accordingly, the majority ruled, the ordinances were invalid when enacted and later repealed, under a 1901 law that repealed all previous local enactments other than police or municipal regulations. In a separate concurring opinion, Judge E. Barrett Prettyman opined that even if the laws were "municipal" in nature and validly enacted, they had been abandoned by nonenforcement.

As a rationale for the court's move, Stephens noted that the ordinances had lain dormant for seventy-eight years, amid the local "custom of race disassociation." The choice to enforce them now ranked as a legislative one. "Such a decision were better left, we think, to the Congress."

The four dissenting judges took the opposite view. In an opinion written by Judge Charles Fahy (a Georgia native and former US solicitor general) they said the antidiscrimination ordinances regulated a local activity: "the serving of food at a fixed location within the District." As for local "custom," Fahy noted that there had been a shift toward equal treatment—the very practice the ordinances embraced—in the armed services, the government, and even in local restaurants.

The Coordinating Committee issued a press release that quoted Terrell. "I consider today's majority decision in the Thompson Restaurant case a tragedy for the United States. Clearly the matter is up to the Supreme Court to resolve."

9

Eat Anywhere

President Dwight D. Eisenhower filed toward the center of the US House, flanked by senators Robert A. Taft, the Ohio Republican, and Lyndon B. Johnson, a Texas Democrat. Applause rang out across the chamber, extending into an ovation that lasted more than a minute. Thirteen days after the inaugural, just after 12:30 p.m. on February 2, 1953, Eisenhower was giving his first State of the Union address.

Since the swearing-in, Eisenhower had hunkered inside the White House, leaving only once, the previous day, for a Sunday-morning service at the National Presbyterian Church and a private tour of the National Gallery of Art's Japanese collection. Around noon on February 2, the president, clad in a three-piece suit, climbed into a limousine with the First Lady and a Secret Service agent and reversed the inaugural route back to the Capitol. Now, Vice President Nixon and Speaker Joseph W. Martin Jr., a Massachusetts Republican, sat in high-backed chairs behind him, against an American flag backdrop. Looking down on them, from the gallery's front row, the First Lady had settled into place with her mother, Elivera Doud.

In the gallery, where onlookers clustered in doorways and lined the stairs, and in the chamber were an array of notables: Winifred E. Reed, the justice's wife; Alice Roosevelt Longworth, Theodore Roosevelt's sixty-eight-year-old daughter; Margaret Chase Smith, a Maine Republican who numbered as the Senate's sole female member, or in the *Washington Post*'s argot, "the lone lady Senator." Earlier that morning, Chase Smith had told a group of Barnard College students that in forty years, when they reached her age, she expected the Senate's ranks to include more women. She did not venture to predict how many.

At the outset of his speech, broadcast live on radio and television, Eisenhower struck a tone of humility, referring to the "grand labors" of leadership and articulating a few broad themes: global peace, creative enterprise, equal opportunity. He announced "a new, positive" approach to foreign policy, stressing self-help, cooperation, and world trade. He called for deficit reduction, a balanced budget, and an end to wage-and-price controls. Near the end of his remarks, in a passage dedicated to civil rights, he invoked his stature as a former soldier who last appeared before a joint session of Congress in 1945, after Germany's surrender. "Our civil and social rights form a central part of the heritage we are striving to defend on all fronts and with all our strength," he said. "To be true to one's own freedom is—in essence—to honor and respect the freedom of all others."

From there, Eisenhower turned to equality, the "cardinal ideal" in the nation's heritage, and called for parity of rights for all citizens, regardless of race, color, and creed. He linked discrimination to "the persistence of distrust and of fear in the hearts of men," rather than regional or sectional bias. He did not waver, however, about the urgency of the mission. "This makes all the more vital the fighting of these wrongs by every individual, in every station of life, in his every deed."

Yet unlike his Democratic predecessor, Eisenhower did not endorse—or even mention—federal civil rights legislation. Nor did he refer to the federal judiciary, where, across the street at the Supreme Court, the justices were pondering the future of segregated public education. Rather, he called for presidential leadership and "friendly" relations with the states and cities. "Much of the answer lies in the power of fact, fully publicized, of persuasion, honestly pressed, and of conscience, justly aroused."

While he did not intend to propose federal legislation, Eisenhower pledged to use the authority of his office to end segregation in the District of Columbia, including the federal government and the military. He received tepid applause. He touted home rule for Washington residents and recommended appointing two more D.C. commissioners, so "all elements of our population" could gain representation. "This will be a first step toward insuring that this Capital provide an honored example to all communities of our Nation," he said.

Nine days after the speech, on February 11, Eisenhower denied an executive-clemency bid by Julius and Ethel Rosenberg—the husband and wife convicted, in March 1951, of conspiring to disclose nuclear-defense secrets to the Soviet Union. Judge Irving R. Kaufman of the federal district court in New York sentenced them to death, a sanction upheld on appeal. In a statement denying the Rosenbergs a reprieve, Eisenhower said their crime was worse than murder, since they had betrayed the nation and "the cause of freedom, for which free men are fighting and dying at this very hour."

Meanwhile, on February 20, the Corporation Counsel's Office—in its enforcement role, charged with authority for prosecuting violations of local ordinances—asked the Supreme Court to review *Thompson*. Behind the scenes, Eisenhower's Justice Department had prodded Vernon West and Chester Gray to appeal their loss in the D.C. Circuit—a setback, at least in Philip Elman's view, they might otherwise have let stand. In a twenty-page petition for a writ of certiorari, filed by West and Gray and quietly crafted, in part, by Elman, the office said that *Thompson* raised substantial national and local questions about racial discrimination and congressional power to grant home rule. Indeed, they wrote, Washington's racial segregation posed an issue of such importance that the president had addressed the topic in his State of the Union address, which they quoted at length.

The Justice Department weighed in with a *Thompson* friend-of-the-court brief on March 10, urging the Supreme Court to review the case and uphold the antidiscrimination laws. The department's papers, filed under the imprimatur of Attorney General Herbert Brownell Jr., bore the names of Robert L. Stern, the acting solicitor general, and Philip Elman, who drafted the submission. Brownell—a Nebraska native, who had worked as a corporate lawyer in New York—had observed the mechanics of Jim Crow during his first day in the capital, when he saw a restaurant owner deny service to an African American family. In his brief, Brownell said the D.C. Circuit's rulings were "clearly erroneous" and the underlying constitutional and statutory questions were "obviously not of mere local concern." Rather, *Thompson* raised national issues warranting the Court's review, he wrote, also quoting Eisenhower's State of the Union speech.

Brownell and West filed a joint "suggestion" three days later, on March 13, asking the Court to expedite *Thompson*. The justices had not yet resolved whether they would review the case. Nor had the restaurant's attorneys even filed their papers opposing the certiorari petition. But in three paragraphs, Brownell and West said the justices would serve "the public interest" by deciding *Thompson* before the end of the current term, which expired in June. If the Court granted the petition on April 6, they wrote, it could hear oral arguments during the week of April 27.

Thompson's responded to the joint filing first, on March 17, with opposition equally worded in three terse paragraphs. Any notion of advancing the case was "premature," wrote the restaurant's attorneys, since their answer to the certiorari petition, which they were in the process of drafting, would demonstrate the absence of any constitutional issue. As for the substance, they added, Brownell and West were seeking "an advisory opinion upon a hypothetical question which may not arise in the future." Nor had Brownell and West shown why the Court should place *Thompson* ahead of other pending matters—an apparent reference to *Brown* and the school cases—which, unlike *Thompson*, raised questions of national importance.

The restaurant's attorneys addressed the substantive claims on March 26, with their opposition to the certiorari petition, urging the justices to abstain. *Thompson* raised no legal errors, no constitutional questions, no issues of national concern, and nothing "worthy of review," they said. The entire proceeding, they wrote, raised a local matter of statutory construction: whether the legislative assembly had later repealed the antidiscrimination laws of 1872 and 1873. Under their approach, the answer was yes, echoing the D.C. Circuit. The Reconstruction-era laws were not mere "police" or municipal regulations; they converted the failure to serve everyone into a criminal offense, depriving restaurant owners of their contractual right to accommodate whomever they pleased. The purpose of the Reconstruction-era laws, they added, was to alter "by legislative fiat" the mores of Washington residents—the white populace—and impose "a policy of social equality." Thus, as "civil rights legislation," the Reconstruction-era laws had been repealed in 1901—along with all nonmunicipal enactments—and the D.C. Circuit had disposed of the case properly.

On April 6, the Supreme Court unveiled a series of orders and rulings, a staple of its Monday routine. By a four-to-four vote, the justices issued an order expelling Abraham J. Isserman, one of the *Dennis* defense lawyers, from the Supreme Court bar, the roster of attorneys admitted to practice before the tribunal. (Isserman, who accused the trial judge of "judicial misconduct," had been imprisoned in 1952 for contempt and disbarred.) Separately, the Court denied an appeal by "Tokyo Rose," a Japanese American convicted of treason for broadcasting propaganda from Japan to US troops during World War II. And, in a two-sentence directive, the justices agreed to hear Mary Church Terrell's test case, now known as No. 617, *District of Columbia v. John R. Thompson Co., Inc.*

The order did not illuminate why, in the waning weeks of the term, the justices added *Thompson* to a docket already strained by the school-segregation cases and the Rosenberg appeals. But, with less than three months remaining before they scattered for summer recess, they conveyed a sense of urgency. Instead of holding *Thompson* until the fall, the Court did as Brownell and West suggested, assigning the case for oral argument on April 27.

Attorneys for both sides had worked on Terrell's test case for more than three years, weathering three rounds of briefing and argument in three separate forums. Now they found themselves slated to appear before the US Supreme Court, the final arbiter, in less than a month. Under the timetable proposed by Brownell and West, opposed by Thompson's and adopted by the Court, they had three weeks to write, type, print, bind, and file briefs—and prepare to defend them before the justices.

★ ★ ★ ★ ★

That same morning, a crowd gathered on the South Lawn of the White House, an expanse of greenery overlooking the Washington Monument and the Mall. As gray skies hinted at the prospect of rain, boys and girls, parents and guardians, streamed through the gates of the executive mansion for the Easter Egg Roll. Inside, white and yellow fragments dotted the grass, remnants of shells and hard-boiled yolks. A public address system blared lost-and-found announcements: a sweater, a husband, a silver pin, a teddy bear.

Beginning with the administration of Rutherford B. Hayes, who relocated the egg roll from the Capitol to the White House in 1878, successive presidents and first ladies had traced their signatures on the annual Easter Monday gathering. Florence Harding donned a Girl Scout uniform. Eleanor Roosevelt, the first egg-roll hostess to embrace the broadcast medium, greeted radio listeners in 1933. But since 1941, when more than 50,000 enthusiasts mobbed the executive mansion, the egg roll, historically open to all, without regard to race, had withstood a twelve-year hiatus, derailed by World War II, postwar food shortages, and President Truman's White House renovation project.

Eisenhower ushered the White House Easter Egg Roll into the atomic age, with roughly 10,000 guests—white and black—converging in the president's backyard. At 11:00 a.m., he stepped onto the South Portico and greeted the revelers, assuring them that he planned to join them, but he wouldn't sign any autographs. Moments later, he plunged into the crowd, flanked by a wedge of Secret Service and police officers.

Out on the lawn, Dwight David Eisenhower II, the president's five-year-old grandson, and Barbara Anne, his three-year-old granddaughter, scouted for eggs. A young girl, clad in a frilly dress, skirted the Secret Service detail and stood behind the First Grandchildren, staring. Photographers held cameras aloft, straining to capture an image of Ike, surrounded by a sea of faces and bodies. Fifteen minutes after emerging, the Eisenhowers retreated back inside the White House. David, who had lost half his eggs in the process, burst into tears.

The next day, the *Afro-American* paired headlines reading "Thousands Roll Eggs on White House Lawn" and "Supreme Court Will Review 'Lost Laws' Case Decision." Underneath, the editors ran a black-and-white photograph: three African American girls, clad in dress shoes and anklets, eyeing the contents of their straw baskets. The South Portico soared behind them.

★ ★ ★ ★ ★

Mary shared her thoughts with the *Afro* a few days later. In the immediate aftermath of the D.C. Circuit's ruling, she and the Coordinating Committee had redoubled their efforts, unveiling new initiatives. In late January, they launched a petition drive, urging Eisenhower and the District Commissioners to honor the president's vow to eradicate Jim Crow in the capital. As citizens of Washington, we are "sick of segregation," the petition read. "It is wrong and indefensible."

In early February, while Eisenhower was finalizing his State of the Union speech, Terrell had rallied supporters, encouraging them to subsidize the committee's efforts with financial contributions. She lobbied Baptist and other ministers to endorse "some form of action," including a possible march to the Lincoln Memorial. On Sunday, February 8, six days after the State of the Union, she sat on the Capitol steps for a prayer service spearheaded by the *Afro*, where roughly 2,000 participants sought divine guidance for the Supreme Court justices in the school-segregation cases. In March, though, after Brownell had filed *Thompson* friend-of-the-court papers, Mary shelved discussions of a march, ceding the spotlight and the battleground to the attorneys.

Now, in her *Afro* interview, she indulged in statesmanship, hailing the Supreme Court for its interest in her case. "It is the only thing to do to make Washington the true capital of the country called the democracy of the world," she said. "I feel that whatever decision the Supreme Court reaches will be a just one, making Washington a truly great capital."

★ ★ ★ ★ ★

From his third-floor NAACP office on West 43rd Street, near Times Square, Thurgood Marshall was mobilizing. For several years, he and his staff had devoted themselves to the school cases, working tirelessly to manage the logistical, evidentiary, and strategic burden of litigating four separate challenges, in four different jurisdictions, and pursue them all the way to the

Supreme Court. In late January, after the D.C. Circuit's *Thompson* decision, Marshall pivoted to the capital—a strategy Houston and Randolph had championed more than a decade earlier. During a speech at the Shoreham Hotel, Marshall questioned Washington's legitimacy as a global symbol of democracy, one steeped in racism. "But no one can seriously deny that it is a typical example of democracy in the United States," he said. "No one would deny that the basic reason for withholding the vote to the citizens of the District of Columbia is that a sizable portion of these voters are colored."

Later that spring, with the Supreme Court expediting *Thompson*, Marshall and his colleagues scrambled, seeking consent from the attorneys to file a friend-of-the-court brief. On April 18, after Thompson's Restaurant rejected their overture, they filed a five-page motion, typeset and printed in New York, asking the justices for permission to participate with a written submission. If the Court upheld the D.C. Circuit, African Americans in Washington would "lose vital and precious personal rights," the NAACP wrote, as would tourists, who encountered the capital's segregated hotels and restaurants. "The District of Columbia symbolizes American democracy." So long as Washington sanctioned racial discrimination by law, efforts to eliminate it elsewhere would meet "stiff resistance," they added. "Once it is clear, however, that racial discrimination in our capital has no legal warrant, the great mass of national opinion seeking to eliminate racial barriers will be swelled with new moral strength and vigor."

★ ★ ★ ★ ★

Brownell, Stern, and Elman filed an eighty-nine-page brief on April 23, one week before oral argument. Paragraph by paragraph, they defended the Reconstruction-era ordinances, with texts ranging from the Federalist Papers to the Fifteenth Amendment, and authority originating from Alaska to Wyoming. Throughout, they buttressed their central assertion: the laws were validly enacted and never repealed.

As a threshold matter, Brownell and Elman reframed the debate, steering away from the D.C. Circuit's distinction between "general legislation" and "municipal regulation," which they dismissed as irrelevant. The real issue in the case, they said—the test of the Reconstruction-era laws' validity—was whether Congress had empowered Washington's local lawmakers to enact civil rights ordinances, and, if so, whether Congress had done so as a valid and constitutional delegation of its own exclusive jurisdiction over the federal capital. Congress, they wrote, did have exclusive jurisdiction over Washington, but "exclusive" did not mean "non-delegable." Congress, moreover, under the Organic Act of 1871, properly delegated broad legislative authority to Washington, covering "all rightful subjects of legislation." And pursuant to that delegation they wrote, the capital's local government had "full authority to legislate on subjects of local concern," including local laws prohibiting racial discrimination in public accommodations. Municipal governments around the country, they noted, had also chosen to pass such laws, much as they had enacted other regulations to promote the public health and welfare of their citizens.

In a twenty-two-page section, Brownell and Elman dismantled the centerpiece of the D.C. Circuit's majority opinion: the alleged difference between "general legislation" and "municipal regulation." Chief Judge Stephens had, of course, invoked this distinction to invalidate the ordinances. Congress, he reasoned, had only delegated municipal powers to the District government; civil rights legislation exceeded the confines of "municipal regulation" and verged into the realm of "general legislation," where only Congress had authority to act—meaning the ordinances, as passed by Washington's local lawmakers, were invalid and Washington restaurants could keep segregating.

Brownell and Elman confronted Stephens's rationale directly. Neither the Constitution nor previous Supreme Court decisions supported the view that congressional power to delegate legislative authority to Washington hinged on the difference between "general legislation" and "municipal regulation," they wrote. On the contrary, the concept arose in the context of "ordinary municipalities," where matters such as domestic relations and estate administration warrant uniform treatment and fall within the province of "general legislation" by the state. Local matters, by contrast, absent statewide law to the contrary, qualify as appropriate subjects for "municipal regulation."

Brownell and Elman then turned to the facts. Washington, they wrote, was no "ordinary municipality." Rather, the capital blended elements of a city and state and functioned like a territory, meaning the geographical rationale for distinguishing between "general" and "municipal" did not apply. Moreover, under previous Supreme Court decisions, they added, Congress only retained for itself, and did not delegate authority to the capital to address, "national matters": declaring war, raising armies, regulating interstate commerce. And none of those was at issue in *Thompson*.

In a five-line order dated April 27, the Court denied the NAACP's request. The justices furnished no explanation. In *Thompson*, they had banished Marshall and the NAACP to the sidelines.

★ ★ ★ ★ ★

At 3:20 p.m. on April 30, Chester Gray rose to address the Supreme Court. A fifty-four-year-old Pittsburgh native with a receding hairline and horn-rimmed glasses, Gray had gravitated to the capital during World War I, when he enlisted in the navy and served as a confidential secretary to Franklin D. Roosevelt, then an assistant secretary. Later, after graduating from National University School of Law, a predecessor of what became George Washington University Law School, Gray worked as a secretary to Justice James C. McReynolds. Now, as a twenty-five-year veteran of the Corporation Counsel's Office, Gray readied to argue *Thompson* one more time—and for the last time.

In and around the capital, with temperatures predicted to climb to 80 degrees, spring had arrived. Residents adjusted to daylight saving time, ushered in earlier that morning, and the loss of an hour of sleep. The *Post's* front page featured the previous day's highlights: Democrats blasting Eisenhower on his one hundredth day in office for "drift" and "creeping McCarthyism"; Attorney General Brownell announced, during his first press conference, he had identified sixty-two new groups for inclusion on the Justice Department's subversives list, including the Committee for the Negro in the Arts and the Labor Council for Negro Rights. And in Winchester, Virginia, about seventy-five miles northwest of the capital, residents awaited the coronation of Kathryn Eisenhower, the president's nineteen-year-old niece, as queen of the annual apple-blossom festival.

Before Gray, massed in a line, loomed the eight justices. Ensconced in black leather-upholstered chairs (the seat for Justice Jackson, sidelined by illness, was vacant), they were dwarfed by the scale of their surroundings. At their backs, towering overhead, was the backdrop conceived by Cass Gilbert (who also designed Oberlin College's Finney Chapel and Yakima's Northern Pacific Railroad Depot): four Ionic columns, fashioned from Ligurian marble, imbued with amber tones. Along the wall, interspersed among the columns, hung cascades of red velvet drapery. As in a theater, the curtains demarcated the boundary between the proscenium, where the justices presided and faced the public, and the rest of the Court, into which they retreated after argument, slipping behind the curtains, to deliberate in secret. At the lectern, advocates stood facing the center of the mahogany bench.

Behind Gray, a waist-high bronze railing demarcated the space reserved for members of the public, like a communion rail. There, among the rows of spectators, sat Mary—recently named "Mother of the Year" by the Howard University Women's League—and Reverend Jernagin. Earlier in the month, Jernagin had traveled to Korea and converted twenty-one servicemen, black and white, to Christianity. On the perimeter, flanking the audience on both sides, eight identical Ionic columns were grouped in pairs, facing each other across the chamber, evoking balance and rationality. At the front of the room, over the bench and facing the spectators, a marble frieze celebrated law and government, channeled from antiquity: a male warrior; an American eagle; a carved tablet, etched with numerals representing the first ten amendments in the Bill of Rights; and a huddled group of females and citizens, invoking the protection of a judge.

Gray opened by tracing a straightforward path to reversal: deference to Washington on its own laws. The D.C. Circuit had failed to consider the ordinances' legislative history and the time period during which they were enacted, he said; and, though the Constitution gave Congress exclusive jurisdiction over Washington, Congress retained the right to delegate local lawmaking to the District, sparing lawmakers the burden of serving as the capital's day-to-day city council. Indeed, he argued, when Congress passed the Organic Act of 1871—reorganizing the District and vesting it with broad legislative authority—civil rights legislation, such as the antidiscrimination laws, fell within the activities Washington could regulate on its own.

Chief Justice Vinson, who had sat on the D.C. Circuit before his elevation to the Supreme Court, quizzed Gray about legislative history: elements Chief Judge Stephens should have considered; whether Congress retained any powers to legislate under the Organic Act; if it delegated authority why had Congress enacted legislation governing Washington, including streetcar measures, between 1865 and 1870. Gray parried by arguing that the local legislative council had less power then, before the Organic Act.

The Court had allotted Gray an hour, but after forty-eight minutes, he yielded to Elman, who appeared at the lectern at 4:00 p.m. As he had in his brief, Elman distilled a how-to narrative for upholding the antidiscrimination laws. Congress gave Washington comprehensive legislative powers, he said, and the Constitution only barred other states from regulating the capital; it did not prevent Washington's local government from passing its own local laws.

Vinson steered Elman to the second issue, whether the statutes had been repealed. "That is rather important," he pointed out. For Elman, whose brief devoted more than thirty pages to the topic, Vinson had posed an easy question. "Repeals by implication are not favored," he said. "They must rest on a clear and manifest purpose to repeal." Halfway through his argument, the Court adjourned for the day.

★ ★ ★ ★ ★

When the justices reconvened the next day at 12:05 p.m., Elman reposi-
tioned himself at the lectern, poised to resume his argument at the midpoint.
This time, several justices—Vinson, Burton, Frankfurter, and Reed—peppered him with questions, exploring potential weaknesses, seeking clarifica-
tions, hinting to their colleagues about where they stood. Vinson probed
more deeply about legislative history. Reed pointed out that the D.C. commissioners had not enforced the ordinances, prompting a rejoinder from
Justice Minton. African Americans hadn't insisted on enforcement, he said;
the commissioners hadn't been remiss because they hadn't been asked.

Elman nudged his argument forward. Confusion about the statutes contributed to Washington's enforcement failure, he said, but the capital had not repealed or abandoned them. "It would be most extraordinary that the District
Commissioners, by some inaction on their part[,] had it in their power to
repeal an enactment having the force of an Act [sic] of Congress," he said.

Ringgold Hart, the attorney for Thompson's, assumed his place at 12:40
p.m. Hart, a Georgetown University law school alumnus, had served in
Gray's capacity, as the principal assistant Corporation Counsel, several decades earlier. Now a named partner in a Washington law firm, he sought to
defend his victory in the D.C. Circuit. The Reconstruction-era laws, he said
in his brief, were invalidly enacted, expressly repealed, impliedly repealed,
and constitutionally suspect because they discriminated against businesses
"without any reasonable basis."

But Hart read aloud from a previous decision by the Court, and this
seemed to tax the justices' patience, sparking interruptions. Burton asked
whether a territorial legislature could enact laws like the antidiscrimination
ordinances. Black followed up with a related query: whether Congress
could delegate to Washington the right to pass its own legislation. Both
questions led Hart to address the rationale of the D.C. Circuit's majority
opinion, the alleged distinction between "general" legislation and "municipal" regulation—to which Hart's brief had devoted more than half its thirty-
three pages. Congress could only delegate municipal lawmaking authority,
he said—meaning fire prevention, sanitation, public health, and public safety—
a province his brief dubbed "mere police regulations."

At its best, Hart's theory of *Thompson* seized the national stake in eradicating a segregated capital and converted it to his advantage. In his brief,
citing the president's vow to end Washington's Jim Crow, Hart had written
that a local statute spawning such national interest had to qualify as "legislation,"
not mere "municipal" regulation. In other words, he claimed, if discrimination

in Washington rose to the level, as a national priority, of rating a mention during Eisenhower's State of the Union message, only Congress could enact laws on that subject for the capital.

Black, a former trial lawyer, bore down, wielding a point from Brownell's brief: even if Washington only had authority over "municipal regulation," the ordinances reflected a valid exercise of that privilege; they fell within the capital's police powers to promote public safety, health, and welfare by regulating the restaurant industry, from construction and occupancy to sanitary conditions. Why does that delegation from Congress—meaning municipal authority—not include power to enact these ordinances? Black asked. Then he asked Hart to justify his distinction between regulating a restaurant's hours of operation and imposing a duty of service.

Hart equivocated. It hinged, he said, on the nature of the professed right. After an interjection from Frankfurter, Black circled back, as if cross-examining a hostile witness. Again, he asked whether Washington had authority, under its police powers, to pass the ordinances. The Reconstruction-era civil rights laws exceeded the local legislature's regulatory mandate because they placed a novel obligation on restaurant owners, Hart said, meaning the duty to serve everyone.

At its core, Hart's logic echoed his certiorari opposition papers and his brief, where, he wrote, the ordinances interfered with restaurants' "freedom to contract or not to contract with whom they pleased," imposing on them "a duty to sell to all." But his rationale, with its intimation of white supremacy, had already failed to persuade at least four of the justices, the minimum number required to vote in favor of granting certiorari. As a cultural matter, moreover, Hart had delved into terrain familiar to generations of southern whites, reared to consider African Americans socially inferior. With his appeal to the sanctity of contracts and his repudiation of "social equality," Hart had swayed a majority of the D.C. Circuit, including Chief Judge Stephens. But to Justice Black, who claimed a distant relationship through maternal forebears to Justice Harlan, the *Plessy* dissenter, it proved anathema. Black quizzed Hart about a pair of late-nineteenth-century laws buried in a footnote of Brownell's brief. The first, enacted in 1887, gave the District's commissioners the "usual and reasonable" police-power authority over matters such as traffic, taxi fares, and litter. The second, passed by Congress in 1892, granted the commissioners authority to enact reasonable regulations necessary to protect the health and "comfort" of the capital's residents. On its face, it applied to "all persons" in Washington.

Hart, whose expertise hewed toward tax and zoning matters, had no way of knowing the extent to which the justices had evolved even in the short time since *Henderson, Sweatt,* and *McLaurin.* Through no fault of his own, their *Bolling* and *Brown* deliberations remained off-limits, including Frankfurter's bid to postpone reargument in *Bolling* until after Eisenhower took office. Other than decoding signals from the bench—an exercise that could flummox even experienced practitioners—Hart had no way of divining their emerging consensus, especially about segregation in Washington. Still, he either ignored or misread the cues, making matters worse. Comfort of the people would not include allowing a member of "the colored race" to dine in "a white restaurant," he said. Black disagreed, saying he did not see anything more related to people's comfort. Hart did not flinch.

"They have their own restaurants," he replied, meaning facilities that catered to African Americans.

"I am talking about the comfort of people," said Black. If you mean all the people, he added, that power is broad enough to authorize a legislature to pass an act to promote their comfort. "I can think of nothing affecting comfort much more than having a nice place to eat and sleep."

Hart soldiered on, fielding follow-up queries from Frankfurter and Black. But the damage to his credibility defied repair. Even Burton, renowned among colleagues for his equanimity, radiated skepticism.

Burton wondered aloud if the distinction itself were beyond the power of definition. He meant, presumably, the alleged difference between "general" legislation and "municipal" regulation. More than a decade earlier, as a senator, Burton had denounced as unconstitutional—and vowed to vote against—any proposed laws that discriminated against African Americans, including a bill that would have required segregated playgrounds in Washington. Now, Burton's inquiry reverberated with subtext, challenging the soundness of the decision below and, by implication, Jim Crow's culture of line drawing and exclusion.

Hart agreed—meaning the distinction was indeed beyond definition. With that he acknowledged the indefensibility of the lower court's premise and conceded the D.C. Circuit's majority opinion.

Now, out of candor or frustration or both, Hart went a step further. Even Congress could not enact such legislation, he maintained. It was as if he had reached back seven decades, to 1883, and conjured the rationale of the *Civil Rights Cases*: Congress had no authority to intrude upon states' rights—or in this instance, the province of the voteless capital—and require equal service in restaurants, without regard to race. Hart's written submissions had mined a similar vein of anachronism, citing the Civil Rights Act of 1875, neglecting to acknowledge *Henderson*, *Sweatt*, and *McLaurin*.

As he broached the sixty-minute mark, Hart shifted topics, arguing, as he had in his brief, that the ordinances had been repealed. In his written filing, Hart had offered a variety of explanations to support his premise, including the one used by Judge Prettyman in his concurring opinion in the D.C. Circuit: the Reconstruction-era laws had been abandoned by nonenforcement. The civil rights laws had lain dormant for years, he had written; they had "become obsolescent and been forgotten" and had been "resurrected" in *Thompson*. Closing his argument before the justices, he pressed the point again, telling the Court the ordinances had been revived for this case.

★ ★ ★ ★ ★

Brownell, Stern, and Elman filed a supplemental memorandum the next day, May 2. With their submission, they were following up on the notion—alluded to by Hart at the end of his argument and stated in his brief—that the ordinances, over the decades, had lapsed into obscurity and obsolescence and, therefore, irrelevance. They were acting "out of an abundance of caution," they wrote, "in order to dispel any possible doubts that may have arisen during the oral argument" about "the general availability" of the Reconstruction-era ordinances to the public and lawyers in Washington. As their filing made plain, they had looked into whether someone who undertook basic research in a Washington library could find the ordinances, contained in bound, published volumes of local laws enacted in 1872 and 1873.

It was not just a legal issue. In its *Thompson* coverage, the local press referred to the Reconstruction-era ordinances as the "lost" laws, a shorthand reference that spoke to a sense of puzzlement, or perhaps cynicism, about why the ordinances had languished for so long. *Thompson*, of course, had changed that.

During a colloquy with Vinson before the Court took *Thompson* under advisement, Chester Gray had made a concession: even he had not known about the Reconstruction-era laws until 1947, when Charles Hamilton Houston asked him to search the Corporation Counsel's safe for the original bound volume. (Houston was then on the research committee for the Rosenwald-funded report.) After hearing Gray's admission, Vinson balked, asking if he had to check a secure vault to find the District's laws. Gray confirmed that had happened in this case. "Well, if they are locked up in a safe with the key in your pocket, they aren't lost," Vinson said, sparking laughter in the courtroom.

Based on their inquiries, Brownell and Elman wrote, reported, bound volumes—containing the text of the Reconstruction-era laws—were in several locations: the Library of Congress, the D.C. Public Library, the bar association's library in the federal courthouse, the Justice Department's library, and the Supreme Court's library. With a four-page memo, one that did not cite a single Supreme Court decision, they cemented their point. "It is respectfully submitted, therefore, that there is no basis whatsoever for any inference that these laws were 'lost,' or that it was necessary to pry into musty archives or other obscure places not accessible to the bar and the public generally, in order to ascertain and verify their existence and continuing vitality."

Justice Douglas filed into the conference room on May 6. His notebook paper now bore the *Thompson* name.

Throughout the winter and into the spring, Douglas had tacked among court business and other diversions, including his impending divorce from his wife, Mildred. He delivered to Doubleday the final chunk of his new manuscript, *North from Malaya*, cashed a $9,785 royalty check for *Beyond the High Himalayas*—a sum equivalent to more than one-third of his salary as a justice—and vacationed in Arizona, where he shot a mountain lion. He fielded publicity requests for *North from Malaya*, scheduled for release on May 28, and asked his editor for at least a one-year hiatus—under a contract that required him to generate four books in five years. He visited Joseph P. Kennedy in Palm Beach, traveled to Panama, and, back in Washington, planned a possible two-month Himalayan trek with Robert F. Kennedy, the former SEC chairman's twenty-seven-year-old son. In private, after producing four nonfiction projects in three years, Douglas flashed glints of exhaustion and anxiety, stewing about his health, his taxes, and—saddled with divorce-related debt—his shortage of funds.

Inside the conference room, Douglas inscribed his colleagues' impressions on *Thompson*. Vinson said he was "inclined to reversal." Black showed no such indecision. He felt they should reverse per curiam, meaning an unsigned opinion rendered by the Court as a whole, the judicial equivalent of a slam-dunk. Washington's failure to enforce the laws was "irrelevant," Black said. Reed said he would affirm, parroting the restaurant's logic. As the remaining justices spoke, however, Reed emerged, again, as an outlier. One by one, Frankfurter, Burton, Clark, and Minton said they would reverse.

As the lone segregation proponent, Reed absorbed the implications. Like Chief Judge Stephens, who lived in an apartment at the Sheraton Park Hotel, Justice Reed lived at the Mayflower Hotel, and neither he nor his wife cooked. After the conference, parsing the impact in personal terms, he reportedly said: "Why—why this means that a nigra can walk into the restaurant at the Mayflower Hotel and sit down to eat at the table right next to Mrs. Reed!"

★ ★ ★ ★ ★

Douglas composed his first draft of the *Thompson* opinion by hand, before turning the pages over to a typist. At the outset, he crafted an introduction, rooting the decision in the arena of civil rights. This is a criminal proceeding, he wrote, based on the refusal of Thompson's Restaurant to serve "three well-behaved and respectable members of the Negro race" solely because of their race and color. He crossed out "three" and substituted "certain"; he drew a line through "well-behaved and respectable." He did not identify Mary Church Terrell or her test-case compatriots, though their names dotted the record, memorialized in the agreed statement of facts from the trial court and in the brief filed by Thompson's.

Within the Court, Douglas had not jockeyed for the mantle of leader, intellectual or otherwise, though not for lack of confidence in his own ability. With his globetrotting and writings, his position-taking and personal indiscretions, he had shouldered the risk of alienating his colleagues, or at least on occasion forfeiting their goodwill. Frankfurter and Jackson, in particular, suspected him of pining after the presidency, notwithstanding his statement to the contrary in his September 25, 1951, letter to Truman, the substance of which surfaced in the press the day after the *New York Times Magazine* ran "Black Silence of Fear."

Still, as the *Thompson* conference and oral arguments suggested, the justices had all but rejected the restaurant's position and the D.C. Circuit's approach—and with them, the culture of line-drawing and race-based exclusion, of whites-only dining rooms and Jim Crow counters, the anachronism of a midcentury democratic capital adhering to segregation. Even a narrowly crafted *Thompson* ruling, confined to the facts and Reconstruction-era laws, would reverberate—in Washington, across the South, and abroad. And Douglas, for all his flaws and idiosyncrasies, had intellectual gravitas. Well before some of his colleagues, he had signaled his readiness to repudiate *Plessy*. With his draft concurrence in *Henderson*, he had anticipated the

Court's current focus on racial classifications in Washington's public schools and restaurants. Since then, including the *Brown* and *Bolling* conference, he had persisted in his views.

Like *Thompson*, *Bolling* had placed before the justices the issue of segregated Washington, filtered through its separate schools—one system for whites, another for blacks. But *Bolling*, unlike *Thompson*, did not stand alone. The Court had bundled *Bolling* with the four other school-segregation cases, including *Brown*, and within the Court's internal deliberations, they remained a group, teeming with the complexities of overruling *Plessy*, of directing white and black schoolchildren to sit side by side.

Thompson, with its specific factual and legal posture, would not overrule *Plessy*, but it would send a signal, one the justices, with their rushed consideration and expedited decision-making, were ready to transmit. They had found consensus in Washington's Jim Crow restaurants and a vehicle for expressing it in *Thompson*. For all his impulsivity, Douglas had the capacity to generate a lawyerly, technical opinion. In *Thompson*, he summoned the discipline to write one.

In a paragraph, Douglas compressed the case's procedural history, its path through the local courts and the D.C. Circuit, before turning to substance. Three years after abandoning his *Henderson* concurrence, he emulated Elman's brief. Washington's legislative power extended to "all 'rightful subjects of legislation'" within the capital, he wrote, and Congress, pursuant to its constitutional authority over Washington, had leeway to delegate lawmaking power to the District, as it could with a US territory. Though a majority of the judges on the court of appeals were persuaded otherwise, he added, Washington's delegated power was as broad as the police power of a state. "And certainly so far as the federal constitution is concerned, there is no doubt that legislation which prohibits discrimination on the basis of race in the use of facilities serving a public function is within the police power of the states."

After citing the Federalist Papers and James Madison—citations that also appeared in Elman's brief—Douglas announced the Court's ruling: Washington had the power, as delegated by Congress, to enact a law barring discrimination against African Americans by restaurants in the District of Columbia. Page by page, he disposed of the remaining issue, whether the antidiscrimination laws had been abandoned or repealed. Here again, he largely echoed Elman's reasoning. Failure of the executive branch to enforce a law does not result in its modification or repeal, he said, and Washington had not enacted any other ordinance to withdraw or alter the contested ones.

As if to remind readers, he backtracked to his starting point, saying the laws prescribe "in terms of civil rights, the duties of restaurants to members of the public." At the end, three pages later, Douglas skipped a line. On the right side of the page, underneath the text, he wrote one word and underlined it: "Reversed."

★ ★ ★ ★ ★

Frankfurter turned to school segregation on May 27, two days after the Court denied a petition for certiorari in *Rosenberg*. Without success, Frankfurter had urged his colleagues to grant the Rosenbergs' petition and review the case. Now, he maneuvered for the result that eluded him and the Court in *Rosenberg*: delay. With a pair of communications, he laid the foundation for the outcome he had favored since December: scheduling *Brown*, *Bolling*, and the other cases for reargument.

In a typeset memorandum, Frankfurter told the other justices he had drafted a set of inquiries for the attorneys. His five "suggested questions," some boasting two to four subparts, did not reveal the Court's position on the issues, he said; rather, they pointed "in opposite directions," with some favoring one side and some the other. Even to the extent the interrogatories probed about remedies, suggesting the Court had resolved the issues on the merits, Frankfurter looked ahead. The critical factor in these cases, he wrote, is "psychological." "Time, in turn, is the ameliorative factor in the process of adjustment."

Separately, Frankfurter prepared a typed missive to the justices, describing a letter he had received that morning. He did not identify the correspondent, other than to convey his status as an eminent source and practitioner, "especially well informed" about the Court's history and workings. This person, Frankfurter wrote, wondered why the Court did not resurrect the practice, discontinued since Chief Justice Hughes, of tabling cases over the summer, not rushing to resolve them in the spring. The implication, at least for the school cases, and for Frankfurter, was that change was coming too fast.

★ ★ ★ ★ ★

Douglas sent *Thompson* to the printer on May 29, the day after the *New York Times* hailed *North from Malaya* as "uncommonly stimulating reading." In New York that same day, Judge Kaufman scheduled the Rosenbergs' execution for the week of June 15. On June 1, as Britons readied for the coronation of Elizabeth II, the first woman to ascend to the throne in 116 years, Douglas prepared a statement for Reuters, heralding a report that a British expedition, led by Edmund Hillary, had reached the summit of Mount Everest. Douglas also circulated to the other justices his sixteen-page, single-spaced draft opinion in *Thompson*.

Three of Douglas's FDR-era colleagues responded with handwritten notes, etched on their copies of the *Thompson* draft. On the back of the last page, Frankfurter scrawled one word: "Yes." Jackson asked for a revision indicating his noninvolvement in the argument and conference. Black angled, still, for an unsigned reversal—a reproach to the D.C. Circuit and the restaurant. In his message, he criticized them, not Douglas's draft. "I think all the contentions here are frivolous and that the opinions of the court of appeals puff up nothing into an apparent big something," he wrote. "Under the circumstances, I go along although I hate to dignify these frivolous conclusions."

Over the next few days, Douglas fielded typed notes, memorialized on Supreme Court letterhead, from his remaining colleagues. Burton and Clark signaled their agreement on June 2. Minton relayed his approval on June 3, the 145th anniversary of the birth of Jefferson Davis, the former Confederate president, marked at the Capitol with services at his statue. On June 5, the day after Frankfurter circulated a revised version of his "suggested questions," Vinson sent his *Thompson* vote to Douglas, noting his agreement as well.

★ ★ ★ ★ ★

Frankfurter drafted a letter to Vinson dated Monday, June 8. The document, the lawyerly equivalent of a memorandum to file, synthesized Frankfurter's view of the justices' consensus, forged during several conferences, about the school-segregation cases. With an eye trained on shaping the order itself, Frankfurter said he wanted to ensure that the Court's directive contained, in a "single 'package,'" the items they had discussed.

First, he wrote, as if negotiating a settlement with opposing counsel, all five cases would be set for reargument. Second, the Court would direct the attorneys to respond to questions addressing the merits and remedy; the queries would not disclose the Court's thinking, or, as he said, "tip the mitt." Third, he added, Attorney General Brownell would be invited to participate. Finally, he wrote, the Court would hand down the order with *Thompson*.

With a glance toward posterity, Frankfurter explained the justification for soliciting Brownell's involvement. The reason did not stem from "tactics or 'public-relations,'" he wrote. Rather, it reflected pragmatism—a notion he attributed to Justice Jackson, "very early" in their deliberations: the Eisenhower administration, unlike the Truman White House, might incur responsibility for enforcing the Court's decision; accordingly, it should face that responsibility as part of the adjudicative process. He also suggested how the order should read: "The Attorney General of the United States is invited to take part in the oral argument and to file an additional brief if he so desires."

★ ★ ★ ★ ★

From the bench, on June 8, 1953, Douglas began reading. The Court had convened, near the end of its term, to issue orders and opinions, not to hear oral arguments. Joseph Forer, Mary Church Terrell's lawyer, sat in the audience. At the back of the courtroom, facing the bench, an allegorical frieze depicted a standoff between good and evil, with Justice, a classically draped female, holding her sheathed sword. "This is a criminal proceeding," Douglas said, against Thompson's Restaurant, for refusing to serve "certain members of the Negro race" at one if its Washington, D.C. locations. Paragraph by paragraph, Douglas recited the decision's text. At the top of page 9, he validated the assumption Terrell and her attorneys had made from the beginning: the antidiscrimination ordinances had "survived" and remained part of the capital's "governing body of laws."

That's when Forer knew: they had won. At the end of the opinion, Douglas reinforced the point, saying the laws remained "presently enforceable."

In the end, the eight justices had aligned unanimously in *Thompson*. They remained polarized on internal dissent, subversives, and McCarthy-era excess, from *Isserman* to the Rosenbergs. But in *Thompson*, repudiating the capital's segregated restaurants by an 8-to-0 vote, they endowed their rebuke with the full weight of their institutional prestige. Even Reed joined the majority. In a twist of irony, so, too, did Justice Clark, who, in his previous role as attorney general, had affixed the subversive label to the Civil Rights Congress, which recruited Mary to launch *Thompson* in the first place.

Separately, the Court issued an order restoring all five school-segregation cases, including *Bolling*, to the docket, assigning them for oral argument on October 12. The Court instructed the attorneys to address a series of queries—tracking Frankfurter's suggestions—including whether the Court had authority, when interpreting the Fourteenth Amendment, to abolish segregated public schools, and, if segregated schools were unconstitutional, how it should fashion a remedy. "Would a decree necessarily follow," the Court said, that "Negro children should forthwith be admitted," or could the Court, pursuant to "its equity powers," sanction "an effective gradual adjustment" to integration? In New York, Thurgood Marshall and his colleagues scrapped their summer vacation plans.

★ ★ ★ ★ ★

On the other end of the phone, an *Afro* reporter broke the news. At first, Mary struggled for words. She and her committee had tried to remain "hopeful and patient," she said, "praying for a favorable decision." Eventually, she alighted on a theme she had pressed from the outset: the shame of a Jim Crow capital. It would have been "a great tragedy" for the country, and would have hurt its reputation, had the Supreme Court not decided against Thompson's Restaurant, she said. "I hate to think [w]hat an adverse decision would have meant to the whole of our group[,] but more especially to our children who have to grow up feeling that they were inferior to other people."

That afternoon, the *Washington Evening Star* splashed the news about *Thompson* across its front page, summarizing the opinion and rehashing the oral argument. Meanwhile, the *Washington Post* unleashed a team of reporters to canvass for reactions. Brownell commended the Court's opinion as "a significant forward step" toward achieving Eisenhower's antisegregation program. Gray posed for a photograph, holding a bound volume of the statutes. Mary, looking ahead to another birthday, found vindication. "I will be 90 on the 23rd of September and will die happy that children of my group will not grow up thinking they are inferior because they are deprived of rights which children of other racial groups enjoy."

Among the vanquished, the decision sparked resignation and acceptance. E. F. Colladay, general counsel for the Washington Board of Trade, the capital's business-trade group, said he was "surprised and disappointed." Even Thompson's folded. "We're going to start serving colored people immediately," said Harding Balance, the manager of the Fourteenth Street cafeteria. The chain's Washington superintendent, Sylvester Becker, phoned corporate headquarters in Chicago for guidance. "It's the law and we'll abide by it," Becker told the *Afro*.

★ ★ ★ ★ ★

At 8:30 p.m., the chairman of the capital's board of commissioners, Samuel Spencer, appeared on a local thirty-minute program, *Your Commissioners Report* on WMAL-TV. Spencer, who consulted with West earlier in the day about the Court's decision, used the broadcast to prepare the public. Restaurants must follow the ordinances "immediately," he said. The Washington Restaurant Association issued a statement, saying the Supreme Court had ruled, segregation violated the law, and members should comply with the decision.

On S Street, telegrams streamed into Mary's home. "CONGRATULA-TIONS ON YOUR SUP[E] RB FIGHT AND VICTORY," read one. An official from Delta Sigma Theta sorority cabled from Cincinnati, thanking Mary for her "UNTIRING AND MILITANT EFFORTS." From New York, an *Ebony* magazine editor, Allan Morrison, wired to say he would arrive in Washington the next day to coordinate a formal photograph of Mary at Cedar Hill, Frederick Douglass's home, for an upcoming issue.

The next morning, the *Post* and the *Afro* featured *Thompson* on their front pages. "D.C. Café Segregation Killed; Decision on Schools Postponed," read the *Post's* headline. The *Afro* distilled the Court's ruling: "Eat Anywhere."

★ ★ ★ ★ ★

Mary Church Terrell filed into Thompson's Restaurant three days later, wearing a two-piece aqua dress and a red hat. Beyond the glass doors, she assembled with veterans of her previous outings: David Scull, Geneva Brown, and Reverend Jernagin. As they wound through the cafeteria line, patrons stared. Reporters and photographers hovered. Passersby gathered outside, gazing through the window.

Four days had elapsed since the Supreme Court unveiled *Thompson*, two since the Metropolitan Police began enforcing it. Across the capital, while attorneys still worked to block the Rosenbergs' executions, pockets of resentment smoldered. A Washington resident, Mary Smith, typed a letter to Justice Douglas, saying he must be a "Negro," since "NO WHITE MAN OF HONOR would sell out the white women of his country to the BLACK RACE." A Georgia Democrat, Representative William McDonald Wheeler, introduced a bill to repeal the antidiscrimination ordinances. Given the political atmosphere—a reference to the Eisenhower administration—he entertained little hope of success. "But feeling the way I do, there was no sense in just sitting around and doing nothing," he said. Day by day, the *Post* noted the absence of disorder, the lack of complaints.

Inside Thompson's, Mary did what white customers had always done: she helped herself. From the jumble of choices, she selected soup, cake, and coffee. Jernagin, the juice and fitness enthusiast, had fasted before their mid-afternoon foray, and from a caloric standpoint, he splurged: meat, shortcake, macaroni, tomato juice.

At the cashier's desk, the manager, Harding Balance, commandeered Mary's tray and carried it into the dining area. His gesture conveyed deference and respect, courtesies to which she had always thought herself entitled. Now, by virtue of the Supreme Court's intercession, she had earned them.

Mary sat down at a square table, in an open space packed with patrons who were eating family-style, side by side. An empty coat rack hovered at the opposite end of the room. A toddler gazed out from a booster seat. Seated with Scull and Jernagin, Mary ate her soup and fielded questions. Flashbulbs popped. Another minister, the Reverend Dr. Graham G. Lacey, the pastor of Central Presbyterian Church, sat with them. Lacey, a friend of Jernagin, had arrived at Thompson's before Mary and her party so that he could monitor their progress. "It's like another Emancipation," he said.

That morning, the *Post*'s front page featured a speech that Eisenhower had given in South Dakota the previous day to a national convention of Young Republicans at Mount Rushmore. With the granite heads of George Washington, Thomas Jefferson, Abraham Lincoln, and Theodore Roosevelt looming as a backdrop, Eisenhower touted the demise of Washington's segregated restaurants, announcing that it was one of his administration's key accomplishments. "We have taken substantial steps toward insuring equal civil rights to all of our citizens, regardless of race or creed or color," he said. "And in the District of Columbia, before the bar of the Supreme Court, the attorney general has successfully appealed for the upholding of laws barring segregation in all public places in our National Capital."

Long before Eisenhower and his advisors encamped in the capital, Mary Church Terrell had slogged through the courts, weathering defeats, setbacks, and delays. She had waited more than five decades for this moment, since *Plessy* stamped her and millions of others with the taint of inferiority, saddling her with the twin burdens of sex and race. This was her recompense: for the railway officials who steered her to the Jim Crow car; for the drug-store soda fountain clerk who refused to serve her; for the dime-store manager who denied her a slice of pie.

Inside Thompson's, a photographer logged an image of Mary, surrounded by evidence of her repast: plates, a bowl, a sugar dispenser. The *Afro* ran the photograph at the top of the front page four days later. Underneath, in a separate story, Mary responded to the president's Mount Rushmore remarks. "I am greatly opposed to the Eisenhower administration taking credit for opening the restaurants," she said. "It had nothing to do with it."

Epilogue
Until Full and Final Victory

After *Thompson*, a Highland Beach neighbor reported to Mary, children clustered on the pier in the dark one evening, chatting about integration: its benefits and complexities; what they had done and where they had gone since the decision. Two African American men, including Dr. Frederick Patterson, the Tuskegee president, dined at the White House as invitees of President Eisenhower. As the *Afro-American* noted on July 28, they were the executive mansion's first black dinner guests since President Theodore Roosevelt hosted Booker T. Washington in 1901.

Mary composed a note to Justice Black from Highland Beach on July 30. "Highly Esteemed Judge Hugo Black," she opened. As she explained, Black's sister-in-law, Virginia Durr, had written her a letter, and she wanted to respond but had left the correspondence in Washington. She wondered if he would be so kind as to furnish the address.

Durr, a progressive southerner and ex-Washingtonian, had returned to Alabama with her husband, Clifford Durr, a former New Deal attorney, Rhodes Scholar, and president of the National Lawyers Guild. Virginia had written to Mary at the end of June, hailing her *Thompson* win. Before signing off, Terrell addressed Justice Black directly. "Please forgive me[,] but I cannot finish this letter without telling you I thank God from the depths of my heart that you are a member of the United States Supreme Court!!!"

Black responded the next day. "I had your letter and appreciated what you said," he wrote simply. He had forwarded Terrell's note, which she enclosed, to Mrs. Durr in Montgomery, Alabama, he added. And he supplied the address.

In August, a CIA-sponsored coup ousted Iran's prime minister, Mohammed Mossadegh, and installed Shah Mohammed Rezi Pahlavi. Attorney General

Brownell, meanwhile, vowed to blacklist the National Lawyers' Guild, whose members had represented Mary and her colleagues in *Thompson* and the Rosenbergs—who were executed in Sing Sing's electric chair on June 19, 1953. Brownell announced his intentions during the American Bar Association's Diamond Jubilee meeting in Boston, where delegates convened on August 23 for Mass in Holy Cross Cathedral, a reception at the Harvard Club, and a concert given by the Boston Symphony. Before disbanding, they sanctioned a resolution supporting disbarment of Communist lawyers. Chief Justice Vinson, who attended the ABA conference, died of a heart attack in his Washington, D.C., apartment two weeks later, in the early morning hours of September 8.

Ebony ran an essay by Mary, titled "I Remember Frederick Douglass," in the October issue, a month after publishing a seven-page profile of Thurgood Marshall. Only in the caption of a full-page photograph, where she posed with a bust of Douglass in the background, did the editors acknowledge her Supreme Court victory, noting that *Thompson* had "ended discrimination in Washington eating places." Her piece, commissioned after *Thompson* as a human-interest story, spilled across eight pages. Terrell shared her recollections of the former slave and abolitionist: Sunday tea in the Cedar Hill living room; croquet with her husband and Douglass on the Cedar Hill lawn; Douglass's wife, Helen Pitts Douglass, kneeling at his feet and fixing an errant lock of his hair.

On Mary's ninetieth birthday, she and Reverend Jernagin and two other colleagues, William Nixon, a retired teacher, and Arline D. Hays, an elderly white woman, launched a drive to banish Jim Crow from the capital's movie theaters. They began, after lunch at Longchamps Restaurant, with an outing to Loew's Capitol Theatre. To their surprise, they were admitted without objection. Still, Mary signaled her determination to banish segregation everywhere in Washington. "If I live to see integration in the schools here, then I can die in peace!" she said.

For her formal birthday celebration, a luncheon on October 10, more than seven hundred guests poured into the Statler Hotel's presidential room. It was the same room in which then-congressman Nixon had spoken on January 27, 1950, the day Thompson's first refused to serve Mary and her peers. Clad in a two-piece blue dress with diamond earrings and an orchid corsage, she had prepared brief remarks, announcing that every movie house in the capital was now admitting customers without regard to race. The theater campaign had been the "shortest and pleasantest" of her career, she said in her statement. The restaurant crusade, on the other hand, had been the "longest and hardest."

In a speech, Walter White hailed Mary as "a great American," who had struggled for "full equality" for everyone. Communists were wrong to say peace and equality could emanate only from Soviet totalitarianism. Thanks to Mary's "distinguished role," the democratic change in Washington had flowed from the Supreme Court, without violence or bloodshed. After acknowledging Charles Hamilton Houston, dubbing him "another gallant fighter" for democracy, White looked ahead: to the Supreme Court's decision in the school-segregation cases; to democracy's "unfinished business"; and, a decade hence, to 1963, when life for black Americans would be very different. Let us derive strength and faith from the example of Mary Church Terrell and Charles H. Houston, White said, so that when we gather here again on the Emancipation Proclamation's centennial, to honor Mrs. Terrell on her hundredth birthday, we will be able to say, "The job is finished."

During the festivities, Mary posed for a photograph with Paul Robeson, who had donated $90 to a Mary Church Terrell fund, unveiled that day, to eliminate segregation in Washington. He and his wife, Eslanda, had also sent written tributes to the luncheon committee, praising Mary for her leadership and perseverance. "Certainly no one in our contemporary life more exemplifies our courage, our integrity, our militant demands for full citizenship and full freedom," he wrote. In the photograph, Robeson beamed, staring into the camera; Mary looked slightly downward, her eyebrows arched, her chin lifted, with the trace of a smile.

★ ★ ★ ★ ★

Mary started a new diary in January 1954. It was an Oberlin appointment calendar, furnished by the college president. In her opening entry, dated December 30, 1953, she wrote about receiving the Philadelphia Citizens Award from the Philadelphia Cotillion Society, an African American philanthropic entity. Previous recipients of the prize, known as the Diamond Cross of Malta, included Marian Anderson, Mary McLeod Bethune, and Eleanor Roosevelt. For the ceremony, which Mary attended twelve days after leading an Atlanta march on behalf of Rosa Lee Ingram, the Georgia woman convicted of killing a white man, she wore a floor-length gown and white gloves.

As the new year unfolded, while an informant told the Federal Bureau of Investigation's Washington field office that the Coordinating Committee was infiltrated but not controlled by the Communist Party, Mary lined her calendar with engagements: beef stew with Phyllis, a church dinner with Nettie Swift, chicken à la king with her Saturday bridge club. In early February, she entertained a visit from her nephew Thomas, who was stationed in Korea. On February 6, after Thomas left for California, she turned to her journal. "I shall never see him again."

Two weeks later, Mary rode an afternoon train to New York, where she attended a George Washington's birthday dance held by the Utility Club, Inc., a community-service organization. As one of two recipients of the Seagram Vanguard Award, she fielded acclaim for her efforts to eliminate racial barriers in the nation's capital and "her inspiration to people everywhere." The group's president, who wore a colonial-style gown and wig, posed for a photograph with Mary and the second honoree, Thurgood Marshall, who was hailed for his "outstanding leadership."

Mary Church Terrell wrote her last diary entry on March 7, 1954, about misplacing the box for her Cross of Malta and then finding it, with the help of her bridge club's hostess. By early May, Mary was struggling to get out of bed. After nine decades, her health was failing. Just before Mother's Day, she canceled a trip to Atlanta, where she had planned to lead a crusade in support of Rosa Lee Ingram.

★ ★ ★ ★ ★

On Monday, May 17, reporters assembled in the Supreme Court's pressroom. In the courtroom, the justices convened at noon and trudged through routine fare: bar admissions, which consumed about thirty minutes, and a trio of opinions, read by Justices Clark and Douglas. Then, as Douglas reached the end of his recitation, Harold Willey, the clerk, routed a message from the chamber upstairs down to the pressroom through a pneumatic chute. Banning E. Whittington, the press officer, donned a suit jacket. "Reading of the segregation decisions is about to begin in the court room," he announced.

On the bench, at 12:52 p.m., Chief Justice Earl Warren began reciting the text of a single opinion, the Court's combined resolution of *Brown*, *Briggs*, and the cases from Virginia and Delaware. Warren, a former California governor (and vice presidential candidate, with Thomas Dewey), had joined the Court the previous fall, when President Eisenhower had tapped him to replace Fred Vinson. All eight associate justices arrayed themselves on either side of Warren, including Jackson, back in Court for the first time since suffering a heart attack. Across the chamber, facing the bench, a cross section of official and unofficial Washington had congregated: Attorney General Brownell; former secretary of state Dean Acheson; Chief Justice Warren's wife, Nina. Other than several attorneys, including Thurgood Marshall, James Nabrit, and George Hayes, the session had drawn few African Americans.

With unadorned declarative sentences, Warren recounted the facts and legal history, from ratification of the Fourteenth Amendment to *Plessy*, *Sweatt*, and *McLaurin*. Fixing the case in the present, he stressed "the importance of education to our democratic society": citizenship and military service, "cultural values" and "professional training", normal adjustment and success in life. "Such an opportunity, where the state has undertaken to provide it, is a right which must be made available to all on equal terms." From there, having hinted at the outcome, Warren framed the issue: whether segregating children in public schools, "solely on the basis of race," deprived black American students of equal educational opportunities, even if the physical structures were equal. "We believe that it does."

By a unanimous vote, the justices resolved the question they had dodged in *Sweatt* and *McLaurin*. And, relying on the NAACP's evidence, which they cited in a footnote, they repudiated *Plessy* and its rationale, saying legalized segregation inflicted psychological harm on children, denoting their inferiority and undermining their motivation to learn. Any contrary language in *Plessy*, they said, "is rejected."

When Warren finished reading *Brown*, he turned to *Bolling*, the Washington case. He traced the legal framework, pivoting to due process and the Fifth Amendment since, as he explained, the Fourteenth Amendment only applied to the states. "Classifications based solely upon race must be scrutinized with particular care, since they are contrary to our traditions, and hence constitutionally suspect," he read. Then, after some additional background on the law, he said Washington's segregated public schools were not reasonably related to any proper governmental objective, and they arbitrarily deprived African American children of their liberty in violation of the Fifth Amendment's due process clause. Given *Brown*, which held that the Fourteenth Amendment barred states from operating segregated schools, he added, "it would be unthinkable that the same Constitution would impose a lesser duty on the Federal Government."

Still, for all the resonance of the opinions in *Brown* and *Bolling*, for all the power of the Court's unanimity in both decisions, the justices fell short. Instead of imposing a remedy, they punted, invoking and acknowledging "the great variety of local conditions," the "considerable complexity" inherent in shaping a decree. They ordered another reargument to take place in the fall, devoted to the topic of formulating relief, and instructed the attorneys to respond to Questions 4 and 5 from their previous directive, released with *Thompson* almost a year earlier, on June 8, 1953. By doing so, the justices signaled their own ambivalence about whether to order immediate desegregation or permit a more gradual transition. They also invited Brownell and the southern states to appear at the reargument, as friends of the Court.

Before an hour had elapsed, Voice of America began saturating Eastern Europe with foreign-language broadcasts about the decision, starting with Albania at 2:15 p.m., and, fifteen minutes later, Yugoslavia and Ukraine. At 6 p.m., as morning dawned in the Far East, the VOA blanketed Asia: Japan, Korea, Vietnam, and China—in Mandarin, Cantonese, and Amoy dialects. "They have been told that the Negro in the United States is still practically a slave and a declassed citizen," an unnamed official told the *New York Times*, referring to earlier anti-American propaganda. On the record, in a separate account, the *Times* garnered Acheson's reaction to the ruling: "great and statesmanlike."

★ ★ ★ ★ ★

On May 27, ten days after Chief Justice Warren read the *Brown* and *Bolling* decisions, Senator James Eastland of Mississippi emerged on the Senate floor. During a sixty-minute speech before a handful of colleagues, Eastland said the Supreme Court had become "indoctrinated and brainwashed by Left-wing pressure groups." He honed in on Justices Black and Douglas, invoking a dossier of their transgressions, dating back to five years before *Henderson*, *Sweatt*, and *McLaurin*. Eastland said Black had received an award from the Southern Conference for Human Welfare, which he called "a notorious Communist-front organization." Relying on an *Afro-American* article about the event, which took place at the Statler Hotel in 1945, Eastland quoted remarks by Charles Hamilton Houston, who had commended Black as "a great stabilizing force" in the African American struggle for equal rights. At the banquet, Eastland said, white jurists and black leaders had sat together at the same table.

As for Douglas, Eastland relied on a sampling of newspaper coverage. He noted his receipt of a $1,000 public service award from the Sidney Hillman Foundation in December 1952 and Douglas's statement, in September 1951, about recognizing Red China. Douglas had become, to a "shocking" extent, "the creature of leftish groups," announced Eastland; his conduct raised "a presumption of tainted justice."

Eastland, who briefly practiced law before plunging into politics, also exploited the Court's failure to require immediate enforcement of desegregation, answering its call for southern input with an endorsement of states' rights and white supremacy. As Hugo Black had feared, Eastland summoned, on the South's behalf, a spirit of defiance. Southern governors were accountable only to their voters and state legislatures, not to the Supreme Court, he warned, and if necessary they might call out the militia to preserve order. "Let me make this clear," he said. "The South will retain segregation."

★ ★ ★ ★ ★

By early June, Nettie Swift was urging Mary to rally. In a handwritten note from New York, where Nettie had prepared a message to be read at the seventieth anniversary of the AAUW's Washington branch, she told Terrell to take any measures needed to improve her health. "Keep up your courage, my Dear. And may the good Lord bless you and keep you."

After *Brown* and *Bolling*, Mary posed for a photograph, seated upright, with the *Afro-American* in her lap. Across the front page, in type visible over her shoulder, the editors chronicled the Supreme Court's unanimous opinion—and Thurgood Marshall's victory—as the most important case in a generation. "Mix Schools" read the headline.

At sunset, on July 22, an ambulance pulled up outside Mary's home in Highland Beach. She had stopped taking her morning swim, withdrawn, even, from conversations about *Brown*. In an Annapolis hospital, she died of cancer two days later, two months shy of her ninety-first birthday.

Before her funeral, scheduled as an afternoon service at Lincoln Temple Congregational Church, Mary's body lay in state at the National Association of Colored Women, inside the organization's headquarters at 1601 R Street, NW. Black and white, young and old, they came, several hundred in all. Doctors and attorneys, teachers and domestics, they filed past her open coffin. A woman recited a prayer and made the sign of the cross. A young boy and girl brought a bouquet of flowers. "She was our buddy," they told a reporter for the *Afro-American*.

From a suite on West 125th Street in Harlem, about a block from the Apollo Theater, Paul Robeson's office issued a press release. Due to a concert engagement at the International Peace Arch in Blaine, Washington, located on the U.S.-Canadian border, he would be unable to attend Mary Church Terrell's funeral, he said. But in his statement, Robeson extolled her for her distinction and her friendship, someone who inspired and emboldened him. "In her unceasing militant struggle for the full citizenship of her people," he said, "Mary Church Terrell leaves us a rich heritage and a noble example—an example to be followed by us all until full and final victory."

On Thursday, July 29, 1954, mourners began streaming into Lincoln Temple Congregational, at 11th and R Streets, NW, around 10:30 a.m. Flower arrangements lined both sides of the rostrum. A team of five police officers—black and white—reserved an entire block for the funeral procession, which consisted of thirty-four cars.

At 1:00 p.m., when the service began, more than seven hundred persons had packed into the church. The temperature hovered near 100 degrees. Mourners waved cardboard fans. The overflow crowd spilled into the Sunday-school rooms, onto the front entrance, and into the street. Outside and in the basement, loud speakers transmitted the ceremony. Inside the church, in a section for dignitaries, sat representatives from the National Association of Colored Women, Delta Sigma Theta Sorority, the AAUW, the NAACP, and the Coordinating Committee, as well as students and teachers from Robert H. Terrell Junior High School. George Hayes, one of the *Bolling* attorneys, served as an honorary pallbearer. Mary's family was there, too: her half-sister Annette; her daughters Phyllis Terrell Langston and Mary Terrell Beaudreau, who had remarried (after her first husband died) and settled in Los Angeles. Terrell's nephew Thomas had not been able to join them.

From organ prelude to recessional, the service lasted only about thirty minutes. The choir sang "O Love That Will Not Let Me Go." There were readings from the Book of Psalms and Revelations. Instead of delivering a eulogy, the Reverend Charles Shelby Rooks read one of Terrell's obituaries. When it was over, Phyllis, now fifty-six, filed out, wearing a dark dress and gloves. A nurse, clad in a white uniform, followed behind her. Mary came next, with Lathall Langston, Phyllis's husband. Annette—who had held the train of Mary's wedding gown—trailed behind, accompanied by a nurse of her own. Later, Phyllis spoke to the *Chicago Defender*. "We requested the simplest of congregational services because mother has already been eulogized so much that there is nothing left to say," she said. Her mother would have wanted it that way, she added.

★ ★ ★ ★ ★

For all its restraint, Mary Church Terrell's funeral still sparked controversy, a protocol breach emanating from official Washington—the city she had called home for more than sixty years, the city she had long bemoaned for its southern outlook on race, the city she had, with *Thompson*, transformed. Queried about whether the Eisenhower administration planned to send a condolence message to Terrell's service, the White House had demurred, saying the president had not known her. Maxwell M. Rabb, an associate White House counsel, attended on his own, unofficially, and found a seat in a reserved pew. An elderly gentleman from the funeral home—the same enterprise that had coordinated Robert Terrell's service—ejected him, not knowing who he was. George Hayes steered Rabb to a place among the pallbearers.

A few days later, Rabb appeared before the National Association of Colored Women, whose members had collected in Washington for their twenty-ninth biennial convention, drawing an array of speakers, including Vice President Nixon. Rabb read a statement from First Lady Mamie Eisenhower. Mary Church Terrell, a lifelong Republican until just before Eisenhower's election, had not lived to hear his wife's tribute. Nor had she lived to see the vice president, whose hunt for Communist subversives had fueled recriminations against her and other black activists, address the organization she had helped found in *Plessy*'s aftermath. Nor had she lived to hear Nixon hail the Supreme Court's decision in *Brown*—and apparently neglect to mention her win in *Thompson*. But someone, Phyllis perhaps, saved an article from the black press about the First Lady's remarks and added it, with its photos of Mary and the First Lady, to Robert Terrell's papers, amid clippings about *Thompson* and Mary's receipt of the Cross of Malta. "For more than sixty years[,] her great gifts were dedicated to the betterment of humanity, and she left a truly inspiring record," Mamie Eisenhower said in her statement. "Her life was the epitome of courage and vision and a deep faith—an example worthy of emulation by all who love their fellow men."

Mary Church Terrell's life had begun in the year of the Emancipation Proclamation and ended two months after *Brown*. She had lived through the aftermath of Reconstruction and the attendant despair and activism, from Amenia to the Marian Anderson concert. She had endured retrenchment, insult, deprivation, indignity, hardship, and loss. With *Thompson*, she had triumphed, achieving vindication that paved the way for public school integration nationwide.

And she had done it all from Washington, D.C., the nation's democratic heart and symbolic soul. She had defied the capital's entrenched southern culture, its deference to racial separatism and exclusion. With a pair of Reconstruction-era laws, with the Supreme Court's intercession, she had prevailed, reshaping Washington's image from Dixie backwater to global beacon, for all the people.

Acknowledgments

This book would not exist without the help of many generous, knowledgeable, and dedicated people around the country.

At the Library of Congress, I relied extensively on collections in the Manuscript Reading Room, the Newspaper and Current Periodical Reading Room, and the Law Library Reading Room. The specialists and professionals who work there helped me day after day and year after year, in person, by phone, and by email, and they have my respect and thanks. I am particularly grateful to Jeffrey M. Flannery in the Manuscript Division for his responsiveness and courtesy at every stage of this project.

The Moorland-Spingarn Research Center at Howard University was also vital to researching and writing this book, especially its holdings related to Charles Hamilton Houston, Mary Church Terrell, and Paul Robeson. I am indebted to Joellen ElBashir, Dr. Tywanna Whorley, Dr. Kenvi C. Phillips, and Richard Jenkins for their assistance, and to Dr. Clifford L. Muse Jr., the university archivist, and Seth Kronemer at Howard University School of Law.

Jean and Raymond L. Langston provided invaluable assistance from Highland Beach, Maryland. They answered my questions, shared their insights, and gave me access to their collection of Mary Church Terrell diaries, letters, and papers, which they have since donated to Oberlin College. They have my profound gratitude.

Relatives of Mary Church Terrell's colleagues during the *Thompson* era were also generous with their time and wisdom, including Thai Jones, the grandson of Annie Stein, who is also the author of a nonfiction book about three generations of his family's activism and a journalism school classmate of mine; Eleanor Stein, Annie's daughter; and Shanelle Rein and Richard Rein, who are the granddaughter and son, respectively, of David Rein, one of the attorneys for Mary Church Terrell.

In Washington and beyond, many people helped me track down documents and information and confirm facts, including Patricia McCabe

Estrada and McKinley Cooper in the Supreme Court's Public Information Office; Felicia Wivchar in the Office of Art and Archives in the clerk's office of the US House; Ann Kessler at the Kiplinger Research Library, Historical Society of Washington, D.C.; the Reverend Jonathan V. Newton at the Metropolitan AME Church in Washington; Andrea Watson at Terrell Place; Michelle Hammer at Harpers Ferry National Historical Park; Guinevere Roper at the National Park Service; Stephanie Sager at the Harpers Ferry Historical Association; Raymond Traietti and Tania deLuzuriaga at Harvard University; Robin Carlaw at the Harvard University Archives in Pusey Library; Lesley Schoenfeld and Jane Kelly at the Harvard Law School Library; Kenneth M. Grossi and Louisa C. Hoffman at the Oberlin College Archives; Randy Sowell and Pauline Testerman at the Harry S. Truman Library; Edwin G. Frank and Christopher Ratliff at the University of Memphis Libraries; Yi-Fun Hsueh, president of the Harvard Club of Washington, D.C.; Diane Donham and Leelyn Johnson at the Library of Michigan; Gordon E. Hogg and Ruth Bryan at the University of Kentucky Libraries; Elizabeth E. Hilkin at the University of Texas School of Law; Linda Fariss at the Indiana University Maurer School of Law; Elizabeth L. Plummer and Tutti Jackson at the Ohio History Connection; Nathaniel Janick at the Martha's Vineyard Museum; Karen Wahl at George Washington University Law School; and Daniel J. Linke and Sara Logue at the Seeley G. Mudd Manuscript Library at Princeton University. In addition, Alexander Wheeler provided research assistance.

Tim Bent, Alyssa O'Connell, Gwen Colvin, Amy Whitmer, and Keely Latcham at Oxford University Press contributed immeasurably to this book, including rigorous, comprehensive, and thoughtful edits. They made my work infinitely better. Betsy Lerner, my agent, was invaluable from the outset and whenever I needed her. I am lucky to have the benefit of her wisdom, good sense, and sense of humor. Many thanks as well to Karen Wolny and Luba Ostashevsky for their support and professionalism.

For generosity of spirit, I would like to thank my husband, Robert. I could not have done this without him, and not just because he sharpened my writing and my thinking when I needed him most. He is a prize. My mother, also a source of inspiration, never wavered in her enthusiasm and commitment. I am grateful to her and to friends and family near and far, including Ellen Moulier and Jennifer Hardman Turner, who always make me laugh, the Washington cats who occasionally herd, and the late, lamented Tray Mitchell, who, I suspect, would have been my friend anywhere. For various acts of goodwill, encouragement, and kindness along the way, I am also grateful to my brothers, my stepson Dylan, my nieces and nephews, Sam Freedman, George Haj, LynNell Hancock, Mary Slattery Johnson, Lisa Soghor, Kerry Sheridan, Melanie D. G. Kaplan, Emily Paulsen, Mary Tabor Engel, Andrea Worden, Dan de Visé, Crystal Howard, Gregg Lange, Terri Sewell, Davison M. Douglas, Dr. Keith M. Lindgren, Dr. John T. Queenan, and the incomparable Jake. Holger Griebl translated Mary Church Terrell's German-language diaries, which she kept during her studies in Berlin and Florence. Finally, Martha Atwater, to whom this book is dedicated, for her extraordinary spirit. As one very small example, she encouraged me as a writer before and after I actually became one. I am grateful to her, grateful to have known the gift of her friendship.

Notes

AA	*Afro-American* (Washington, D.C./Baltimore, Maryland)
AAUW	American Association of University Women
AC	*Atlanta Constitution*
ACWIAWW	*A Colored Woman in a White World*, by Mary Church Terrell
ADW	*Atlanta Daily World*
AS	Annie Stein, CCEDCADL
AST	*Austin Statesman and Tribune*
BC	*Boston Courant*
BCDM	*Battle Creek Daily Moon* (Battle Creek, Michigan)
BCE	*Battle Creek Enquirer* (Battle Creek, Michigan)
BDG	*Boston Daily Globe*
BJ	*Boston Journal*
BT	*Boston Transcript*
BTW	Booker T. Washington
BTWLOC	Booker T. Washington Papers, Library of Congress
CA	*Colored American*
CCEDCADL	Coordinating Committee for the Enforcement of the D.C. Anti-Discrimination Laws
CCP	*Cleveland Call and Post*
CD	*Chicago Defender*
CDT	*Chicago Daily Tribune*
CG	*Cleveland Gazette*
CHH	Charles Hamilton Houston
CHHHUMS	Charles Hamilton Houston Papers, Howard University, The Moorland-Spingarn Research Center
CLA	*Cleveland Advocate*
CNC	*Charleston News and Courier*
CPD	*Cleveland Plain Dealer*
CRC	Civil Rights Congress
CRCPS	Civil Rights Congress Papers, Schomburg Center for Research in Black Culture
CSM	*Christian Science Monitor*

CT	*Chicago Tribune*
CWL	Colored Woman's League
DD	*Daily Defender*
DDE	Dwight D. Eisenhower
DFP	*Detroit Free Press*
DOJ	Department of Justice
EA	Edith Allen, Secretary to WOD
FDR	Franklin D. Roosevelt
FF	Felix Frankfurter, Supreme Court Justice
FFHLS	Felix Frankfurter Papers, Harvard Law School
FFLOC	Felix Frankfurter Papers, Library of Congress
FI	*Friends' Intelligencer*
FMV	Fred M. Vinson, Chief Justice, US Supreme Court
FWT	*Fort Worth Telegram*
HC	*Hartford Courant*
HDC	*Hartford Daily Courant*
HHB	Harold H. Burton, Supreme Court Justice
HHBLOC	Harold H. Burton Papers, Library of Congress
HLB	Hugo L. Black, Supreme Court Justice
HLBLOC	Hugo L. Black Papers, Library of Congress
HST	Harry S. Truman
IS	*Indianapolis Star*
JRF	Julius Rosenwald Fund
LAT	*Los Angeles Times*
LMC	Lincoln Memorial Commission
MC	*Memphis Commercial*
MCT	Mary Church Terrell
MCTHB	Mary Church Terrell Papers. Highland Beach, Maryland, private collection, since donated to Oberlin College
MCTHUMS	Mary Church Terrell Papers, Howard University, The Moorland–Spingarn Research Center
MCTJ	*Mary Church Terrell Journal*
MCTLOC	Mary Church Terrell Papers, Library of Congress
MLK	Martin Luther King Jr. Memorial Library, Washington, D.C.
NA	*Nashville American*
NAA	*National Afro-American*
NAACPLOC	NAACP Papers, Library of Congress
NACW	National Association of Colored Women
NARADC	National Archives and Records Administration, Washington, D.C.
NB	*Nashville Banner*
NJG	*New Journal and Guide*
NNPA	National Negro Press Association
NNS	*Newport News Star*
NOI	*New Orleans Item*

NS	Nettie Swift (Mrs. Clarence F.)
NYA	*New York Age*
NYAN	*New York Amsterdam News*
NYEJ	*New York Evening Journal*
NYEP	*New York Evening Post*
NYG	*New York Globe*
NYHT	*New York Herald Tribune*
NYJ	*New York Journal*
NYOC	*New York Observer and Chronicle*
NYS	*New York Sun*
NYT	*New York Times*
PC	*Pittsburgh Courier*
PDW	*People's Daily World*
PI	*Philadelphia Inquirer*
PIHULS	Phineas Indritz Papers, Howard University School of Law
PJ	*Providence Journal*
PPR	*Pioneer Press*
PRHUMS	Paul Robeson Papers, Howard University, The Moorland-Spingarn Research Center
PT	*Philadelphia Tribune*
RHJ	Robert H. Jackson, Supreme Court Justice
RHJLOC	Robert H. Jackson Papers, Library of Congress
RHT	Robert H. Terrell
RHTLOC	Robert H. Terrell Papers, Library of Congress
RNCSNC	Report of the National Committee on Segregation in the Nation's Capital
RRC	Robert R. Church
RRM	Robert R. Moton
RRMLOC	Robert R. Moton Papers, Library of Congress
RW	Roy Wilkins, NAACP
SFC	*San Francisco Chronicle*
SLPD	*St. Louis Post-Dispatch*
TA	*The Advance*
TAC	Thomas A. Church
TCC	Tom C. Clark, Supreme Court Justice
TDJ	*Topeka Daily Journal*
TM	Thurgood Marshall, NAACP
TR	Theodore Roosevelt
TRLOC	Theodore Roosevelt Papers, Library of Congress
TS	*The Sun* (also *Baltimore Sun*) (Baltimore, Md.)
UMLRRC	University of Memphis Libraries, Robert R. Church Family Papers
WA	*Washington American*
WB	*Washington Bee*
WCCS	War Camp Community Service

WE	*Washington Eagle*
WES	*Washington Evening Star*
WGH	Warren G. Harding
WH	*Washington Herald*
WHS	The Historical Society of Washington, D.C.
WHT	William Howard Taft
WHTLOC	William Howard Taft Papers, Library of Congress
WLP	William L. Patterson
WOD	William O. Douglas
WODLOC	William O. Douglas Papers, Library of Congress
WP	*Washington Post*
WPTH	*Washington Post, Times Herald*
WSJ	*Wall Street Journal*
WSS	*Washington Sunday Star*
WT	*Washington Tribune*
WTC	William T. Coleman Jr.
WTH	*Washington Times Herald*
WTI	*Washington Times*
WW	Walter White, NAACP

Unless otherwise noted, citations to information from Mary Church Terrell's journal are from her journals and diaries contained with her papers at the Library of Congress.

PROLOGUE: JANUARY 27, 1950

page 3. Thompson's Restaurant: See Affidavits, circa Jan. 27, 1950, in MCTLOC (one for each participant). These affidavits provide details about the incident inside Thompson's on January 27, 1950, including the manager's conversation with Jernagin and Terrell. They were prepared at Forer and Rein after the incident at the restaurant. See MCT, untitled document with written recollections of *Thompson*, Apr. 6, 1954, in MCTLOC [hereafter, "Written Recollections"]. Other sources for this scene include: *WP*, Jan. 31, 1950; *AA*, Feb. 11, 1950; Thai Jones, *A Radical Line: From the Labor Movement to the Weather Underground, One Family's Century of Conscience* (New York: Free Press, 2004), 97; *WES*, Jan. 27, 1950; *NYAN*, June 20, 1953 (interior photos).

page 3. Streetcar tracks: See *WP*, Jan. 28, 1950 (photograph).

page 3. Monumental boulevards and spaces: See The National Committee on Segregation in the Nation's Capital, *Segregation in Washington: A Report of the National Committee on Segregation in the Nation's Capital* (Chicago, 1948), 1–2 [hereafter "RNCSNC"].

page 3. Details of Fourteenth Street: WHS, Photograph Nos. 3173–3246, July 23, 1950; *WP*, Jan. 28, 1950 (exterior photo of Thompson's); *PC*, circa Mar. 31, 1950, reprinted in Dennis Brindell Fradin and Judith Bloom Fradin, *Fight On!: Mary*

Church Terrell's Battle for Integration (New York: Clarion Books, 2003), 131 (photo of Thompson's exterior).

page 3. Men in fedoras jaywalking: See *WP*, Jan. 28, 1950 (photo outside Thompson's).

page 3. Somewhere else: The business district's center was on Seventh Street. See Kate Masur, *An Example for All the Land: Emancipation and the Struggle over Equality in Washington, D.C.* (Chapel Hill: University of North Carolina Press, 2010), 114.

page 3. Charter member: See MCT Affidavit, circa Jan. 27, 1950, ¶2; National Negro Committee, Program, Second Annual Conference, May 12–14, 1910, in MCTLOC (listing Mary Church Terrell as a committee member); William English Walling to MCT, July 26, 1910, in MCTHUMS; MCT, *ACWIAWW*, 234; *MCTJ*, Oct. 22, 1949, in MCTHB; Envelope, postmarked Oct. 28, 1949, in MCTLOC (with her handwriting, marked "*Save*" and "Du Bois says I am a founder of the NAACP").

page 5. Washington background: Sources include Phineas Indritz, "Racial Ramparts in the Nation's Capital," 41 Georgetown L. J. 297, 297, and n11, 301 (Mar. 1953) [hereafter "Indritz, Ramparts"]; RNCSNC, 4–6 (discrimination against diplomats from African, Caribbean, and Latin nations as well as India).

page 4. Thompson's background: *WSJ*, Nov. 26, 1949; *WSJ*, Nov. 26, 1949; *CDT*, Mar. 5, 1950; T. Jones, *A Radical Line*, 97.

page 4. Thrift: MCT to RHT, Aug. 12, 1900, in MCTLOC.

page 4. Down the block: See *National Council of American-Soviet Friendship, Inc. v. McGrath*, Petition for Writ of Certiorari, US Supreme Court, October Term, 1949, No. 7, filed Jan. 23, 1950.

page 4. Without charge: See AS to MCT, June 6, 1950, in MCTLOC; "For Immediate Release," news release, May 25, 1951, in MCTLOC.

page 4. Hand-picked: AS to MCT, Jan. 5, 1950, in MCTLOC; CCEDCADL, Minutes, Executive Committee Meeting, Jan. 18, 1950, in MCTLOC.

page 4. Jernagin background: *AA*, Mar. 1, 1958; *DD*, Feb, 24, 1958; *AA*, June 10, 1952; *CCP*, Mar. 1, 1958; *ADW*, Jan. 23, 1944; *PC*, Nov. 13, 1943; *ADW*, Nov. 11, 1943.

page 4. Letterhead: David Scull to MCT, Apr. 3, 1951, in MCTLOC.

page 5. "the fighting parson": *AA*, Mar. 1, 1958.

page 6. Regret: MCT, "If I Were Young Again," *Negro Digest*, Sept. 1943, 58, in MCTLOC.

page 6. Washington history: Sources include Constance McLaughlin Green, *The Secret City: A History of Race Relations in the Nation's Capital* (Princeton: Princeton University Press, 1967), 13, 20–21, 29–32, 41, 59–60, 67, 70–72, 78–80; Masur, *An Example for All the Land*, 7, 15, 17–18, 23, 25–26, 41, 45, 101, 106–7, 130–31, 161–62, 171–72, 177; 207, 213, 218–19, 250–51; *WP*, Dec. 13, 2012; The Smithsonian Anacostia Museum and Center for African American History and Culture, *The Black Washingtonians: The Anacostia Museum Illustrated Chronology* (Hoboken, N.J.: John Wiley & Sons, 2005), 42–45 [hereafter "*The Black Washingtonians*"].

page 6. Jurisdiction over: US Const., art. I, §8, cl. 17.

page 6. "revolting sight": Green, *The Secret City*, 20.

page 6. "gangs of Negroes": Ibid.

page 7. "deleterious influence": Green, *The Secret City*, 31.

page 7. Model of: Masur, *Example for All the Land*, 23.

page 7. "the national shame": National Archives and Records Administration, Featured Documents, "The District of Columbia Emancipation Act," http://www .archives.gov/exhibits/featured_documents/dc_emancipation_act/.

page 8. "Colored Persons": Masur, *Example for All the Land*, 45, 101, 106–7.

page 8. Universal men's suffrage: Ibid., 11, 18, 130; Green, *The Secret City*, 80.

page 8. Voting rights/political background: Masur, *Example for All the Land*, 10–12, 130, 148, 158–61, 207, 213, 218–19, 250–51; Green, *The Secret City*, 80, 91, 96, 104, 111–12, 162; Indritz, "Post Civil War Ordinances Prohibiting Racial Discrimination in the District of Columbia," 42 Georgetown L. J. 179, 202 (Jan. 1954); Indritz, Ramparts, 304–5 and n31.

page 8. Transform race relations: Masur, *Example for All the Land*, 131, 172.

page 8. Background on ordinances: Green, *The Secret City*, 94, 96, 108–9; Masur, *Example for All the Land*, 161–63, 171–72; T. Jones, *A Radical Line*, 94; Gladys Byram Shepperd, *Mary Church Terrell: Respectable Person* (Baltimore: Human Relations Press, 1959), 22; *District of Columbia v. John R. Thompson Co., Inc.*, No. 617, Brief for the United States as Amicus Curiae, filed Apr. 23, 1953 [hereafter "DOJ *Thompson*"].

page 9. Police court: Indritz, Ramparts, 306; *District of Columbia v. John R. Thompson Co., Inc.*, 81 A.2d 249, 259–60n5 (D.C. Mun. App. 1951). While one district supreme court case in 1872 might be construed as undermining one of the ordinances (see Masur, *Example for All the Land*, 230), the Municipal Court of Appeals in *Thompson* found that in none of the earlier cases was "the validity of the act" passed upon.

page 9. Reasons unrelated: Indritz, Ramparts, 306; *District of Columbia v. John R. Thompson Co., Inc.*, 81 A.2d 249, 259–60n5 (D.C. Mun. App. 1951).

page 9. Not expressly repealed: Indritz, Ramparts, 305; *District of Columbia v. John R. Thompson Co., Inc.*, 81 A.2d 249, 259–60n5 (D.C. Mun. App. 1951); RNCSNC, 18; DOJ *Thompson*, 15.

page 9. Out of fashion, into disuse: See Indritz, Ramparts, 306–7.

page 9. Racist proclivities: See Indritz, Ramparts, 307.

page 9. Little incentive: Indritz, Ramparts, 308.

page 9. Washington in 1950: RNCSNC, 12, 13, 26, 55, 79, 15, 16, 82; Indritz, Ramparts, 298n2, 303.

page 10. "And photographs": *WES*, June 4, 1949, in HHBLOC.

page 10. Courting support: See *PT*, Jan. 17, 1950; *NYT*, Jan. 5, 1950.

page 10. State of the Union: HST, "Annual Message to the Congress on the State of the Union," Jan. 4, 1950, http://www.presidency.ucsb.edu/ws/?pid=13567.

page 10. First had in 1948: HST, "Special Message to the Congress on Civil Rights," Feb. 2, 1948, http://www.presidency.ucsb.edu/ws/?pid=13006; David McCullough, *Truman* (New York: Touchstone, 1993), 586–88.

page 10. Supper speech: HST, "Remarks at a Supper for Democratic Senators and Representatives," Washington, D.C., Jan. 12, 1950, http://www.presidency.ucsb.edu/ws/index.php?pid=13479.

page 11. Civil rights plank: Democratic Party Platform of 1948, July 12, 1948, http://www.presidency.ucsb.edu/ws/index.php?pid=29599.

page 11. "We can't": HST, "Remarks to a Delegation from the National Emergency Civil Rights Mobilization Conference," Washington, D.C., Jan. 17, 1950, http://trumanlibrary.org/publicpapers/viewpapers.php?pid=586.

page 11. Inertia: See Indritz, Ramparts, 298–303.

page 11. State Department, Congress, abroad: *WP*, Jan. 26, 1950; *WP*, Jan. 27, 1950.

page 11. "Women's News": *WP*, Jan. 27, 1950.

page 11. Georgetown salons: See Louis Menand, "Table Talk: How the Cold War Made Georgetown Hot," review of *The Georgetown Set* by Gregg Herken, *The New Yorker*, Nov. 10, 2014; Sally Quinn, "In a New Play, the Washington Hostess Lives Again," *WP*, May 16, 2014.

page 11. Hiss background: Sources include *WP*, Jan. 26, 1950; *NYT*, Jan. 26, 1950; *WES*, Jan. 27, 1950; *WP*, Jan. 28, 1950; Michael J. Ybarra, *Washington Gone Crazy: Senator Pat McCarran and the Great American Communist Hunt* (Hanover, N.H.: Steerforth Press, 2004), 487; McCullough, *Truman*, 651, 759.

page 11. Washington on January 27: For details see *WES*, Jan. 27, 1950; *WP*, Jan. 27, 1950.

page 11. High-priority target: *WP*, Jan. 26, 1950.

page 11. "As a Negro": Ibid.

page 11. Nixon floor speech: *CDT*, Jan. 27, 1950.

page 12. Jam-packed day: HST, "Remarks to the Women's Patriotic Conference on National Defense," Washington, D.C., Jan. 26, 1950, http://www.presidency.ucsb.edu/ws/index.php?pid=13579. For details, see *WP*, Jan. 26, 1950; *WES*, Jan. 27, 1950; *WP*, Jan. 28, 1950.

page 13. "I want this": *WP*, Jan. 28, 1950.

page 13. In the law office: MCT, Written Recollections, Apr. 6, 1954, in MCTLOC.

page 13. Enforcement authority: See DOJ *Thompson*, 101; Indritz, Ramparts, 304.

page 13. Not known: See Philip Elman and Norman Silber, "The Solicitor General's Office, Justice Frankfurter, and Civil Rights Litigation, 1946–1960: An Oral History," 100 Harvard L. Rev. 817, 831 [hereafter "Elman, Oral History"]; Richard Kluger, *Simple Justice: The History of Brown v. Board of Education and Black America's Struggle for Equality* (New York: Vintage Books, 1977), 579.

page 13. "may still be": RNCSNC, 18.

page 13. "Communist front": *TS*, Jan. 23, 1950.

page 13. Urging them: *WP*, May 17, 1949; Donald M. Murtha to John Russell Young, May 16, 1949, in PIHULS.

page 13. New York headquarters: See Memorandum to All Sponsoring Organizations from RW and Arnold Aronson, Dec. 21, 1949, in NAACPLOC.

page 13. Little attention: For several years, the Julius Rosenwald Fund had tried to encourage the NAACP to participate actively in its study of segregation in Washington, with limited success. See, for example, Will W. Alexander to WW, Mar. 25, 1946, in NAACPLOC. Washington civil rights leaders, including the NAACP's branch in the capital, supported the study, but NAACP leaders in New York were cautious. See TM to WW, Jan. 20, 1947, in NAACPLOC; Memorandum to WW from Leslie Perry, Jan. 21, 1947, in NAACPLOC; William H. Hastie to WW, Jan. 20, 1947, in NAACPLOC; TM to WW, Jan. 24, 1947, in NAACPLOC.

page 13. Special counsel: See Memorandum to All Sponsoring Organizations from RW and Arnold Aronson, Dec. 21, 1949, in NAACPLOC (titles on letterhead).

page 13. National policy: See James T. Patterson, *Brown v. Board of Education: A Civil Rights Milestone and Its Troubled Legacy* (New York: Oxford University Press, 2002), 12–14.

page 13. More pressing: See Patterson, *Brown v. Board of Education*, 12–14; *NJG*, Jan. 21, 1950 (*Sweatt* and *Henderson*).

page 13. Segregated public graduate schools: See, for example, Memorandum to Messrs. Hastie, Hill, Houston, Johnson, Martin, Ming, and Nabrit from TM, Oct. 19, 1948, in CHHHUMS; Memorandum to Messrs. Hastie, Houston, Ming, and Nabrit from TM, Apr. 29, 1949, in CHHHUMS.

page 14. Communist-front: See Memorandum to All Sponsoring Organizations from RW and Arnold Aronson, Dec. 21, 1949, in NAACPLOC; D. H. Dowdal to RW, Jan. 8, 1950, in NAACPLOC.

page 14. Held sway: See Memorandum to All Sponsoring Organizations from RW and Arnold Aronson, Dec. 21, 1949, in NAACPLOC; McCullough, *Truman*, 586, 588.

page 14. Virtually alone: See *WP*, May 17, 1949; William L. Houston to Roy Wilkins, Nov. 6, 1949, in NAACPLOC.

page 14. Terrell background: Sources include *WP*, Oct. 28, 1891; MCT, *A Colored Woman in a White World* (Amherst, N.Y.: Humanity Books, 2005), 8–16 (Ham foreword), 20, 31–32, 37–38, 43–44, 49, 56, 64, 72, 74, 92–99, 135, 141–43, 157–62; Shepperd, *Mary Church Terrell*, 21–23; Roland M. Baumann, *Constructing Black Education at Oberlin College: A Documentary History* (Athens, Ohio: Ohio University Press, 2010), 68; *General Catalogue of Oberlin College, 1833–1908* (Oberlin, 1909), 218, 366; Preston Lauterbach, *Beale Street Dynasty: Sex, Song, and the Struggle for the Soul of Memphis* (New York: W.W. Norton, 2015), 1–183.

page 14. Envisioned: See Lauterbach, *Beale Street Dynasty*, 2–3, 50–51, 180–81.

page 14. Oberlin background: Sources include Henry Louis Gates Jr., *Life Upon These Shores: Looking at African American History, 1513–2008* (New York: Alfred A. Knopf, 2011), 73; Baumann, *Constructing Black Education at Oberlin College*, 1–2,

16–18; Oberlin College, About Oberlin, "Early History," http://new.oberlin.edu/about/history.dot.

page 14. Other establishments: See RHT to M. G. Gibbs, Aug. 10, 1916, in MCTLOC; MCT, *ACWIAWW*, 462–65. Since *ACWIAWW* was written long after many of the events it describes, I supplement it, as much as possible, with contemporaneous accounts and documents.

page 14. Gentility: Editorial, *The Independent*, July 14, 1904, 108; Shepperd, *Mary Church Terrell*, 4.

page 14. Light-skinned: *BCE*, Nov. 2, 1907.

page 14. Some southerners: *MCTJ*, Apr. 9, 1908, in MCTLOC; *MCTJ*, Jan. 28, 1908, in MCTLOC; *MCTJ*, Feb. 4, 1909, in MCTLOC; *MCTJ*, May 6, 1948, in MCTHB.

page 14. Including white women: See Maude Spier Brubaker to MCT, Oct. 10, 1946, in MCTLOC.

page 14. "I have never": MCT, *ACWIAWW*, 471; see MCT, *ACWIAWW*, 29, 75.

page 14. Seethed: See Rayford Ellis to MCT, Oct. 31, 1947, in MCTLOC; *MCTJ*, Feb. 14, 1948, in MCTHB.

page 15. Truman press conference: HST, The President's News Conference, Washington, D.C., Jan. 27, 1950, http://www.presidency.ucsb.edu/ws/index.php?pid=13601Conference; McCullough, *Truman*, 761.

page 15. Compromise: *WP*, Jan. 26, 1950.

page 15. "awesome weapon": *WP*, Jan. 27, 1950; see Ybarra, *Washington Gone Crazy*, 487.

page 15. String of letters: WOD to Claire Sweany, Jan. 27, 1950, in WODLOC; WOD to Charles Mussared, Jan. 27, 1950, in WODLOC; WOD to George C. McGhee, Jan. 27, 1950, in WODLOC.

page 15. World travel: See WOD to Robert S. Allen, Jan. 20, 1950, in WODLOC.

page 15. Foreign affairs: WOD, *The Court Years*, 288–89.

page 16. "He has summarized": WOD to George C. McGhee, Jan. 27, 1950 in WODLOC.

page 16. Douglas background: Sources include Bruce Allen Murphy, *Wild Bill: The Legend and Life of William O. Douglas* (New York: Random House, 2003), xv, 10–12, 14–15, 18, 20–24, 272–78, 282–86; WOD to FMV, Nov. 1, 1949, in RHJLOC; WOD, *Go East Young Man*, xi, 8, 17–18, 31–33, 54, 59, 63–64, 97–98, 100–102, 117, 124, 127–34, 139, 156–74, 257–95; Jean Edward Smith, *FDR* (New York: Random House, 2007), 338; McCullough, *Truman*, 300; William O. Douglas, *The Court Years, 1939–1975: The Autobiography of William O. Douglas* (New York: Random House, 1980), 4, 41, 288–89; Jeffrey Rosen, *The Supreme Court: The Personalities and Rivalries That Defined America* (New York: Times Books/Henry Holt and Co., 2007), 142–43, 169–70; "The Work Sheet," unidentified newspaper clipping, June 8, 1948, in HHBLOC; EA to Stan [Sparrowe], May 31, 1951, in WODLOC; WOD to Stanley E. Sparrowe, Mar. 20, 1953, in WODLOC; WOD to Everett Sutphin, Apr. 1, 1950, in WODLOC.

page 16. Butler denounced: *NYT*, Nov. 30, 1922.

page 16. Robeson background: Martin Duberman, *Paul Robeson: A Biography* (New York: The New Press, 1995), 5–6, 24, 34, 53–55; WOD, *Go East Young Man*, 138–39; Victor S. Navasky, *Naming Names* (New York: Penguin Books, 1981), 187–88.

page 17. Old men: William O. Douglas, *Go East Young Man, The Early Years: The Autobiography of William O. Douglas* (New York: Vintage Books, 1983), 465; WOD, *The Court Years*, 7.

page 17. Schemes: WOD to FDR, June 23, 1939, in WODLOC; WOD to FDR, Sept. 19, 1939, in WODLOC; WOD to FDR, Nov. 10, 1939, in WODLOC; WOD to FDR, Aug. 22, 1940, in WODLOC.

page 17. "shackled and sad": WOD to John J. Hooker, Oct. 19, 1948, in WODLOC.

page 17. Nightlife: EA to Hon. Hussein Ala, Oct. 13, 1950, in WODLOC; Memorandum from EA to WOD, Feb. 5, 1953, in WODLOC; Message from EA to WOD, Feb. 4, 1953, in WODLOC.

page 17. western hats: EA to Hamley & Co., Oct. 23, 1950, in WODLOC.

page 17. Bourbon, Scotch: See, for example, *CPD*, circa Mar. 19, 1950, in HHBLOC; *WP*, Jan. 26, 1950 (ad); WOD to Damon Trout, May 2, 1949, in WODLOC.

page 17. Cigarettes: See, for example, *WP*, Jan. 26, 1950.

page 17. Slump-shouldered: See HST Library, State Department Photograph, WOD with Prime Minister Mohammed Mossadegh, Nov. 5, 1951, Accession No. 66–8018, http://www.trumanlibrary.org/photographs/view.php?id=3287.

page 17. Cajoled: WOD to Robert S. Allen, Jan. 20, 1950, in WODLOC.

page 18. Truman poker buddy: McCullough, *Truman*, 511; see Gilbert King, *Devil in the Grove: Thurgood Marshall, the Groveland Boys, and the Dawn of a New America* (New York: Harper Perennial, 2013), 342.

page 18. "rusty": WOD to FMV, Nov. 20, 1949, in RHJLOC.

page 18. "Save a luncheon": WOD to Harold L. Ickes, Dec. 20, 1949, in WODLOC.

page 18. Lamented: WOD to Thurman Arnold, Jan. 19, 1950, in WODLOC.

page 18. Wire photo: FF to RHJ, n.d., enclosing photograph dated circa Nov. 5, 1949, in RHJLOC.

page 18. Hobbyhorse: See FF to RHJ, n.d., written on *NYHT* hobbyhorse photo of WOD, in RHJLOC.

page 18. Postponed: FMV to WOD, Oct. 17, 1949, in WODLOC (delaying *Henderson*).

page 18. Robeson railed: *ADW*, Oct. 20, 1949.

page 18. Fell short: See Rosen, *The Supreme Court*, 149; Elman, Oral History, 844 (Frankfurter's nicknames for colleagues, including "the *Chamer*," meaning "fool," for Reed, and "Yak" for WOD).

page 18. "Cheer up": FF to RHJ, n.d., enclosing photograph dated circa Nov. 5, 1949, in RHJLOC.

page 18. "From your": FF to RHJ, n.d., written on *NYHT* hobbyhorse photo of WOD, in RHJLOC.

page 18. Rifle: EA to WOD, Jan. 5, 1950, in WODLOC.

page 18. Official: EA to WOD, Jan. 5, 1950, in WODLOC; WOD to Gerald Dooher, Jan. 24, 1950, in WODLOC.

page 18. Traveled with: WOD, *Strange Lands and Friendly People* (New York: Harper & Brothers 1951), xv; WOD to Gerald Dooher, Jan. 24, 1950, in WODLOC.

page 18. Taxes: EA to WOD, Jan. 25, 1950, in WODLOC; EA to WOD, Jan. 5, 1950, in WODLOC.

page 18. "It is a": EA to WOD, Jan. 5, 1950, in WODLOC.

page 18. "And your checkbook": EA to WOD, Jan. 5, 1950, in WODLOC.

page 19. "This makes it": Ickes to WOD, Jan. 6, 1950, in WODLOC.

page 19. Sensed a reaction: MCT, Written Recollections, Apr. 6, 1954, in MCTLOC.

page 19. Something had happened: Ibid.

page 19. Usher in: See Masur, *Example for All the Land*, 261.

CHAPTER 1: ON TO THE BATTLEFIELD

page 20. Harvard's 1884 Commencement: Sources include *NYT*, June 21, 1884; *BDG*, June 26, 1884; *NYT*, June 26, 1884.

page 20. Sanders Theatre: Sources include *BDG*, June 26, 1884; *NYT*, June 26, 1884; Henry Van Brunt, "Harvard Memorial Hall and Sanders Theatre," *The Harvard Register*, Mar. 1880, IVA.

page 20. Applause: Wilbur P. Thirkield, "Letter from Boston: Negro Orator at the Harvard University Commencement," circa July 24, 1884, in RHTLOC. Thirkield later served as president of Howard University.

page 21. Son of former slaves: *HDC*, May 28, 1884.

page 21. Written his speech: RHT, "The Negro Race in America Since Its Emancipation," Cambridge, Mass., June 25, 1884, in RHTLOC. All quotations are from this source.

page 21. Memorial Hall: Sources include Van Brunt, IVA.

page 21. "Give their proud": Harvard University, Office for the Arts at Harvard, "History of Memorial Hall," https://www.fas.harvard.edu/~memhall/history.html.

page 21. Fabled regiment: James M. McPherson, *Battle Cry of Freedom: The Civil War Era* (New York: Oxford University Press, 2003), 686.

page 21. Background on Terrell: Sources include *HDC*, May 28, 1884; *Friends' Review*, June 7, 1884, 710; *Robert Heberton Terrell: A Colored Judge of Washington, D.C.*, circa April 1926, in MCTLOC; *NAA*, Feb. 1891, in RHTLOC; *FWT*, Apr. 19, 1908, in MCTLOC; RHT Biography, circa 1901 (handwritten by RHT), in RHTLOC; MCT, *ACWIAWW*, 98.

page 21. White cloths: Kennedy, "Undergraduate Life at Harvard," 53; see Van Brunt, IVA (illustration).

page 21. African American servers: "A Peep at Harvard," *Californian*, Nov. 1880, 476; *WP*, Dec. 25, 1881; Van Brunt, IVA.

page 21. White jackets: See Van Brunt, IVA (illustration).

page 21. Courses and accompaniments: Van Brunt, n1; "A Peep at Harvard," 476; *WP*, Dec. 25, 1881.

page 22. Integrated streetcars: Masur, *An Example for All the Land*, 101–5, 189.

page 22. Integrated schools: Green, *The Secret City*, 101; Masur, *An Example for All the Land*, 189.

page 22. "All were dear": RHT, "The Ancient Greeks," *The Student's Aid*, Mar. 9, 1880, 14, in RHTLOC.

page 22. "And what": Ibid.

page 22. Tweed suits: "A Peep at Harvard," 476.

page 22. Center-parted: Ibid.

page 22. Mannerisms: Ibid.

page 22. Tuition: See Harvard College Bond, Oct. 23, 1880, in MCTHB.

page 22. Menial: *BT*, reprinted in *NYA*, circa June 1884, in RHTLOC.

page 22. Gentleman: Kennedy, "Undergraduate Life at Harvard," 53; *Friends' Review*, 710.

page 22. Tapped him: See Harvard College, "Commencement 1884," Feb. 23, 1884, in RHTLOC.

page 22. Elocution lessons: Ibid.

page 22. Late May: *WP*, May 23, 1884.

page 22. Media outlets: See *The Literary World*, June 14, 1884, 196; "Personals," *The Advance*, June 19, 1884, 413; "News Notes," *Saturday Evening Post*, June 21, 1884, 13.

page 22. "Virginia-born Negro": *The Literary World*, June 14, 1884, 196; "News Notes," *Saturday Evening Post*, June 21, 1884, 13.

page 22. Waiting tables: *HDC*, May 28, 1884; *The Literary World*, June 14, 1884, 196.

page 23. Speaking at commencement: Thirkield, "Letter from Boston," in RHTLOC; *TA*, June 19, 1884, 413 (summa cum laude); "News Notes," *Saturday Evening Post*, June 21, 1884, 13 (ranked in top seven). Because Harvard University records do not generally recognize race, the university's archives can confirm only that Robert H. Terrell spoke at commencement in 1884, not that he was the first African American cum laude graduate or the first African American commencement speaker. E-mail message to author from Robin Carlaw, Nov. 25, 2014.

page 23. Twelve-page: Harvard University, Commencement Program, June 25, 1884, in RHTLOC (in Latin).

page 23. Measured tone: Thirkield, "Letter from Boston," in RHTLOC.

page 23. Silence blanketed: Thirkield, "Letter from Boston," in RHTLOC; *NYG*, circa July 1, 1884, in RHTLOC.

page 23. Solemnity: See Thirkield, "Letter from Boston," in RHTLOC.

page 23. Greek scholar: See Letter of Recommendation from John Williams White for RHT, June 10, 1884, in RHTLOC.

page 23. At least two: "Our Hub Letter: The Graduation and Commencement Season," circa July 1, 1884, in RHTLOC; Harvard University, 1884 Commencement Program, VI, in RHTLOC.

page 23. "My first ballot": See Ward Nine, Garfield & Arthur, Regular Republican Ticket, circa Nov. 1880, in RHTLOC.

page 23. *Civil Rights Cases*: 109 U.S. 3 (1883).

page 24. Incident: *HDC*, Mar. 14, 1883; *BDG*, Mar. 15, 1883.

page 24. J. H. Atwood: *BDG*, Mar. 15, 1883.

page 24. "darkey": Ibid.

page 25. "unendurable": Ibid.

page 25. Applause: *NYG*, circa July 1, 1884, in RHTLOC.

page 25. "honourable record": Letter of Recommendation from John Williams White for RHT, June 10, 1884, in RHTLOC.

page 25. "He has comported": Ibid.

page 25. Terrell and Richard T. Greener: *HC*, Jan. 26, 1885; *CG*, Oct. 13, 1888. Years later, Greener wrote Terrell to congratulate him on his professional achievements. See Richard T. Greener to RHT, Jan. 26, 1914, in MCTHB.

page 25. Harvard College's first black: See "First Black Alumnus's Papers Found," *Harvard Magazine*, Mar. 21, 2012, http://harvardmagazine.com/2012/03/greener -papers-found; *The Black Washingtonians* at 106.

page 26. Rejected: *HC*, Jan. 26, 1885; *CG*, Oct. 13, 1888; Harvard Club of Washington, D.C., Meeting Minutes, Dec. 29, 1884, on file with author.

page 26. Resigned: *CG*, Oct. 13, 1888.

page 26. "There was nothing": *HC*, Jan. 26, 1885.

page 26. "This sort of": Ibid.

page 26. "Andalusian": Editorial, *The Independent*, July 14, 1904, 107; see MCT, *ACWIAWW*, 127.

page 26. "This is a": MCT to "Fannie," [no last name] July 19, 1888, in MCTLOC. All quotations are from this source.

page 26. *City of Berlin*: MCT, *ACWIAWW*, 99; Souvenir List, The Short Trip, Steamship *City of Berlin*, July 21, 1888, in MCTLOC.

page 27. Background on Mary Church: Sources include Preston Lauterbach, *Beale Street Dynasty*, 1–2, 16, 25, 28, 32–34, 37–40, 45–46, 50–51, 70–72; MCT, *ACWIAWW*, 10–11 (Ham foreword), 31–36, 38–41, 49–71; MCT to RHT, Oct. 27, 1912, in MCTLOC; RRC to MCT, Oct. 15, 1875, in Oberlin College Archives, Lawson-Merrill Papers, Box 5 (she lived at 143 Groveland).

page 27. Brothels: Lauterbach, *Beale Street Dynasty*, 2, 51, 113, 180. It is unclear whether Mary Church Terrell knew about her father's businesses; he kept his children insulated from his affairs, at least until he died, when his son, Robert R. Church Jr., assumed responsibility for them. See Lauterbach, *Beale Street Dynasty*, 69, 72, 179–80. But she lived in her father's home after she graduated from Oberlin, from the fall of 1884 until the summer of 1885, and, as she later wrote. she knew he was not "a saint." MCT, *ACWIAWW*, 36, 90–93.

page 27. Did not recognize: Lauterbach, *Beale Street Dynasty*, 28. In drafts of *ACWIAWW*, Mary Church Terrell wrote that Captain Church had acknowledged Robert Church as his son. See MCT, *ACWIAWW*, Drafts, n.d., 5, 26, in MCTLOC. But Ransdell, her publisher, warned that Captain Church's relatives might sue her because she had no proof of paternity. See *MCTJ*, Mar. 1, 1940, in MCTHB. In her published memoir, she did not mention the relationship between the two men. See MCT, *ACWIAWW*, 32.

page 27. Gunshot wounds: Lauterbach, *Beale Street Dynasty*, 25, 70.

page 27. Headaches: Lauterbach, *Beale Street Dynasty*, 70, 175, 326n12; MCT, *ACWIAWW*, 36.

page 27. "violent temper": MCT, *ACWIAWW*, 36.

page 27. "Mollie": MCT, *ACWIAWW*, 43.

page 28. Oberlin background: Sources include Eugene Tuttle, *Our Continent*, Dec. 20, 1882, 737, 739–40; see Gates, *Life Upon These Shores*, 73–76; Shepperd, *Mary Church Terrell*, 22; Baumann, *Constructing Black Education at Oberlin College*, 1–2, 15–19, 24–25, 29–31, 35, 63 (photo), 72; Tony Horwitz, *Midnight Rising: John Brown and the Raid That Sparked the Civil War* (New York: Picador, 2011), 114, 124, 162–63, 289, 291; McPherson, *Battle Cry of Freedom*, 206.

page 28. "the reformer's aggressive": Tuttle, *Our Continent*, 739; see Baumann, *Constructing Black Education at Oberlin College*, 17–18.

page 27. Radicals and fanatics: Tuttle, *Our Continent*, 739; see Baumann, *Constructing Black Education at Oberlin College*, 16–18.

page 28. Mary Church at Oberlin: Sources include MCT to Henry C. King, Jan. 26, 1914, in MCTLOC; MCT, *ACWIAWW*, 71–72 (and Drafts of *ACWIAWW* in MCTLOC); Baumann, *Constructing Black Education at Oberlin College*, 69, 75, 84, 108, 101, 103; Gates, *Life Upon These Shores*, 76; *Oberlin Review*, Mar. 15, 1884, in MCTLOC.

page 29. The Bruces: Lawrence Otis Graham, *The Senator and the Socialite: The True Story of America's First Black Dynasty* (New York: HarperCollins, 2006), 7, 87–97, 102; MCT, *ACWIAWW*, 81; Deborah Gray White, *Too Heavy a Load: Black Women in Defense of Themselves, 1894–1994* (New York: W.W. Norton, 1999), 48 (photo); Lauterbach, *Beale Street Dynasty*, 45.

page 29. Visiting the Bruces: MCT, *ACWIAWW*, 81–82.

page 29. Met Douglass: MCT, *ACWIAWW*, 83.

page 29. "struggles to resist": MCT, College Writings, 1880–1884, in MCTLOC.

page 29. "to improve": Ibid.

page 29. Rarity: See MCT, "Introduction to Address on Woman Suffrage Delivered to Teachers of the Public Schools of Washington," Washington, D.C., Apr. 12, 1910, in MCTLOC.

page 29. Could not understand: See MCT, *ACWIAWW*, 92.

page 29. Horace and the *Odyssey*: See Church, Mary Eliza, Student Grade Recorder, Book XII, 391, in Oberlin College Archives.

page 29. Knew the stereotypes: See MCT, "Woman Suffrage," Apr. 12, 1910, in MCTLOC.

page 29. Inattentiveness: See MCT, *ACWIAWW*, 157.

page 30. Same day as Terrell: *CDT*, June 26, 1884; *BDG*, June 26, 1884.

page 30. Both parents skipped: MCT, *ACWIAWW*, 80.

page 30. In Paris: See *MCTJ*, Aug. 26, 1888–Sept. 24, 1888, in MCTLOC.

page 30. A semester of French: Church, Mary Eliza, Student Grade Recorder, 391.

page 30. Church and Terrell teaching: Sources include MCT, *ACWIAWW*, 96–99; *The Black Washingtonians* at 118.

page 31. Switzerland: See *MCTJ*, Sept. 25, 1888–Feb. 11, 1889, in MCTLOC; MCT, *ACWIAWW*, 102–4.

page 31. Howard Law 1889 graduation: Sources include *WES*, May 27, 1889; *WP*, May 28, 1889; *WES*, May 28, 1889; Everett O. Alldredge, *Centennial History of First Congregational United Church of Christ, Washington, D.C., 1865–1965* (Baltimore: Port City Press, circa 1965), 13–14 and photos; Law Department of Howard University, Class of '89 Commencement Program, n.d., in RHTLOC.

page 31. German and Italian: See MCT, *ACWIAWW*, 105–33; MCT to RHT, March [n.d.], 1889, in MCTHB; *MCTJ*, Sept. 22, 1889–April 28, 1890, in MCTLOC.

page 32. Douglass background: Sources include *WP*, Jan. 24, 1889; *WP*, Mar. 3, 1889; *DFP*, Jan. 22, 1889; *WP*, Inaugural Number, circa March 1889; *SLPD*, Mar. 2, 1889.

page 32. Girded: *WP*, Jan. 4, 1889.

page 32. Frequent guest: RHT, "The Peerless Douglass," Washington, D.C., Apr. 2, 1895, in RHTLOC.

page 32. "a week's reading": *NYA*, Mar. 7, 1895, in RHTLOC.

page 32. "comprehensive": Frederick Douglass, *Three Addresses: On the Relations Subsisting Between the White and Colored People of the United States* (Washington: Gibson Bros., 1886), 24, in RHTLOC.

page 32. "With the respect": Douglass, *Three Addresses*, cover page, in RHTLOC; see also Frederick Douglass to the Editor of the *Independent*, Apr. 24, 1892, in MCTHB.

page 32. "vast change": *FI*, Jan. 12, 1889.

page 32. "virtue": Ibid.

page 32. "I only ask": Ibid.

page 32. "We love our": Ibid.

page 33. Speculation: *LAT*, Jan. 4, 1889; *WP*, Feb. 3, 1889.

page 33. "It is quite": *LAT*, Jan. 4, 1889.

page 33. "a good representative": Rep. Henry Cabot Lodge to Hon. William Windom, May 27, 1889, in RHTLOC.

page 33. "men of character": RHT, "Parting Remarks on Behalf of the Class of 1889, Howard University Law School," Washington, D.C., May 27, 1889, in RHTLOC. This is the source of all quotes.

page 33. "We represent": Ibid.

page 33. "von D.": See, for example, *MCTJ*, Jan. 18, 1890, in MCTLOC; MCT, *ACWIAWW*, 122, 125–26. For her reaction to her father's decision, see *MCTJ*, March 1890, in MCTLOC (in German).

page 33. "Mary has been": Lauterbach, *Beale Street Dynasty*, 180–81.

page 34. "My dear Sir": RHT to RRC, Jan. 6, 1891, in MCTLOC. This is the source of all quotes.

page 34. With a reference: See RRC, "Reply to Suitor in Germany," Feb. 24, 1890, in UMLRRC.

page 34. Wedding details: Sources include MCT and RHT, Wedding Invitation, Oct. 28, 1891, in RHTLOC; *MC*, Oct. 29, 1891, in RHTLOC; MCT, *ACWIAWW*, 139; Lauterbach, *Beale Street Dynasty*, 96, 98–99; Shepperd, *Mary Church Terrell*, 20.

page 34. Remarried: Lauterbach, *Beale Street Dynasty*, 70; Pamela Palmer, ed., *The MVC Bulletin*, The Robert R. Church Family of Memphis: Guide to the Papers with Selected Facsimiles of Documents and Photographs, No. 10 (1979): 14, 22 (photograph of the Lauderdale home) [hereafter "*MVC Bulletin*"].

page 35. "with malice aforethought": The *Free Speech*, circa Oct. 28, 1891, in RHTLOC.

page 35. "Robert Terrell weds": *WP*, Oct. 29, 1891.

page 35. "the most notable": Ibid.

page 35. Wedding presents: *NYA*, circa Dec. 31, 1891, in RHTLOC.

page 35. Diamond ring worth: *BC*, Nov. 1891, in RHTLOC.

page 35. Washstand set: *NYA*, circa Dec. 31, 1891, in RHTLOC.

page 35. Broken off: MCT to RHT, n.d., in MCTHB; see MCT to RHT, "Vendredi Matin," n.d., circa Oct. 24, 1891, in MCTHB. No letter communicating the rupture itself appears to have survived.

page 35. Overture: She thought she received a job offer. See MCT, *ACWIAWW*, 137–38; *WP*, Oct. 29, 1891. However, her discussions about the position might not have advanced to the point of a formal employment offer. See Memorandum, Mrs. Mary Church Terrell '84, Dec. 26, 1933, in Oberlin College Archives, Box 1028, Folder 2.

page 35. Wedding portrait: See MCT Photograph, circa Oct. 28, 1891, in MCTHUMS.

page 35. Wrong choice: See MCT, *ACWIAWW*, 137–38. For her thoughts generally about her suitability for work and about class differences between spouses, see *MCTJ*, Jan. 20, 1916, in MCTHB and *MCTJ*, Mar. 30, 1916, in MCTHB.

page 35. *Ringwood's*: See MCT, "The History of the Club Women's Movement," *The Aframerican Woman's Journal*, Summer and Fall, 1940, 37, in MCTLOC.

page 36. "Berto": *MCTJ*, Apr. 23, 1905, in MCTLOC.

page 36. Miscarriage: Edward Andress Hibbard, *Fortieth Anniversary Report (Report X) of the Secretary of the Class of 1884 of Harvard College*, June 1924, 102, in RHTLOC; MCT to RHT, Aug. 1, 1892, in MCTHB.

page 36. Fear: See Telegram from RRC to RHT, June 9, 1892, in MCTHB; Telegram from Annie Church to RHT, June 10, 1892, in MCTHB.

page 36. "at all doubtful": TAC to RHT, June 11, 1892, in MCTLOC.

page 36. "come over": Ibid.

page 36. Appetite: RRC to RRT, July 3, 1892, in MCTLOC; see Annie Church to RHT, June 14, 1892, in MCTHB.

page 36. Left: MCT to RHT, July 22, 1892, in MCTHB.

page 36. Well-being: See MCT to RHT, July 26, 1892, in MCTHB; MCT to RHT, Aug. 24, 1892, in MCTHB; MCT to RHT, Aug. 25, 1892, in MCTHB; MCT to RHT, Sept. 1, 1892, in MCTHB; MCT to RHT, Sept. 2, 1892, in MCTHB.

page 36. Affection: See, for example, MCT to RHT, July 27, 1892, in MCTHB; MCT to RHT, Aug. 1, 1892, in MCTHB; MCT to RHT, Sept. 4, 1892, in MCTHB.

page 36. Remain near: MCT to RHT, Sept. 5, 1892, in MCTHB.

page 36. Deferred: MCT to RHT, Sept. 7, 1892, in MCTHB.

page 36. Reform: See MCT to RHT, Aug. 23, 1892, in MCTHB; MCT to RHT, Sept. 5, 1892, in MCTHB; MCT to RHT, Sept. 10, 1892, in MCTHB.

page 36. Beneath him: See MCT to RHT, Nov. 8, 1892, in MCTHB.

page 36. "the chief attribute": RHT, "Republican Campaign Speech 1892," in RHTLOC.

page 37. Terrell lost: Acting Secretary (name illegible) to RHT, May 19, 1893, in RHTLOC.

page 37. Capital Savings Bank: See M. Sammye Miller, "An Early Venture in Black Capitalism: The Capital Savings Bank in the District of Columbia, 1888–1902," *Records of the Columbia Historical Society, Washington, D.C.* 50 (1980): 359–66.

page 37. Ten-year reunion: *Harvard College, Decennial Report of the Secretary*, June 1894, 43, in RHTLOC.

page 37. "Southern Mob Rule": RHT, "Introducing Ida Wells Barnett—To Deliver an Address on Lynching, 1893," in RHTLOC.

page 37. "persistent and systemic agitation": Ibid.

page 37. "best citizens": Ibid.

page 37. Dispatches: *NYA*, circa Jan. 13, 1894, in RHTLOC; *NYA*, Dec. 12, 1895, in RHTLOC.

page 37. "What a miserable": *NYA*, Nov. 29, 1894, in RHTLOC.

page 37. "iron impartiality": *NYA*, May 26, 1895, in RHTLOC; see Edmund Morris, *The Rise of Theodore Roosevelt* (New York: Random House, 2001), 451, 455.

page 38. Two girls and a boy: MCT, *ACWIAWW*, 141–43; Harvard College Class of 1884, *Report X*, 102.

page 38. Colored Woman's League: Sources include MCT, *ACWIAWW*, 185–86; White, *Too Heavy a Load*, 23, 27 (in 1892, with others); MCT, *ACWIAWW*, 14 (Ham foreword); *Fourth Annual Report of the Colored Woman's League of Washington, D.C., for the year ending January 1, 1897*, in MCTLOC.

page 38. "the best interests": Act of Incorporation, Constitution and Bylaws, The Colored Woman's League, Jan. 11, 1894, in MCTLOC.

page 38. *Plessy v. Ferguson*: 163 U.S. 537 (1896).

page 38. Envoy: Gates, *Life Upon These Shores*, 202.

page 38. Engineering a legal challenge: Ibid.

page 38. "'Jim Crow' car case": *TS*, May 19, 1896; *PI*, May 19, 1896; *SFC*, May 19, 1896.

page 39. Harlan background: Patterson, *Brown v. Board of Education*, xxii; Rosen, *The Supreme Court*, 80, 83.

page 39. *Dred Scott v. Sandford*: 60 U.S. 393 (1857).

page 39. Only dissent in *Civil Rights Cases*: 109 U.S. at 26 (Harlan, J., dissenting); Rosen, *The Supreme Court*, 95.

page 39. Mid-July: Sources include CWL, *Fourth Annual Report*, 7 (July 14–16); *NYA*, July 30, 1896, in RHTLOC; MCT, "The History of the Club Women's Movement," *The Aframerican Woman's Journal*, Summer and Fall 1940, 34–38, in MCTLOC; Program, First Annual Convention of the National League of Colored Women, July 14–16, 1896, in MCTLOC. For background also see MCT, *ACWIAWW*, 187–89; White, *Too Heavy a Load*, 22–23.

page 40. "the highest plane": NACW, *Minutes of the National Association of Colored Women*, Nashville, Tenn., Sept. 15–18, 1897, 6, in MCTLOC.

page 40. "pilgrimage": CWL, *Fourth Annual Report*, 8. They also went to Cedar Hill. Ibid.

page 40. brick engine house: Horwitz, *Midnight Rising*, 156–80, 285; McPherson, *Battle Cry of Freedom*, 201–7.

page 40. "our peculiar trials": See MCT, "President's First Address," Nashville, Tenn., Sept. 15, 1897, in MCTLOC (handwritten draft). All quotations are from this source.

page 40. "savage instinct": RHT, letter-to-the-editor, *CA*, circa July 26, 1896, in RHTLOC.

page 40. "teach men how": Ibid.

page 40. "these splendid women": *NYA*, July 30, 1896, in RHTLOC.

page 40. "race problem": Ibid.

page 40. "Women in": Ibid.

page 40. "lifting as we": MCT, *An Address Delivered Before the National American Woman Suffrage Association, Feb. 1898* (Washington, D.C., 1898), 15.

page 41. "every child born": MCT, "Greetings from the NACW to the Congress of Mothers," n.d., in MCTLOC.

page 41. Friends warned: MCT, *ACWIAWW*, 196.

page 41. "Populists and": *WP*, July 19, 1896, in RHTLOC.

page 41. "in cordial sympathy": William McKinley to RHT, July 25, 1896, in RHTLOC.

page 41. Hanna and McKinley background: Sources include Morris, *The Rise*, 404–5, 558, 565–66, 568, 571–76, 583–84; Edmund Morris, *Theodore Rex* (New York: Random House, 2001), 38–39; *CA*, Aug. 22, 1897, in RHTLOC.

page 41. "party managers": *WP*, July 19, 1896, in RHTLOC.

page 41. "ornamental": Ibid.

page 41. "begin too soon": Ibid.

page 41. "this large class": Ibid.

page 41. "treated with": Ibid.

page 41. "open question": M. A. Hanna to RHT, July 30, 1896, in RHTLOC.

page 41. "I will give": Ibid.

page 42. Speculation about: *WB*, n.d., in RHTLOC; *CA*, Mar. 20, 1897, in RHTLOC.

page 42. Public Comfort: Chairman [name illegible] to RHT, Dec. 23, 1897, in RHTLOC.

page 42. Roosevelt coveted: Morris, *The Rise*, 561.

page 42. Prowess: Morris, *The Rise*, 566, 573–76.

page 42. "You, I know": Theodore Roosevelt to RHT, June 10, 1897, in TRLOC.

page 42. "politician of": *CA*, Aug. 22, 1897, in RHTLOC (with handwritten note that reads, "Editorial by R. H. Terrell").

page 42. "Any good paying": Mss. 70 George A. Myers Papers, Letter from RHT to George Myers, Aug. 27, 1898: Ohio History Connection.

page 42. "Of course": Ibid.

page 42. Teaching and debt: Source includes *BJ*, Nov. 13, 1901, in RHTLOC; *CA*, Nov. 16, 1901, in RHTLOC; John R. Lynch to RHT, Aug. 6, 1910, in RHTLOC; RHT to RRC, Apr. 23, 1902, in UMLRRC.

page 42. Principal: Superintendent of Schools [name illegible] to RHT, Apr. 29, 1899, in RHTLOC.

page 42. "grace of bearing": *CA*, Feb. 17, 1900.

page 42. "ineffable charm": Ibid.

page 43. "her rare ability": *CA*, June 9, 1900.

page 43. "the 'female Booker T'": Chautauqua, Danville, Ill. Aug. 2–16, 1900, in RHTLOC.

page 43. "dear little": MCT to RHT, Aug. 12, 1900, in MCTLOC.

page 43. "a sense of": Ibid.

page 43. "I enjoy": Ibid.

page 43. "thrift": Ibid.

page 43. Salary stalled: Superintendent of Schools to RHT, Apr. 29, 1899, in RHTLOC.

page 43. "Then, too": MCT to RHT, Aug. 12, 1900, in MCTLOC.

CHAPTER 2: THE GREATEST WOMAN THAT WE HAVE

page 44. "Please call": Telegram from BTW to RHT, Nov. 4, 1901, in RHTLOC.

page 44. Background on Washington: Sources include Booker T. Washington, *Up From Slavery* (New York: Dover Publication, 1995), iii, 1, 101; Gates, *Life Upon These Shores*, 189; C. Vann Woodward, *The Strange Career of Jim Crow: A Commemorative Edition* with afterword by William S. McFeely (New York: Oxford University Press, 2002), 82.

page 44. Background on Atlanta Expo: Sources include BTW, *Up From Slavery*, 101–2, 105–6; Gates, *Life Upon These Shores*, 201; Atlanta History Center Album, Fred L. Howe 1895 Cotton States and International Exposition Photographs, http://album.atlantahistorycenter.com/store/Category/437-fred-1-howe-1895 -cotton-states-and-international-exposition-photographs.aspx.

page 44. "Coonville": Atlanta History Center Album, Fred L. Howe 1895 Cotton States and International Exposition Photographs, VIS 145.71.01, "Craps at

Coonville 'Now Seben Come Eleben,'" http://album.atlantahistorycenter.com
/store/Products/85125-craps-at-coonville-now-seben-come-eleben.aspx.

page 44. "Craps": Ibid.

page 44. "a new era": See BTW, *Up From Slavery*, 106–9.

page 44. "ornamental gewgaws": BTW, *Up From Slavery*, 107.

page 44. "common occupations": Ibid.

page 45. "No race can": Ibid.

page 45. "grievances": Ibid.

page 45. "opportunities": Ibid.

page 45. "northern philanthropists": BTW, *Up From Slavery*, 108; see Morris, *T. Rex*,
48, 49.

page 45. "a constant stream": BTW, *Up From Slavery*, 108.

page 45. "The wisest among": Ibid.

page 45. "No race": BTW, *Up From Slavery*, 108–9.

page 45. "The man who": *NYA*, circa Mar. 22, 1896, in RHTLOC.

page 45. honorary masters: *NYT*, June 25, 1896.

page 45. "what a blessed privilege": BTW to RHT, July 19, 1896, in RHTLOC.

page 45. "This action": Ibid.

page 45. Theodore Roosevelt background: Sources include Morris, *T. Rex*, 3–4, 6,
37–39, 43, 47–49, 52–53; Morris, *The Rise*, xxiii, 5, 7–9, 11, 15–29, 33–48, 52–54,
67, 77, 116, 143–44, 147–48, 467–69, 492–94, 523, 533 (photo), 703; Vann Woodward,
The Strange Career of Jim Crow, 6, 69–70; Doris Kearns Goodwin, *The Bully Pulpit:
Theodore Roosevelt, William Howard Taft, and The Golden Age of Journalism* (New York:
Simon & Schuster, 2013), 321, 745.

page 46. Inferior: See Morris, *T. Rex*, 52–53.

page 46. Long run: See BTW, *Up From Slavery*, 107–9; *NYA*, Jan. 3, 1901, in
RHTLOC; Morris, *T. Rex*, 48.

page 46. "the higher and better": *NYA*, Jan. 3, 1901, in RHTLOC.

page 46. "Negro loafer": Ibid.

page 47. "superior": See Morris, *T. Rex*, 47, 52.

page 47. Washington dinner: Sources include Morris, *T. Rex*, 52–54; Goodwin, *The
Bully Pulpit*, 321; Deborah Davis, *Guest of Honor: Booker T. Washington, Theodore
Roosevelt, and the White House Dinner That Shocked a Nation* (New York: Atria
Books, 2012), 189–202.

page 47. Southern delegations boycotted: *WP*, Oct. 19, 1901, in RHTLOC.

page 47. Erupted: Ibid.

page 47. "The President's attempt": "The Same Old South," circa Oct. 1901, in
RHTLOC.

page 47. "No self-respecting": Ibid.

page 47. Washington lobbied: See *WES*, circa Nov. 12, 1901, in RHTLOC; *NYEP*,
Nov. 13, 1901, in RHTLOC; *CA*, Nov. 16, 1901, in RHTLOC; *WP*, Nov. 15,
1901, in RHTLOC; *NYJ*, Nov. 13, 1901, in RHTLOC.

page 47. Nominated: See *NYJ*, Nov. 13, 1901, in RHTLOC; *WES*, circa Nov. 12,
1901, in RHTLOC; *BDG*, Nov. 18, 1901, in RHTLOC.

page 47. Son of a: See *TS*, Aug. 12, 1869; *CA*, Nov. 16, 1901, in RHTLOC; *NYA*, circa Nov. 13, 1901, in RHTLOC.

page 47. "particularly acceptable": *WES*, circa Nov. 12, 1901, in RHTLOC.

page 47. "common-sense": *NYEP*, Nov. 13, 1901, in RHTLOC.

page 47. "Fewer negroes": Ibid.

page 48. Loan: Based on correspondence between Robert H. Terrell and Robert R. Church, it appears that Terrell arranged for a loan, through his father-in-law, to repay approximately $2,000 that Terrell had borrowed from Capital Savings Bank. See RHT to RRC, Apr. 23, 1902, in UMLRRC; RHT to RRC, Nov. 8, 1902, in UMLRRC; RHT to RRC, Mar. 16, 1909, in UMLRRC. Capital Savings Bank failed in November 1902 and was placed into receivership in early 1903. See Miller, An Early Venture, 364–65. According to Miller, "misappropriations and looting by several" directors contributed to the bank's collapse, but "fragmentary" evidence and "a conspiracy of silence" among those with knowledge of the bank's operations precluded a complete understanding of what happened, including the extent to which Robert H. Terrell was aware of the bank's financial situation or whether he and other directors had "knowingly approve[d] risky loan ventures" that benefited themselves and their friends. Terrell's law and real estate partner, John R. Lynch, was a director, as was Terrell's friend, Whitefield McKinlay. See Miller, An Early Venture, 363–65. For later correspondence between Terrell and his father-in-law about real estate matters in Washington, see RRC to RHT, n.d., circa 1909, in UMLRRC; RRC to RHT, May 6, 1912, in UMLRRC; RRC to Whitfield [*sic*] McKinlay, May 6, 1912, in UMLRRC.

page 48. Background on August, 10, 1904: Sources include *WES*, Aug. 11, 1904; *MCTJ*, July–Aug. 1904, in MCTLOC; MCT, *ACWIAWW*, 238, 244–45; *WP*, May 29, 1904; *WP*, June 14, 1904; *WP*, July 19, 1904; *WP*, June 19, 1904; *The CA Magazine*, Aug. 1904, 531, in RHTLOC; MCT to RHT, July 1, 1904, in MCTHB.

page 48. "notable success": BTW to John C. Dancey, Aug. 1, 1904, in MCTLOC.

page 48. "hit of the congress": *WP*, July 19, 1904.

page 49. "ease of manner": Editorial, *The Independent*, July 14, 1904, 108.

page 49. "Lynching": MCT, "Lynching from a Negro's Point of View," *The North American Review*, June 1904, 853.

page 49. "A thousand": RHT to MCT, May 11, 1904, in MCTLOC.

page 49. $75.00 payment: David A. Munro to RHT, May 12, 1904, in MCTLOC.

page 49. "wrong-headed" and "morbid": *Harper's Weekly*, June 18, 1904, 928, in MCTLOC.

page 49. "the greatest woman": Lewis H. Douglass to MCT and RHT, June 30, 1904, in MCTLOC.

page 49. "Tell her": Ibid.

page 49. "the cold neutrality": See RHT, Bench Notebook, circa 1902, with his hand-written inscription on the cover page, in RHTLOC.

page 49. "one of the great": RHT, "Theodore Roosevelt," *The CA Magazine*, Aug. 1904, 542, in RHTLOC.

page 49. "Think we can": "Ned" [at *NYA*] to RHT, July 12, 1904, in MCTLOC.

page 49. First person: See MCT, "Address at Reception given in My Honor at the Metropolitan Church," Washington, D.C., Aug. 10, 1904, in MCTLOC.

page 49. "The sound of my": Ibid. All subsequent quotations from this speech are from this source.

page 50. Activities in Berlin: *TS*, June 12, 1904; *WP*, June 14, 1904; *WP*, June 19, 1904.

page 50. Countess of Warwick: *MCTJ*, July 18, 1904, in MCTLOC.

page 50. "the guest of honor": *WP*, Aug. 11, 1904.

page 50. "a triumph for": Ibid.

page 51. "it was time to": Laura Terrell Jones to RHT, Oct. 6, 1904, in MCTLOC.

page 51. "very fine café": Haydee Campbell to MCT, Sept. 15, 1904, in MCTLOC.

page 51. Niagara Movement background: Sources include Green, *The Secret City*, 167–68; Gates, *Life Upon These Shores*, 237–40.

page 51. Background on Du Bois: W. E. B. Du Bois, *The Souls of Black Folk* (New York: Barnes & Noble Books, 2005), 37, 41–42, 45–47. For Niagara disciples, Washington was anathema. See W. E. Burghhardt Du Bois, *The Amenia Conference: An Historic Negro Gathering*, Troutbeck Leaflets, No. 8 (Amenia, N.Y.: September 1925), 5–6, in MCTLOC [hereafter, "Du Bois, *Amenia*"].

page 51. "attitude of": Du Bois, *The Souls of Black Folk*, 41.

page 51. "gospel of": Ibid.

page 51. "insist": Du Bois, *The Souls of Black Folk*, 44.

page 52. "Persistent manly": Gates, *Life Upon These Shores*, 239.

page 52. Allegiance: Mary had admired Washington, too, especially after her husband's appointment to the bench. See MCT to RHT, July 4, 1902, in MCTHB; MCT to RHT, Aug. 26, 1902, in MCTHB. Du Bois, on the other hand, struck her as aloof. See MCT to RHT, circa Jan. 1906, in MCTHB.

page 52. Recently confirmed: *MCTJ*, Dec. 15 and 19, 1905, in MCTLOC.

page 52. Brownsville background: Sources include *WP*, Aug. 16, 1906; Morris, *T. Rex*, 453–55, 466–68; Goodwin, *The Bully Pulpit*, 511–12; Davis, *Guest of Honor*, 253; *NYT*, Nov. 29, 1906; *NYT*, Nov. 25, 1906; *NYT*, Nov. 27, 1906; *NYT*, Dec. 12, 1906; *WP*, Feb. 18, 1907.

page 52. "black ruffians": *WP*, Aug. 16, 1906 (quoting Houston *Post*).

page 52. "brutes": Ibid.

page 52. "citizens guard": *WP*, Aug. 17, 1906.

page 53. "slights": *WP*, Aug. 22, 1906; see *WP*, Nov. 20, 1906, in MCTLOC.

page 53. "cockiness": See "A Review of the World," *Current Literature*, Jan. 1907, 1 (quoting an undated *New York Times* story); see Morris, *T. Rex*, 455; Davis, *Guest of Honor*, 254.

page 53. "race hatred": Morris, *T. Rex*, 454.

page 53. "without honor": Morris, *T. Rex*, 467; "A Review of the World," *Current Literature*, Jan. 1907, 1 (quoting Taft report).

page 53. "participated in": Morris, *T. Rex*, 467.

page 53. Puzzled: See *CT*, Nov. 21, 1906, in MCTLOC; *NYT*, Nov. 18, 1906, in MCTLOC.

page 53. Labored to regain: See Morris, *T. Rex*, 455; see Goodwin, *The Bully Pulpit*, 513.

page 53. Sided with Brownsville's whites: Morris, *T. Rex*, 455; see Goodwin, *The Bully Pulpit*, 513.

page 53. After the midterm: *CT*, Nov. 21, 1906, in MCTLOC; Morris, *T. Rex*, 467; Goodwin, *The Bully Pulpit*, 512.

page 53. No hearing: See *WP*, Nov. 20, 1906, in MCTLOC; Morris, *T. Rex*, 465.

page 53. Investigators cited: See *CT*, Nov. 21, 1906, in MCTLOC; see Morris, *T. Rex*, 464–65.

page 53. Failure to implicate: See *WP*, Nov. 20, 1906, in MCTLOC; *CT*, Nov. 21, 1906, in MCTLOC.

page 53. Conspiracy: See *WP*, Nov. 20, 1906, in MCTLOC; see Morris, *T. Rex*, 455, 464–65.

page 53. Unfit for service: See *CT*, Nov. 21, 1906, in MCTLOC; Morris, *T. Rex*, 464–65.

page 53. Menace: See *CT*, Nov. 21, 1906, in MCTLOC.

page 53. Revered: See MCT, "The Social Functions During Inauguration Week," *The Voice of the Negro*, April 1905, 241–42, in MCTLOC.

page 53. "Teddy": MCT to RHT, June 25, 1902, in MCTLOC.

page 53. "returned the salute": Ibid.

page 54. Washington acknowledged: Morris, *T. Rex*, 467.

page 54. Outcast: Morris, *T. Rex*, 467; see Goodwin, *The Bully Pulpit*, 515; W. E. B. Du Bois, "The President and the Soldiers," *The Voice*, Dec. 1906, 552–53; MCT, "The Disbanding of the Colored Soldiers," *The Voice*, Dec. 1906, 554–58.

page 54. Background on November 17, 1906: Sources include Morris, *T. Rex*, 468, 471; Goodwin, *The Bully Pulpit*, 511–15; *NYT*, Nov. 18, 1906, in MCTLOC; *WP*, Nov. 20, 1906, in MCTLOC; MCT, "Secretary Taft and the Negro Soldiers," *The Independent*, July 23, 1908, 189 [hereafter "MCT, Negro Soldiers"]; Ham, Debra Newman, "African-American Activist Mary Church Terrell and the Brownsville Disturbance," *Trotter Review* 18 no. 5 (2009): 33–34 [hereafter "Ham, Brownsville"]; MCT, *ACWIAWW*, 310–11. Unless otherwise indicated, this account of events in Taft's office, including her conversations with Carpenter and Taft, is based on Terrell's recollection.

page 54. John Milholland: On February 1, 1906, Mary Church Terrell appeared as one of several speakers at a meeting, sponsored by the Constitution League at Cooper Union in New York, to protest disfranchisement of southern blacks. According to the *New York Times*, which called her the most "bitter" of the speakers, she ignored several requests from Milholland to end her remarks. *NYT*, Feb. 2, 1906; see MCT to RHT, Feb. 3, 1906, in MCTHB.

page 55. All you want: MCT, Negro Soldiers, 189–90. Mary Church Terrell put this in quotes, but she wrote this article several months after the conversation, so I am paraphrasing. She also recounts the conversation in *ACWIAWW*, 311, using all capital letters for "all."

page 55. Is that *all*: MCT, Negro Soldiers, 190; MCT, *ACWIAWW*, 311. Terrell put this in quotes, but I am paraphrasing.

page 55. Sarcasm and smile: MCT, *ACWIAWW*, 311; MCT, Negro Soldiers, 190 ("merry twinkle"); Goodwin, *The Bully Pulpit*, 513 ("merry twinkle").

page 55. Administrative prowess: See Goodwin, *The Bully Pulpit*, 390, 395–96.

page 55. Long aspired: See Morris, *T. Rex*, 457–58; Goodwin, *The Bully Pulpit*, 14–15, 50, 215, 387.

page 55. Like his father: Goodwin, *The Bully Pulpit*, 26.

page 55. Roosevelt knew: *MCTJ*, Dec. 18, 1905, in MCTLOC; MCT, *ACWIAWW*, 318; see Lauterbach, *Beale Street Dynasty*, 135.

page 55. Impulsivity: Goodwin, *The Bully Pulpit*, 380.

page 55. "New York Repub.": Cable from WHT to TR, Nov. 17, 1906, in TRLOC. All subsequent quotations are from this source.

page 56. Newspapers trumpeted: *AC*, circa Nov. 17, 1906, in MCTLOC; *PJ*, Nov. 18, 1906, in MCTLOC; *WP*, Nov. 18, 1906, in MCTLOC; *WES*, Nov. 18, 1906, in MCTLOC; *WH*, Nov. 18, 1906, in MCTLOC.

page 56. "one of the leading": *NYT*, Nov. 18, 1906, in MCTLOC.

page 56. "At her request": *WP*, Nov. 18, 1906, in MCTLOC.

page 56. "The First Established": *WES*, Nov. 18, 1906, in MCTLOC (with Romeike logo).

page 56. "exceeded": *NYT*, Nov. 18, 1906, in MCTLOC.

page 56. "presidential authority": Ibid.

page 56. As the *Post*: *WP*, Nov. 20, 1906, in MCTLOC.

page 56. "You have not": Andrew Humphrey to MCT, Nov. 20, 1906, in MCTLOC.

page 56. "*Esto*": Ibid.

page 56. "Discharge is not": Morris, *T. Rex*, 471; Goodwin, *The Bully Pulpit*, 514.

page 56. "I care nothing": Morris, *T. Rex*, 471; Goodwin, *The Bully Pulpit*, 514; see *CT*, Nov. 21, 1906, in MCTLOC.

page 56. In private: See "Memorandum for the President" [no author credited], Nov. 27, 1906, in TRLOC; Morris, *T. Rex*, 471–73.

page 57. "a very necessary": Albert Bushnell Hart to TR, Nov. 26, 1906, in TRLOC.

page 57. Asking Taft: Morris, *T. Rex*, 471–73.

page 57. "earned the": Du Bois, "The President and the Soldiers," 553.

page 57. "insist": Ibid.

page 57. "And so for": MCT, "The Disbanding of the Colored Soldiers," 558.

page 57. Nobel: Sources include Telegram from Loevland [*sic*] to TR, Dec. 10, 1906, in TRLOC; Cable from "Peirce" to TR, Dec. 10, 1906, in TRLOC; Morris, *T. Rex*, 473, 723n473; Davis, *Guest of Honor*, 148.

page 57. Investigation: *NYT*, Nov. 21, 1906; *NYT*, Nov. 25, 1906; Ham, Brownsville, 32; see Telegram from Gilchrist Stewart to TR, Dec. 8/9, 1906, in TRLOC.

page 57. Shared with Foraker: Morris, *T. Rex*, 471.

page 57. "I hope the": MCT to [Gilchrist] Stewart, Dec. 10, 1906, in MCTLOC. Terrell did not use Stewart's first name, but she and Stewart met with Roosevelt about Brownsville the following day, on December 11, 1906. See *WES*, Dec. 12, 1906, in MCTLOC.

page 57. "lawless and murderous": Morris, *T. Rex*, 474.

page 57. "conclusive": Morris, *T. Rex*, 474.

page 58. "utterly inadequate": Morris, *T. Rex*, 474.

page 58. "intolerable": MCT, "What It Means to Be Colored in the Capital of the United States," *The Independent*, Jan. 24, 1907, 181, in MCTLOC; see MCT, *ACWIAWW*, 425–38. The article was based on a speech she had given in Washington on October 10, 1906. See The Library of America, Story of the Week, MCT, "What It Means to Be Colored in the Capital of the United States," reprinted from *American Speeches: Political Oratory from Abraham Lincoln to Bill Clinton* (The Library of America, 2006), 204–12, http://www.loa.org/images/pdf/Terrell_What_It_Means.pdf.

page 58. "And surely": MCT, "What it Means," 186.

page 58. Nineteenth-century article: MCT, "Peonage in the United States: The Convict Lease System and the Chain Gangs," *The Nineteenth Century and After*, August 1907, 306–22, in MCTLOC.

page 58. "trumped-up charges": MCT, "Peonage in the United States," 306, in MCTLOC.

page 58. "only partially": Ibid. For similar language, see MCT, "Service Which Should be Rendered the South," *The Voice of the Negro*, March 1905, 185, in MCTLOC. For her earlier references to convict labor see MCT, "A Plea for the White South by a Coloured Woman," *The Nineteenth Century and After*, July, 1906, 76–77, in MCTLOC. For more on convict labor, see Lauterbach, *Beale Street Dynasty*, 77–78.

page 59. "But there": Oswald Garrison Villard to MCT, Sept. 19, 1907, in MCTLOC.

page 59. "the great": *NYA*, circa Sept. 19, 1907, in RHTLOC.

page 59. "We should do": Ibid.

page 59. Brewer background: J. Gordon Hylton, "The Judge Who Abstained in *Plessy v. Ferguson*: Justice David Brewer and the Problem of Race," 61 Miss. L. J. 315 (1991).

page 59. "a Caucasian nation": Hylton, "The Judge Who Abstained," 316–17.

page 59. "leading woman": Untitled clipping, Oct. 25, 1907, in MCTLOC.

page 59. Flecks of gray: See Willard French, "Mrs. Mary Church Terrell," The *Lyceumite and Talent*, Nov. 1907, 8, in MCTLOC.

page 59. Terrell's Congregationalism: *MCTJ*, Dec. 26, 1909, in MCTLOC; MCT, *ACWIAWW*, 63.

page 60. Congregationalists in the audience: See *NYOC*, Oct. 31, 1907; "The Cleveland Meetings," *TA*, Oct. 24, 1907.

page 60. "The Strongest": *NYT*, Oct. 15, 1907, in MCTLOC; *WES*, Oct. 14, 1907, in MCTLOC. According to an undated, untitled clipping, this was a new speech for her lecture tour. See untitled clipping, circa Oct. 14, 1907, MCTLOC.

page 60. "practically healed": *CPD*, Oct. 15, 1907, in MCTLOC.

page 60. pressed before: See MCT, "Service Which Should be Rendered," 183–84, in MCTLOC; MCT, "A Plea for the White South," 82–83. She had criticized the North before, too, for its "silence" and "neutrality" about the disfranchisement of southern blacks. See *NYT*, Feb. 2, 1906.

page 60. "vices": *CPD*, Oct. 15, 1907, in MCTLOC.

page 60. "scare crow": Ibid.

page 60. "bugaboo": Ibid.

page 60. "poison[ed]": Ibid.

page 60. "Those who": *WTI*, Oct. 17, 1907.

page 60. "grateful": *NYT*, Oct. 15, 1907, in MCTLOC.

page 60. "And while": Ibid.

page 60. "It is one": Ibid.

page 60. barely registered: *WES*, Oct. 14, 1907, in MCTLOC; *NYT*, Oct. 15, 1907, in MCTLOC; *TS*, Oct. 15, 1907.

page 61. "Colored Woman Raps": *CPD*, Oct. 15, 1907.

page 61. Released a report: *WTI*, Oct. 17, 1907.

page 61. "South Poisons": Ibid.

page 61. "Colored Troops": Ibid.

page 61. "worthy": *WH*, Oct. 18, 1907, in MCTLOC.

page 61. "uplift": Ibid.

page 61. "merit": Ibid.

page 61. "hot air": *WB*, circa Oct. 17, 1907, in MCTLOC.

page 61. Whites-only: *MCTJ*, Jan. 28, 1908, in MCTLOC; *MCTJ*, Feb. 16, 1909, in MCTLOC; *MCTJ*, Mar. 31, 1909, in MCTLOC; *MCTJ*, June 10, 1909, in MCTLOC.

page 61. Skin lightener: MCT to RHT, July 24, 1910, in MCTLOC.

page 61. "There is as much": *WB*, circa Oct. 17, 1907, in MCTLOC.

page 61. "ill-advised": *NYA*, Oct. 24, 1907, in MCTLOC.

page 61. "agitate": Ibid.

page 62. "If some": Ibid.

page 62. Purity Congress background: Sources include untitled clipping, circa Oct. 14, 1907, in MCTLOC; National Purity Federation, Program of the National Purity Congress, Battle Creek, Mich., Oct. 31 to Nov. 6, 1907, in MCTLOC.

page 62. "The theater": *BCDM*, Nov. 2, 1907.

page 62. "Purity!": *BCE*, Nov. 2, 1907.

page 62. "the condition": Ibid.

page 62. Several times: MCT, Lynching from A Negro's Point of View, 857, 865; *TDJ*, Feb. 21, 1907, in MCTLOC; *FI*, Oct. 28, 1905, 681; *MCTJ*, Oct. 18, 1905, in MCTLOC.

page 63. "relations": *BCE*, Nov. 2, 1907.

page 63. "many supposedly": Ibid.

page 63. "some": Ibid.

page 63. "a pure life": Ibid.

page 63. "constant temptations": Ibid.

page 63. "The only": Ibid.

page 63. "The lives": Ibid.

page 63. "Negro speaker": Ibid.

page 63. "sarcasm": Ibid.

page 63. "scornful curl": Ibid.

page 63. "easily pass": Ibid.

page 63. "furious invective": *NOI*, Nov. 2, 1907, in MCTLOC.

page 63. No servant girl: Ibid.

page 63. Boston to New Orleans: *NOI*, Nov. 2, 1907; *WP*, Nov. 2, 1907; *BT*, Nov. 2, 1907; *NB*, Nov. 2, 1907; *NA*, Nov. 2, 1907; *CNC*, Nov. 2, 1907; *TS*, Nov. 2, 1907.

page 63. "no servant girl": *WP*, Nov. 2, 1907.

page 63. Negative reaction: *NA*, Nov. 3, 1907, in MCTLOC.

page 63. Clarification: *NB*, Nov. 7, 1907, in MCTLOC; *IS*, Nov. 7, 1907, in MCTLOC.

page 63. "the majority": *NB*, Nov. 8, 1907, in MCTLOC.

page 63. Twin letters: *NA*, Nov. 14, 1907, in MCTLOC; *CNC*, Nov. 14, 1907, in MCTLOC.

page 63. "no servant girl": Ibid.

page 63. "no such": Ibid.

page 64. "I have never": Ibid.

page 64. Heflin and streetcar bill: Sources include *CDT*, Feb. 23, 1908; *WP*, Oct. 7, 1908 in RHTLOC; *LAT*, Mar. 28, 1908; *NYT*, Mar. 28, 1908; *TS*, Mar. 28, 1908; US Senate, Senate History, 1921–1940, "Cotton Tom's Last Blast," http://www .senate.gov/artandhistory/history/minute/Cotton_Toms_Last_Blast.htm.

page 64. "un-American": *CDT*, Feb. 23, 1908.

page 64. "evil": Ibid.

page 64. "I would not": Ibid.

page 64. Heflin and Lundy incident: Sources include *NYT*, Mar. 28, 1908; *LAT*, Mar. 28, 1908; *TS*, Mar. 28, 1908; *NYT*, Aug. 5, 1909. Heflin was later indicted on three counts of assault, but the second victim failed to appear before the grand jury and the indictment was quashed. *NYT*, Aug. 5, 1909.

page 65. "It is said": *TS*, Mar. 28, 1908.

page 65. "supernatural strength": Ibid.

page 65. Cocaine: Ibid.

page 65. Boarded a Washington streetcar: See *MCTJ*, July 27–28, 1908, in MCTLOC.

page 66. About money: MCT to RHT, June 25, 1902, in MCTLOC; MCT to RHT, July 13, 1902, in MCTLOC; MCT to RHT, May 19, 1903, in MCTHUMS; see MCT to RHT, Aug. 1, 1914, in MCTHB.

page 66. Like sisters: See Phyllis Terrell and Mary Terrell, Photograph, n.d., in MCTHUMS, Box 102–17.

page 66. Springfield riot background: Gates, *Life Upon These Shores*, 241–42.

page 67. Financial assistance: See, for example, RHT to RRC, Apr. 23, 1902; RHT to RRC, Mar. 16, 1909, in UMLRRC; MCT to RHT, Aug. 1, 1914, in MCTHB.

page 67. "It is all bad": MCT to RHT, May 19, 1903, in MCTHUMS.

page 67. "I wish you" : Ibid.; see MCT to RHT, "Vendredi Matin," n.d., circa Oct. 24, 1891, in MCTHB; MCT to RHT, July 1, 1904, in MCTHB; *MCTJ*, Sept. 9, 1916, writing about Nov. 27, 1907, in MCTHB.

page 67. At the mercy: See RHT, "Remarks at the Dinner of the Class of 1884," circa 1914, in RHTLOC.

page 67. Unaware of any: *WP*, Oct. 7, 1908.

page 67. "On this matter": W[illiam] Hayward to RHT, Sept. 12, 1908, in RHTLOC.

page 68. "I know that": RHT to WHT, Nov. 4, 1908, in WHTLOC.

page 68. Inaugural Committee: Corcoran Thom to RHT, Dec. 8, 1908, in RHTLOC.

page 68. Van Rensselaer Cruger: *MCTJ*, Sept. 9, 1905, in MCTLOC.

page 69. Lottery winnings: *MCTJ*, Feb. 3, 1889, in MCTLOC; MCT, *ACWIAWW*, 116.

page 69. Roughly 10 percent: See *PPR*, circa Nov. 15, 1901, in RHTLOC.

CHAPTER 3: THEY COME STANDING ERECT

page 70. "I try to be": MCT to RHT, Aug. 15, 1909, in MCTLOC.

page 70. "I feel like": Ibid.

page 70. "because she": Ibid. Mary had noted similar problems during a previous summer vacation. See MCT to RHT, July 27, 1907, in MCTHB.

page 70. "kisses and hugs": MCT to RHT, Aug. 15, 1909, in MCTLOC.

page 71. Deeded half: *MCTJ*, Sept. 7, 1909, in MCTLOC; see Indenture between Robert R. Church and Anna Church and MCT, July 29, 1909, in MCTHB; RRC to RHT, n.d., circa 1909, in UMLRRC.

page 71. Pinchback: See Graham, *The Senator and the Socialite*, 8.

page 71. Crab salad and tongue: *MCTJ*, Sept. 19, 1909, in MCTLOC.

page 71. Platform: *MCTJ*, Oct. 4, 1909, in MCTLOC.

page 71. Exhaustion: *MCTJ*, Sept. 23, 1909, in MCTLOC; *MCTJ*, Oct. 26, 1909, in MCTLOC; see *MCTJ*, Nov. 19, 1909, in MCTLOC.

page 71. New York: *MCTJ*, Nov. 10, 1909, in MCTLOC.

page 71. A total of $1,218: *MCTJ*, Nov. 17, 1909, in MCTLOC.

page 71. Europe: *MCTJ*, Nov. 17 and 18, 1909, in MCTLOC; see also Mrs. William M. McDonald to MCT, Nov. 23, 1909, in MCTLOC.

page 71. Anonymous book: *MCTJ*, Nov. 19, 1909, in MCTLOC.

page 71. Trauma: MCT, *ACWIAWW*, 39, 151.

page 71. Municipal Court: *AA*, Apr. 10, 1909.

page 72. Antitrust: *Annual Report of the Attorney General of the United States for the Year 1909* (Washington: GPO, 1909), 3–5.

page 72. Anonymous letter: Letter to the President, Dec. 1, 1909, in RHTLOC.

page 72. Trail of litigation: See *WP*, July 22, 1905; see RHT to RRC, Apr. 23, 1902, in UMLRRC.

page 72. "rascality": Letter to the President, Dec. 1, 1909, in RHTLOC.

page 72. Denied: RHT to the Attorney General, Dec. 10, 1909, in RHTLOC. But see Miller, An Early Venture, 364–65 ("misappropriations and looting by several" directors contributed to the bank's collapse, but "fragmentary" evidence and "a conspiracy of silence" among those with knowledge of the bank's operations precluded a complete understanding of what happened, including the extent to which Robert H. Terrell was aware of the bank's financial situation or whether he and other directors had "knowingly approve[d] risky loan ventures" from which they and their friends benefited).

page 72. Withdrawn: *MCTJ*, Dec. 15, 1905, in MCTLOC; *MCTJ*, Dec. 16, 1905, in MCTLOC; *MCTJ*, Dec. 19, 1905, in MCTLOC.

page 72. Background on NAACP: Gates, *Life Upon These Shores*, 240, 242–43; http://www.naacp.org/pages/naacp-history.

page 72. Little role or recognition: See Program, National Negro Committee, May 12, 1910, and May 14, 1910, in MCTLOC; William English Walling to MCT, July 26, 1910, in MCTHUMS.

page 73. "the awful conditions": MCT to RHT, June 4, 1909, in MCTLOC.

page 73. "I don't care": Ibid.

page 73. "official assistant": *MCTJ*, June 18, 1909, in MCTLOC.

page 73. Valet: Brooks served as a valet to Taft, Wilson, and Harding. See John Milton Cooper Jr., *Woodrow Wilson: A Biography* (New York: Alfred A. Knopf, 2009), 196–97, 420, 579; A. Scott Berg, *Wilson* (New York: G. P. Putnam's Sons, 2013), 271, 280, 700; John W. Dean, *Warren G. Harding* (New York: Times Books/Henry Holt, 2004), 139.

page 73. "seconded": "President Taft's Address," newspaper clipping, circa June 18, 1909, in MCTLOC.

page 73. "great influence": "President Taft's Address," newspaper clipping, circa June 18, 1909, in MCTLOC; *MCTJ*, June 18, 1909, in MCTLOC; see *MCTJ*, Jan. 8, 1908, in MCTLOC; *MCTJ*, June 3, 1908, in MCTLOC.

page 74. Her husband's foes: MCT to "Mr. Carpenter," Dec. 15, 1909, in WHTLOC. It is unclear what Mary Church Terrell knew about her husband's role, if any, in the collapse of Capital Savings Bank, or about any financial assistance her father provided to help him pay off any debts he owed to the bank. See RHT to RRC, Apr. 23, 1902, in UMLRRC; RHT to RRC, Nov 8, 1902, in UMLRRC; RHT to RRC, Mar. 16, 1909, in UMLRRC; RRC to RHT, n.d., circa 1909, in UMLRRC; MCT to RHT, Aug. 1, 1914, in MCTHB.

page 74. "I feel sure": MCT to "Mr. Carpenter," Dec. 15, 1909, in WHTLOC.

page 74. Reappointed and confirmed: *Congressional Record*, Jan. 5, 1910, 322; *Congressional Record*, Jan. 11, 1910, 505.

page 74. "I have not": WHT to RHT, Mar, 2, 1910, in RHTLOC.

page 74. "Nobody resigns": Ibid.

page 74. Taft inaugural: William H. Taft, Inaugural Address, Mar. 4, 1909, http://www.presidency.ucsb.edu/ws/?pid=25830. All quotations are from this source. See also Morris, *T. Rex*, 550–53.

page 75. Previously occupied: *AC*, Mar. 17, 1909.

page 75. "professional politicians and": *CDT*, Mar. 25, 1909.

page 75. "constantly conservative": Ibid.

page 75. Would not appoint: John R. Lynch to RHT, Mar. 10, 1910, in RHTLOC.

page 75. Black "mammy" memorial: *TS*, Apr. 24, 1910.

page 75. "one of the grandest": Ibid.

page 75. "pure, unselfish": Ibid.

page 75. "the old black": *WP*, May 3, 1910 (quoting the *NYS*).

page 75. "enjoyed her": Ibid.

page 75. "To Southerners": Ibid.

page 76. "dear old 'mammy'": MCT, Lynching from a Negro's Point of View, 856.

page 76. "social equality": Ibid.

page 76. History of openness: Jill Nelson, *Finding Martha's Vineyard: African Americans at Home on an Island* (New York: Doubleday, 2005), 22–23, 28.

page 76. Palmer's Skin Success: MCT to RHT, July 24, 1910, in MCTLOC.

page 76. "If I had": Ibid.

page 76. "Optimism": RHT, "Address by Robert H. Terrell Before the Cleveland Association of Colored Men, Aug. 1, 1910," in RHTLOC.

page 76. "I am frank": RHT to BTW, Aug. 10, 1910, in BTWLOC.

page 76. Domestic relations: George William Cook to RHT, June 6, 1911, in RHTLOC.

page 76. "necessaries": Prof. Robert H. Terrell, Howard Law School, Domestic Relations Examination, Feb. 3, 1912, in RHTLOC.

page 77. Black Cabinet: *AA*, Apr. 13, 1912.

page 77. "until it reaches": RHT, "Address to Howard University Law School [class of] 1912," in RHTLOC.

page 77. "I believe": Ibid.

page 77. "a sufferer": Ibid.

page 77. Inheritance reportedly worth: *CD*, Oct. 5, 1912; see S. M. Neely to TAC, Jan. 29, 1913, in MCTHB; Last Will and Testament of R. R. Church Dec'd, filed Sept. 11, 1912, in MCTHB; Lauterbach, *Beale Street Dynasty*, 179–80.

page 77. She knew: See Lauterbach, *Beale Street Dynasty*, 179–80; S. M. Neely to MCT, Feb. 14, 1913, in MCTHB.

page 78. Leased: MCT to RHT, June 10, 1919, in MCTLOC; see MCT, *ACWIAWW*, 284.

page 78. Girls told: MCT, *ACWIAWW*, 284.

page 78. Woodrow Wilson background: Sources include Jill Lepore, "The Tug of War," review of *Wilson*, by A. Scott Berg, *The New Yorker* (Sept. 9, 2013); see Smith, *FDR*, 99, 100n., 662n6; Gates, *Life Upon These Shores*, 252; Cooper, *Woodrow Wilson*, 198–99.

page 78. Du Bois endorsed: Gates, *Life Upon These Shores*, 252.

page 78. Predicted: RHT to George A. Myers, Nov. 7, 1912, Mss. 70, George A. Myers Papers, Ohio History Connection.

page 78. "new freedom": Green, *The Secret City*, 171.

page 78. "fair and just treatment": Ibid.

page 78. Agenda: Smith, *FDR*, 100 and 662n6; MCT to the US Senate, circa Jan. 1915, in MCTLOC.

page 78. Dominated the cabinet: Cooper, *Woodrow Wilson*, 204; Berg, *Wilson*, 261–65.

page 78. Cabinet meeting: Smith, *FDR*, 661n3; see Berg, *Wilson*, 306–7.

page 78. Burleson denounced: Cooper, *Woodrow Wilson*, 205; Berg, *Wilson*, 306.

page 78. Segregation by Wilson administration: See Berg, *Wilson*, 306–12; Green, *The Secret City*, 171–75; RNCSNC, 60–61; Cooper, *Woodrow Wilson*, 204–6; Smith, *FDR*, 661n3, 662n6.

page 78. Admissions regimen: Smith, *FDR*, 100n.; Berg, 155–57.

page 79. Unseated: Smith, *FDR*, 99; Green, *The Secret City*, 171.

page 79. One of the two: See Green, *The Secret City*, 171; *AA*, Jan. 22, 1916.

page 79. Dispersal: RHT to MCT, Sept. 25, 1913, in MCTLOC; see MCT to RHT, Sept. 28, 1913, in MCTHB; MCT to RHT, Oct. 10, 1913, in MCTHB; RHT to MCT, Oct. 14, 1913, in MCTHB.

page 79. Even with an old friend: See RHT to George A. Myers, Dec. 19, 1913, Mss. 70, George A. Myers Papers, Ohio History Connection.

page 79. Rented space: See RHT to MCT, Sept. 25, 1913, in MCTLOC; RHT to MCT, Oct. 14, 1913, in MCTHB; RHT to George Myers, Dec. 19, 1913, Ohio History Connection; see *MCTJ*, Feb. 7, 1916, in MCTHB.

page 79. "My dear, dear Wife": RHT to MCT, Sept. 25, 1913, in MCTLOC.

page 79. "in spite": Ibid.

page 79. "your home": Ibid.

page 79. "This will be": Ibid.

page 79. Nagi: RHT to MCT, Sept. 25, 1913, in MCTLOC; MCT to RHT, Mar. 22, 1915, in MCTLOC.

page 79. "turmoil": RHT to MCT, Sept. 25, 1913, in MCTLOC.

page 79. "a family council": Ibid.

page 79. "break up a": Ibid.

page 79. In part: There were other considerations, including her decision to leave her husband and her desire to remove Phyllis from Washington. See MCT to RHT, Sept. 28, 1913, in MCTHB; MCT to RHT, Oct. 24, 1913, in MCTHB; RHT to MCT, Oct. 6, 1913, in MCTHUMS. In a handwritten draft of her memoir, Terrell wrote that Howard University met her academic standards, but she did not want her girls "to think 'black' all the days of their lives." MCT, *ACWLAWW*, Draft, n.d., 25, in MCTLOC.

page 79. Hoped: See MCT to RHT, Sept. 28, 1913, in MCTHB.

page 79. In particular: Ibid.; see MCT to RHT, Oct. 24, 1913, in MCTHB.

page 79. Denials and explanations: Florence Fitch to MCT, Nov. 4, 1913, in MCTLOC; Henry C. King to MCT, Jan. 24, 1914, in MCTLOC; Henry C. King to MCT, Feb. 4, 1914, in MCTLOC.

page 79. Avoid offending: MCT to Florence Fitch, Oct. 1913, in MCTLOC; MCT to Henry C. King, Jan. 26, 1914, in MCTLOC. Phyllis and Mary Terrell were able to socialize with white students because Helen Swift, the daughter of Mary Church Terrell's Oberlin friend, Nettie Swift, had befriended Mary. See MCT to RHT, Oct. 24, 1913, in MCTHB; MCT to RHT, Sept. 7, 1892, in MCTHB; *MCTJ*, Mar. 20–21, 1916, in MCTHB.

Page 79. Parted: See MCT to RHT, Sept. 28, 1913, in MCTHB; RHT to MCT, Sept. 27, 1913, in MCTHUMS.

page 79. Once in pencil: RHT to MCT, Sept. 27, 1913, in MCTHUMS.

page 79. Expenses: RHT to MCT, Oct. 6, 1913, in MCTHUMS; see MCT to RHT, Sept. 28, 1913, in MCTHB; MCT to RHT, Oct. 10, 1913, in MCTHB. Mary later claimed that she had paid the girls' Oberlin expenses from her savings. See MCT to RHT, Aug. 1, 1914, in MCTHB.

page 79. Racial bias: See MCT to RHT, Oct. 24, 1913, in MCTHB.

page 80. Gossip: RHT to MCT, Sept. 25, 1913, in MCTLOC (in postscript); RHT to MCT, Oct. 26, 1913, in MCTHUMS.

page 80. Reminded: RHT to MCT, Oct. 26, 1913, in MCTHUMS.

page 80. Angled for her to visit: RHT to MCT, Nov. 20, 1913, in MCTLOC.

page 80. Floors and shades: Ibid.

page 80. Fantasized: RHT to MCT, Oct. 19, 1913, in MCTHUMS.

page 80. Efforts to contest: See RHT to MCT, Oct. 19, 1913, in MCTHUMS; RHT to MCT, Oct. 26, 1913, in MCTHUMS; RHT to MCT, Oct. 28, 1913, in MCTHUMS; RHT to MCT, Nov. 9, 1913, in MCTHUMS.

page 80. Mu-So-Lit: RHT to MCT, Oct. 19, 1913, in MCTHUMS.

page 80. "a wrong thing": RHT to MCT, Oct. 28, 1913, in MCTHUMS.

page 80. Food poisoning: RHT to MCT, Nov. 14, 1913, in MCTLOC.

page 80. "some hashery": Ibid.

page 80. Pulse, diet, mortality: RHT to MCT, Nov. 14, 1913, in MCTLOC.

page 80. Whether Wilson: Ibid.

page 80. White and black: William L. Houston to James C. McReynolds, Dec. 4, 1913, in RHTLOC; John E. Laskey to the Attorney General [McReynolds], Dec. 4, 1913, in RHTLOC.

page 80. "You are never": RHT to MCT, Nov. 14, 1913, in MCTLOC.

page 80. "I am still": RHT to George Myers, Dec. 19, 1913, Mss. 70, George A. Myers Papers, Ohio History Connection.

page 81. "I am sorry": *NYEJ*, circa Jan. 22, 1914, in RHTLOC.

page 81. Wilson sent: Telegram from RRC [Jr.] to RHT, Apr. 25, 1914, in MCTLOC; see Confirmation of Robert H. Terrell, 63rd Cong., 2d sess., *Congressional Record* 12004 (July 18, 1914).

Page 81. "It is": Telegram from BTW to RHT, Feb. 19, 1914, in RHTLOC.

page 81. At the Y: See Telegram from RRC [Jr.] to RHT, Mar. 4, 1914, in MCTLOC; RHT to George Meyers, July 17, 1914, Mss. 70, George A. Myers Papers, Ohio History Connection. But see Telegram from RRC [Jr.] to RHT,

Mar. 25, 1914, in MCTLOC (directed to 421 T St.); Telegram from RRC [Jr.] to RHT, Apr. 25, 1914, in MCTLOC (directed to 421 T St.).

page 81. Might collapse: MCT to Senator Burton, Mar. 20, 1914, in MCTLOC (from 421 T St.).

page 81. "After struggling": Ibid.

page 81. Bankruptcy: *AA*, May 29, 1915; RHT to [illegible] Davis, Sept. 15, 1915, in RHTLOC.

page 81. Sympathized: *AA*, May 29, 1915.

Page 81. Retreated: She had already shared her displeasure with him in private. See MCT to RHT, Aug. 1, 1914, in MCTHB.

page 81. Lecture in lieu: RHT to MCT, June 5, 1915, in MCTLOC; MCT, *ACWIAWW*, 224, 285.

page 81. Supervised completion: See RHT to MCT, June 7, 1915, in MCTLOC.

page 81. Background on Highland Beach: Sources include MCT to TAC, Aug. 10, 1917, in MCTLOC; Green, *The Secret City*, 209.

page 82. Substitute teacher: MCT, *ACWIAWW*, 280.

page 82. McReynolds forced: *AA*, Jan. 22, 1916.

page 82. "national preparedness": Green, *The Secret City*, 182.

page 82. Jim Crow section: Ibid.

page 82. Segregating troops: Ibid.

page 82. Background on People's: *WH*, Aug. 28, 1915.

page 82. "generally are fair-minded": *AST*, circa Nov. 15, 1915, in RHTLOC.

page 82. "I can't see": RHT to M. G. Gibbs, Aug. 10, 1916, in MCTLOC.

page 83. "For fourteen years": Ibid.

page 83. "We do not care": M. G. Gibbs to RHT, July [*sic*] 12, 1916, in MCTLOC.

page 83. "We appreciate your": Ibid.

page 83. Du Bois hoped: Du Bois, *Amenia*, 7–9.

page 84. "Social Discrimination": Amenia Conference Program, Aug. 24–26, 1916, in MCTLOC.

page 84. "The Negro in": Ibid.

page 84. "Dis cote": Political Cartoon, "The Record in the U.S. Senate Will Prove That Woodrow Wilson Did Appoint this Negro Terrell as Judge of the City Court of Washington, D.C.," n.d., with handwritten note indicating it was used in Georgia during the 1916 election by Progressives to siphon support from Wilson, in MCTHUMS.

page 84. World War I background: Cooper, *Woodrow Wilson*, 389; Gates, *Life Upon These Shores*, 255; *CD*, Sept. 15, 1917; Green, *The Secret City*, 187; *WP*, Mar. 1, 1999; see Kluger, *Simple Justice*, 110.

page 85. "the present emergency": George W. Cook to MCT, Nov. 14, 1917, in MCTLOC.

page 85. Liberty Loan Committee: RHT, Certificate of Appointment, Sept. 25, 1918, in RHTLOC.

page 85. Fifth: See *AA*, Apr. 26, 1918.

page 85. "Since you gave": RHT to TR, May 3, 1918, in TRLOC.

page 85. "That's mighty": TR to RHT, May 7, 1918, in RHTLOC.

page 85. As did Mary: MCT, "The Racial Worm Turns," circa 1920, in MCTLOC.

page 85. Safe place for: NNS, Sept. 27, 1918, in RHTLOC.

page 85. "We were all": Sgt. Bernard G. Cooper to RHT, Nov. 18, 1918, in RHTLOC.

page 86. "The Negroes": Eugene K. Jones to "Gentlemen" of the WCCS, Nov. 15, 1918, in MCTLOC.

page 86. Fear of Bolshevism: See Green, The Secret City, 191n7.

page 86. Declaration of loyalty: Letter from [illegible], Associate Secretary, to MCT, Nov. 26, 1918, in MCTLOC.

page 86. Struggling to build: See Annette Church to MCT, Mar. 8, 1918, in MCTLOC; RHT to MCT, Feb. 24, 1919, in MCTLOC.

page 86. "I shall be": MCT to Phyllis and Mary Terrell, circa Nov. 27, 1918, in MCTLOC.

page 86. "Believe me": Ibid.

page 86. "worry a poor": Ibid.

page 86. "Home Ain't": Ibid.

page 86. After nightfall: WP, July 20, 1919.

page 86. Background on 1919 Riot: Sources include WP, July 20, 1919; WES, July 20, 1919; NYT, July 20, 1919; Green, The Secret City, 190–93 and n7; Berg, Wilson, 670; WP, July 21, 1919; WES, July 21, 1919; NYT, July 21, 1919; WP, July 22, 1919; NYT, July 22, 1919; WP, Mar. 1, 1999; William M. Tuttle Jr., Race Riot: Chicago in the Red Summer of 1919 (New York: Atheneum, 1970), 29.

page 86. Returned from Paris peace conference: Cooper, Woodrow Wilson, 508; Berg, Wilson, 604.

page 86. Retired to the Mayflower: NYT, July 22, 1919; see Cooper, Woodrow Wilson, 510; Berg, Wilson, 615.

page 86. "Murder Bay": Masur, An Example for All the Land, 57; WP, Mar. 1, 1999.

page 87. "sowing the seeds": WP, Mar. 1, 1999.

page 87. "colored maniac": AA, July 11, 1919.

page 87. "clean up": WP, July 20, 1919; WES, July 20, 1919; see NYT, July 21, 1919.

page 87. Taft unearthed: See CD, June 3, 1922.

page 87. "three of them": WP, July 20, 1919.

page 87. "a few hotheads": WP, July 21, 1919.

page 87. "arena": WP, July 21, 1919.

page 88. "clean-up": Ibid.

page 88. "to pale into": Ibid.

page 88. Unrested and unwell: See WP, July 22, 1919.

page 88. Telling the press: WP, July 22, 1919; NYT, July 22, 1919; Cooper, Woodrow Wilson, 510; Berg, Wilson, 615.

page 88. Staff canceled: WP, July 22, 1919.

page 88. Gun dealers: Ibid.

page 88. New wave: Sources include *NYT*, July 22, 1919; *WP*, July 22, 1919; *WES*, July 22, 1919.

page 88. Howard Theater's roof: *WP*, Mar. 1, 1999.

page 88. "Many of the": *NYT*, July 22, 1919.

page 88. "the good women": *WES*, July 22, 1919; *WP*, July 23, 1919.

Page 88. "rape demons": *WES*, July 22, 1919.

page 88. "a national scandal": *WES*, July 22, 1919; *WP*, July 23, 1919.

page 88. "green whisky": *WP*, July 22, 1919.

page 89. Segregate streetcars: *WP*, July 23, 1919.

page 89. Officials knew: *WES*, July 22, 1919.

page 89. That evening: Sources include *NYT*, July 23, 1919; *WP*, July 23, 1919; *WES*, July 23, 1919; *WP*, July 24, 1919; *NYT*, July 24, 1919.

page 89. "What a spectacle": *WP*, July 23, 1919.

page 89. Withdraw their ambassadors: See ibid.

page 89. "Most of them": *NYT*, July 23, 1919.

page 89. "ran amuck": *WES*, July 27, 1919.

page 89. Lobbied Attorney General: *AA*, Aug. 1, 1919.

page 90. Chicago unrest: Tuttle, 32; Gates, *Life Upon These Shores*, 263.

page 90. "S.S. of": *WES*, July 28, 1919.

page 90. "sharpshooter": *WES*, July 28, 1919.

page 90. "We went": *WES*, July 28, 1919.

page 90. Jernagin: *The Black Washingtonians*, 145.

page 90. "This is a": *AA*, Aug. 8, 1919.

page 90. Annual salary: Letter to MCT from J. E. [illegible], Aug. 9, 1919, in MCTLOC.

page 90. More than two dozen: Berg, *Wilson*, 609.

page 90. More than one hundred died: Cooper, *Woodrow Wilson*, 510.

page 90. Thousands more: Ibid.

page 90. Mainly African Americans: Ibid.

page 90. Field secretary: *CSM*, July 4, 1919.

page 90. "Red Summer": Cooper, *Woodrow Wilson*, 510; Berg, *Wilson*, 609.

page 90. High blood pressure: RHT to MCT, Apr. 26, 1917, in MCTHUMS; RHT to MCT, Feb. 10, 1919, in MCTHUMS; RHT to MCT, Mar. 6, 1919, in MCTHB; Telegram from Mary Church to MCT, July 28, 1920, in MCTHB.

page 90. Diet: See RHT to MCT, Feb. 10, 1919, in MCTHUMS.

page 90. Juggled: *CLA*, Dec. 13, 1919; Program, Schenley High School Auditorium, Feb. 27, 1920, in RHTLOC; RHT to MCT, Apr. 20, 1920, in MCTLOC.

page 90. A much-revised: See RHT, "The Negro Today," signed and dated May 1920, Washington, D.C., in RHTLOC.

page 91. "The Negro problem": Ibid.

page 91. "our duty": Ibid.

page 91. "equal and exact": Ibid.

page 91. "our fight": Ibid.

page 91. "Black Men": Ibid.

CHAPTER 4: AN EXAMPLE FOR ALL THE WORLD

page 92. "the full import": RHT to MCT, Aug. 19, 1920, in MCTLOC.

page 92. RNC enlisted: Coleman DuPont to Robert J. Nelson, Sept. 22, 1920, in MCTLOC.

page 92. Real battleground: *NYT*, Dec. 21, 1919; *NYT*, Oct. 22, 1920; *NYT*, Oct. 23, 1920; *NYT*, Sept. 27, 1920.

page 92. "negro domination": *NYT*, Oct. 22, 1920.

page 93. Harding background: Sources include James David Robenalt, *The Harding Affair: Love and Espionage During the Great War* (New York: Palgrave Macmillan, 2009), 13–17, 28, 77, 100, 125, 156, 190, 202, 286, 338, 340, 343–44, 347; Dean, *Warren G. Harding*, 5, 7, 9, 12, 21, 24, 26–27, 44–45; *NYT*, June 21, 1920; *NYT*, June 18, 1920; *NYT*, Aug. 12, 2015 (genetic tests confirm Harding fathered a child out of wedlock).

page 93. "the Duchess": Robenalt, *The Harding Affair*, 28; Dean, *Warren G. Harding*, 21.

page 93. "old-fashioned": *NYT*, Dec. 21, 1919.

page 93. The Aunt Jemima: See National Photo Company, "Inez P. McWhorter (Harding Cook)," June 15, 1920, Library of Congress, Prints and Photographs Division, Call No. LC-F8–8498, http://www.loc.gov/pictures/item/npc2007001825/.

page 93. Front-porch campaign: *NYT*, July 4, 1920; Dean, *Warren G. Harding*, 69–70.

page 93. McKinley flagpole: Dean, *Warren G. Harding*, 69.

page 94. Harding's departure: *NYT*, July 4, 1920; *WP*, July 4, 1920.

page 94. Douglas Fairbanks: *NYT*, July 4, 1920.

page 94. Acceptance speech: *NYT*, July 23, 1920. All quotations are from this source.

page 94. "Social Justice Day": Telegram from Mrs. Richard Edwards to MCT, Sept. 26, 1920, in MCTLOC; see Social Justice Day, "Information for Visiting Women," Oct. 1, 1920, in MCTLOC.

page 94. Monthly rent: Billie Goines to MCT, Oct. 7, 1920, in MCTLOC.

page 94. "I did not": RHT to MCT, circa Sept. 27, 1920 (handwritten note on Edwards telegram).

page 94. "You had better": Ibid.

page 95. "strong utterances": MCT to MT and PT, n.d., written on Sept. 30, 1920, in MCTLOC.

page 95. "jump into": Ibid.

page 95. "Look after": Ibid.

page 95. Vantage point: MCT to Eva Chase, Oct. 6, 1920, in MCTLOC.

page 95. Chautauqua circuit: Robenalt, *The Harding Affair*, 29, 323.

page 95. Hoarse: *WP*, Oct. 1, 1920.

page 95. "the shack": Dean, *Warren G. Harding*, 74; Tarulli H.D. Media Group, "Warren G. Harding: America's 29th President," uploaded on June 20, 2011 (shown to visitors at the Warren G. Harding Home in Marion, Ohio, with archival film footage), https://www.youtube.com/watch?v=4z_1xMxCWDM.

page 95. Social Justice Day: Sources include *WP*, Oct. 1, 1920; *NYT*, Oct. 2, 1920; *WP*, Oct. 2, 1920; *TS*, Oct. 2, 1920; *WP*, Sept. 25, 1920.

page 95. Fur stole: Indiana Historical Society Photograph, "Warren G. Harding and Marie Edwards of Peru, Indiana at the Social Justice Day in Marion, Ohio," Oct. 1, 1920, Item M0612_Box5_K14, http://images.indianahistory.org/cdm /singleitem/collection/V0002/id/1200.

page 96. "an army of": WP, Oct. 2, 1920.

page 96. "equal pay": Ibid.

page 96. Swarmed: Ibid.

page 96. "There is nothing": NYT, Oct. 2, 1920.

page 96. "public welfare": WP, Oct. 2, 1920.

page 96. "the best channel": RHT to MCT, Oct. 6, 1920, in MCTLOC.

page 96. "a walkover": Ibid.

page 96. "theater fiends": RHT to MCT, Feb. 24, 1919, in MCTLOC.

page 96. "travel anywhere": Ibid.

page 96. "He must begin": RHT to MCT, Oct. 6, 1920, in MCTLOC.

page 96. "I am too": Ibid.

page 97. "This time next": MCT to WGH, Oct. 30, 1920, in MCTLOC.

page 97. "I know you": Ibid.

page 97. "That is all": Ibid.

page 97. "Every colored man": MCT, "Campaign Speech made at Newport, RI," Oct. 12, 1920, in MCTLOC.

page 97. "It will": MCT to WGH, Oct. 30, 1920, in MCTLOC.

page 97. "It will": Ibid.

page 98. Voted in Marion: See Dean, Warren G. Harding, 76.

page 98. Watermelon: Photograph, "Cook at Warren G. Harding home," n.d. [during 1920 presidential campaign], No. OHS:AL05327.tif, Ohio Pix, Ohio History Connection. http://cdm16007.contentdm.oclc.org/cdm/singleitem/collection /p267401coll132/id/11944/rec/3.

page 98. More than 60 percent: Cooper, Woodrow Wilson, 571; Berg, Wilson, 693.

page 98. Most commanding: Berg, Wilson, 693; LePore, Tug of War, 81.

page 98. Slipped inquiries: "Marie" [no last name] to MCT, Jan. 6, 1921, in MCTLOC; Anna Church to MCT, Dec. 28, 1920, and Jan. 4, 1921, in MCTLOC.

page 98. Panel charged: Letter from Chairman [name illegible], Committee on Information to MCT, Jan. 10, 1921, in MCTLOC.

page 98. Dispense: Library of Congress, "'I do Solemnly Swear...': Presidential Inaugurations," Telegram from WGH to Hon. Edward B. McLean, circa Jan. 12, 1921, http://memory.loc.gov/cgi-bin/ampage?collId=pin_mssmisc&fileName= pin/pin3901/pin3901page.db&recNum=0&itemLink=r?ammem/pin:@ field%28NUMBER+@band%28mssmisc+pin3901%29%29&linkText=0.

page 98. African American caddy: See Photograph, "President Warren G. Harding on the Golf Course," Harding Memorial Association Collection, St. Augustine, Fla., Feb. 1921, P 146, Box 12, Folder 2 Ohio Pix, Ohio History Connection.

page 98. Strawberry shortcake: NYT, Feb. 5, 1921.

page 98. "fairplay": AA, Mar. 4, 1921.

page 98. "Woodrow Wilson leaves": Ibid.

page 98. "No President": Ibid.

page 98. "Big Inauguration Contest": *AA*, Mar. 4, 1921.

page 98. Wilson's exit: Sources include Berg, *Wilson*, 639–42; *NYT*, Mar. 5, 1921; *WP*, Mar. 5, 1921.

page 99. Harding's inauguration: Sources include *NYT*, Mar. 5, 1921; *WP*, Mar. 5, 1921; *WES*, Mar. 4, 1921; Architect of the Capitol, "About the Grounds," http://www.aoc.gov/capitol-grounds/about-grounds.

page 99. George Washington's Bible: *WP*, Mar. 5, 1921.

page 99. "era of good": WGH, "Inaugural Address," Mar. 4, 1921, http://www.presidency.ucsb.edu/ws/index.php?pid=25833.

page 99. "Our supreme task": Ibid.

page 100. Public access: *WP*, Mar. 5, 1921; *WES*, Mar. 5, 1921.

page 100. By decree: Berg, *Wilson*, 657.

page 100. "one of our": *CD*, Mar. 12, 1921.

page 100. "It seems all right": *NJG*, June 18, 1921.

page 100. Shuttered: For background on Robert R. Church, the NAACP, and the Republican Party in 1920, see Lauterbach, *Beale Street Dynasty*, 202, 233, 237–40; *NJG*, June 18, 1921.

page 100. Unable: See *MCTJ*, Mar. 14, 1921, in MCTHB; *MCTJ*, May 18, 1921, in MCTHB; *MCTJ*, Nov. 30, 1921, in MCTHB.

page 100. Reconciled: See *MCTJ*, Jan. 10, 1915, in MCTLOC; *MCTJ*, Jan. 25, 1915, in MCTLOC; *MCTJ*, Feb. 6–7, 1916, in MCTHB; RHT and MCT, Invitation, Twenty-Fifth Wedding Anniversary, Oct. 25, 1916, in MCTHB; RHT to MCT, Dec. 7, 1916, in MCTHB; RHT to MCT, July 11, 1917, in MCTHB; RHT to MCT, Mar. 6, 1919, in MCTHB; RHT to MCT, Aug. 7, 1919, in MCTHB.

page 100. Separate accounts: See *WT*, Oct. 22, 1926, in MCTLOC.

page 100. Togetherness: See *MCTJ*, June 19, 1921, in MCTHB; *MCTJ*, Sept. 17, 1921, in MCTHB; *MCTJ*, Sept. 19, 1921, in MCTHB; *MCTJ*, Oct. 2, 1921, in MCTHB; *MCTJ*, Oct. 11, 1921, in MCTHB; *MCTJ*, Nov. 2, 1921, in MCTHB.

Page 100. "Chairman of the Chairman": *MCTJ*, Jan. 25, 1915, in MCTLOC.

page 100. Difficulties: See *MCTJ*, Jan. 4, 1921, in MCTHB; *MCTJ*, Feb. 23, 1921, in MCTHB; *MCTJ*, June 27, 1921, in MCTHB. For examples of separate schedules and separateness, see *MCTJ*, July 10, 1921, in MCTHB; *MCTJ*, Sept. 11, 1921, in MCTHB; *MCTJ*, Sept. 23, 1921, in MCTHB; *MCTJ*, Nov. 26, 1921, in MCTHB.

page 101. "I believe that": RHT to WHT, Aug. 13, 1921, in WHTLOC.

page 101. "I am glad": Ibid.

page 101. "I am glad": WHT to RHT, Aug. 19, 1921, in WHTLOC.

page 101. "I am far": RHT to MCT, March 19, 1922, in MCTHUMS. For her response, see MCT to RHT, March [no date], 1922, in MCTHB.

page 101. Real estate: See Last Will and Testament of R. R. Church, filed Sept. 11, 1912, in MCTHB; Lauterbach, *Beale Street Dynasty*, 179–80.

page 101. "some of the": TAC to MCT, Mar. 6, 1922, in MCTLOC.

page 102. "New York is wild": Ibid.

page 102. "sick": MCT to TAC, Mar. 21, 1922, in MCTLOC.

page 102. "ignorant": Ibid.

page 102. Invitation: The Lincoln Memorial Commission, Invitation to the Dedication Ceremony, circa May 16, 1922, in RHTLOC.

page 102. "in charge of": LMC, "Acceptances Should Be Mailed before May 22, 1922," [separate insert], circa May 16, 1922, in RHTLOC.

page 102. Naval radio: WES, May 30, 1922.

page 102. Details: WHT to C. O. Sherrill, May 14, 1922, in WHTLOC; C. O. Sherrill to WHT, May 19, 1922, in WHTLOC; Henry Bacon to WHT, May 28, 1922, in WHTLOC; WHT to Robert T. Lincoln, May 23, 1922, in WHTLOC.

page 102. "Shall have to": Telegram from WHT to Robert R. Moton, May 23, 1922, in WHTLOC. Subsequent quotations are from this source.

page 103. Moton wired: Telegram from Robert R. Moton to WHT, May 24, 1922, in WHTLOC.

page 103. Dedication ceremony: Sources include WP, May 31, 1922; WES, May 30, 1922; WP, May 30, 1922; NYT, May 31, 1922; Philip B. Kunhardt III, Peter W. Kunhardt, and Peter W. Kunhardt Jr., Looking for Lincoln: The Making of an American Icon (New York: Alfred A. Knopf, 2008), 450; Adam Fairclough, "Civil Rights and the Lincoln Memorial: The Censored Speeches of Robert R. Moton (1922) and John Lewis (1963)," The Journal of Negro History 82, no. 4 (Autumn 1997): 408–16.

page 103. Spaces rivaling: LMC, The Lincoln Memorial and the Development of Potomac Park, enclosed in C. O. Sherrill to WHT, May 19, 1922, in WHTLOC; see WP, May 31, 1922.

page 103. Section Five: AA, June 2, 1922.

page 103. East Potomac Golf Course: Green, The Secret City, 198–99.

page 104. "that lying nigger": Alice Dunbar-Nelson, edited by Gloria T. Hull, Give Us Each Day: The Diary of Alice Dunbar-Nelson (New York: W.W. Norton, 1986), 87.

page 104. abolitionist forebears: Dean, Warren G. Harding, 19–20, 75–76. Editors refused to publish the allegations. See NYT, Oct. 23, 1920; Dean, Warren G. Harding, 75–76; Robenalt, The Harding Affair, 14, 26. Recent genetic testing found that Harding had no African ancestry. See NYT, Aug. 12, 2015.

page 104. "Linc": CD, June 10, 1922; but see Dunbar-Nelson, Give Us Each Day, 87 ("Link").

page 104. likelihood: CD, June 10, 1922.

page 104. McKinlay background: TS, July 22, 1910; AA, June 2, 1922; CSM, July 21, 1910; AA, Aug. 6, 1910; CD, June 10, 1922; Davis, Guest of Honor, 185–87, 189; see Miller, An Early Venture, 363–65; RRC to Whitfield [sic] McKinlay, May 6, 1912, in UMLRRC.

page 104. "coal black": TS, July 22, 1910.

page 104. "Well, think": AA, June 2, 1922.

page 104. Walked out: For details see *AA*, June 2, 1922; *CD*, June 10, 1922.

page 104. Originally drafted: RRM, "Address of Robert Russa Moton at the Dedication of the Lincoln Memorial," Washington, D.C., May 30, 1922, in RRMLOC (marked "Address as revised" and previous draft, marked, "Address as originally written," May 17, 1922). All cites are to this source, for both speeches.

page 106. Confederate veterans and Union soldiers: *WP*, May 31, 1922.

page 106. Frail and unsteady: Ibid.

page 107. Cavalcade: Ibid.

page 107. Proprietary dignity: See C-Span, "Lincoln Memorial Dedication, May 30, 1922" (Courtesy: National Archives), http://www.c-span.org/video/?286716–1/lincoln-memorial-dedication [hereafter "C-Span video"]; Thomas Mallon, "Set in Stone," review of *Looking for Lincoln*, by Philip B. Kunhardt III et al., *The New Yorker*, Oct. 13, 2008 ("proprietary pleasure").

page 107. "a disgraceful page": *AA*, Apr. 13, 1912.

page 107. "greatest act": *AA*, Sept. 28, 1912.

page 107. "living lie": Ibid.

page 107. "Christ-like character": *NYT*, May 31, 1922; *WP*, May 31, 1922.

page 107. "brotherly love": *WP*, May 31, 1922.

page 107. "Here is a": Ibid.

page 107. "rejoiced": *WP*, May 31, 1922.

page 107. Cheer rose: Ibid.

page 107. Recorded: *WP*, May 31, 1922; C-Span video.

page 107. Visitors climbed: *WP*, May 31, 1922.

page 108. "a concession": George Murray to WHT, June 1, 1922, in WHTLOC.

page 108. "entirely out of": Ibid.

page 108. "no such *segregation*": WHT to George Murray, June 4, 1922, in WHTLOC (emphasis original).

page 108. "If colored people": Ibid.

page 108. "most shocking": "Resolution of Protest Adopted by the District of Columbia Branch of the N.A.A.C.P. Against the Segregation of Colored People at the Dedication of the Lincoln Memorial," *enclosed with* Letter from [illegible NAACP President] to WHT, June 7, 1922, in WHTLOC.

page 108. "When juster": Editorial, *CD*, June 10, 1922.

page 109. "alarmed": *CD*, circa June 10, 1922, in RHTLOC.

page 109. "worried": Ibid.

page 109. Her home: See MCT, Indenture, circa Dec. 7, 1920, in MCTHB.

page 109. Remedies: Carl Wilson to RHT, June 10, 1922, in RHTLOC; Harrison T. Davis to RHT (no date), in RHTLOC; Allie M. Jones to MCT, June 17, 1922, in MCTLOC; W. R. Rodgers to RHT, June 12, 1922, in RHTLOC.

page 109. "Wisdom, Uprightness and Learning": "Warren G. Harding, Appointment of Robert H. Terrell," June 22, 1922, in RHTLOC.

page 109. "about the only": Emmett Scott to RHT, June 26, 1922, in RHTLOC.

page 109. The dog: RHT to MCT, March 21, 1923, in MCTLOC.

page 109. Harvard's freshman dorms: Hamilton Fish to RHT, Jan. 17, 1923, in RHTLOC.

page 109. War veterans: *CD*, Apr. 21, 1923.

page 109. Senate's blessing: *CD*, Mar. 10, 1923.

page 109. "as if": Annette Church to MCT, Jan. 3, 1924, in MCTLOC.

page 109. Segregated bathing: "Dear Friend" Letter from Norman L. McGhee, Jan. 19, 1923, in MCTLOC.

page 109. Short stories: Letter from [illegible, The Frank A. Munsey Co.] to MCT, Feb. 6, 1923, in MCTLOC.

page 110. "Colored women": MCT, letter-to-the-editor, *WES*, Feb. 10, 1923; MCT, letter-to-the-editor, *WH*, Feb. 15, 1923, in MCTLOC. For more personal insights, see *MCTJ*, Mar. 17, 1948, in MCTHB.

page 110. "Surely in their": MCT, letter-to-the-editor, *WES*, Feb. 10, 1923.

page 110. "a change and": MCT to RHT, circa Feb. 26, 1923, in MCTLOC. She did not date this letter, which she wrote from Jacksonville. Her itinerary called for three days in Jacksonville, from February 26, 1923, to February 28, 1923.

page 110. In private: N. B. Young to RHT, May 7, 1923, in RHTLOC.

page 110. "I miss you": RHT to MCT, Mar. 26, 1923, in MCTHUMS.

page 110. Second stroke: *AA*, Dec. 26, 1925, in RHTLOC.

page 110. Relatives urged: Anna Church to MCT, May 29, 1923, in MCTLOC; Annette Church to MCT, June 1, 1923, in MCTLOC; Annette Church to MCT, Jan. 3, 1924, in MCTLOC.

page 110. Canceled: Emmett Scott to RHT, Oct. 18, 1923, in RHTLOC.

page 110. Floral arrangement: J. Burlis to RHT, Jan. 12, 1924, in RHTLOC.

page 110. Car accident: Eula Edwards to MCT, Aug. 29, 1923, in MCTLOC; *WT*, Aug. 4, 1923, in MCTLOC.

page 110. "fine catch": MCT to RHT, Mar. 25, 1923, in MCTLOC; Mary Louise Church, Wedding Reception Invitation, June 27, 1923, in MCTHB.

page 110. Cross burning: *NYT*, Apr. 3, 1924; *NYT*, Apr. 4, 1924; *TS*, Apr. 4, 1924.

page 110. Racial restrictive covenants: See NAACP, *15th Annual Report of the National Association for the Advancement of Colored People for 1924* (Jan. 1925), 21–22, in MCTLOC [hereafter "NAACP 1924 Report"].

page 110. Real estate discrimination: MCT, *ACWIAWW*, 150–51, 154–55.

page 111. Though sympathetic: Harriot Stanton Blatch to MCT, Nov. 23, 1920, in MCTLOC.

page 111. "the whole civilized": MCT, "Remarks Made at Meeting Called by Kelly Miller at the John Wesley A.M.E. Church to Protest Against Segregation," Washington, D.C., Apr. 14, 1924, in MCTLOC.

page 111. "Our chief duty": Ibid.

page 111. Fortieth reunion: MCT to RHT, June 10, 1924, in MCTLOC.

page 111. "agitation": NAACP 1924 Report, 47.

page 111. "to reward": Ibid.

page 112. Listened: Eula Edwards to MCT, June 15, 1924, in MCTLOC.

page 112. Regrets: Robert Mattingly to MCT, Jan. 14, 1925, in MCTLOC.

page 112. Lecturer: See Mary Anderson to E. J. Henning, Dec. 12, 1924, *enclosed with* C. Bascom Slamp to MCT, Dec. 16, 1924, in MCTHUMS.

page 112. Fretted: MCT to TAC, Jan. 1, 1925, in MCTLOC.

page 112. Salary: MCT to RHT, June 10, 1924, in MCTLOC.

page 112. Mary's name: NAACP 1924 Report, 54–55, 1. She may have been focused on other concerns, including the Memphis real estate she had inherited from her father. See *MCTJ*, Apr. 10, 1921, in MCTHB; MCT to RHT, March [no date], 1922, in MCTHB; Anti-Segregation Drive, Sponsored by the Colored Women of Washington, Dec. 20–28, 1925, in MCTLOC.

page 112. Check for $1,180: See Statement, Van Court Rental Agency, Mar. 17, 1925, in MCTLOC; see D. S. Van Court to MCT, Sept. 24, 1935, in MCTLOC.

page 112. Radio fitness: Arthur E. Bagley to MCT, Nov. 25, 1925, in MCTLOC.

page 112. Asthma attack: *CD*, circa Dec. 25, 1925, in RHTLOC.

page 113. Would never recover: Anna Church to MCT, Dec. 21, 1925, in MCTLOC.

page 113. Life-insurance claim: D. Harris to MCT, Dec. 21, 1925, in MCTLOC.

page 113. "It is impossible": Arthur Froe to MCT, Dec. 21, 1925, in MCTLOC.

page 113. Houston announced: *WES*, Dec. 21, 1925, in RHTLOC.

page 113. Honored the university: Ibid.

page 113. Adjourned: Order of the Municipal Court of the District of Columbia, Sitting In Banc, Dec. 22, 1925, in RHTLOC.

page 113. Robert's funeral: Sources include *WA*, Dec. 24, 1925, in RHTLOC; *WE*, Dec. 26, 1925, in RHTLOC; *AA*, Dec. 26, 1925; *NJG*, Dec. 26, 1925, in RHTLOC.

page 113. Honorary pallbearers: McGuire's Funeral Home, Automobile List, circa Dec. 24, 1925, in RHTLOC.

page 113. "During his": *WA*, Dec. 24, 1925, in RHTLOC.

page 113. Terrells together: *WE*, Dec. 26, 1925, in RHTLOC. Her husband's doctor would later sue her to collect $75—reflecting Robert's unpaid medical bills, dating back to May 1924. In a court filing, she said she had neither requested nor agreed to pay for her husband's medical services, which were "on his own account" and "out of his fund." *WT*, Oct. 22, 1926, in MCTLOC.

CHAPTER 5: THE RADICALIZATION OF MARY CHURCH TERRELL

page 114. Started her memoirs: *MCTJ*, Jan. 3, 1927, in MCTLOC.

page 114. "Dubois [*sic*] doesn't": MCT to TAC, Jan. 10, 1926, in MCTLOC.

page 114. "Don't Laugh!": MCT to TAC, Mar. 1, 1926, in MCTLOC.

page 114. "It seems to us": Herbert Jenkins to MCT, June 29, 1926, in MCTHUMS.

page 114. Candor and disclosure: *MCTJ*, Feb. 28, 1927, in MCTLOC.

page 115. Reader's report: Herbert Jenkins to MCT, Apr. 15, 1927, in MCTHUMS.

page 115. Brevity: Ibid.

page 115. Seven-page letter: *MCTJ*, Apr. 21, 1927, in MCTLOC.

page 115. Three operations: See *MCTJ*, Jan. 26, 1915-Mar. 27, 1915, in MCTLOC;
  RHT to MCT, Feb. 13, 1915, in MCTHB. She did not disclose the reason for the
  third operation, other than to refer to it in her diary, on February 1, 1915, as the
  "big" one. Though the nature of the third operation remains unclear, it may have
  been a hysterectomy. See Alison M. Parker, "'The Picture of Health': The Public
  Life and Private Ailments of Mary Church Terrell," *Journal of Historical Biography*
  13 (Spring 2013): 164–207, 182, www.ufv.ca/jhb.

page 115. Covered: See RHT to MCT, Feb. 16, 1915, in MCTHUMS.

page 115. Application: Copy of Application, Inter-Ocean Casualty Co., May 31,
  1924, in MCTLOC.

page 115. The "WHOLE" truth: MCT to Mr. Latham, Oct. 19, 1939, in MCTLOC.

page 115. Anonymously: See *MCTJ*, July 31, 1909, in MCTLOC (as if it happened
  to other women); *MCTJ*, Nov. 19, 1909, in MCTLOC. She also wrote a handful
  of articles for the *Colored American*, using the byline "Euphemia Kirk." See *CA*,
  Feb. 3, 1900; *CA*, Mar. 10, 1900; *CA*, Mar. 17, 1900.

page 116. Focus on: See MCT, *ACWIAWW*, 71–133, 237–48.

page 116. Omitting: See MCT, *ACWIAWW*, 31, 224, 285, 196.

page 116. "Shall I": MCT, *ACWIAWW*, handwritten draft, n.d., 2, in MCTLOC.

page 116. "obstacles": MCT, *ACWIAWW*, typed draft, n.d., 364, in MCTLOC.

page 116. "barriers": Ibid.

page 116. "opportunities": Ibid.

page 116. incident: MCT, *ACWIAWW*, handwritten draft, n.d., 22, in MCTLOC.

page 116. Rejections: She did publish short fiction in the *Crisis*. See MCT, "Aunt
  Dinah and Dilsey Discuss the Problem," *The Crisis* 25, no. 4 (Feb. 1923): 159, in
  MCTLOC.

page 116. "unconvincing": Munsey [illegible] to MCT, Feb. 6, 1923, in MCTLOC.

page 116. "uninteresting": Ibid.

page 116. "the art of": Ibid.

page 116. "story interest": Leah Sewell to MCT, May 31, 1922, in MCTLOC.

page 116. "I can't say": Joel E. Spingarn to MCT, May 24, 1922, in MCTLOC.

page 116. S Street apartments: *MCTJ*, June 23, 1931, in MCTHUMS; *MCTJ*, July
  1, 1931, in MCTHUMS.

page 116. Ground floor: See *MCTJ*, Aug. 8, 1931, in MCTHUMS; *MCTJ*, Dec. 31,
  1931, in MCTHUMS.

page 116. Daybed: *MCTJ*, June 24, 1931, in MCTHUMS.

page 116. Card parties: See, for example, *MCTJ*, Jan. 12, 1935, in MCTLOC; *MCTJ*,
  Jan. 15, 1935, in MCTLOC; *MCTJ*, Jan. 25, 1935, in MCTLOC.

page 116. Shopping: See, for example, *MCTJ*, Feb. 25, 1935, in MCTLOC; *MCTJ*,
  Mar. 26, 1935, in MCTLOC.

page 116. Debt: See, for example, *MCTJ*, Aug. 5, 1931, in MCTHUMS; *MCTJ*,
  Aug. 10, 1931, in MCTHUMS.

page 116. Involved: See, for example, *MCTJ*, Feb. 13, 1935, in MCTLOC.

page 117. "DeP": See *MCTJ*, Dec. 4, 1931, in MCTHUMS. Approximately three
  months into his first term, DePriest alienated southern congressional colleagues

by eating in the members' cafeteria with Congresswoman Ruth Hanna McCormick, a white Illinois Republican who was the daughter of former Senator Mark Hanna. See Newspaper Clipping, circa May 25, 1929, in MCTLOC. Later that year, Mary Church Terrell worked on McCormick's unsuccessful campaign for election to the US Senate, speaking to black voters in Illinois. See MCT, *ACWIAWW*, 397–400.

page 117. Say goodbye: *MCTJ*, June 29, 1931, in MCTHUMS.

page 117. Admired her: *MCTJ*, Dec. 4, 1931, in MCTHUMS.

page 117. Fumed: *MCTJ*, Dec. 26, 1931, in MCTHUMS.

page 117. Prayed it would continue: *MCTJ*, Dec. 31, 1931, in MCTHUMS.

page 117. Relief: *MCTJ*, Jan. 1, 1934, in MCTHUMS.

page 117. Refusal: *MCTJ*, May 27, 1934, in MCTHUMS.

page 117. Tenants: See, for example, *MCTJ*, Mar. 6, 1934, in MCTHUMS; *MCTJ*, Mar. 8, 1934, in MCTHUMS.

page 117. Lightbulbs: *MCTJ*, Mar. 30, 1934, in MCTHUMS.

page 117. Honorary degree: See, for example, *MCTJ*, Jan. 8–9, 1934, in MCTHUMS.

page 117. Lump: *MCTJ*, Aug. 24, 1934, in MCTHUMS; *MCTJ*, Aug. 28, 1934, in MCTHUMS.

page 117. Impending marriage: See, for example, *MCTJ*, July 14, 1934, in MCTHUMS.

page 117. administrative and clerical jobs: See, for example, *MCTJ*, Jan. 15, 1934, in MCTHUMS.

page 117. Laid off: See, for example, *MCTJ*, Apr. 24–25, 1934, in MCTHUMS.

page 117. Heart and blood pressure: *MCTJ*, Aug. 30, 1934, in MCTHUMS.

page 117. "*Psychoneurosis*": *MCTJ*, Aug. 30, 1934, in MCTHUMS.

page 117. Alone in a cafeteria: *MCTJ*, Nov. 29, 1934, in MCTHUMS.

page 117. Separation: See *MCTJ*, Nov. 28, 1934, in MCTHUMS.

page 117. Weighed whether or not: *MCTJ*, Dec. 8, 1934, in MCTHUMS.

page 117. "At my wit's end": *MCTJ*, Dec. 9, 1934, in MCTHUMS.

page 117. Should have started rewriting: *MCTJ*, Feb. 28, 1935, in MCTLOC.

page 117. Acceptable to whites: *MCTJ*, Feb. 27, 1935, in MCTLOC.

page 117. "greatly improved": *MCTJ*, Mar. 15, 1935, in MCTLOC (quoting letter).

page 117. "fascinating": Ibid. (quoting letter).

page 117. Expressing reservations: Ibid.

page 117. London agent: *MCTJ*, Mar. 17, 1935, in MCTLOC.

page 118. "interesting": Herbert F. Jenkins to MCT, Apr. 11, 1935, in MCTHUMS.

page 118. "far too long": Ibid.

page 118. Window seat: See *MCTJ*, May 21, 1931, in MCTHUMS.

page 118. Rosenwald Fund: *WSS*, Mar. 19, 1935, in MCTLOC.

page 118. "I fear I am": MCT to TAC, Apr. 11, 1935, in MCTLOC. Though she does not mention Little, Brown's decision in her note to her brother, her diary indicates that she received the rejection letter, which is dated April 11, on April 11.

page 118. "You have let": Ibid. In 1921, Stuyvesant Press published Thomas's non-fiction book, titled *The Roller*, which was about breeding and caring for canaries. See *MCTJ*, Feb. 2, 1921, in MCTHB; MCT, *ACWIAWW*, 74.

page 118. "an artist": MCT to TAC, Apr. 11, 1935, in MCTLOC.

page 118. "a missionary": Ibid.

page 118. "a reformer": Ibid.

page 119. "It is quite": Ibid.

page 119. "I love her": *MCTJ*, Apr. 14, 1935, in MCTLOC.

page 119. "Banish my": *MCTJ*, Jan 1, 1935, in MCTLOC (the prayer is dated April 18, 1935).

page 119. "From worry": Ibid.

page 119. Mary spotted: *MCTJ*, April 9, 1939, in MCTHUMS.

page 119. Black limousine: *WP*, Apr. 10, 1939.

page 119. Anderson concert: Sources include *WP*, Apr. 10, 1939; *WES*, Apr. 19, 1939; *NYT*, Apr. 10, 1939; *AA*, Apr. 15, 1939; *CD*, Apr. 15, 1939; Nancy J. Weiss, *Farewell to the Party of Lincoln: Black Politics in the Age of FDR* (Princeton: Princeton University Press, 1983), 256–57, 259, 261–62; Kosti Vehanen, *Marian Anderson: A Portrait* (Westport, Conn.: Greenwood Press, 1970), 239, 242–44.

page 119. Once in a century: *WP*, Apr. 10, 1939; see Weiss, *Farewell to the Party of Lincoln*, 257.

page 119. After church: Details are from *MCTJ*, April 9, 1939, in MCTHUMS.

page 119. Mink coat: *WES*, Apr. 10, 1939.

page 119. Mink-trimmed hat: *CD*, Apr. 15, 1939.

page 119. Sat together: See *WES*, Apr. 10, 1939; *WP*, Apr. 10, 1939; Vehanen, *Marian Anderson*, 239 (photo).

page 120. White House vetted: Weiss, *Farewell to the Party of Lincoln*, 262.

page 120. Lindbergh: *WP*, Apr. 10, 1939.

page 120. Ickes background: Smith, *FDR*, 323n; Weiss, *Farewell to the Party of Lincoln*, 36, 51–52, 256–57.

page 120. DAR denied: *NYT*, Apr. 10, 1939.

page 120. School board banished: *AA*, Feb. 23, 1939.

page 120. Outrage over Nazi Germany: Ibid.

page 120. *Kristallnacht*: Smith, *FDR*, 426.

page 120. Resignation: See *AA*, Mar. 4, 1939; Weiss, *Farewell to the Party of Lincoln*, 261.

page 121. "an act of insanity": *AA*, Mar. 11, 1939 (quoting Jackson *Daily News*).

page 121. "We love": Ibid.

page 121. Shifted public opinion: Ibid.

page 121. Proposed an outdoor concert: Smith, *FDR*, 402; Weiss, *Farewell to the Party of Lincoln*, 259.

page 121. White suggested: Weiss, *Farewell to the Party of Lincoln*, 259–60.

page 121. Ickes agreed: Smith, *FDR*, 402; Weiss, *Farewell to the Party of Lincoln*, 260.

page 121. Roosevelt consented: Smith, *FDR*, 402; Weiss, *Farewell to the Party of Lincoln*, 260.

page 121. In Hyde Park: *WES*, Apr. 10, 1939; Weiss, *Farewell to the Party of Lincoln*, 261.

page 121. Warm Springs: *NYT*, Apr. 10, 1939.

page 121. Ethicist: See Weiss, *Farewell to the Party of Lincoln*, 256.

page 121. NBC's live broadcast: *WES*, Apr. 10, 1939.

page 121. "In this great": *WP*, Apr. 10, 1939. All quotes from Ickes speech are from this source.

page 121. Applause: *WP*, Apr. 10, 1939.

page 121. southern Democrats: Smith, *FDR*, 400–401.

page 121. Trod carefully: See Smith, *FDR*, 402.

page 121. Anderson at the podium: See *WP*, Apr. 10, 1939 (photo); *WES*, Apr. 10, 1939 (photo); Vehanen, *Marian Anderson*, 244–46; Weiss, *Farewell to the Party of Lincoln*, 263 (photo); Lost_ Shangri_La_Horizon, "Marian Anderson: The Lincoln Memorial Concert," Apr. 9, 1939, published Nov. 17, 2010, http://www.dailymotion .com/video/xfo81h_marian-anderson-the-lincoln-memorial-concert-1939_ shortfilms (newsreel footage).

page 121. Encampment: Vehanen, *Marian Anderson*, 239 (photo).

page 121. Men in overcoats: *WES*, Apr. 10, 1939 (photo).

page 122. Ten organs: Vehanen, *Marian Anderson*, 245.

page 122. Range, warmth, emotional resonance: *WES*, Apr. 10, 1939.

page 122. Carrying for blocks: *NYT*, Apr. 10, 1939.

page 122. Latecomers stopped and doffed: *WES*, Apr. 10, 1939.

page 122. Like a sigh: See *WES*, Apr. 10, 1939.

page 122. Floodlights: *WES*, Apr. 9, 1939.

page 122. Justice Hugo L. Black arrived: *WP*, Apr. 10, 1939; *WES*, Apr. 10, 1939.

page 122. "You don't know": *WES*, Apr. 10, 1939; see *CD*, Apr. 15, 1939; *NYT*, Apr. 10, 1939 (slightly different version of the quote).

page 122. "The immensity": *WES*, Apr. 10, 1939; see *CD*, Apr. 15, 1939; *WP*, Apr. 10, 1939.

page 122. Black velvet and violet: *MCTJ*, Apr. 9, 1939, in MCTHUMS.

page 122. Receiving line: *AA*, Apr. 15, 1939.

page 122. "The Lord certainly": *MCTJ*, Apr. 9, 1939, in MCTHUMS.

page 122. Spiritual awakening: See *MCTJ*, May 1, 1936, in MCTLOC; *MCTJ*, May 29–June 8, 1936, in MCTLOC.

page 123. "I shall tell you": MCT to PT, May 27, 1936, in MCTLOC.

page 123. False teeth: *MCTJ*, Nov. 12–19, 1934, in MCTHUMS.

page 123. Glasses: *MCTJ*, Sept. 10, 1931, in MCTHUMS.

page 123. Hearing tests: *MCTJ*, Sept. 4, 1934, in MCTHUMS.

page 123. "God forbid": *MCTJ*, Dec. 30, 1936, in MCTLOC.

page 123. Only religious revival: See Joint Committee on Delinquency and Crime, Minutes, circa Jan. 24, 1937, 2, in MCTLOC.

page 123. Seized and auctioned: see Lauterbach, *Beale Street Dynasty*, 290–91; *MTCJ*, Mar. 11, 1940, in MCTHB.

page 123. Lunch: *MCTJ*, Apr. 12, 1939, in MCTHUMS.

page 123. "anticlimax": Ibid.

page 123. "more harm than good": Ibid.

page 123. Douglas swearing-in: *NYT*, Apr. 18, 1939; *WP*, Apr. 18, 1939; *WES*, Apr. 17, 1939.

page 124. Boy Scout mien: *WES*, Apr. 17, 1939 (photo).

page 124. "almost bombastically": The Supreme Court Historical Society, History of the Court, "Homes of the Court," http://www.supremecourthistory.org/history-of-the-court/home-of-the-court/.

page 124. Elsewhere: *WP*, Apr. 17, 1939; *WES*, Apr. 17, 1939; *WP*, Apr. 18, 1939. In their stories, the *Post* and the *Star* refer to the team as the Nationals or the Nats, though the *Star* also called them the Senators.

page 124. "unconventional": *NYT*, Apr. 17, 1939.

page 124. "do equal right": US Supreme Court, "Text of the Oaths of Office for Supreme Court Justices," http://www.supremecourt.gov/about/oath/textofthe oathsofoffice2009.aspx.

page 124. "present": *Kessler v. Strecker*, 307 U.S. 22, 30 (1939) (italics deleted).

page 124. Refused to speak to or stand: Rawn James Jr., *Root and Branch: Charles Hamilton Houston, Thurgood Marshall, and the Struggle to End Segregation* (New York: Bloomsbury Press, 2013), 116; see Kluger, *Simple Justice*, 114.

page 125. "That he is an": *NYT*, Apr. 18, 1939; *Kessler*, 307 U.S. at 36.

page 125. "During the rest": *NYT*, Apr. 18, 1939.

page 125. On her own: See *MCTJ*, Jan. 13, 1940, in MCTHB; *MCTJ*, Jan. 15, 1940, in MCTHB; *MCTJ*, Jan. 16, 1940, in MCTHB. The final blow was a rejection by Macmillan. See *MCTJ*, Jan. 13, 1940, in MCTHB. She agreed to pay more than $1,400 to self-publish her memoir. See *MCTJ*, Mar. 20–21, 1940, in MCTHB.

page 125. Other titles: See Ransdell, Inc., "Books You Should Know About," circa 1941, in MCTLOC; Ransdell, Inc. Catalogue, Fall and Winter 1940–41, in MCTLOC.

page 125. "Many thanks": Radiogram from MCT to H. G. Wells, Apr. 18, 1940, in MCTLOC. But see *MCTJ*, Apr. 17, 1940, in MCTHB.

page 125. "artless": H. G. Wells, Introduction to *A Coloured Woman in the Great White World*, Apr. 9, 1940, 2, in MCTLOC [hereafter "Wells, Intro"].

page 125. "loose and ample assemblage": Wells, Intro., 1.

page 125. in favor: See *MCTJ*, Apr. 19, 1940, in MCTHB; *MCTJ*, June 5, 1940, in MCTHB.

page 125. "discreet faltering from explicitness": Wells, Intro., 2.

page 125. "When, as my reward": Wells, Intro., 3.

page 125. Terrell reviewed: See *MCTJ*, May 22, 1940, in MCTHB.

page 125. Houston background: See William P. Jones, *The March on Washington: Jobs, Freedom, and the Forgotten History of Civil Rights* (New York: W. W. Norton, 2013), xv–xvi; Green, *The Secret City*, 227–30; Kluger, *Simple Justice*, 105–10, 116, 125–30, 160–61, 165, 201–2, 212; James, *Root and Branch*, 19–24, 30–35, 39–46, 52–54, 116; *WP*, Apr. 23, 1950; King, *Devil in the Grove*, 42; Patterson, *Brown v. Board of Education*, 12, 15–16; *The Black Washingtonians*, 188–93; *PC*, Sept. 17, 1938.

page 126. Swiveled: James, *Root and Branch*, 116.

page 126. McReynolds dissent: See *Missouri ex rel. Gaines v. Canada*, 305 U.S. 337 (1938); Kluger, *Simple Justice*, 213.

page 126. Future challenges: See Patterson, *Brown v. Board of Education*, 16; Kluger, *Simple Justice*, 213.

page 126. Mary gave $5: See Charles E. Russell to MCT, Dec. 16, 1938, in MCTLOC.

page 126. Leaving Marshall: See James, *Root and Branch*, 126, 130, 153; Kluger, *Simple Justice*, 214.

page 127. Soliciting donors: Kluger, *Simple Justice*, 161–63.

page 127. Economic justice: See James, *Root and Branch*, 129.

page 127. Understood better: Kluger, *Simple Justice*, 162–63.

page 127. First peacetime draft: W. Jones, *The March on Washington*, 27.

page 127. Urging Roosevelt: CHH to FDR, June 10, 1940, in CHHHUMS.

page 127. Thanked: James Rowe Jr. to CHH, June 25, 1940, in CHHHUMS.

page 127. Segregated inaugural: Emergency Committee on Inaugural Jim Crowism, "The Honorable Jim Crow Attends the Inaugural," Jan. 19, 1941, in CHHHUMS; see The Inaugural Committee and the Committee on Special Entertainment, Invitation to a "Musical by Negro Artists," Jan. 20, 1941, in WODLOC.

page 127. March on Washington: *AA*, Jan. 25, 1941; W. Jones, *The March on Washington*, 1–3; Duberman, *Paul Robeson*, 252.

page 127. "first class citizenship": W. Jones, *The March on Washington*, xv.

page 127. State of the Union: W. Jones, *The March on Washington*, 2.

page 127. "would wake up": *AA*, Jan. 25, 1941.

page 127. Reception: *WT*, Feb. 1. 1941, in MLK/MCT and RHT.

page 127. Knew otherwise: See *MCTJ*, Dec. 24, 1940, in MCTHB; *MCTJ*, Dec. 26, 1940, in MCTHB.

page 127. trimmed: *MCTJ*, June 5, 1940, in MCTHB; see MCT, *ACWIAWW* (Washington, D.C.: Ransdell Inc., 1940), preface by H.G. Wells, i–ii [hereafter "MCT, *ACWIAWW*, Ransdell"]. Gone, for example, was the following: "This is a rambling book. It is a loose and ample assemblage of reminiscences of very unequal value. It is definitely an artless book." Wells, Intro, 1–2; see MCT, *ACWIAWW*, Ransdell, i.

page 127. *Afro-American*'s favorable: *AA*, Nov. 2, 1940, in MCTLOC.

page 127. "on hand": Eleanor Roosevelt to MCT, Mar. 24, 1941, in MCTLOC.

page 128. Frustrated: See *MCTJ*, Dec. 23, 1940, in MCTHB.

page 128. Declaration: Initiating Group, A Statement on the Position of the Negro People in America, "To the Negro People: A Statement on Our Present Position in America," Apr. 11, 1941, in MCTLOC.

page 128. Robeson background: Duberman, *Paul Robeson*, 54–155.

page 128. Pullman-car image: A. Philip Randolph to MCT, Apr. 26, 1941, in MCTLOC.

page 128. "It is the growing": *AA*, Apr. 12, 1941.

page 128. "to gird for": *AA*, June 7, 1941.

page 128. FDR summoned: Smith, *FDR*, 493–94. Details of the meeting are from this source unless otherwise noted.

page 128. Scheduled for July 1: *AA*, May 10, 1941.

page 128. Wary of alienating: Smith, *FDR*, 493; see Green, *The Secret City*, 254; Kluger, *Simple Justice*, 218.

page 128. Silent processional: *CD*, June 28, 1941; *CD*, May 17, 1941; *AA*, May 10, 1941.

page 129. Propaganda: See Green, *The Secret City*, 254.

page 129. 1919 riot: Smith, *FDR*, 494; see W. Jones, *The March on Washington*, 56.

page 129. Executive order: Smith, *FDR*, 494; *NYT*, June 26, 1941; Kluger, *Simple Justice*, 219; *WP*, June 26, 1941; *WES*, June 26, 1941; Gates, *Life Upon These Shores*, 299. FDR's directive, Executive Order 8802, established "a Committee on Fair Employment Practice." It was referred to as the Committee on Fair Employment Practices, or the FEPC. See *Henderson*, US Brief, 4, *Henderson*, Record 90; Green, *The Secret City*, 258–60.

page 129. Called off: *WP*, June 26, 1941; *WES*, June 26, 1941.

page 129. Blacks in World War II: Gates, *Life Upon These Shores*, 302–4.

page 129. Capital Transit issues: Green, *The Secret City*, 256–60.

page 129. "last resort": *CD*, July 3, 1943.

page 130. "nerve center": Ibid.

page 130. "financial and economic": Ibid.

page 130. "the classic second-class citizens": Ibid.

page 130. Isolation: See MCT, "Colored Women and World Peace," 1932, in MCTLOC, written on behalf of the Women's International League for Peace and Freedom.

page 130. Retreat: In 1940, for example, she maintained a public profile through ceremonial events such as a dinner for the National Negro Congress and a Republican tea, but she also played bridge and went to movies. See *MCTJ*, Feb. 28, 1940, in MCTHB; *MCTJ*, Feb. 29, 1940, in MCTHB; *MCTJ*, Mar. 14, 1940, in MCTHB; *MCTJ*, Apr. 20, 1940, in MCTHB; *MCTJ*, May 26, 1940, in MCTHB.

page 130. Equal Rights Amendment: See Women's Joint Legislative Committee for Equal Rights to The Honorable Frederick Van Nuys, May 8, 1943, in MCTLOC.

page 130. Tuskegee Airmen: MCT, "The Negro Soldier Today and in the Past," Washington, D.C., Feb. 14, 1944, in MCTLOC.

page 130. At Houston's behest: CHH to "Dear Friend," Apr. 2, 1943, in MCTLOC.

page 130. Old regret: MCT, "If I Were Young Again," *Negro Digest*, Sept. 1943, 58, in MCTLOC.

page 130. Applied: *MCTJ*, Oct. 8, 1946, in MCTHB; "Facts About Mrs. Mary Church Terrell's Application for Membership in the Washington Branch, A.A.U.W.," Oct. 24, 1946, in MCTLOC; Mrs. Clarence F. Swift, letter to the editor, *WP*, May 7, 1948.

page 130. Reinstatement: See *MCTJ*, Oct. 8, 1946, in MCTHB; *MCTJ*, Nov. 8, 1946, in MCTHB; *MCTJ*, Oct. 10, 1946, in MCTHB; MCT, "How and When the College Alumnae Club Was Founded," *The Journal of the College Alumnae Club of Washington*, n.d., 3–5, in MCTLOC. In this article, Terrell writes that she and several other black women belonged to the alumnae club for white women, but graduates of historically black colleges were not eligible for admission, so she and other black women formed a separate club of their own in 1910.

page 130. Effort to test: Mrs. Clarence F. Swift, letter to the editor, *WP*, May 7, 1948; see *MCTJ*, Nov. 8, 1946, in MCTHB.

page 130. Dinners: See *MCTJ*, Mar. 28, 1946, in MCTHB; *MCTJ*, May 24, 1946, in MCTHB.

page 130. Voted: Maude Spier Brubaker to MCT, Oct. 10, 1946, in MCTLOC; *MCTJ*, Oct. 10, 1946, in MCTHB.

page 130. Government integrated: Green, *The Secret City*, 231, 261–62.

page 131. Bilbo background: *AA*, Aug. 4, 1945; *PC*, May 25, 1946; RNCSNC, 88; Howard Whitman, "Washington—Disgrace to the Nation," *Woman's Home Companion*, Feb. 1950, 45; *ADW*, March 19, 1946.

page 131. *Morgan v. Virginia*: 328 U.S. 373 (1946). Mary Church Terrell attended the oral argument in the Supreme Court. See *MCTJ*, Mar. 27, 1946, in MCTHB.

page 131. "helpless pawn": RNCSNC, 88 (quoting *WES*, Sept. 4, 1946).

page 131. Loyalty order: See McCullough, *Truman*, 486, 521, 523, 531, 550–53; *WP*, Mar. 23, 1947; *NYT*, Mar. 23, 1947; *WES*, Mar. 24, 1947.

page 132. Plan to saturate: *NYAN*, Mar. 29, 1947; CORE, *Conference Report*, June 13–15, 1947, in NAACPLOC; see *PC*, June 21, 1947; *ADW*, June 22, 1947; *CCP*, June 28, 1947; *AA*, June 28, 1947.

page 132. CORE: W. Jones, *The March on Washington*, xvii, 60–61.

page 132. Howard students: W. Jones, *The March on Washington*, 58, 64–65; see Kluger, *Simple Justice*, 130.

page 132. "Suspected of 'Communist'": *CD*, June 21, 1947, in RHTLOC.

page 132. "holy warfare": MCT, "Address of Welcome to the 38th Annual Conference of the NAACP," Washington, D.C., June 24, 1947, in MCTLOC.

page 132. First president: McCullough, *Truman*, 569.

page 132. Blistering: *WES*, June 30, 1947.

page 132. Flags: See *WP*, June 30, 1947 (photo).

page 132. "reached a turning point": *WP*, June 30, 1947.

page 132. "And when": Ibid.

page 132. CORE volunteers: See *CD*, Aug. 23, 1947.

page 133. Bemoaned: See *AA*, Aug. 2, 1947.

page 133. "Let us remember": RNCSNC, 4 (quoting *WES*, Aug. 21, 1947, which, in turn, quoted *Trud*, a Russian newspaper).

page 133. HUAC released: *PC*, Sept. 13, 1947.

page 133. CRC background: See, for example, CRC, Invitation, Mar. 29, 1946, in NAACPLOC; Gloster Current to Walter White, May 2, 1946, in NAACPLOC; George Marshall to Dear Friend, Aug. 8, 1946, in NAACPLOC; Roy Wilkins to Walter White, May 1, 1946, in NAACPLOC; King, *Devil in the Grove*, 154.

page 133. Observer not delegate: TM to Milton Kaufman, Apr. 23, 1946, in NAACPLOC.

page 134. "nuisance" not a "front": Memorandum from Marian Wynn Perry to WW, May 7, 1946, in NAACPLOC.

page 134. "a CP outfit": RW to D. Ellis Byrd, May 25, 1946, in NAACPLOC; see Navasky, *Naming Names*, 36.

page 134. Warned: RW to D. Ellis Byrd, May 25, 1946, in NAACPLOC.

page 134. Clark's removal: CRC, *Action Bulletin*, July 3, 1946, in NAACPLOC.

page 134. Oust Bilbo: George Marshall to WW, Sept. 25, 1946, in NAACPLOC.

page 134. "intolerable": *WES*, Oct. 29, 1947.

page 134. Shameful: *WP*, Oct. 30, 1947.

page 134. "failure of democracy": *WP*, Oct. 30, 1947.

page 134. "a symbol of democracy": Ibid.

page 134. "renewed faith": Ibid.

page 134. So-called: See Rayford Ellis to MCT, Oct. 31, 1947, in MCTLOC (hand-written note).

page 134. "brutal": Ibid.

page 134. "God have mercy": Ibid.

page 134. Not new: See Navasky, *Naming Names*, 22.

page 134. Subversives list: *AA*, Dec. 13, 1947.

page 135. Presidential election of 1948: See Patterson, *Brown v. Board of Education*, 2; Mary L. Dudziak, *Cold War Civil Rights: Race and the Image of American Democracy* (Princeton: Princeton University Press, 2000), 85–86; McCullough, 587–88.

page 135. northern blacks: See Patterson, *Brown v. Board of Education*, 2; Dudziak, *Cold War Civil Rights*, 86.

page 135. Truman civil rights message: McCullough, *Truman*, 586–87.

page 135. "We have lots of work": CHH, "The Highway," *AA*, Apr. 3, 1948.

page 135. School-crossing guards: *NYT*, May 14, 1948; *NYHT*, May 14, 1948; *WES*, May 14, 1948; *CD*, May 22, 1948; *AA*, May 22, 1948; *PC*, May 22, 1948.

page 135. *Hurd v. Hodge*: 334 U.S. 24 (1948).

page 136. Refused to answer: *WES*, May 31, 1948; *WES*, June 1, 1948.

page 136. White House picket: *PC*, May 15, 1948.

page 136. "terrorism": *NYT*, June 3, 1948.

page 136. "The struggle for": Ibid.

page 136. "We will take": Ibid.

page 136. Walter White warned: WW to CHH, May 27, 1948, in NAACPLOC.

page 136. Name graced: See *BDG*, May 7, 1948. Robeson's name was on the letterhead of the Civil Rights Congress. See William Lawrence to Dear Friend, May 7, 1948, in NAACPLOC.

page 136. No patience: See CHH to Roger Baldwin, June 21, 1948, in NAACPLOC.

page 136. "a jim-crow": *AA*, June 12, 1948.

page 136. "We have no": Ibid.

page 136. "we are not": Ibid.

page 136. "But some": Ibid.

page 136. CORE endorsed: *PT*, June 29, 1948.

page 136. "If, as the": *PC*, July 24, 1948.

page 136. Truman's executive order: *NYT*, July 27, 1948; Dudziak, *Cold War Civil Rights*, 86; Patterson, *Brown v. Board of Education*, 2.

page 136. Subsidized: CHH, "Along the Highway," *AA*, Dec. 18, 1948; see JRF, Executive Committee Minutes, July 3, 1946, in CHHHUMS; JRF, Executive Committee Minutes, Oct. 31, 1946, in CHHHUMS.

page 137. "blot on our nation": See RNCSNC, cover page.

page 137. "Symbol of Democracy": RNCSNC, 4.

page 137. "I would rather": Ibid.

page 137. Research committee: RNCSNC, 92.

page 137. "mysteriously disappeared": RNCSNC, 18.

page 137. "some lawyers": Ibid.

page 137. Views on race: McCullough, *Truman*, 247.

page 137. Oregon senator: *AA*, Dec. 18, 1948; *WP*, Dec. 28, 1948.

page 137. Propaganda: *WES*, Dec. 11, 1948.

page 137. Publicity drive: See CHH, A Radio Forum with David Brinkley, *America United*, NBC, Dec. 19, 1948, in NAACPLOC; *MCTJ*, Dec. 29, 1948, in MCTHB.

page 137. Suing: *AA*, Dec. 18, 1948; see *WP*, Dec. 28, 1948.

page 137. "No self-respecting": CHH, "Along the Highway," *AA*, Dec. 18, 1948.

page 137. "All he asks": Ibid.

page 137. "We had that right": Ibid.

page 137. "but merely": Ibid.

page 137. "rubbing": *CD*, Dec. 25, 1948.

page 137. "planning a trick or so": Ibid.

page 137. Regulation: *WP*, Dec. 28, 1948; Green, *The Secret City*, 296.

page 138. "As far as": *WP*, Dec. 28, 1948.

page 138. "If such": Thomas G. Buchanan Jr. to MCT, Dec. 27, 1948, in MCTLOC.

page 138. "Once the": Ibid.

page 138. Terrell and Patterson background: Sources include WLP to MCT, May 10, 1934, in MCTLOC; WLP to MCT, May 15, 1934, in MCTLOC; *MCTJ*, Dec. 20, 1948, in MCTHB; WLP to MCT, Dec. 22, 1948, in MCTLOC; *ADW*, Dec. 29, 1948.

page 138. Honorary degrees: *MCTJ*, June 14, 1948, in MCTHB; James M. Nabrit Jr. to MCT, Apr. 21, 1948, in MCTLOC; "Stevenson Gives Five Honorary Doctorates," *Oberlin Review*, June 14, 1948, in RHTLOC.

page 138. "responsible": Thomas G. Buchanan Jr. to MCT, Dec. 27, 1948, in MCTLOC.

page 138. "serious and dignified": Ibid.

page 139. "We ask you": Ibid.

page 139. Ignored warnings: See *MCTJ*, Feb. 11, 1949, in MCTHB; MCT, "Remarks Made by MCT at the Elks Civil Rights Meeting, Feb. 11 and 12, 1949," Washington, D.C., in MCTLOC. A year earlier, Terrell had been warned about the alleged Communist leanings of Robeson, with whom she worked on the Council on African Affairs, which promoted solidarity against apartheid and colonialism in Africa. See *MCTJ*, Feb. 11, 1948, in MCTHB. She was then diagnosed with shingles, which her doctor attributed to nerves. See *MCTJ*, Apr.

16, 1948, in MCTHB. Robeson canceled a visit to her house. See *MCTJ*, Apr. 20, 1948, in MCTHB. A few weeks after that, Terrell began tossing some of her letters. See *MCTJ*, May 11, 1948, in MCTHB; *MCTJ*, May 22, 1948, in MCTHB.

page 139. Backed out: See *MCTJ*, Apr. 6, 1949, in MCTHB; *MCTJ*, Apr. 11, 1949, in MCTHB; *MCTJ*, Apr. 14, 1949, in MCTHB; *MCTJ*, May 3, 1949, in MCTHB; *WES*, Apr. 14, 1949.

page 139. Several news outlets: See *WP*, Apr. 21, 1949; *NYT*, Apr. 21, 1949; Duberman, *Paul Robeson*, 342.

page 139. Starting with the AP: Duberman, *Paul Robeson*, 342; see *WP*, Apr. 21, 1949.

page 139. "would fight any enemy": *WP*, Apr. 22, 1949.

page 139. The truth: See *MCTJ*, Apr. 11, 1949, in MCTHB; *MCTJ*, Apr. 14, 1949, in MCTHB; *WES*, Apr. 14, 1949; *MCTJ*, Apr. 27, 1949, in MCTHB; *MCTJ*, May 3, 1949, in MCTHB.

Page 139. Could not afford: *ADW*, Apr. 22, 1949.

page 139. Strained her health: *AA*, Apr. 23, 1949, in MCTLOC.

page 139. "distorted": Duberman, *Paul Robeson*, 350.

page 139. Three-judge panel: *WP*, June 14, 1949.

page 139. Had enough: See *PC*, July 2, 1949, in RHTLOC; *MCTJ*, June 13, 1949, in MCTHB; *MCTJ*, June 19, 1949, in MCTHB; *MCTJ*, June 27, 1949, in MCTHB.

page 140. "A time comes": MCT, "[Remarks to the] National Committee to Free the Ingram Family," New York, June 22, 1949, in MCTLOC.

page 140. "we are afraid": Ibid.

page 140. "agitators": Ibid.

page 140. "Most of the injustices": Ibid.

page 140. "Every LEGAL means": Ibid.

page 140. "we are tired": Ibid.

page 140. "women representing": Editorial, *NYT*, June 25, 1949; see "No Capital Gains," *Time*, July 4, 1949, 39, in MCTLOC.

page 140. "silly": Duberman, *Paul Robeson*, 360; *NYT*, July 19, 1949; *WP*, July 19, 1949.

page 140. "We can win": Duberman, *Paul Robeson*, 360; *NYT*, July 19, 1949; *WP*, July 19, 1949.

page 140. Petitioned: "A Petition to the Human Rights Commission of the Social and Economic Council of the United Nations, and to the General Assembly of the United Nations, and to the Several Delegations of the Member States of the United Nations," circa Sept. 19, 1949, in MCTLOC; see House Committee on Un-American Activities, Report on the Communist "Peace" Offensive: A Campaign to Disarm and Defeat the United States," 82nd Cong., 1st sess., 1951, H. Rep. 378, 45 [hereafter "HUAC Peace Report"] (saying Du Bois sponsored a UN appeal on the Ingrams' behalf on Sept. 17, 1949).

page 140. "No better": MCT, "Mrs. Terrell's Speech—Presentation of Ingram Brief," Sept. 19, 1949, in MCTLOC.

page 140. Lent her name: See CHH, "Statement on the Appearance of Paul Robeson in Washington," Sept. 23, 1949, in CHHHUMS; *MCTJ*, Oct. 4, 1949, in MCTHB; *MCTJ*, Oct. 13, 1949, in MCTHB.

page 141. "with the same": *ADW*, Oct. 20, 1949.

page 141. Heart attack: *CD*, Apr. 29, 1950; King, *Devil in the Grove*, 195–96; James, *Root and Branch*, 212.

page 141. His son's correspondence: William L. Houston to Roy Wilkins, Nov. 6, 1949, in NAACPLOC.

page 141. Soviet Embassy: *AA*, Nov. 19, 1949.

page 141. When Douglas returned: FMV to WOD, Feb. 1. 1950, in WODLOC.

page 141. Spurred articles: *WP*, Apr. 27, 1948; *NYT*, Apr. 27, 1948.

page 141. "Segregation is always a humiliating experience,...": WTC Jr. to FF, Aug. 5, 1949, 23, in FFLOC.

page 141. Houston's son: Kluger, *Simple Justice*, 279–80.

page 142. "We shall see": Memorandum to All Sponsoring Organizations from RW and Arnold Aronson, Dec. 21, 1949, in NAACPLOC.

CHAPTER 6: SEGREGATION WILL GO

page 143. King dialed his boss: *ADW*, Feb. 2, 1950.

page 143. Do nothing: Ibid.

page 143. Mulling the laws' validity: *ADW*, Feb. 2, 1950; *NJG*, Feb. 4, 1950.

page 143. Haywood background: Personal History of Margaret A. Haywood, circa July 4, 1949, in MCTLOC.

page 143. Rein background: *NYT*, Aug. 15, 1979; *WP*, Aug. 15, 1979.

page 144. Forer background: *WP*, June 23, 1986.

page 144. Opposing: See *WP*, May 18, 1948 (ad).

page 144. Defending: *NYT*, Aug. 15, 1979.

page 144. Upholding: Cert. Petition, *National Council of American-Soviet Friendship, Inc. v. McGrath,* No. 7, Oct. Term 1949 (filed Jan. 23, 1950), 9.

page 144. $300 legal fee: FBI File, "David Rein," June 19, 1947, private collection, in the author's possession.

page 144. "No. 1 Communist": *NYT*, Mar 29, 1949; *WP*, July 10, 1947; Navasky, *Naming Names*, 36–37.

page 144. Asking: Cert. Petition, *National Council of American-Soviet Friendship, Inc.,* 2–6.

page 144. Potential to upend: See *WP*, Mar. 18, 1952.

page 144. progressives: Forer also served as chairman of the Progressive Party of the District of Columbia, a post previously held by Arthur Stein, Annie Stein's husband. See Call to the Fifth Annual Convention of the Progressive Party of the District of Columbia, Oct. 25, 1953, in MCTLOC.

page 144. Communist front in 1944: *WP*, Jan. 23, 1950.

page 144. "in effect": *WP*, May 17, 1949; see Donald M. Murtha to Hon. John Russell Young, May 16, 1949, in PIHULS.

page 144. Accusing the FBI: *WP*, Jan. 23, 1950; *TS*, Jan. 23, 1950.

page 144. Reasonably soon: See *ADW*, Feb. 2, 1950; *NJG*, Feb. 4, 1950.

page 144. "Case filed": *WP*, Jan. 31, 1950.

page 144. "*complaint*": Ibid.

page 145. "known" Communists: Navasky, *Naming Names*, 23; Ybarra, *Washington Gone Crazy*, 490; see McCullough, *Truman*, 765.

page 145. "If the laws": Editorial, *WP*, Feb. 24, 1950.

page 145. "How this community": Ibid.

page 145. Keep segregating: *WES*, Feb. 28, 1950.

page 145. Only Scull: Ibid.

page 145. Flu outbreak: WOD to Jane Wager, Mar. 27, 1950, in WODLOC.

page 145. Health and fitness: See, for example, WOD to Dr. Fred Otten, Mar. 28, 1950, in WODLOC; WOD to Eric Sevareid, Mar. 29, 1950, in WODLOC; WOD to Francis Biddle, Mar. 31, 1950, in WODLOC.

page 145. Mountain lion hunt: WOD to Jane Wager, Mar. 27, 1950, in WODLOC; WOD to Eric Sevareid, Mar. 29, 1950, in WODLOC.

page 145. Mexican expeditions: See WOD to General Jose P. Botello, Mar. 28, 1950, in WODLOC.

page 145. Baboquivari: See WOD to Jane Wager, Mar. 27, 1950, in WODLOC; WOD to Eric Sevareid, Mar. 29, 1950, in WODLOC.

page 145. Rock samples: EA to James Boyd, Mar. 27, 1950, in WODLOC.

page 146. Informing his wife: Murphy, *Wild Bill*, 288–89; see EA to Elon Gilbert, Apr. 24, 1950, in WODLOC.

page 146. Gridiron Dinner: WOD to Thomas L. Stokes, Mar. 30, 1950, in WODLOC.

page 146. Stag Yakima party: See WOD to Miss S. I. Anthon, Mar. 29, 1950, in WODLOC; WOD to Damon Trout, Mar. 29, 1950, in WODLOC.

page 146. Perlman and Elman: See Kluger, *Simple Justice*, 277.

page 146. Friend-of-the-court brief: Dudziak, *Cold War Civil Rights*, 91; Brief for the United States, *Shelley v. Kraemer* and *Hurd v. Hodge*, Nos. 72 et al., Dec. 5, 1947.

page 146. *Shelley v. Kraemer*: 334 U.S. 1 (1948).

page 146. For the first time: Kluger, *Simple Justice*, 277.

page 146. Jettison: See Brief for the United States, *Henderson v. Interstate Commerce Comm'n*, No. 25, Oct. 5, 1949, 10–11, 36, 40 [hereafter "DOJ *Henderson*"].

page 146. "wrong as a matter": See Memorandum for the United States as Amicus Curiae, *McLaurin v. Oklahoma State Regents for Higher Education* and *Sweatt v. Painter*, Nos. 33 and 34, Feb. 9. 1950, 9 [hereafter, "DOJ *McLaurin*"].

page 146. *Henderson* resonated: For facts and procedural history of the case, see DOJ *Henderson*, 3–9.

page 146. "any undue": Interstate Commerce Act, 49 U.S.C. 1, Section 3 (1) (appended to Southern Railway Brief).

page 146. Embarrassed him: See *Henderson*, Transcript of Record, Feb. 17, 1949, 105–6.

page 147. Assault: See DOJ *Henderson*, 10–11, 25–26, 40, 63–66; *CSM*, Apr. 8, 1950.

page 147. "erroneous" and "obsolete": DOJ *Henderson*, 11.

page 147. "the same treatment": DOJ *Henderson*, 10.

page 147. "The phrase": DOJ *Henderson*, 11.

page 147. "social": DOJ *Henderson*, 41.

page 147. "The Amendment": DOJ *Henderson*, 42.

page 147. "master-race psychology": DOJ *Henderson*, 56; see ibid. at 34–35n30.

page 148. "thin disguise": DOJ *Henderson*, 63 (quoting Harlan's *Plessy* dissent, 163 U.S. at 562).

page 148. "most complicated task": DOJ *Henderson*, 63.

page 148. "subterfuges": Ibid.

page 148. "'Separate but equal'": DOJ *Henderson*, 65.

page 148. Hearing details: *CD*, Apr. 15. 1950; CCEDCADL, "Press Release: For PMs," Mar. 30, 1950, in MCTLOC.

page 148. "Mrs. Terrell": Thai Jones, e-mail message to author, Feb. 28, 2015.

page 149. Annie and Arthur Stein background: Sources include T. Jones, *A Radical Line*, 15–32, 50–68, 91–106; AS to MCT, Feb. 2, 1950, in MCTLOC; Marvin Caplan, "Trenton Terrace Remembered: Life in a 'Leftist Nest,'" *Washington History* 6, no. 1 (Spring/Summer 1994): 46–65.

page 149. "Those who are": CCEDCADL, "Press Release: For PMs," Mar. 30, 1950, in MCTLOC.

page 149. "They are trying": Ibid.

page 149. Stipulated: See *District of Columbia v. John R. Thompson Co., Inc.*, No. 99150, Agreed Statement of Facts, circa Mar. 31, 1950, 1–2, in NARADC. The attorneys also stipulated, "upon information and belief," that four prosecutions under the 1872 law had yielded convictions in police court, but all were later reversed in the D.C. Supreme Court or *nolle prossed* and there had been no prosecutions since 1872 under that law. But see *Thompson*, 81 A.2d at 259n5 (noting there were five prosecutions, not four). In addition, the attorneys stipulated that as far as they could discern from the official record there had "never" been any attempted prosecutions under the 1873 law.

page 149. Under advisement: *CD*, Apr. 15, 1950; CCEDCADL, "TO ALL FRIENDS OF CIVIL LIBERTIES," circa Apr. 1, 1950, in MCTLOC.

page 149. Declining: John S. Wood to MCT, Mar. 31, 1950, in MCTLOC.

page 150. Oral argument background: *AA*, Apr. 15, 1950; *CSM*, Apr. 8, 1950, in RHJLOC; *WP*, Apr. 4, 1950.

page 150. Clark recusal: See *Henderson*, 339 U.S. at 826; *WES*, June 5, 1950.

page 150. McGrath lacked: See WOD, *The Court Years*, 249; Kluger, *Simple Justice*, 277.

page 150. DNC chairman: See McCullough, *Truman*, 593, 627, 713.

page 150. Political calculus: See McCullough, *Truman*, 590–91, 713.

page 150. "The betting": *WP*, Apr. 2, 1950.

page 150. More egalitarian future: See *WP*, Apr. 4, 1950.

page 151. "a reality": Ibid.

page 151. "peace and order": *CSM*, Apr. 8, 1950, in RHJLOC; *WP*, Apr. 4, 1950.

page 151. Laughter: *CSM*, Apr. 8, 1950, in RHJLOC; *WP*, Apr. 4, 1950.

page 151. Renowned: WOD, *The Court Years*, 180–81; Patterson, *Brown v. Board of Education*, 50.

page 151. "Then the way": *CSM*, Apr. 8, 1950, in RHJLOC; *WP*, Apr. 4, 1950.

page 151. Hobbs background: *NYT*, June 3, 1952.

page 151. "the kiss of death": Hobbs, *Henderson* Amicus Brief, Dec. 6, 1949, 5 [hereafter, "Hobbs, *Henderson*"].

page 151. "absurd": Hobbs, *Henderson*, 5.

page 151. "impossible": Ibid.

page 151. "for the best interests of all!": Hobbs, *Henderson*, 9.

page 151. Scripture: Hobbs, *Henderson*, 6 (citing 1 Cor. 8:13).

page 151. "first author": *CSM*, Apr. 8, 1950, in RHJLOC; *WP*, Apr. 4, 1950.

page 151. "they would echo": *WP*, Apr. 4, 1950.

page 151. Another era: See *CSM*, Apr. 8, 1950, in RHJLOC; *WP*, Apr. 4, 1950; *WES*, June 5, 1950.

page 151. Conference background: See Mark Tushnet and Katya Levin, "What Really Happened in *Brown v. Board of Education*," 91 Columbia L. Rev. 1867 (Dec. 1991) [hereafter "Tushnet"]; WOD, Conference Notes, Nos. 25 (*Henderson*); 34 (*McLaurin*); 44 (*Sweatt*), Apr. 8, 1950, in WODLOC. Unless otherwise indicated, references to this conference come from WOD's notes and from Tushnet, particularly pages 1887 to 1892. For conferences in general, see WOD, *The Court Years*, 144–45, 246, 248; Kluger, *Simple Justice*, 586–89.

page 152. Work ethic he admired: WOD, *The Court Years*, 248; see McCullough, *Truman*, 264, 287.

page 152. Senate colleague: McCullough, *Truman*, 216.

page 152. Chewing tobacco: See Patterson, *Brown v. Board of Education*, 49; Kluger, *Simple Justice*, 585.

page 152. Ribald humor: See Sherman Minton to WOD, Oct. 17, 1951, in WODLOC.

page 152. Geographical split: See Kluger, *Simple Justice*, 587–88.

page 153. Issues hovered over the conference: See Tushnet, 1887.

page 153. Opponents: Tushnet, 1889.

page 153. Segregationists: See Tushnet, 1889.

page 153. Appearance of McGrath: See Tushnet, 1889.

page 153. "wise": Tushnet, 1890.

page 153. "more harm than good": WOD, *Henderson* Notes, Apr. 8, 1950, in WODLOC.

page 153. "fluid enough to join": Tushnet, 1890.

page 154. "commingling": Tushnet, 1888.

page 155. Reed's notes on Douglas: See Tushnet, 1889n118.

page 155. would confront and overturn: Tushnet, 1889.

page 155. Keep fighting: Kluger, *Simple Justice*, 517–18.

page 155. Justices Black and Clark: *CD*, May 6, 1950; *AA*, May 6, 1950; King, *Devil in the Grove*, 196.

page 155. Terrell summoned: Earlier that spring, before Houston died but while he was still incapacitated, she revised typed drafts that were dated April 3, adding her handwritten changes. See MCT to John S. Woods, Apr. 3, 1950, in MCTLOC.

page 155. Not overtly: Mary Church Terrell had been seen in Washington with CRC officials. See Newspaper Clipping "Search for Missing Civil Rights Law for Nation's Capital Gets Under Way," n.d. (photo), in MCTLOC.

page 155. "The real subversives": MCT, "Statement of Mrs. Mary Church Terrell, NACW," May 5, 1950, published in Hearings Before the Committee on Un-American Activities on H.R. 3903 and H.R. 7595, House, 81st Cong., 2nd sess., 1950, 2360, 2361.

page 156. "murder": Ibid., 2361; see also MCT to Hon. John S. Wood, Apr. 3, 1950, in MCTLOC (two drafts with MCT's handwritten edits).

page 156. Flashing doubts: HHB to FF, Sept. 21, 1945, in FFLOC.

page 156. Work and gym regimen: See, generally, HHB Diary, in HHBLOC; Newspaper clipping "Burton Finds Job Tough, Exacting," n.d., circa Mar. 25, 1951, in HHBLOC.

page 156. Languished: "The Work Sheet," unidentified newspaper clipping, June 8, 1948, in HHBLOC.

page 156. First since Taft: PD, July 2, 1948, in HHBLOC.

page 156. Annotated: See HLB to HHB, May 1, 1946, in HHBLOC; WOD to HHB, May 1, 1946, in HHBLOC; FF to HHB, Mar. 27, 1946, in HHBLOC; FF to HHB, Nov. 20, 1946, in HHBLOC.

page 156. Only Republican: Kluger, Simple Justice, 588.

page 156. Sympathized with: HHB to WW, Mar. 15, 1941, in HHBLOC; HHB to WW, Jan. 2, 1942, in HHBLOC; AA, Mar. 14, 1942; Editorial, WES, June 4, 1949, in HHBLOC.

page 156. Intellects and personalities: CSM, "A Court of Fierce Individualists," n.d., circa June 1949, in HHBLOC; Kluger, Simple Justice, 582–85.

page 156. Coached: See, for example, FF to HHB, Mar. 20, 1946, in HHBLOC.

page 156. Only dissent: CCP, June 8, 1946; Morgan v. Virginia, 328 U.S. 373 (1946).

page 156. Chatted with Douglas: See EA to WOD, Dec. 12, 1949, in WODLOC.

page 156. Loyalist and drudge: Drew Pearson, "Merry-Go-Round: High Court Taking Turn to Right," circa Sept. 10, 1949, in HHBLOC.

page 156. Collection: PD, Nov. 15, 1948, in HHBLOC; PD, circa May 27, 1949, in HHBLOC; CSM, Dec. 3, 1949, in HHBLOC.

page 157. Of assistance: TCC, Memorandum to the Conference from Mr. Justice Clark, Apr. 7, 1950, in FFLOC, WODLOC, and in RHJLOC.

page 157. "But what segregation": WOD, Memorandum from Mr. Justice Douglas, circa May 31, 1950, in HHBLOC and RHJLOC [hereafter, "Douglas, Henderson Memo"].

page 157. "a constitutional sanction": Ibid.

page 157. "But I see": Ibid.

page 157. "This case": Ibid.

page 157. "a dissent": HHB Diary, May 31, 1950, in HHBLOC.

page 157. "It will be": FF, Memorandum for the Conference, May 31, 1950, in RHJLOC, WODLOC, and HHBLOC [hereafter "Frankfurter, *Henderson* Memo"].

page 157. "Brother Burton": Ibid.

page 158. Mutual admiration: See FF to WOD, circa Nov. 26, 1938, in WODLOC.

page 158. Curdled: Philip Elman to FF, circa Aug. 24, 1945, in FFHLS; Rosen, *The Supreme Court*, 147.

page 158. "As you know": FF to WOD, Dec. 20, 1949, in FFLOC.

page 158. Constitutional scholar: Patterson, *Brown v. Board of Education*, 50.

page 158. "Tabular analysis": FF to FMV, Dec. 13, 1946, in FFLOC.

page 158. Oral opinions: FF to FMV, Feb. 3, 1949, in FFLOC.

page 158. Proposed amendments: FF to FMV, Dec. 26, 1946, in FFLOC; FF to FMV, Dec. 27, 1946, in FFLOC; FF to FMV, Dec. 28, 1946, in FFLOC.

page 158. Douglas fled: WOD to Frank Stanton, May 26, 1950, in WODLOC; WOD to Joseph P. Kennedy, Apr. 20, 1950, in WODLOC.

page 158. Outdoors: WOD, Memorandum to the Conference, Jan. 11, 1951, in WODLOC; WOD to Patricia Kane, Jan. 2, 1951, in WODLOC; WOD, *The Court Years*, 308–9, 182; WOD to E. C. Blackburn, Apr. 10, 1950, in WODLOC; WOD, *Strange Lands and Friendly People* (New York: Harper & Brothers, 1951), 148–49.

page 158. Wildflowers: WOD to Lowell Pinkerton, Jan. 12. 1950, in WODLOC.

page 158. Grasses: WOD to Elon Gilbert, May 29, 1950, in WODLOC.

page 158. Lichen: WOD to Dr. George A. Llano, Apr. 21, 1950, in WODLOC.

page 158. Rebuffed: McCullough, *Truman*, 635–37; Rosen, *The Supreme Court*, 144; WOD, *The Court Years*, 289–90; Murphy, *Wild Bill*, 259–64.

page 158. "number two man": Murphy, *Wild Bill*, 264; see McCullough, *Truman*, 637; Rosen, *The Supreme Court*, 144.

page 158. Oliver Wendell Holmes Jr.: See FF to HHB, Dec. 5, 1946, in HHBLOC; FF to HHB, Dec. 13, 1946, in FFLOC; WOD, *The Court Years*, 134; Rosen, *The Supreme Court*, 147.

page 158. Judicial restraint: FF to HHB, Dec. 13, 1946, in FFLOC; Patterson, *Brown v. Board of Education*, 48; WOD, *The Court Years*, 22, 55, 134; Rosen, *The Supreme Court*, 147–49.

page 158. Bulwark: WOD, *The Court Years*, 48, 52–53, 55, 96, 101; Patterson, *Brown v. Board of Education*, 48.

page 158. *Terminiello v. City of Chicago*: 337 U.S. 1 (1949).

page 158. "unreasonable discriminations": *Henderson*, Draft Op., circa May 26, 1950, 8, in RHJLOC.

page 159. "at most symbolic": Ibid.

page 159. "identical tickets": Ibid.

page 159. "No one single": FF to HHB, May 26, 1950, in HHBLOC.

page 159. "symbolic": See DOJ *Henderson*, 30 and n24; *Henderson*, Draft Op., circa May 26, 1950, 8, in RHJLOC.

page 159. Black's sense: Dudziak, *Cold War Civil Rights*, 106–7.

Page 159. "the constitutionality": *Plessy*, 163 U.S. at 551; see Kluger, *Simple Justice*, 523 (noting that *Bolling v. Sharpe*, which challenged segregation in Washington, D.C., schools, brought *Plessy* "full circle").

page 160. "yellow Star of David": WOD, *Henderson* Draft Concurring Opinion, Printer's Copy, June 5, 1950, 6, in WODLOC.

page 160. "social equality": WOD, *Henderson* Draft Concurring Opinion, 7.

page 160. "legal equality": Ibid.

page 160. "color-blind": Ibid.

page 160. "ruling class": Ibid.

page 160. "caste": Ibid.

page 160. "our standards of equality": Ibid.

page 160. "There can be no": Ibid.

page 160. "the attached pages": WOD to HHB, June 3, 1950, in HHBLOC (enclosing the first three pages of a *Henderson* draft concurrence).

page 160. "Never circulated": See WOD, *Henderson* Draft Concurring Opinion, Printer's Copy, June 5, 1950, in WODLOC (annotation).

page 161. the last minute: See HHB Diary, June 5, 1950, in HHBLOC.

page 161. *Henderson*: 339 U.S. 816 (1950).

page 161. Contrary to advice: "HL" and "NC" to HHB Re: *Henderson*, May 31, 1950, in HHBLOC.

page 161. "The division": HHB, "Statement from the bench by Mr. Justice Burton," June 5, 1950, 5, in HHBLOC; see *Henderson*, 339 U.S. at 825.

page 161. Douglas kept: *Henderson*, 339 U.S. at 826.

page 161. Later that day: See *WES*, June 5, 1950.

page 161. *Sweatt*: 339 U.S. 629 (1950).

page 161. *McLaurin*: 339 U.S. 637 (1950).

page 161. "commingle": *McLaurin*, 339 U.S. at 641.

page 161. "on his own merits": *McLaurin*, 339 U.S. at 642.

page 161. "I hope": See Telegram from H. C. Valentine to HHB, June 5, 1950, in HHBLOC.

page 161. "I also hope": Ibid.

page 161. "Are these": Ibid.

page 161. "U.S. Taxpayer": J. S. Shelton to HHB, June 5, 1950, in HHBLOC.

page 161. "identical tickets": Ibid.

page 161. "identical accommodations": Ibid.

page 161. "a big fuss": Ibid.

page 161. NAACP statement: *CDT*, June 6, 1950.

page 162. "As long as": Ibid.

page 162. *Our World* Statement: MCT, "Concerning the Supreme Court's Decision Opening Southern Institutions to Colored Students," circa June 1950, in MCTLOC.

page 162. "We gave them": *WES*, June 7, 1950, in HHBLOC (Vinson's dialogue balloon).

page 162. Father of the Year: *LAT*, May 26, 1950, in HHBLOC.

page 162. "We have never": TM to WLP, June 9, 1950, in NAACPLOC.

page 162. "The complete destruction": *ADW*, June 11, 1950.

page 162. "every legal": See NAACP, Resolution Adopted by the 41st Annual Conference, Boston, Mass., June 23, 1950, in NAACPLOC.

page 163. "short-lived": *District of Columbia v. John R. Thompson, Co., Inc.*, Criminal No. 99150, In the Municipal Court for the District of Columbia, Opinion of the Court, July 10, 1950, 5, 7, in NARADC.

page 163. "a real problem": *Thompson*, July 10, 1950, 12.

page 163. "old municipal regulations": Ibid.

page 163. "Police action": McCullough, *Truman*, 782.

page 163. "Radio Moscow": *WP*, July 12, 1950.

page 163. "disgracefully inadequate": Editorial, *WES*, July 12, 1950.

page 163. "If the abandonment": Ibid.

CHAPTER 7: THIS THING CAN BE LICKED

page 164. Not guilty: See *Thompson*, July 10, 1950, 12.

page 164. Declined: See Information, In the Municipal Court for the District of Columbia, Aug. 1, 1950, in NARADC.

page 164. *Courier* portrait: *PC*, Aug. 5, 1950, in PIHULS; see *AA*, Aug. 5, 1950.

page 164. Bore down: See *AA*, Nov. 21, 1950; AS to MCT, Dec. 5, 1950, in MCTLOC; *AA*, Dec. 5, 1950; AS to MCT, Dec. 12, 1950, in MCTLOC.

page 164. Like Houston: Kluger, *Simple Justice*, 160–61.

page 164. eighty-seventh birthday: *AA*, Oct. 3, 1950; T. Jones, *A Radical Line*, 99.

page 164. *Afro* photographer: *AA*, Oct. 3, 1950.

page 164. Asked Perlman: See Philip B. Perlman to MCT, Oct. 27, 1950, in MCTLOC.

page 164. Internal Security Act: See Ybarra, *Washington Gone Crazy*, 484; Navasky, *Naming Names*, 22–23.

page 164. "Red invasion army": Editorial, *WES*, July 12, 1950.

page 165. "60-ton Russian-made tanks": Ibid.

page 165. Exceeding Mundt-Nixon: Ybarra, *Washington Gone Crazy*, 489; Navasky, *Naming Names*, 22.

page 165. Never enacted: Ybarra, *Washington Gone Crazy*, 489.

page 165. Compelled to register: Navasky, *Naming Names*, 22.

page 165. Subversive Activities Control Board: Ibid.

page 165. Presidentially proclaimed: Navasky, *Naming Names*, 23.

page 165. Detain: Ibid.; American Civil Liberties Union, *Civil Liberties*, April 1952, 4, in MCTLOC.

page 165. "The course proposed": HST, "Veto of the Internal Security Bill," Sept. 22, 1950, http://trumanlibrary.org/publicpapers/viewpapers.php?pid=883.

page 165. "one of the most absurd": Ybarra, *Washington Gone Crazy*, 527.

page 165. A little more than twenty-four hours: Ybarra, *Washington Gone Crazy*, 526–33.

page 165. Overrode: Ybarra, *Washington Gone Crazy*, 529–33.

page 165. Only forty-eight House members and ten senators: Ybarra, *Washington Gone Crazy*, 529, 533.

page 165. Later that fall: *NYT*, Dec. 31, 1950; *NYT*, Dec. 17, 1950; see McCullough, *Truman*, 814–18.

page 165. Decreed: *NYT*, Dec. 17, 1950; see McCullough, *Truman*, 833.

page 165. "menace": HST, Proclamation 2914, "Proclaiming the Existence of a National Security Emergency," Dec. 16, 1950, http://www.presidency.ucsb.edu/ws/?pid=13684.

page 165. "communist aggression": Ibid.

page 165. "all citizens": Ibid.

page 165. Kresge's picket: T. Jones, *A Radical Line*, 99; *AA*, Dec. 30, 1950; *AA*, Dec. 5, 1950.

page 165. Management refused: *AA*, Nov. 21, 1950; *AA*, Dec. 5, 1950.

page 165. "Don't Buy": *AA*, Dec. 30, 1950.

page 165. Announcing: MCT and Randolph T. Blackwell to "Dear Friend," Jan. 15, 1951, in MCTLOC.

page 165. "The enemy is": J. Howard McGrath to MCT, Feb. 2, 1951, in MCTLOC.

page 166. "race problem": See MCT to J. Howard McGrath, Feb. 8, 1951, in MCTHUMS.

page 166. "I wish the": Ibid.

page 166. "Man to Man": *WP*, Feb. 19, 1951.

page 166. "We can't afford": Ibid.

page 166. Rally: *NYT*, Feb. 1, 1951.

page 166. Edited memoirs: NS to MCT, Dec. 12, 1938, in MCTLOC; *MCTJ*, May 11, 1940, in MCTHB.

page 166. Prodded her: See *MCTJ*, May 22, 1939, in MCTHUMS.

page 166. Separate headquarters: *WP*, Jan. 7, 1950.

page 167. Loyalty boards probing: WOD, *The Court Years*, 57–62.

page 167. Tastes in music, theater, art: WOD, *The Court Years*, 61–62.

page 167. Loyalty oaths: Navasky, *Naming Names*, 335.

page 167. Probe: Memorandum from TM to the Office, Feb. 12, 1951, in NAACPLOC; King, *Devil in the Grove*, 207–9.

page 167. Tastes inclined: See AAUW, Washington Branch, *Monthly Newsletter*, Mar. 1950, 1–2, in MCTLOC.

page 168. Philip Morrison background: *NYT*, Apr. 26, 2005; *LAT*, Apr. 26, 2005; *WP*, Apr. 26, 2005.

page 168. "agitator": *NYHT*, Aug. 6, 1950, in NAACPLOC.

page 168. A cause embraced: Navasky, *Naming Names*, 25; Kluger, *Simple Justice*, 160.

page 168. "I am not a Communist": See MCT, "Address for the Maryland Committee for Peace," Baltimore, Md., Oct. 6, 1950, in MCTLOC.

page 168. No one had denounced: See Navasky, *Naming Names*, 85.

page 169. "'peace' offensive": HUAC Peace Report, 1.

page 169. "the most dangerous hoax": Ibid.

page 169. "known": HUAC Peace Report, 51; see Navasky, *Naming Names*, 189.

page 169. As many as eighty: HUAC Peace Report, 107.

page 169. "tremendously obsessed": HUAC Peace Report, 44.

page 169. "fellow traveler": HUAC Peace Report, 43.

page 169. "distinct preference": HUAC Peace Report, 45.

page 170. "outstanding leader": Ibid.

page 170. "the great mass": Ibid.

page 170. Five times: See HUAC Peace Report, 57, 112, 126, 135, 151.

page 170. "affiliated with such": HUAC Peace Report, 57.

page 170. With Jernagin and Brown: HUAC Peace Report, 125–26.

page 170. She and Patterson: HUAC Peace Report, 112.

page 170. "our country's destiny": Mid-Century Conference for Peace, [untitled] news release, May 17, 1950, in MCTLOC.

page 170. American Peace Crusade: HUAC Peace Report, 135.

page 170. *Joint Anti-Fascist Refugee Committee v. McGrath*: 341 U.S. 123 (1951). All citations are to this source.

page 171. "Publication of": See Federal Bureau of Investigation, "FBI Records: The Vault," O. John Rogge, Part 4 of 11, 104, https://vault.fbi.gov/rosenberg-case /o.-john-rogge/o.-john-rogge-part-04-of-06/view.

page 171. Safeguarded: Ibid.

page 172. "Negro Leaders Accused": *ADW*, May 2, 1951.

page 172. "pink": Ibid.

page 172. Phone number: AAUW, *Washington Branch Yearbook, 1952–1953*, in MCTLOC.

page 172. Reversed: See *District of Columbia v. John R. Thompson Co., Inc.*, 81 A.2d 249, 256 (May 24, 1951).

page 172. "This decision": See CCEDCADL, untitled news release, May 25, 1951, in MCTLOC.

page 172. "Of course": Ibid.

page 172. Planned a mass meeting: June 15th Mass Meeting Committee, Minutes, May 29, 1951, in MCTLOC.

page 173. Had announced: *AA*, June 2, 1951.

page 173. *Afro* coverage: *AA*, May 29, 1951; *AA*, May 26, 1951; *AA*, June 2, 1951.

page 173. Did not appear: *AA*, Apr. 14, 1951.

page 173. *Dennis*: 341 U.S. 494 (1951).

page 174. "intended to initiate": *Dennis*, 341 U.S. at 497.

page 174. "properly and constitutionally": *Dennis*, 341 U.S. at 497.

page 174. Horses, porters: WOD to Robert E. Motz, May 5, 1951, in WODLOC.

page 174. Dalai Lama: WOD to Ken McCormick, May 7, 1951, in WODLOC.

page 174. "occupied an exalted position": *Dennis*, 341 U.S. at 584 (Douglas, J., dissenting).

page 174. "This has been": *Dennis*, 341 U.S. at 585 (Douglas, J., dissenting).

page 174. "We have deemed it": Ibid.

page 174. Metropolitan Baptist background: *WP*, Sept. 29, 1982.

page 175. "to celebrate the": MCT, "Mass Meeting," Washington, D.C., June 15, 1951, in MCTLOC. All quotations are from this source.

page 176. "only labor": *PDW*, June 1951, in HHBLOC.

page 176. "But I am no longer": MCT, Mass Meeting, June 15, 1951, in MCTLOC.

page 176. "psychological roadblocks": *NYT*, June 27, 1951.

page 176. Reception: *ADW*, June 30, 1951.

page 177. "Make no compromise": *NYT*, June 29, 1951.

page 177. Vote of 262 to 55: *WP*, July 1, 1951.

page 177. Support for Du Bois: Ibid.

page 177. "complete uniformity": CRC, "Excerpts from Resolutions Adopted by NAACP 42nd Annual Convention, Atlanta, Ga.," news release, circa June 30, 1951, in NAACPLOC.

page 177. Fundraising drive: *AA*, June 2, 1951; *CD*, June 16, 1951.

page 177. "or other activities": Ibid.

page 177. "in any manner": Ibid.

page 177. Josephine Baker background: *AA*, July 10, 1951; Dudziak, *Cold War Civil Rights*, 67–77; Mary L. Dudziak, "Josephine Baker, Racial Protest, and the Cold War," *The Journal of American History* (Sept. 1994): 546–48, 550–52; *AA*, July 7, 1951 (photo); see *PT*, July 10, 1951; *NYAN*, July 14, 1951; *AA*, July 3, 1951; *AA*, July 10, 1951.

page 178. Ordered soda: *AA*, July 7, 1951; *NYAN*, July 14, 1951; *PT*, July 10, 1951.

page 178. Hecht's background: *WP*, Nov. 13, 1941, in MLK; *WP*, Nov. 16, 1941, in MLK; *WES*, Sept. 30, 1934, in MLK; WDN, Apr. 11, 1956, in MLK; *WES*, May 21, 1952, in MLK; WDN, Apr. 11, 1956, in MLK; *WES*, Nov. 6, 1934, in MLK; *WES*, Aug. 5, 1951, in MLK (1901 ad); WDN, Nov. 5. 1951, in MLK; *WP*, Apr. 26, 1950, in MLK.

page 178. "Stouts": *WP*, July 1, 1951.

page 178. "Associates": WDN, Apr. 11, 1956, in MLK; *WES*, May 21, 1952, in MLK.

page 178. No African American sales staff: See S. Walter Shine to C. B. Dulcan, Jan. 16, 1952, in MCTLOC.

page 178. Brand Names Retailer of the Year: *WES*, Apr. 17, 1952, in MLK.

page 178. 1950 sales: Hecht's reported sales of $85.3 million in 1950, and $92 million for the fiscal year ended January 31, 1952. See *WP*, Apr. 25, 1952, in MLK.

page 178. Fifth largest: *WP*, Apr. 26, 1950, in MLK.

page 178. Confronted: See CCEDCADL, Minutes, circa Apr. 18, 1951, in MCTLOC; *AA*, May 22, 1951; T. Jones, *A Radical Line*, 102.

page 178. Segregated lunch counter: See T. Jones, *A Radical Line*, 102; MCT and Alice Trigg to Dear Friend, Apr. 30, 1951, in MCTLOC.

page 178. not to alter: See, for example, MCT to Dear Friend, Apr. 30, 1951, in MCTLOC; *AA*, Apr. 24, 1951; T. Jones, *A Radical Line*, 102.

page 178. Boycott: See CCEDCADL, Minutes, circa Apr. 18, 1951, in MCTLOC.

page 178. Both stores: MCT to Dear Friend, Apr. 30, 1951, in MCTLOC.

page 178. Cancel: See MCT to Dear Friend, Apr. 30, 1951, in MCTLOC; *AA*, May 22, 1951.

page 178. "The men who": *WP*, June 6, 1951, in MLK.

page 179. "Sitdowns": *AA*, June 12, 1951.

page 179. Every hour, six: CCEDCADL, *Progress Report*, July 1951, in PIHULS.

page 179. Dying in Korea: *PT*, July 10, 1951; Dudziak, "Josephine Baker," 550.

page 179. Washington is the: This is a paraphrase based on several sources. *NYAN*, July 14, 1951 (not a quote); *PT*, July 10, 1951; see Dudziak, "Josephine Baker," 550.

page 179. Hecht's would abide: *PT*, July 10, 1951; *CD*, July 14, 1951.

page 179. "I went exploring": *AA*, July 7, 1951.

page 179. "Once our people": *CD*, July 14, 1951.

page 179. Quietly: see *AA*, July 3, 1951.

page 179. "a serious flaw": Memorandum for the United States as Amicus Curiae, In the US Court of Appeals for the District of Columbia Circuit, *John R. Thompson Co., Inc. v. District of Columbia*, 2 [hereafter, "SG's Memo"].

page 179. "The United States": SG's Memo, 2.

page 179. "It must": Ibid.

page 179. Picket line: CCEDCADL, Minutes of the meeting of the Hecht Boycott Committee, July 11, 1951, in MCTLOC; AS to MCT, July 20, 1951, in MCTLOC; *PC*, July 28, 1951, in PIHULS; *PC*, Jan. 26, 1952, in MLK; T. Jones, *A Radical Line*, 102–3.

page 179. "In every field": Mary McLeod Bethune, "The Tides of Democracy are Running Strong Once Again in Washington," *CD*, July 14, 1951. The next day, Mary Church Terrell's nephew, Thomas, expressed concerns about her possible approval of a strategy to foment mass protests at Washington restaurants, which could damage her reputation or lead to allegations that she was affiliated with Communists. TAC [Jr.] to MCT, July 15, 1951, in MCTHB.

page 180. Truman declined to comment: *AA*, July 31, 1951.

page 180. "the only logical": *NYT*, Sept. 1, 1951; see Murphy, *Wild Bill*, 307.

page 180. "on the books": *AA*, Sept. 15, 1951.

page 180. Top story: See "Contents: The Cover," *New York Times Magazine*, Jan. 13, 1952, 4.

page 180. Bestsellers list: See "The Best Sellers," *New York Times Book Review*, Jan. 13, 1952, 8.

page 180. "drift": WOD, "The Black Silence of Fear," *New York Times Magazine*, Jan. 13, 1952, 7.

page 181. "I think he ought": *NYT*, Sept. 1, 1951; see Murphy, *Wild Bill*, 307; McCullough, *Truman*, 588.

page 181. "We're really at war": *NYT*, Sept. 1, 1951.

page 181. "*Personal*": HST to WOD, Sept. 13, 1951, in WODLOC.

page 181. "continued interest": Ibid.

page 181. "somewhat embarrassed": HST to WOD, Sept. 13, 1951, in WODLOC; see Murphy, *Wild Bill*, 308.

page 181. "that cut throat": HST to WOD, Sept. 13, 1951, in WODLOC; see Murphy, *Wild Bill*, 308.

page 181. "Since you are on": HST to WOD, Sept. 13, 1951, in WODLOC; see Murphy, *Wild Bill*, 308.

page 181. "I have returned": WOD to HST, Sept. 25, 1951, in WODLOC.

page 181. "The day may": Ibid.

page 181. "much better": HST to WOD, Oct. 2, 1951, in WODLOC.

page 181. "clear the air": Ibid.

page 181. Condemning British control: See WOD, *Strange Lands and Friendly People*, 119.

page 181. Had embarked: See, for example, WOD, *Strange Lands and Friendly People*, 119.

page 181. Lt. Col. Vernon Walters: Henry R. Appelbaum, "Vernon Walters—Renaissance Man: In Memoriam," Central Intelligence Agency Library, posted Apr. 14, 2007, https://www.cia.gov/library/center-for-the-study-of-intelligence/csi-publications/csi-studies/studies/vo146no1/article01.html.

page 181. Documented: See, for example, HST Library Photograph, "Prime Minister Mossadegh, of Iran on the steps of the Supreme Court building," Nov. 5, 1951, Accession No, 66–8015, http://www.trumanlibrary.org/photographs/view.php?id=3291.

page 182. "only as a by-stander": WOD to HST, Nov. 12, 1951, in WODLOC. All quotations are from this source.

page 182. Mossadegh asked: HST Library and Museum, "The Oil Crisis in Iran, 1951–1953," HST to Mohammed Mossadegh, with related material, Nov. 14, 1951, http://www.trumanlibrary.org/whistlestop/study_collections/iran/documents/index.php?documentid=1–13&pagenumber=1&cid=43 (includes Mohammed Mossadegh to HST, Nov. 9, 1951).

page 182. More time: Ibid. (HST to Mohamed Mossadegh, Nov. 14, 1951).

page 182. "I'm reading it": HST to WOD, Nov. 19, 1951, in WODLOC.

page 182. "an ominous trend": WOD, "The Black Silence of Fear," *New York Times Magazine*, Jan. 13, 1952, 7.

page 182. "back regions": Ibid.

page 182. Foot, horseback, jeep: See WOD, *Strange Lands and Friendly People*, xiii.

page 182. "must be secretly aligning": WOD, "Black Silence," 37.

page 182. "magnified and exalted": Ibid.

page 182. "character assassination": Ibid.

page 182. "Those who are unorthodox": Ibid.

page 182. "Everyone who": Ibid.

page 182. Atop a stool: *PC*, Jan. 26, 1952, in MLK.

page 182. *Afro* reporter: *AA*, Jan. 19, 1952, in MLK.

page 182. $6 million in business: *AA*, Jan. 19, 1952, in MLK; see *PC*, Jan. 26, 1952, in MLK (suggesting the policy changed after a store inventory showed a loss of sales during the boycott).

page 182. Hecht's denied: *AA*, Jan. 19, 1952, in MLK.

page 183. 60 percent: *WP*, Dec. 3, 1952, in MLK.

page 183. Two weeks before: See *WP*, Apr. 25, 1952, in MLK.

page 183. Issued: CCEDCADL to Dear Friend, "Victory at Hecht's!" circa Jan. 14, 1952, in MCTLOC.

page 183. "Why don't you": *AA*, Jan. 19, 1952.

page 183. highly unusual: See Phineas Indritz, "Racism in the Nation's Capital," *The Nation*, Oct. 18, 1952, 356, in NAACPLOC.

page 183. White sale: *WP*, Jan. 16, 1952.

page 183. Ham sandwich: *AA*, Jan. 19, 1952.

page 183. Pie: *PC*, Jan. 26, 1952, in MLK; *AA*, Jan. 19, 1952.

page 183. Coffee with cream and sugar: *PC*, Jan. 26, 1952, in MLK.

page 183. "We're second-class": *AA*, Jan. 19, 1952.

page 183. Photograph: *AA*, Jan. 19, 1952.

page 184. Internal security emergency: *WP*, Jan. 17, 1952; *TS*, Jan. 17, 1952.

page 184. Prevent D.C. blacks and whites: *NYT*, Feb. 20, 1986.

page 184. "reliable information": *WP*, Jan. 17, 1952.

page 184. "If we are": *TS*, Jan. 17, 1952.

page 184. "404 Rif3ewie3 EDrive": NS to MCT, Feb. 25, 1952, in MCTLOC.

page 184. "Hurrah": Ibid.

page 184. "The world does": Ibid.

page 184. "keep pushing": Ibid.

page 185. "I wonder": Ibid.

CHAPTER 8: A BIGGER STEP IS IN ORDER

page 186. Photograph: *AA*, June 10, 1952.

page 186. Two-year boycott: CCEDCADL, Copy of Memo Sent to the Home Office, G.C. Murphy Co., Apr. 24, 1952, in MCTLOC.

page 186. Shock: MCT to Walter G. Shaw, Apr. 24, 1952, in MCTLOC.

page 187. Fall argument calendar: *AA*, June 14, 1952.

page 187. Howard graduation background: Sources include *AA*, June 17, 1952; *AA*, Apr. 29, 1952; AAUW, Washington Branch, *Monthly Newsletter*, April 1952, 3, in MCTLOC.

page 188. *Steel Seizure*: See *Youngstown Sheet & Tube Co. v. Sawyer*, 343 U.S. 579 (1952); McCullough, *Truman*, 897–901.

page 188. African American diplomatic posts: *AA*, June 14, 1952.

page 188. Truman's speech: HST, "Commencement Address at Howard University," June 13, 1952, http://www.presidency.ucsb.edu/ws/?pid=14160. All quotations are from this source.

page 189. radio spot: Broadcast Script, Delivered over Station WUST, Washington, D.C., June 15, 1952, in MCTLOC. All quotations are from this source. It is unclear whether this transcription was prepared before or after the broadcast.

page 190. Hero worship: *MCTJ*, June 12, 1927, in MCTLOC (Lindbergh); MCT, *ACWIAWW*, 59–60 (John Brown).

page 190. Requested a slice: For details of the incident, see *AA*, June 28, 1952.

page 190. Newly sworn-in: *AA*, May 6, 1952 (photo), in MCTLOC.

page 190. Guardianship dispute: See *MCTJ*, Mar. 5, 1937, in MCTHUMS; *MCTJ*, Apr. 8 1937, in MCTHUMS; *MCTJ*, Apr. 10, 1937, in MCTHUMS.

page 190. Didn't want: *MCTJ*, Mar. 5, 1937, in MCTHUMS.

page 190. Allowance: *MCTJ*, Apr. 5, 1952, in MCTLOC; TAC [Jr.] to MCT, Aug. 10, 1952, in MCTLOC (spending money).

page 190. Rent: TAC [Jr.] to MCT, Aug. 10, 1952, in MCTLOC.

page 190. Job: Ibid.

page 190. Draft issues: See *MCTJ*, June 22–24, 1952, in MCTLOC; *MCTJ*, June 28, 1952, in MCTLOC.

page 190. Air force commission: *MCTJ*, June 23, 1952, in MCTLOC.

page 191. "Aren't you ashamed": *AA*, June 28, 1952.

page 191. "You know": Ibid.

page 191. Truman's top choice: See McCullough, *Truman*, 903–7.

page 191. Bowed to: See McCullough, *Truman*, 905.

page 191. Sparkman background: *NYT*, Nov. 17, 1985.

page 191. "colossal blunder": Ibid.

page 191. Democratic platform: See Democratic Party Platform of 1952, July 21, 1952, http://www.presidency.ucsb.edu/ws/index.php?pid=29600.

page 192. Lacked specifics: See NAACP, "Eisenhower Stands Firm Against Federal FEPC," news release, Aug. 28, 1952, in NAACPLOC.

page 192. "BUT DON'T BUY": MCT to Ministers of the Gospel, Aug. 28, 1952, in MCTLOC.

page 192. Informant told: Memorandum to FBI Director from SAC, WFO (100–14005), Nov. 15, 1957, on file with author, DocId. No. 59166586. Less than a year later, on Feb. 18, 1953, an FBI informant alerted the Washington Field Office about Annie Stein's decision to leave the Coordinating Committee and return to New York. See T. Jones, *A Radical Line*, 90.

page 192. Agreed to integrate: For details, see *AA*, Sept. 6, 1952.

page 192. "Today, every": MCT to Dear Friend, Sept. 3, 1952, in MCTLOC.

page 192. Truman signed: See *AA*, Sept. 13, 1952.

page 192. Ill-conceived: Ibid.

page 192. Control vandalism: Editorial, *AA*, Sept. 20, 1952.

page 193. "The greatest legendary": *AA*, Sept. 23, 1952.

page 193. Checkers Speech background: Sources include Jean Edward Smith, *Eisenhower in War and Peace* (New York: Random House, 2012), 531–32, 538–39; McCullough, *Truman*, 759; *AA*, Sept. 27, 1952.

page 193. "honesty and integrity": PBS, American Experience, "Primary Resources: Nixon's Checkers Speech," Sept. 23, 1952, http://www.pbs.org/wgbh/americanexperience/features/primary-resources/nixon-checkers/. All quotes are from this source.

page 193. Racially restrictive covenant: *AA*, Sept. 27, 1952.

page 194. Sparkman and others: *AA*, Oct. 4, 1952.

page 194. Forged his candidacy: See Smith, *Eisenhower*, 544–45 (TV ads); McCullough, *Truman*, 913.

page 194. Allegedly fired: *AA*, Oct. 7, 1952; *AA*, Aug. 30, 1952.

page 194. "We both": *AA*, Oct. 14, 1952.

page 194. "We know": Ibid.

page 194. Referendum on Truman: See McCullough, *Truman*, 909–12; Smith, *Eisenhower*, 546–47.

page 194. "Jim Crow Sparkman": *AA*, Oct. 25, 1952.

page 194. Byrnes: Ibid.

page 194. "born a Republican": "Statement by Mary Church Terrell on Stevenson Candidacy, Oct. 30, 1952," enclosed with Mrs. James H. Rowe Jr. to MCT, Oct. 30, 1952, in MCTLOC.

page 195. "Governor Stevenson has": District Stevenson-Sparkman Club, untitled news release, Oct. 30, 1952, enclosed with Mrs. James H. Rowe Jr. to MCT, Oct. 30, 1952, in MCTLOC.

page 195. "If Governor Stevenson": "Statement by Mary Church Terrell on Stevenson Candidacy, Oct. 30, 1952," enclosed with Mrs. James H. Rowe Jr. to MCT, Oct. 30, 1952, in MCTLOC.

page 195. "Mrs. Terrell, 89": *WES*, Oct. 30, 1952.

page 195. Election results: Smith, *Eisenhower*, 546, 548, 843n67; McCullough, *Truman*, 913.

page 195. *Brown* argument: Sources include *AA*, Dec. 13, 1952; *WP*, Dec. 9, 1952.

page 195. *Bolling*: For background on the case and the attorneys, see Kluger, *Simple Justice*, 515–23, 539.

page 196. Urging the Court: See Brief for the United States as Amicus Curiae, Nos. 8, 101, 191, 413, 448 (Dec. 2, 1952), at 17–26 [hereafter "DOJ *Brown*"].

page 196. Elman and Frankfurter: Elman, Oral History, 843, 832, 847, 844.

page 196. "particularly acute": DOJ *Brown*, 4.

page 196. "This city": DOJ *Brown*, 4.

page 196. "a true symbol": DOJ *Brown*, 4 (quoting HST, Message to the Congress, Feb. 2, 1948, H. Doc. No. 516, 80th Cong., 2d sess., 5).

page 196. "a failure of democracy": DOJ *Brown*, 4 (quoting *To Secure These Rights*, Report of the President's Committee on Civil Rights [1947], 89).

page 196. "Although progress is being": DOJ *Brown*, 8 n. 6 (quoting Dean Acheson, Dec. 2, 1952); see Elman, Oral History, 818; Vann Woodward, *The Strange Career of Jim Crow*, 132 (quoting Acheson letter).

page 196. Potential spectators: For details see *AA*, Dec. 13, 1952.

page 196. Battling a cold: *MCTJ*, Dec. 2–5 1952, in MCTLOC.

page 197. That day and into the next: See *NYT*, Dec. 11, 1952; *WP*, Dec. 11, 1952; *NYT*, Dec. 12, 1952; *WP*, Dec. 12, 1952.

page 197. *Bolling* originated: See Kluger, *Simple Justice*, 522–23, 577–80; *WP*, Dec. 11, 1952; *NYT*, Dec. 11, 1952.

page 197. Refusal to admit: See Kluger, *Simple Justice*, 521; *WP*, Dec. 11, 1952; *NYT*, Dec. 11, 1952.

page 197. Failure to state a claim: See Kluger, *Simple Justice*, 522; *NYT*, Dec. 11, 1952; DOJ *Brown*, 14.

page 197. Fifth Amendment: See Kluger, *Simple Justice*, 521–22; *WP*, Dec. 11, 1952; DOJ *Brown*, 14.

page 197. "explicit and mandatory": DOJ *Brown*, 16.

page 197. "a grave and difficult": Ibid.

page 197. Remand: Ibid.

page 197. "its own independent choice": DOJ *Brown*, 17.

page 198. Split his hour: Kluger, *Simple Justice*, 578. For information about Hayes, see Kluger, *Simple Justice*, 578; *WP*, Dec. 11, 1952; *NYT*, Dec. 11, 1952.

page 198. Congress never required: Kluger, *Simple Justice*, 578; see *WP*, Dec. 11, 1952.

page 198. "pure racism": Kluger *Simple Justice*, 578; see *WP*, Dec. 11, 1952.

page 198. Vinson defended: Kluger, *Simple Justice*, 578; see *WP*, Dec. 11, 1952.

page 198. "a matter of politics": Kluger, *Simple Justice*, 578.

page 198. Nabrit argument: Kluger, *Simple Justice*, 578–79.

page 198. *Korematsu*: 323 U.S. 214 (1944).

page 198. "just as precious": Kluger, *Simple Justice*, 578.

page 198. "I assert": Ibid.

page 198. Korman background and argument: Kluger, *Simple Justice*, 579–80.

page 198. Out of benevolence: Kluger, *Simple Justice*, 579.

page 198. Reviled: Kluger, *Simple Justice*, 580; Elman, Oral History, 837.

page 198. controversial: See, for example, Kluger, *Simple Justice*, 580; Elman, Oral History, 837. Even more than twenty years later, Elman recalled his disbelief when he realized Korman was invoking *Dred Scott* to defend Washington's segregated schools.

page 198. "the mere reflex": Kluger, *Simple Justice*, 580 (quoting *Dred Scott*).

page 198. Only Congress: Kluger, *Simple Justice*, 580.

page 199. "You either have": Ibid.

page 199. "We submit": Ibid.

page 199. "Segregation in D.C.": Editorial, *AA*, Dec. 13, 1952.

page 199. "Gentler Sex": Ibid.

page 199. DeLaine: Ibid.

page 199. "I don't anticipate": Ibid.

page 199. "hypocrisy": Editorial, *AA*, Dec. 13, 1952. This was published with the byline: "The Executive Board of the Co-Ordinating Committee for the Enforcement of the D.C. Anti-Discrimination Laws, MRS. MARY CHURCH TERRELL, Chairman."

page 199. "Will we who": Ibid.

page 199. "long overdue": Ibid.

page 199. "A bigger step": Ibid.

page 199. Equipped: See WOD Conference Notes, Dec. 13, 1952, in WODLOC; see also Mark Tushnet, "What Really Happened in *Brown v. Board of Education*,"

91 Columbia L. Rev. 1867, 1880 and n76 (Dec. 1991). This account of the conference is drawn from Douglas's notes and Tushnet, especially pages 1902–8; see also
Kluger, *Simple Justice*, 586–614; Dennis J. Hutchinson, "Unanimity and Desegregation: Decisionmaking in the Supreme Court, 1948–1958," 68 Georgetown
Law J. 1 (1979).

page 199. Botanist: See WOD, *Beyond the High Himalayas* (Garden City, N.Y.:
Doubleday 1952), 12 (pressed several hundred botanical specimens in the Himalayas).

page 200. Successful: See "Best Seller List," *New York Times Book Review*, Dec. 7,
1952, BR8 (No. 10 on general list).

page 200. Two sections: WOD to Ken McCormick, Dec. 5, 1952, in WODLOC.

page 200. Travels throughout Southeast Asia: See WOD to Sheldon D. Clark, Esq.,
Nov. 21, 1952, in WODLOC.

page 200. If he survived: WOD to Ken McCormick, Dec. 2, 1952, in WODLOC.

page 200. The rest: Ibid.

page 200. Trekking through: See Robert Trumbull, review of *Beyond the High
Himalayas*, by WOD, *New York Times Book Review*, Sept. 21, 1952, BR3; WOD,
Beyond the High Himalayas, 7–9.

page 200. Walter Cronkite: EA to Ken McCormick, Dec. 10, 1952, in WODLOC.

page 200. Book review: EA to Francis Brown, Dec. 10, 1952, in WODLOC.

page 200. Recognized expert: See Trumbull, review of *Beyond the High Himalayas*, BR3.

page 200. "outside organizations": W. H. Lewis to WOD, Dec. 10, 1952, in
WODLOC.

page 200. "a group of": John Kolitar to WOD, Dec. 10, 1952, in WODLOC.

page 200. "Who is behind": Ibid.

page 200. "Communists? Civil Rights Congress?": Ibid.

page 200. Quarantined: See EA to Mr. and Mrs. J. R. Flood, Dec. 23, 1952, in
WODLOC.

page 200. "No answer": See John Kolitar to WOD, Dec. 10, 1952, in WODLOC;
W. H. Lewis to WOD, Dec. 10, 1952, in WODLOC.

page 201. "very serious": Tushnet, 1903 (quoting Conference Notes of Justice
Clark [Dec. 13, 1952] and Conference Notes of Justice Jackson [Dec. 13, 1952]).

page 201. "serious practical problems": Ibid.

page 201. "battle front": Tushnet, 1904.

page 201. "driven": Ibid.

page 201. "trouble": Tushnet, 1905.

page 201. "informed views": WOD, Conference Notes, No. 8, Dec. 13, 1952, 1
(typed version), in WODLOC.

page 201. "make up": WOD, Conference Notes, No. 8, Dec. 13, 1952, 1 (typed version), in WODLOC.

page 201. "constant progress": WOD, Conference Notes, No. 8, Dec. 13, 1952, 1
(typed version), in WODLOC; see Tushnet, 1905.

page 201. "be left to": WOD, Conference Notes, No. 8, Dec. 13, 1952, 1 (typed version), in WODLOC; see Tushnet, 1905.

page 201. "not fixed": Tushnet, 1905.

page 201. "a body of people": Ibid.

page 201. "gradually disappearing": WOD, Conference Notes, No. 8, Dec. 13, 1952, 1 (typed version), in WODLOC; see Tushnet, 1905.

page 202. All-white: CHH to FF, Dec. 29, 1925, in FFLOC.

page 202. National legal committee: See CHH to FF, Jan. 16, 1937, in FFLOC; Kluger, *Simple Justice*, 281, 601.

page 202. Coexisted, even disregarded: *AA*, Jan. 27, 1940 (whites only movie theater); *NJG*, Nov. 9, 1946 (AVC and SCHW picket).

page 202. Race denoted function and status: See Elman, Oral History, 823–24.

page 202. "intolerable": Tushnet, 1905; see Kluger, *Simple Justice*, 601.

page 202. Nurtured ties: Tushnet, 1883; Elman, Oral History, 832, 844.

page 202. Invoked: WOD, Conference Notes, No. 413 (*Bolling*), Dec. 13, 1952, 1 (typed version), in WODLOC; Tushnet, 1905–6; see Todd C. Peppers, "William Thaddeus Coleman Jr.: Breaking the Color Barrier at the U.S. Supreme Court," *Journal of Supreme Court History* 33 (Nov. 2008): 353–70, 363 [hereafter "Peppers"]; Elman, Oral History, 823–34; see Kluger, *Simple Justice*, 601.

page 202. Assisting Marshall: William T. Coleman Jr. to TM, Dec. 10, 1953, in NAACPLOC; Kluger, *Simple Justice*, 624, 321.

page 202. Mayflower incident: See Peppers, 363; William T. Coleman Jr. with Donald T. Bliss, *Counsel for the Situation: Shaping the Law to Realize America's Promise* (Washington, D.C.: Brookings Institution Press, 2010), 93. Elliot Richardson went on to become President Nixon's attorney general and refused to fire the Watergate special prosecutor, Archibald Cox. See Peppers, 369n33.

page 203. "not serve as": FF to Elliot L. Richardson, Oct. 1, 1952, in FFHLS.

page 203. "promised to change the law": WOD Conference Notes, *Bolling*, Dec. 13, 1952, 1, in WODLOC (typed version).

page 203. "a gain in law": WOD Conference Notes, *Bolling*, Dec. 13, 1952, 1, in WODLOC (typed version); see Elman, Oral History, 832.

page 203. "coercive": WOD Conference Notes, *Bolling*, Dec. 13, 1952, 1, in WODLOC (typed version).

page 203. "sociological": Tushnet, 1906; see WOD Conference Notes, *Brown* (No. 8), Dec. 13, 1952, 1, in WODLOC (typed version); Kluger, *Simple Justice*, 601; Elman, Oral History, 838.

page 203. "all of its history": WOD Conference Notes, *Brown* (No. 8), Dec. 13, 1952, 1, in WODLOC (typed version); see Tushnet, 1906.

page 203. "why what has": WOD Conference Notes, *Brown* (No. 8), Dec. 13, 1952, 1, in WODLOC (typed version).

page 203. Resolution was easy: See Kluger, *Simple Justice*, 603; Tushnet, 1906; WOD Conference Notes, *Bolling*, Dec. 13, 1952, 1, in WODLOC (typed version).

page 203. Could not fashion: Tushnet, 1906; Kluger, *Simple Justice*, 603.

page 203. Irrelevant: Tushnet, 1906.

page 203. Merits beyond dispute: Ibid.

page 203. "application": Ibid.

page 204. "go along":Tushnet, 1907; Kluger, *Simple Justice*, 609.

page 204. "equitable remedies":Tushnet, 1907.

page 204. "delay": WOD Conference Notes, *Brown* (No. 8), Dec. 13, 1952, 2, in WODLOC (typed version).

page 204. "go along": Ibid.

page 204. "Otherwise": Ibid.

page 204. "we should let them": Ibid.

page 204. "more than buildings": Ibid.

page 204. "a habit of mind": Ibid.

page 204. "separate education": Ibid.

page 204. "plenty of time": Ibid.

page 204. "Classification": Ibid.

page 204. "It's invidious": Ibid.

page 204. Eisenhower inaugural: For details see *AA*, Jan. 24, 1953; Program for the Inaugural Ceremonies, Jan. 20, 1953, in WODLOC; *WP*, Jan. 21, 1953; Library of Congress, United Press Photograph, "Chief Justice Frederick Vinson Administering the Oath of Office to Dwight D. Eisenhower on the East Portico of the U.S. Capitol," Jan. 20, 1953, No. 1018022, www.loc.gov/pictures/item/00650983.

page 205. State of the Union: *WP*, Jan. 8, 1953; McCullough, *Truman*, 915.

page 205. "the burdens": HST, "Annual Message to the Congress on the State of the Union," Jan. 7, 1953, http://www.presidency.ucsb.edu/ws/index.php?pid=14379. All quotes are from this source.

page 205. Sunlight gleam on horns: *WP*, Jan. 21, 1953.

page 205. Newly sworn-in: See *WP*, Jan. 21, 1953; Inauguration Ceremonies Program, Jan. 20, 1953, in WODLOC.

page 205. Shared front-row: Program for the Inaugural Ceremonies, Jan. 20, 1953, in WODLOC (seating chart).

page 205. Row D: See Ticket, Inauguration Ceremonies, Jan. 20, 1953, in WODLOC.

page 205. Two Bibles: *WP*, Jan. 21, 1953; Joint Congressional Committee on Inaugural Ceremonies, Swearing-In Ceremony for President Dwight D. Eisenhower, Forty-Second Inaugural Ceremonies, Jan. 20, 1953, http://www.inaugural.senate.gov/swearing-in/event/dwight-d-eisenhower-1953.

page 205. Shook hands: *WP*, Jan. 21, 1953.

page 205. Kissed Mamie: Ibid.

page 205. Mamie's bangs: See *WP*, Feb. 1, 1953 (Hecht's ad).

page 205. Cheered: "President Eisenhower's Inaugural Address (Part 1)," Jan. 20, 1953, https://www.youtube.com/watch?v=xAWJ9slccZg.

page 205. Smiled: Ibid.

page 205. V-shaped salute: *WP*, Jan. 21, 1953.

page 205. Staple: Ibid.

page 205. Departure: See ibid.

page 205. Bow their heads: See ibid.

page 205. Hush: See ibid.

page 205. "Give us": *WP*, Jan. 21, 1953 ("works").

page 205. "Especially": See DDE, Inaugural Address, Jan. 20, 1953, http://www
.presidency.ucsb.edu/ws/?pid=9600. The *Post* did not quote this sentence in its
next-day story, but the *Afro* did. *AA*, Jan. 24, 1953.

page 205. Benediction: Inauguration Ceremonies Program, Jan. 20, 1953, in
WODLOC; *WP*, Jan. 21, 1953.

page 205. Inaugural Parade: For details see *WP*, Jan. 21, 1953; *AA* magazine, Jan. 27,
1953 (photo); Office of the Grand Marshals, Inaugural Parade, Jan. 20, 1953, http://
www.eisenhower.archives.gov/all_about_ike/presidential/1953_inauguration/
1953_inaugural_parade_procession.pdf.

page 205. African Americans marched: See *AA*, Jan. 24, 1953.

page 205. Station break or commercial: *AA*, Jan. 24, 1953. After fielding numerous complaints, the *Afro* asked the station, whose staff director said it was a coincidence.

page 206. Thousands: McCullough, *Truman*, 922. The *Afro's* estimate varied between hundreds and more than 5,000. See *AA*, Jan. 24, 1953.

page 206. Track 9: *AA*, Jan. 24, 1953; Supreme Court of the United States,
"Memorandum," Jan. 20, 1953, in WODLOC.

page 206. *Ferdinand Magellan*: McCullough, *Truman*, 922, 306.

page 206. Home to Missouri: McCullough, *Truman*, 922; *AA*, Jan. 24, 1953.

page 206. Fans milled: For details from Union Station, see *AA*, Jan. 24, 1953, unless
otherwise indicated.

page 206. "Just as nice": *AA*, Jan. 24, 1953.

page 206. "He'd sit": Ibid.

page 206. Truman greeted: *AA*, Jan. 24, 1953; McCullough, *Truman*, 922.

page 206. Arthur Prettyman: *AA*, Jan. 24, 1953; see McCullough, *Truman*, 917.

page 206. "I just had to": *AA*, Jan. 24, 1953.

page 206. "We want Harry": Ibid.

page 206. "For He's a Jolly Good Fellow": Ibid.

page 206. Remarks: See McCullough, *Truman*, 923.

page 206. "a private citizen": *AA*, Jan. 24, 1953 (photo caption).

page 206. FDR's valet: For details about Brooks, see *NYT*, Feb. 5, 1957; *AA*, Jan. 24,
1953; McCullough, *Truman*, 406; *NYT*, Oct. 16, 1947.

page 206. Marveled: *WP*, Jan. 18, 1953; McCullough, *Truman*, 917.

page 206. "Ike" buttons: *AA*, Jan. 24, 1953.

page 206. Justice Burton and his wife: "Burtons at Inaugural Ball," AP photo, circa
Jan. 20, 1953, in HHBLOC.

page 206. Two integrated balls: *AA*, Jan. 24, 1953.

page 206. Trainload from Cleveland: See Courtney Burton, "Inauguration Bulletin,"
circa Jan. 20, 1953, in HHBLOC.

page 207. 5-to-4 vote: *John R. Thompson Co., Inc. v. District of Columbia*, 202 F.2d 579,
589, 591, 593 (D.C. Cir. Jan. 22, 1953).

page 207. All of whom: See Federal Judicial Center, "History of the Federal Judiciary,
Biographical Directory of Federal Judges," http://www.fjc.gov/history/home
.nsf/page/judges.html.

page 207. "custom of race disassociation": *Thompson*, 203 F.2d at 592.

page 207. "Such a decision": Ibid.

page 207. "the serving of food": *Thompson*, 203 F.2d at 599.

page 207. "custom": *Thompson*, 203 F.2d at 601.

page 207. "I consider": CCEDCADL, "Re: Thompson Restaurant Case," news release, Jan. 22, 1953, in MCTLOC; see *AA*, Jan. 31, 1953.

page 207. "Clearly": CCEDCADL news release, Jan. 22, 1953.

CHAPTER 9: EAT ANYWHERE

page 208. Eisenhower State of the Union: Sources include *WP*, Feb. 1, 1953; *WP*, Feb. 3, 1953; see *NYT*, Feb. 3, 1953 (photo); *NYT*, Feb. 2, 1953.

page 208. "the lone lady senator": *WP*, Feb. 3, 1953.

page 208. "grand labors": *WP*, Feb. 3, 1953. All quotes are from this source unless otherwise noted.

page 209. Last appeared: Smith, *Eisenhower*, 446, 430.

page 209. Tepid applause: *WP*, Feb. 3, 1953.

page 209. "the cause of freedom": *NYT*, Feb. 12, 1953; *WP*, Feb. 12, 1953.

page 210. Might otherwise: See Elman, Oral History, 831.

page 210. Certiorari petition: *Thompson*, No. 617, Petition for a Writ of Certiorari, Feb. 20, 1953.

page 210. Crafted, in part: Elman, Oral History, 831. The coauthor was Phineas Indritz.

page 210. Elman drafted: Elman, Oral History, 831.

page 210. Saw a restaurant owner deny: Jim Newton, *Eisenhower: The White House Years* (New York: Doubleday, 2011), 87.

page 210. "clearly erroneous": *Thompson*, Brief for the United States as Amicus Curiae in Support of the Petition for Writ of Certiorari, 8, Mar. 10, 1953 [hereafter, "Brief in Support"].

page 210. "obviously not": *Thompson*, Brief in Support, 2.

page 210. Joint "Suggestion": See *Thompson*, Suggestion That Case Be Advanced, Mar. 13, 1953, in WODLOC, RHJLOC.

page 210. "the public interest": Suggestion, 2.

page 210. "premature": *Thompson*, No. 617, Opposition of Respondent to Suggestion That Case Be Advanced, 1, Mar. 17, 1953.

page 211. "an advisory opinion": Opposition to Suggestion, 1.

page 211. Unlike *Thompson*: Opposition to Suggestion, 2.

page 211. "worthy of review": *Thompson*, No. 617, Brief for Respondent in Opposition to Petition for a Writ of Certiorari, 16, Mar. 26, 1953.

page 211. "by legislative fiat": Opposition Brief, 4.

page 211. "a policy of social equality": Opposition Brief, 5.

page 211. "civil rights legislation": Opposition Brief, 4.

page 211. Orders and rulings: See *WP*, Apr. 7, 1953; *In re Isserman*, 345 U.S. 927 (1953) (Black, J., dissenting from cert. denial); Melvin I. Urofsky, *Division and Discord: The Supreme Court Under Stone and Vinson, 1941–1953* (Columbia: University of South Carolina Press, 1997), 178n69. Isserman, Rein, and Forer filed a joint brief in *Joint-Anti Fascist*. See 341 U.S. at 124.

page 211. *Thompson* Order: *Thompson*, No. 617, October Term 1952, Apr. 6, 1953, in NARADC.

page 211. Strained: See *Rosenberg v. United States*, 346 U.S. 273, 293 (1953) (concurring opinion of Clark, J.); *Rosenberg*, 346 U.S. at 277 (opinion of Vinson, C. J.); Urofsky, *Division and Discord*, 178. Mary Church Terrell spoke at a Rosenberg clemency dinner in New York on March 18, 1953. See MCT, "Rosenberg Clemency Dinner," Mar. 18, 1953, New York, in MCTHB.

page 212. Easter Egg Roll: Sources include *WP*, Apr. 7, 1953; *WES*, Apr. 6, 1953; *AA*, Apr. 7, 1953; *The Black Washingtonians*, 132 (photo).

page 213. "Thousands Roll": *AA*, Apr. 7, 1953.

page 213. "Supreme Court": Ibid.

page 213. South Portico soared: Ibid.

page 213. "sick of segregation": A Petition to the President of the United States and Members of the D.C. Board of Commissioners, n.d., in MCTLOC; *AA*, Jan. 31, 1953.

page 213. "It is wrong": A Petition, n.d., in MCTLOC; *AA*, Jan. 31, 1953.

page 213. "some form of action": MCT to [no name], Feb. 13, 1953, in MCTLOC.

page 213. Lincoln Memorial: MCT to Rev. John H. Robinson, Feb. 7, 1953, in MCTLOC; *AA*, Feb. 28, 1953.

page 213. Prayer service: *AA*, Feb. 7, 1953; *AA*; Feb. 10, 1953.

page 213. "It is the": *AA*, Apr. 14, 1953.

page 213. "I feel": Ibid.

page 213. Devoted themselves: See King, *Devil in the Grove*, 203, 206, 337; Urofsky, *Division and Discord*, 256–57.

page 214. "But no one can": *AA*, Feb. 3, 1953.

page 214. "No one would deny": Ibid.

page 214. "lose vital and precious": NAACP, Motion for Leave to File Brief as Amicus Curiae, 2, Apr. 18, 1953.

page 214. "The District": NAACP Motion, 2.

page 214. "stiff resistance": Ibid.

page 214. "Once it is clear": Ibid.

page 215. "exclusive": *Thompson*, Brief for the United States as Amicus Curiae, 9, Apr. 23, 1953 [hereafter "DOJ *Thompson*"].

page 215. "non-delegable": Ibid.

page 215. "all rightful subjects": DOJ *Thompson*, 8.

page 215. "full authority to": DOJ *Thompson*, 9.

page 215. "ordinary municipalities": DOJ *Thompson*, 33.

page 215. No "ordinary municipality": See DOJ *Thompson* 35, 37.

page 215. "national matters": DOJ *Thompson*, 41.

page 215. Denied NAACP's: *Thompson*, No. 617, Order, Apr. 27, 1953, in NARADC.

page 216. *Thompson* oral argument: Sources include; *WP*, May 1, 1953; *WES*, May 1, 1953; *WP*, May 2, 1953; *AA*, May 5, 1953; *AA*, May 2, 1953; *WES*, May 2, 1953, in RHJLOC; Phineas Indritz, Oral Argument Notes, Apr. 30, 1953 and May 1, 1953, in PIHULS [hereafter "OA Notes"]. Quotations are drawn from newspaper accounts. The Court did not prepare an oral argument transcript.

page 216. Gray background: *WPTH*, Nov. 28, 1965; *WPTH*, July 9, 1956. National University School of Law and George Washington University School of Law combined in 1954 and became known as George Washington University National Law Center, which is now known as George Washington University Law School. Karen Wahl, e-mail message to author, June 2, 2015.

page 216. In and around: See *WP*, Apr. 30, 1953; *WES*, Apr. 30, 1953; *WES*, May 1, 1953 (photo).

page 216. "drift" and "creeping McCarthyism": *WP*, Apr. 30, 1953.

page 216. Eight justices: *WP*, June 9, 1953.

page 216. Courtroom interior: Sources include Kluger, *Simple Justice*, 563–64; author notes, April 23, 2014. Another source was a C-Span "virtual tour" of the Court, with video of the friezes, but the tour no longer appears to be available on C-Span's web site. When reviewed, the link was http://supremecourt.c-span .org/Video/VirtualTour/SC_VT_CourtroomFriezes.aspx.

page 216. Among the rows: See *WP*, May 1, 1953 (courtroom almost full).

page 216. Mary, Jernagin: Shepperd, *Mary Church Terrell*, 88.

page 216. "Mother of the Year": Sadie M. Yancey to MCT, Apr. 20, 1953, in MCTLOC.

page 216. Converted: *AA*, Apr. 25, 1953.

page 217. "That is rather": *WP*, May 1, 1953.

page 217. "Repeals by implication": Ibid.

page 217. "They must rest": Ibid.

page 218. "It would be": *WP*, May 2, 1953.

page 218. "without any reasonable basis": *Thompson*, No. 617, Brief for Respondent, 4, Apr. 28, 1953 [hereafter "Respondent's Brief"].

page 218. More than half: See Respondent's Brief, 6–16, 21–29.

page 218. "mere police regulations": Respondent's Brief, 10.

page 218. At its best: See Respondent's Brief, 9–10.

page 219. Former trial lawyer: Rosen, *The Supreme Court*, 136.

page 219. Point from Brownell's brief: See DOJ *Thompson*, 46–47.

page 219. Why does: See Indritz, OA Notes, 7, May 1, 1953.

page 219. Asked Hart: Ibid.

page 219. It hinged: See ibid.

page 219. "freedom to contract": See Respondent's Brief, 6–7; Certiorari Opposition Brief, 5; see also *Civil Rights Cases*, 109 U.S. at 12, 17.

page 219. "a duty to sell": Certiorari Opposition Brief, 5; Respondent's Brief, 7.

page 219. "social equality": Respondent's Brief, 7.

page 219. Swayed a majority: See Respondent's Brief, 8–9 (quoting Stephens); *Thompson*, 203 F.2d at 579–98.

page 219. Distant relationship to Harlan: See Rosen, *The Supreme Court*, 135.

page 219. Black quizzed: See Indritz, OA Notes, 8, May 1, 1953.

page 219. "usual and reasonable": DOJ *Thompson*, 25n14.

page 219. "comfort": DOJ *Thompson*, 25n14 (citing 1892 law).

page 219. "all persons": Ibid.

page 220. Expertise: *WPTH*, Jan. 19, 1965.

page 220. "the colored race": *AA*, May 5, 1953.

page 220. "a white restaurant": Ibid.

page 220. Black disagreed: *AA*, May 5, 1953.

page 220. "They have their own": Ibid.

page 220. "I am talking": Ibid.

page 220. All the people: Ibid.; see Indritz, OA Notes, 8, May 1, 1953.

page 220. "I can think": *AA*, May 5, 1953.

page 220. Renowned for equanimity: See Urofsky, *Division and Discord*, 154.

page 220. Vowed to vote against: *AA*, Mar. 14, 1942; *CD*, Mar. 14, 1942.

page 220. Beyond definition: Indritz, OA Notes, 9, May 1, 1953.

page 220. Hart agreed: See Indritz, OA Notes, 9, May 1, 1953.

page 220. Conceded the majority opinion: See *Thompson*, 203 F.2d at 588–89, 592–93.

page 220. Even Congress: See Indritz, OA Notes, 9, May 1, 1953.

page 220. *Civil Rights Cases*: See 109 U.S. at 11–12, 25.

page 221. Citing the Civil Rights Act: See Respondent's Brief, 7; Certiorari Opposition, 5.

page 221. Neglecting to acknowledge: See Respondent's Brief, i–iii; Certiorari Opposition, ii.

page 221. Prettyman: See Respondent's Brief, 21; *Thompson*, 203 F.2d at 593–98.

page 221. "become obsolescent and": Respondent's Brief, 20.

page 221. "resurrected": Ibid.

page 221. Revived: See Indritz, OA Notes, 10, May 1, 1953.

page 221. "out of an": Supplemental Memorandum for the United States, 1, May 2, 1953, in RHJLOC and in NARADC [hereafter "Supplemental Memo"].

page 221. "in order to": Supplemental Memo, 1.

page 221. "general availability": Ibid.

page 221. "lost" laws: See *WES*, May 2, 1953, in RHJLOC; *WP*, May 2, 1953; *AA*, May 5, 1953; *AA*, May 9, 1953.

page 221. Had not known: *WP*, May 2, 1953.

page 221. Until 1947: *WP*, June 9, 1953; *WES*, May 2, 1953, in RHJLOC; *WES*, June 8, 1953.

page 221. Charles Hamilton Houston: *WP*, June 9, 1953; *WES*, May 2, 1953, in RHJLOC; *WES*, June 8, 1953; see *WP*, May 2, 1953 ("a District lawyer"); *AA*, May 9, 1953 (same).

page 221. Bound original: See Supplemental Memo, 1.

page 221. On the committee: RNCSNC, 92.

page 221. Secure vault: *WP*, May 2, 1953; *AA*, May 9, 1953.

page 221. "Well, if": *WP*, May 2, 1953; *AA*, May 9, 1953.

page 222. Laughter: *WP*, May 2, 1953; *AA*, May 9, 1953; see *WP*, June 9, 1953 (justices scoffed).

page 222. "It is respectfully": Supplemental Memo, 4.

page 222. Notebook paper: See WOD, Conference Notes, *Thompson*, May 6, 1953, in WODLOC.

page 222. Impending divorce: See Murphy, *Wild Bill*, 295; *CPD*, circa Dec. 14, 1954, in HHBLOC.

page 222. Final chunk: See WOD to Ken McCormick, Jan. 26, 1953, in WODLOC.

page 222. Royalty check: EA to Milton Jones, Feb. 9, 1953, in WODLOC.

page 222. More than one-third: See Murphy, *Wild Bill*, 294.

page 222. Mountain lion: WOD to Helen Strauss, Mar. 4, 1953, in WODLOC.

page 222. Publicity: WOD to Ken McCormick, Jan. 24, 1953, in WODLOC.

page 222. Scheduled for release: WOD to Norman Cleaveland, Mar. 30, 1953, in WODLOC.

page 222. At least a one-year hiatus: See WOD to Ken McCormick, Apr. 1, 1953, in WODLOC.

page 222. Four books in five: Ibid.

page 222. Palm Beach: WOD to Joseph P. Kennedy, Apr. 13. 1953, in WODLOC.

page 222. Panama: WOD to Dr. Alfredo Aleman, Apr. 22, 1953, in WODLOC.

page 222. Himalayan trek: See WOD to Hon. Sheldon T. Mills, Apr. 22, 1953, in WODLOC.

page 222. Four in three: See WOD to Ken McCormick, Apr. 1, 1953, in WODLOC.

page 222. Exhaustion and anxiety: See WOD to R. N. Rahul, May 11, 1953, in WODLOC.

page 222. Health: See WOD to R. N. Rahul, June 5, 1953, in WODLOC; EA to Dr. Roy Hewitt, Jan. 30, 1953, in WODLOC; see Murphy, *Wild Bill*, 295 (impending divorce had a "toll" on Douglas, who began drinking more heavily than usual that spring).

page 222. Taxes: WOD to H. N. Rahul, Jan. 31, 1953, in WODLOC.

page 222. Divorce-related debt: See Murphy, *Wild Bill*, 295.

page 222. Shortage: See WOD to H. N. Rahul, Jan. 31, 1953, in WODLOC; Murphy, *Wild Bill*, 295; WOD to American Security & Trust Co., Apr. 3, 1953, in WODLOC; WOD to American Security & Trust Co., Apr. 13, 1953, in WODLOC.

page 222. "inclined to reversal": WOD, Conference Notes, May 6, 1953, in WODLOC.

page 222. "irrelevant": WOD, Conference Notes, May 6, 1953, in WODLOC. In his diary, Justice Burton graded Elman's performance as "excellent," while Hart's he deemed merely "fair." HHB Diary, May 1, 1953, in HHBLOC.

page 223. Like Stephens: See *WP*, May 29, 1955.

page 223. Lived at the Mayflower: Patterson, *Brown v. Board of Education*, 55; Kluger, *Simple Justice*, 595.

page 223. Did not cook: Kluger, *Simple Justice*, 595.

page 223. "Why—why this means": Patterson, *Brown v. Board of Education*, 55, citing Kluger, *Simple Justice*, 595; ibid.

page 223. "three well-behaved": See *Thompson*, Handwritten Draft, 1, n.d., circa May 25, 1953, in WODLOC.

page 223. "certain": Ibid.

page 223. Names: Agreed Statement of Facts: See *Thompson*, No. 617, Record Extract, 18, Apr. 8, 1953; Respondent's Brief, 2.

page 223. Suspected him: Urofsky, *Division and Discord*, 182; see Murphy, *Wild Bill*, 293 (Douglas, in early 1953, still had hopes of reaching the White House, notwithstanding his pending divorce).

page 224. "all 'rightful subjects'": *Thompson*, Handwritten Draft, 4 (quoting Organic Act).

page 224. "And certainly so": *Thompson*, Handwritten Draft, 12; see DOJ *Thompson*, 47–48.

page 225. "in terms of": *Thompson*, Handwritten Draft, 28.

page 225. "Reversed": *Thompson*, Handwritten Draft, 31.

page 225. Urged: See Murphy, *Wild Bill*, 316; Urofsky, *Division and Discord*, 180.

page 225. Delay: see, for example, Urofsky, *Division and Discord*, 178–80; *Rosenberg*, 346 U.S. at 296, 299 (Black, J., dissenting); *Rosenberg*, 346 U.S. at 305 (Frankfurter, J., dissenting).

page 225. "suggested questions": See FF, "Memorandum for the Conference: *Re: The Segregation Cases*," May 27, 1953, in HLBLOC.

page 225. "in opposite directions": Ibid.

page 225. "psychological": Ibid.

page 225. "Time, in turn": Ibid.

page 225. "especially well informed": FF to "Dear Brethren," May 27, 1953, in FFLOC.

page 225. "uncommonly stimulating": *NYT*, May 28, 1953.

page 225. Kaufman scheduled: See *Rosenberg v. United States*, 346 U.S. at 279.

page 226. Reuters statement: WOD, "Statement dictated to Mr. Rankin of Reuters News Agency," June 1, 1953, in WODLOC.

page 226. Circulated: *Thompson*, No. 617, Draft "as circulated," June 1, 1953, in WODLOC.

page 226. "Yes": FF to WOD, June 1, 1953, in WODLOC.

page 226. Noninvolvement: See RHJ to WOD, n.d., in WODLOC; RHJ to WOD, June 6, 1953, in WODLOC.

page 226. "I think": HLB to WOD, June 2, 1953, in WODLOC (handwritten note).

page 226. "Under the circumstances": Ibid.

page 226. Burton and Clark: HHB to WOD, June 2, 1953, in WODLOC; TCC to WOD, June 2, 1953, in WODLOC.

page 226. Minton: Sherman Minton to WOD, June 3, 1953, in WODLOC.

page 226. Jefferson Davis statue: *WP*, June 7, 1953.

page 226. Revised version: FF, "Memorandum for the Conference: *Re: The Segregation Cases*," June 4, 1953, in WODLOC; see Urofsky, *Division and Discord*, 261n71.

page 226. Noting: FMV to WOD, June 5, 1953, in WODLOC.

page 226. "single 'package'": FF to FMV, June 8, 1953, in FFLOC.

page 226. "tip the mitt": Ibid.

page 226. With *Thompson*: Ibid.

page 227. "tactics or 'public-relations'": Ibid.

page 227. "very early": Ibid.

page 227. "The Attorney General": Ibid.

page 227. Douglas began reading: See Shepperd, *Mary Church Terrell*, 89.

page 227. Orders and opinions: See EA to L.W. Bentley, Apr. 1, 1953, in WODLOC.

page 227. Forer sat: Shepperd, *Mary Church Terrell*, 89.

page 227. "This is a": Shepperd, *Mary Church Terrell*, 89; *Thompson*, 346 U.S. at 102.

page 227. "certain members": *Thompson*, 346 U.S. at 102.

page 227. "survived": *Thompson*, 346 U.S. at 110.

page 227. "governing body of laws": Ibid.

page 227. That's when: See Shepperd, *Mary Church Terrell*, 89.

page 227. "presently enforceable": Shepperd, *Mary Church Terrell*, 90; *Thompson*, 346 U.S. at 118. In reaching its holding about Congress's authority to delegate legislative power to the District, the Court drew analogies to the power of a state to grant "home rule or self-government" to its municipalities, as well as to Congress's authority to delegate power to US territories, suggesting that Congress had the authority to grant self-government to the District. Attorney General Brownell said the decision "removes all doubts" about Congress's power to grant self-government to Washington residents. *WP*, June 9, 1953; see *Thompson*, 346 U.S. at 108, 106-10.

page 228. "Would a decree": *WP*, June 9, 1953 (Question 4).

page 228. "its equity powers": Ibid.

page 228. "an effective gradual": Ibid.

page 228. Scrapped: *AA*, June 9, 1953.

page 228. *Afro* reporter: Ibid.

page 228. "hopeful and patient": Ibid.

page 228. "praying for": Ibid.

page 228. "a great tragedy": Ibid.

page 228. "I hate to think": Ibid.

page 228. *Star* splashed: *WES*, June 8, 1953.

page 228. "a significant": *WP*, June 9, 1953.

page 228. Holding: Ibid.

page 228. "I will be": Ibid.

page 228. "surprised and disappointed": Ibid.

page 228. "We're going to": *AA*, June 9, 1953.

page 228. "It's the law": Ibid.

page 229. At 8:30 p.m.: See *WP*, June 8, 1953.

page 229. "immediately": *WP*, June 9, 1953; *WES*, June 9, 1953.

page 229. Members should: *WP*, June 9, 1953.

page 229. "CONGRATULATIONS": Telegram from Charles and Rhetta Prudhomme to MCT, June 8, 1953, in MCTLOC.

page 229. "UNTIRING AND MILITANT": Telegram from Reber Cann to MCT, June 8, 1953, in MCTLOC.

page 229. Formal photograph: Telegram from Allan Morrison to MCT, June 8, 1953, in MCTLOC.

page 229. "D.C. Café Segregation": *WP*, June 9, 1953.

page 229. "Eat Anywhere": *AA*, June 9, 1953.

page 229. Aqua dress and red hat: *AA*, June 16, 1953.

page 229. Scull, Brown, Jernagin: *WP*, June 13, 1953; *AA*, June 16, 1953.

page 229. Patrons stared: *AA*, June 16, 1953.

page 229. Reporters and photographers: Ibid.

page 229. Gazing through: Ibid.

page 229. Metropolitan Police: *WP*, June 10, 1953.

page 229. Worked: See, for example, Emanuel Bloch and Malcolm Sharp to Chief Judge Thomas Swan, June 10, 1953, in WODLOC; Application for Stay of Execution (June 12, 1953), in WODLOC; Murphy, *Wild Bill*, 319.

page 229. "Negro": Mary Smith to WOD, June 9, 1953, in WODLOC.

page 229. "NO WHITE MAN OF HONOR": Ibid.

page 229. "But feeling": *WP*, June 12, 1953.

page 229. Absence of disorder: *WP*, June 11, 1953; *WP*, June 12, 1953.

page 229. Lack of complaints: *WP*, June 11, 1953; *WP*, June 12, 1953.

page 230. Soup, cake, coffee: *AA*, June 16, 1953; see also *NYAN*, June 20, 1953 (photo of Jernagin, Terrell, and Brown in the cafeteria line).

page 230. Fasted: *AA*, June 16, 1953.

page 230. Midafternoon: See *WP*, June 12, 1953.

page 230. Meat, shortcake, macaroni, tomato juice: *AA*, June 16, 1953.

page 230. Manager commandeered: *AA*, June 16, 1953; see *CD*, Aug. 8, 1953.

page 230. Square table: For this and other details about the scene inside Thompson's, unless otherwise indicated, see *NYAN*, June 20, 1953 (photo).

page 230. Ate soup, fielded questions: *AA*, June 16, 1953.

page 230. Flashbulbs popped: Ibid.

page 230. "It's like another": Ibid.

page 230. "We have taken": *WP*, June 12, 1953; *AA*, June 16, 1953.

page 230. "And in the District": *WP*, June 12, 1953; *AA*, June 16, 1953.

page 231. Image of Mary: *AA*, June 16, 1953.

page 231. "I am greatly": Ibid.

page 231. "It had nothing": Ibid.

EPILOGUE: UNTIL FULL AND FINAL VICTORY

page 232. Children: E. B. Henderson to MCT, June 22, 1953, in MCTLOC.

page 232. White House dinner: *AA*, July 28, 1953.

page 232. "Highly Esteemed": MCT to HLB, July 30, 1953, in HLBLOC.

page 232. Hailing: See Virginia Durr to MCT, June 22, 1953, in MCTLOC.

page 232. "Please forgive": MCT to HLB, July 30, 1953, in HLBLOC.

page 232. "I had your letter": HLB to MCT, July 31, 1953, in HLBLOC.

page 232. CIA-sponsored coup: See *NYT*, Aug. 19, 2013; Tim Weiner, *Legacy of Ashes: The History of the CIA* (New York: Doubleday, 2007), 81–92.

page 232. Installed: See Weiner, *Legacy of Ashes*, 86, 92.

page 233. Blacklist National Lawyers' Guild: *I.F. Stone's Weekly*, Sept. 5, 1953, 2, in CRCPS; see Navasky, *Naming Names*, 37; *WP*, Dec. 1, 1953.

page 233. represented Rosenbergs: *NYT*, Oct. 13, 1989.

page 233. Sanctioned: *I.F. Stone's Weekly*, Sept. 5, 1953, 2.

page 233. Vinson died: *NYT*, Sept. 8, 1953.

page 233. "I remember": MCT, "I Remember Frederick Douglass," *Ebony*, Oct. 1953, 72.

page 233. Marshall profile: "The World's Biggest Law Firm," *Ebony*, Sept. 1953, 17.

page 233. Movie theaters: See *CD*, Oct. 3, 1953; Fradin and Fradin, *Fight On!*, 160.

page 233. "If I live": *CD*, Oct. 3, 1953.

page 233. "shortest and pleasantest": MCT, "Statement to be Read by Mrs. Terrell at the Luncheon," Washington, D.C., Oct. 10, 1953, in MCTLOC.

page 234. "longest and hardest": MCT, "Statement to be Read by Mrs. Terrell at the Luncheon," Washington, D.C., Oct. 10, 1953, in MCTLOC; *AA*, Oct. 24, 1953.

page 234. "a great American": See "Remarks by WW at luncheon Honoring Mrs. Mary Church Terrell on her 90th Birthday," Statler Hotel, Washington, D.C., Oct. 10, 1953, reprinted by Delta Sigma Theta Sorority, n.d., 25, in MCTLOC. All remarks are from this reprint, which looks like a Delta magazine. See also *AA*, Oct. 24, 1953 (several quotes from White's speech).

page 234. "full equality": Remarks by WW, 25.

page 234. "distinguished role": Ibid.

page 234. "another gallant fighter": Remarks by WW, 26.

page 234. "unfinished business": Remarks by WW, 33.

page 234. "The job is finished": Ibid.

page 234. Photo with Robeson: *AA*, Oct. 24, 1953.

page 234. "Certainly no": Paul Robeson to MCT Luncheon Committee, Oct. 6, 1953, in MCTLOC.

page 234. Oberlin calendar: See *MCTJ* (1954), in MCTLOC.

page 234. Philadelphia Citizens Award: Eugene Wayman Jones to MCT, Oct. 14, 1953, in MCTLOC; *PT*, Jan. 2, 1954, in RHTLOC (photo); see also Brenda Dixon Gotthschild, *Joan Myers Brown & the Audacious Hope of the Black Ballerina* (New York: Palgrave Macmillan, 2012), 63–71.

page 234. Previous recipients: Gotthschild, *Joan Myers Brown*, 71.

page 234. Twelve days after: *ADW*, Dec. 18, 1953.

page 234. Informant told: Memorandum to the FBI Director from SAC, WFO, Dec. 23, 1957, 3.

page 235. Stationed in Korea: TAC [Jr.] to Phyllis Terrell Langston, Apr. 11, 1954, in MCTHB.

page 235. Afternoon train: *MCTJ*, Feb. 21, 1954, in MCTLOC.

page 235. "her inspiration to": See *PC*, Mar. 13, 1954, in NAACPLOC (photo); *AA*, Mar. 6, 1954.

page 235. "outstanding leadership": *AA*, Mar. 6, 1954.

page 235. By early May: See *AA*, June 19, 1954, in MCTLOC; Fradin and Fradin, *Fight On!*, 163; TAC [Jr.] to Phyllis Terrell Langston, May 22, 1954, in MCTHB.

page 235. Struggling: Fradin and Fradin, *Fight On!*, 163.

page 235. Canceled: See Telegram to Phyllis Terrell Langston from Maud White Katz, May 6, 1954, in MCTLOC.

page 235. *Brown* decision day: Sources include *NYT*, May 18, 1954; *WP*, May 18, 1954; *TS*, May 18, 1954; Kluger, *Simple Justice*, 700–708.

page 235. Pneumatic chute: "The Negro Strides Toward Full Emancipation," *I.F. Stone's Weekly*, May 24, 1954, in CRCPS; Kluger, *Simple Justice*, 702.

page 235. "Reading of": *NYT*, May 18, 1954; Kluger, *Simple Justice*, 702.

page 235. At 12:52 p.m.: Kluger, *Simple Justice*, 702.

page 235. *Brown*: 347 U.S. 483 (1954). This is the source of all quotations.

page 235. First time: *WP*, May 18, 1954; Kluger, *Simple Justice*, 701.

page 236. Cross section: *WP*, May 18, 1954; *NYT*, May 18, 1954; Kluger, *Simple Justice*, 701; *TS*, May 18, 1954.

page 236. Marshall, Nabrit, Hayes: *WP*, May 18, 1954; *NYT*, May 18, 1954.

page 236. Few African Americans: *WP*, May 18, 1954.

page 236. Relying: See *Brown*, 347 U.S. at 494 and n11 (citing sociological evidence); Kluger, *Simple Justice*, 705–7.

page 236. *Bolling*: 347 U.S. 497 (1954) (This is the source of all quotations); see Kluger, *Simple Justice*, 708.

page 237. Reargument: *Brown*, 347 U.S. at 495; see *WP*, June 9, 1953 (text of five questions).

page 237. Brownell and southern states: *Brown*, 347 U.S. at 496.

page 237. VOA broadcasts: *NYT*, May 18, 1954; see Kluger, *Simple Justice*, 708.

page 237. "They have been told": *NYT*, May 18, 1954.

page 237. "great and statesmanlike": Ibid.

page 237. Eastland Speech: For details see *NYT*, May 28, 1954; Senator Eastland of Mississippi, speaking about the Supreme Court, segregation, and the South, on May 27, 1954, 83rd Cong., 2d session, *Congressional Record*, 6839–45 (enclosed in WOD to Hon. Paul H. Douglas, May 29, 1954) in WODLOC [hereafter, "Eastland Speech"].

page 237. "indoctrinated and brainwashed": *NYT*, May 28, 1954.

page 237. "a notorious": *NYT*, May 28, 1954.

page 237. At the Statler: See CHH, "Mr. Toastmaster, Justice Black, Distinguished Guests, Ladies and Gentleman," Washington D.C., Apr. 3, 1945, in CHHHUMS; *WTH*, Apr. 7, 1945, in CHHHUMS.

page 237. "a great stabilizing": Eastland Speech, 6843 (quoting *AA*, Apr. 14, 1945).

page 237. "shocking": *NYT*, May 28, 1954.

page 237. "the creature": Ibid.

page 237. "a presumption of": Ibid.

page 238. Briefly practiced: See *NYT*, Feb. 20, 1986.

page 238. "Let me": *NYT*, May 28, 1954.

page 238. "The South will": Ibid.

page 238. "Keep up": NS to MCT, June 7, [1954], in MCTHUMS.

page 238. "And may": Ibid.

page 238. "Mix Schools": See *AA*, June 19, 1954, in MCTLOC; Fradin and Fradin, *Fight On!*, 163.

page 238. At sunset: Shepperd, *Mary Church Terrell*, 108.

page 238. Ambulance: Ibid.

page 238. Morning swim: Shepperd, *Mary Church Terrell*, 107.

page 238. Conversations: Ibid.; see *ADW*, Aug. 4, 1954.

page 238. Cancer: MCT, Certificate of Death, July 24, 1954, in MCTHB.

page 238. Lay in state: *AA*, July 31, 1954, in MCTLOC; *ADW*, Aug. 4, 1954; Shepperd, *Mary Church Terrell*, 109.

page 238. Open coffin: *AA*, July 31, 1954, in MCTLOC.

page 238. sign of the cross: Ibid.

page 238. "She was our": Ibid.

page 238. Robeson statement: PR, "Paul Robeson Extols MCT," news release, July 28, 1954, in PRHUMS; *PT*, Aug. 7, 1954.

page 238. "In her unceasing": Ibid.

page 239. Funeral details: See *ADW*, Aug. 4, 1954; *AA*, July 31, 1954, in MCTLOC.

page 239. Black and white officers: *ADW*, Aug. 4, 1954.

page 239. thirty-four cars: *AA*, July 31, 1954, in MCTLOC.

page 239. More than seven hundred persons: *WP*, July 30, 1954 (750) in MLK/MCTRHT; *AA*, July 31, 1954, in MCTLOC.

page 239. "We requested": *CD*, Aug. 7, 1954.

page 239. Would have wanted: Ibid.

page 240. Rabb incident: *CD*, Aug. 14, 1954.

page 240. Nixon: *ADW*, Aug. 12, 1954.

page 240. Neglect to mention: See *ADW*, Aug. 12, 1954.

page 240. "For more than": "First Lady in Tribute to Mrs. Mary C. Terrell," NNPA, n.d., in RHTLOC; *ADW*, Aug. 12, 1954.

page 240. "Her life": "First Lady in Tribute to Mrs. Mary C. Terrell," NNPA, n.d., in RHTLOC. On her ninetieth birthday, Terrell received a written note of congratulations from the First Lady. See Mamie D. Eisenhower to MCT, Oct. 5, 1953, in MCTHUMS. Terrell's friends said the birthday message had given her much happiness. *AA*, July 31, 1954, in MCTLOC.

Note on Sources

This is a nonfiction book, about real people and real events. To the greatest extent possible, I have anchored the narrative in contemporaneous accounts, including letters, diary entries, newspaper articles, speeches, legal briefs, photographs, and other first-person documents, supplemented by my own reporting. Information about sourcing, including primary and secondary sources, is set forth in the chapter notes.

The Library of Congress in Washington, D.C. has much of the archival material I needed to write this book, including the papers of Mary Church Terrell, Robert H. Terrell, Justice William O. Douglas, Justice Hugo L. Black, Justice Harold H. Burton, Justice Felix Frankfurter, Justice Robert H. Jackson, former president and Chief Justice William Howard Taft, President Theodore Roosevelt, Robert R. Moton, Booker T. Washington, and the NAACP. At the Library of Congress, I also used databases, available to on-site researchers, for historical newspapers, congressional reports, and Supreme Court briefs. The digital record helped me fill out the archival one and pursue both sides of Terrell's activism over the decades, as covered in the black and white presses.

Nevertheless, certain elements of the story remain beyond reach. On June 3, 2013, I filed a Freedom of Information Act request with the Federal Bureau of Investigation, asking for records of any surveillance of Terrell, between 1947 and 1954, concerning her alleged ties to the Communist Party or other allegedly subversive groups or individuals. In a letter dated August 21, 2013, the FBI informed me that potentially responsive records had been destroyed on February 16, 1991, pursuant to a court-approved record-retention and disposal plan carried out under the supervision of the National Archives and Records Administration; but other potentially responsive records had been sent to NARA. From NARA, I obtained twelve redacted pages from the fall of 1957, when the FBI's Washington field office received a tip from a confidential informant about Gladys Shepperd, who was researching a book about Terrell. Shepperd, a former president of Delta

Sigma Theta sorority, had been Terrell's neighbor in Highland Beach, Maryland. After rehashing Annie Stein's background in the Communist Party, as well as the allegedly subversive inclinations of Terrell's attorneys, David Rein and Joseph Forer—and after finding nothing subversive about Shepperd—the FBI apparently closed its Shepperd probe in December 1957. She went on to publish her book in 1959.

Throughout this book, I have sometimes referred to Mary Church Terrell by her first name, in part, in the early stages, to distinguish her from her husband, whose last name she shared. Other than her family, who called her "Mollie," those who knew her, including those who worked with her in the struggle to desegregate Washington restaurants, referred to her as "Mrs. Terrell." She was also known, after earning honorary degrees from Oberlin College and Howard University in 1948, as "Dr. Mary Church Terrell." To the extent I use her first name, it is a narrative device, meant with no disrespect, since she is at the center of the story from beginning to end.

I first noticed a reference to the *Thompson* case and Mary Church Terrell online. As a law student, I had read *Brown v. Board of Education*, the Supreme Court's unanimous 1954 decision invalidating segregated public schools. But when I learned about *Thompson*—and Terrell's battles against segregation in the nation's capital—I wondered how she and her case could languish in relative obscurity.

She was born in 1863, the year of the Emancipation Proclamation, and died in 1954, just two months after *Brown*. She published her memoir more than a decade before *Thompson*—a unanimous decision issued a year before *Brown*. She launched her test case in January 1950, almost six years before Rosa Parks helped start the Montgomery, Alabama, bus boycott and a decade before sit-ins rocked lunch counters across the South. Yet history of the civil rights movement, keyed to *Brown* and its aftermath, all but overlooked her. Even *Thompson* failed to mention her by name. It was as if she had disappeared, subsumed by a larger narrative, which, for reasons I understood, tended to begin with *Brown*.

Still, until I began working on this book, I had little insight into Washington's place in the civil rights movement before *Brown*. I viewed Woodrow Wilson as the scholar and public servant whose legacy shaped Princeton University, where I was an undergraduate in the 1980s. I did not know that his administration had segregated federal workers. In the mid- to late 1990s, when I was myself a federal employee, working as an attorney at the Securities and Exchange Commission, I was unaware of battles that had unfolded not far from the agency's headquarters: the 1919 riot, the picketing at Hecht's, Kresge's, and Murphy's, the segregated seating during the Lincoln Memorial's dedication ceremony in 1922. Even when President Barack Obama was inaugurated in 2009, I did not fully appreciate the history he invoked by saying he stood before the country as "a man whose father, less than sixty years ago, might not have been served at a local restaurant."

Even today, Mary Church Terrell's struggle resonates. Terrell was her own protagonist—and she left behind an extensive but incomplete imprint of her life, one that reflected her gifts and idiosyncrasies, her complexities and hardships, and, ultimately, her triumph. It is a privilege to share her story.

Selected Bibliography

This book is based largely on archival records, correspondence, legal documents, journals, and contemporaneous newspaper articles, many of which are located in Washington, D.C., mainly at the Library of Congress. The following works were among the secondary sources I consulted.

Alldredge, Everett O. *Centennial History of First Congregational United Church of Christ, Washington, D.C., 1865–1965*. Baltimore: Port City Press, circa 1965.

Baumann, Roland M. *Constructing Black Education at Oberlin College: A Documentary History*. Athens, Ohio: Ohio University Press, 2010.

Berg, A. Scott. *Wilson*. New York: G. P. Putnam's Sons, 2013.

Coleman, William T., with Donald T. Bliss. *Counsel for the Situation: Shaping the Law to Realize America's Promise*. Washington, D.C.: Brookings Institution Press, 2010.

Cooper, John Milton, Jr. *Woodrow Wilson: A Biography*. New York: Alfred A. Knopf, 2009.

Davis, Deborah. *Guest of Honor: Booker T. Washington, Theodore Roosevelt, and the White House Dinner That Shocked a Nation*. New York: Atria Books, 2012.

Dean, John W. *Warren G. Harding*. New York: Times Books/Henry Holt, 2004.

Douglas, William O. *Beyond the High Himalayas*. Garden City, N.Y.: Doubleday, 1952.

Douglas, William O. *The Court Years, 1939–1975: The Autobiography of William O. Douglas*. New York: Random House, 1980.

Douglas, William O. *Go East Young Man, The Early Years: The Autobiography of William O. Douglas*. New York: Vintage Books, 1983.

Douglas, William O. *Strange Lands and Friendly People*. New York: Harper & Brothers, 1951.

Duberman, Martin. *Paul Robeson: A Biography*. New York: New Press, 1995.

Du Bois, W. E. B. *The Souls of Black Folk*. New York: Barnes & Noble Books, 2005.

Dudziak, Mary L. *Cold War Civil Rights: Race and the Image of American Democracy*. Princeton: Princeton University Press, 2000.

Dunbar-Nelson, Alice. *Give Us Each Day: The Diary of Alice Dunbar-Nelson*. Edited by Gloria T. Hull. New York: W. W. Norton, 1986.

Fradin, Dennis Brindell, and Judith Bloom Fradin. *Fight On!: Mary Church Terrell's Battle for Integration*. New York: Clarion Books, 2003.

Gates, Henry Louis, Jr. *Life Upon These Shores: Looking at African American History, 1513–2008*. New York: Alfred A. Knopf, 2011.

Goodwin, Doris Kearns. *The Bully Pulpit: Theodore Roosevelt, William Howard Taft, and the Golden Age of Journalism*. New York: Simon & Schuster, 2013.

Gotthschild, Brenda Dixon. *Joan Myers Brown & the Audacious Hope of the Black Ballerina*. New York: Palgrave Macmillan, 2012.

Graham, Lawrence Otis. *The Senator and the Socialite: The True Story of America's First Black Dynasty*. New York: HarperCollins, 2006.

Green, Constance McLaughlin. *The Secret City: A History of Race Relations in the Nation's Capital*. Princeton: Princeton University Press, 1967.

Herken, Gregg. *The Georgetown Set: Friends and Rivals in Cold War Washington*. New York: Alfred A. Knopf, 2014.

Horwitz, Tony. *Midnight Rising: John Brown and the Raid That Sparked the Civil War*. New York: Picador, 2011.

James, Rawn, Jr. *Root and Branch: Charles Hamilton Houston, Thurgood Marshall, and the Struggle to End Segregation*. New York: Bloomsbury Press, 2013.

Jones, Thai. *A Radical Line: From the Labor Movement to the Weather Underground, One Family's Century of Conscience*. New York: Free Press, 2004.

Jones, William P. *The March on Washington: Jobs, Freedom, and the Forgotten History of Civil Rights*. New York: W. W. Norton, 2013.

King, Gilbert. *Devil in the Grove: Thurgood Marshall, the Groveland Boys, and the Dawn of a New America*. New York: HarperPerennial, 2013.

Kluger, Richard. *Simple Justice: The History of* Brown v. Board of Education *and Black America's Struggle for Equality*. New York: Vintage Books, 1977.

Kunhardt, Philip B., III, Peter W. Kunhardt, and Peter W. Kunhardt Jr. *Looking for Lincoln: The Making of an American Icon*. New York: Alfred A. Knopf, 2008.

Lauterbach, Preston. *Beale Street Dynasty: Sex, Song, and the Struggle for the Soul of Memphis*. New York: W. W. Norton, 2015.

Masur, Kate. *An Example for All the Land: Emancipation and the Struggle over Equality in Washington, D.C.* Chapel Hill: University of North Carolina Press, 2010.

McCullough, David. *Truman*. New York: Touchstone, 1993.

McPherson, James M. *Battle Cry of Freedom: The Civil War Era*. New York: Oxford University Press, 2003.

Morris, Edmund. *Theodore Rex*. New York: Random House, 2001.

Morris, Edmund. *The Rise of Theodore Roosevelt*. New York: Random House, 2001.

Murphy, Bruce Allen. *Wild Bill: The Legend and Life of William O. Douglas*. New York: Random House, 2003.

Navasky, Victor S. *Naming Names*. New York: Penguin Books, 1981.

Nelson, Jill. *Finding Martha's Vineyard: African Americans at Home on an Island*. New York: Doubleday, 2005.

Newton, Jim. *Eisenhower: The White House Years*. New York: Doubleday, 2011.

Parker, Alison M. "'The Picture of Health': The Public Life and Private Ailments of Mary Church Terrell." *Journal of Historical Biography*, Spring 2013, www.ufv.ca/jhb.

Patterson, James T. Brown v. Board of Education: *A Civil Rights Milestone and Its Troubled Legacy*. New York: Oxford University Press, 2002.

Robenalt, James David. *The Harding Affair: Love and Espionage During the Great War*. New York: Palgrave Macmillan, 2009.

Rosen, Jeffrey. *The Supreme Court: The Personalities and Rivalries That Defined America.* New York: Times Books/Henry Holt, 2007.

Shepperd, Gladys Byram. *Mary Church Terrell: Respectable Person.* Baltimore: Human Relations Press, 1959.

Smith, Jean Edward. *Eisenhower in War and Peace.* New York: Random House, 2012.

Smith, Jean Edward. *FDR.* New York: Random House, 2007.

The Smithsonian Anacostia Museum and Center for African American History and Culture. *The Black Washingtonians: The Anacostia Museum Illustrated Chronology.* Hoboken, N.J.: John Wiley & Sons, 2005.

Terrell, Mary Church. *A Colored Woman in a White World.* Amherst, N.Y.: Humanity Books, 2005.

Terrell, Mary Church. *A Colored Woman in a White World.* Washington, D.C.: Ransdell Inc., 1940.

Tuttle, William M., Jr. *Race Riot: Chicago in the Red Summer of 1919.* New York: Atheneum, 1970.

Urofsky, Melvin I. *Division and Discord: The Supreme Court under Stone and Vinson, 1941–1953.* Columbia: University of South Carolina Press, 1997.

Vehanen, Kosti. *Marian Anderson: A Portrait.* Westport, Conn.: Greenwood Press, 1970.

Washington, Booker T. *Up from Slavery.* New York: Dover, 1995.

Weiner, Tim. *Legacy of Ashes: The History of the CIA.* New York: Doubleday, 2007.

Weiss, Nancy J. *Farewell to the Party of Lincoln: Black Politics in the Age of FDR.* Princeton: Princeton University Press, 1983.

White, Deborah Gray. *Too Heavy a Load: Black Women in Defense of Themselves, 1894–1994.* New York: W. W. Norton, 1999.

Woodward, C. Vann. *The Strange Career of Jim Crow: A Commemorative Edition*, with afterword by William S. McFeely. New York: Oxford University Press, 2002.

Ybarra, Michael J. *Washington Gone Crazy: Senator Pat McCarran and the Great American Communist Hunt.* Hanover, N.H.: Steerforth Press, 2004.

Index